PLACE NAMES OF ALBERTA
Volume IV

COMMITTED TO THE DEVELOPMENT OF CULTURE AND THE ARTS

This book has been published with the help of a grant from the Alberta Foundation for the Arts.

Place Names of Alberta
Volume IV

Northern Alberta

Edited and Introduced by
Merrily K. Aubrey

Alberta Community Development
and
Friends of Geographical Names of Alberta Society
and
University of Calgary Press

© 1996 Alberta Community Development. All rights reserved.

University of Calgary Press
2500 University Drive N.W.
Calgary, Alberta, Canada T2N 1N4

Canadian Cataloguing in Publication Data

Main entry under title:
Place names of Alberta

   Vol. 4 edited and introduced by Merrily K. Aubrey.
   Contents: Vol. 1, Mountains, mountain parks and foothills – v. 2, Southern Alberta – v. 3, Central Alberta – v. 4, Northern Alberta.

   ISBN 0-919813-73-9 (v.1) – ISBN 0-919813-95-X (v.2)
   ISBN 1-895176-44-1 (v.3) – ISBN 1-895176-59-X (v.4)
   ISBN 1-919813-91-7 (set)

   1. Alberta–Gazetteers. 2. Alberta–History, Local.
I. Karamitsanis, Aphrodite, 1961- II. Harrison, Tracey.
III. Aubrey, Merrily K., 1954- IV. Alberta. Alberta Culture and Multiculturalism. V. Geographical Names of Alberta Society. Friends. VI. Alberta. Alberta Community Development.
FC3656.P62 1990   917.123'003   C90-091236-7
F1075.4.P62 1990

Cover photo:
Waterhole post office and stopping place, 1991
Photo by Victoria Lemieux and David Leonard

All rights reserved. No part of this work covered by the copyrights hereon may be reproduced or used in any form or by any means — graphic, electronic or mechanical — without the prior permission of the publisher. Any request for photocopying, recording, taping or reproducing in information storage and retrieval systems of any part of this book shall be directed to the Canadian Reprography Collective, 379 Adelaide Street West, Suite M1, Toronto, Ontario, Canada M5V 1S5.

Typography by Cliff Kadatz.
Printed and bound in Canada by Kromar Printing Ltd.
  ∞ This book is printed on acid-free paper.

For my dear family:
Ken, Arwen, Zyré, Brion,
and especially the memory of Ron and Gisela Aubrey

Table of Contents

Acknowledgements ix

Introduction xi

Explanatory Notes xix

Photo Credits xxi

Maps xxv

Entries 1

Bibliography 237

Appendix: Life on a Survey Crew 245

Glossary 249

Colour Photographs 253

Acknowledgements

A project such as this is done with the aid of many people. First and foremost, I have to thank those who helped with research on the project, namely, Judy Larmour, Barbara Hagensen, Leonel Roldán-Flores, and Chun Hui Zhao. Through their diligent efforts, valuable information was found.

There were several people who pleasantly and patiently put up with my incessant requests for just one more detail. These include the reference staff at the Provincial Archives of Alberta, in particular Marlena Wyman, Karen Rathgeber Mitra, David Leonard, and Ken Kaiser, Maurice Doll and Ron Mussieux at the Provincial Museum of Alberta, Sue Feddema of White Fox Circle, Inc. from Grande Cache, Gordon Reid for information on La Crête, Gracie Thacker at the Fort Chipewyan Historical Society, E. Taylor and Willie Coutereille at Wood Buffalo National Park, and Tom Holt at the Alberta Land Surveyors' Association. I also must thank my counterparts in jurisdictions bordering Alberta for their help with transboundary names. For all who have provided information for this book, thank you.

Editorial work was provided by Martin Lynch, who, from his home in British Columbia, has tirelessly helped on most of the *Place Names of Alberta* series, Bill Shanks, Cliff Kadatz and John King at University of Calgary Press, and Michael Payne, the head of the Research and Publications Program. I am most grateful to Pat Myers for her encouragement and guidance. For their photographic work, appreciation is owed to David Leonard, Victoria Lemieux, Dennis Hyduk at the Provincial Archives of Alberta, and Zyré and Arwen Aubrey-Hébert. I gratefully acknowledge the work of the geographical names co-ordinators before me including Marie Dorsey, Randy Freeman and Aphrodite Karamitsanis.

I wish to thank the Department of Community Development, specifically, Dr. Frits Pannekoek, Director of Historic Sites Service for the continued support of the *Place Names of Alberta* series, along with Les Hurt and Dr. Sandra Thomson, and the two women who edited Volumes I-III, Effie Karamitsanis and Tracey Harrison. Finally, to those who are in great measure responsible for the production of this series – the Friends of Geographical Names of Alberta – *merci, mille fois!* Their dedicated patronage has resulted in a series of books of which Albertans can be proud. Although all of the Friends could be mentioned equally, and have been in earlier volumes, I must mention two who have been of considerable help on this one, Trude McLaren, board member, and Kate Gunn, executive director of the society.

Introduction

How often have you wondered why a place was named as it was? As you read through this book, it will not take long to realise places are not named by chance. Where human beings encounter the land, they name it and, although we tend to name things in predictable fashion, the reasons may be as individual as the person naming it. The names contained in each of Volumes I-III of this series have mirrored the history of its region. *Place Names of Alberta, Volume IV, Northern Alberta*, which completes the series, is no different.

The focus of this volume is on all approved names in northern Alberta, primarily the area north of 55° of latitude. The geographical area covered in this volume is by far the largest of the four, in fact, it covers close to one-half of the entire area of the province. (See page xxvii for the map showing the area covered by this volume.) It is the area where, due to the arrival of fur traders and missionaries, the "Europeans," some of the earliest activities and names are recorded in written form. Because it was an area of sparse settlement, the number of names that have been recorded are by comparison not as great. This large geographic area contains approximately 25 per cent of the province's official names.

As much as possible, there has been an effort to include cross-references between older or unofficial names for officially named features. Due to the unstandardised orthography in many of the first nations' languages, cross-referencing from those languages to official names has been difficult. Where aboriginal names are known, they have been added to the origin information. It is hoped that efforts such as this volume will spark awareness and interest in northern toponymy, and will encourage the recording of geographic names in all the languages of Alberta's north.

In order to fully understand the answer to the question "Why?," it is useful to provide an overview of the trends in naming in northern Alberta. The major influences on Alberta's place names include aboriginal people, explorers, the fur trade, missionaries, surveys, transportation, settlement and industry. A brief look at these factors will explain that trends in naming do exist, and may provide the reader with answers to the inevitable questions of why and when features were named as they were. It also will give insight into the historical perspective provided by toponymy, the study of place names.

The aboriginal people have been in this area of the world the longest, and it is surviving aboriginal names that are the oldest. Some archaeologists believe first nations people have been in this area of the world for at least 12,000 years. The groups that were predominant in the area covered in this volume include the Chipewyan, Cree, and those known historically as the Beaver Indians. Other groups did venture into the territory to follow game or engage in trade with other aboriginal groups or the European fur traders of the Hudson's Bay Company, the Northwest Company, and the X.Y. Company. The Beaver Indians are now found in the north-west part of the province, the Chipewyan in the north-east, and the Cree are to the south of these two groups. Because of their nomadic way of life the boundaries were not fixed.

Aboriginal people most often named their world in a pragmatic way. From the names that survive, it appears that, as a general rule, they did *not* name places after people. They often named features according to physical attributes such as big, little, smoky, stinking; or by the food source that might be available at the site such as jackfish, beaver, buffalo or moose. They journeyed from Point A to Point B, and named the features on their route accordingly. Therefore, if journeys led across different places along a river, the river was not seen as a whole, but rather as a series of distinct, yet interconnected features. One portion might be known as Swift Current River, in another area it might be called Moose River, while in yet another area it would be called Meeting Place River. When this information was recorded by the explorers and scouts, usually one name was used, reflecting European naming convention. A good example of this would be *Athabasca*. This name has been given to a river, lake, town, mountain, pass and waterfalls. According to conventional thought, the name translates to "where there are reeds." This refers only to that area where the river flows into the lake in north-eastern Alberta, which is where the name was recorded by the well-known explorer David Thompson, in the 1790s.

The first nations' people had an oral tradition; history and names were passed by word of mouth from one generation to the next. It was not until they encountered the explorers, fur traders, and missionaries that names were recorded in written form. The French and English speaking fur traders have been here since the late 1700s and they used aboriginal names for geographical features. The Europeans dealt with the various tribal groups, and found it sensible to use those names, or forms of names already known to their suppliers and guides. The French-Canadian voyageurs and traders were some of the first in the area known as Alberta, therefore, it is the French translations of aboriginal names that are some of the first recorded. In 1800 a promontory on Lake Athabasca was referred to by James Mackenzie as Pointe aux Chiens, which now is called by its English translation, Dog Head.

Where you find European settlements, names are more likely to be commemorative. Examples include Fort MacKay and Fort McMurray. Dr. William Morrison MacKay, hired on as a doctor in the Hudson's Bay Company, took on the duties of chief trader and factor at a number of posts before setting up a medical practice in Edmonton in 1898. Fort McMurray was named in 1870 by H.J. Moberly in honour of Chief Factor William McMurray of the HBC. Europeans also liked to name places after places in their homelands, such as Fort Dunvegan and Nottingham House, each of which was named after a place in the British Isles. In this way, the fur traders, who were far away from the land of their birth, brought a bit of home with them.

Early Europeans, because of the business they were in – exploration and exploitation of natural resources – tended to explore, survey and name only those routes needed. They were searching for the most expedient transportation routes by water from the business centres in Montreal and England to the various posts and trading grounds. They were also searching for the fabled route to the Orient. That is why most features were named only along trade routes, which included the major rivers and lakes. Some names that survive today come directly from the fur trade itself. These include places such as Grande Cache, Demicharge Rapids, and Portage River. Other names were recorded by explorers such as David Thompson in the late 1780s-1790s, Alexander Mackenzie in the 1790s, and the Franklin, Ross and Perry expedition of 1818-1820.

The next group to have an impact on toponymy was Roman Catholic missionaries who came primarily from the French order of priests, the Oblates of Mary Immaculate. The first missionary to come to what is now northern Alberta was Father (later Bishop) Alexandre Tâché. He arrived in Fort Chipewyan in 1847 to work with the resident Chipewyan and Cree populations. Some Oblates have been remembered in place names; features such as Petitot River, and communities such as Grouard and Breynat. However, their greatest contribution to Alberta toponymy has been in the their linguistic work. They tirelessly recorded the aboriginal languages, and wrote grammars and dictionaries for native languages. Their systematic recording of the languages give us insight into the names of the past.

With the decline of the fur trade, and the increasing desire to establish a strong British presence, governmental surveying and mapping began in what is now Alberta with the Palliser Expedition between 1857 and 1860. That expedition was concerned with the prairie area to the south in what is now known as the Palliser Triangle. It wasn't until the late 1870s that the first concerted exploration was done in the subject area of this book, under the auspices of the Geological Survey of Canada. The first to work on a systematic natural resource and geological survey was George Mercer Dawson. Although he is best known for his work in British Columbia, he also completed surveys in central and north-western Alberta. His primary concern was geology, he also had to compile information on topography and toponymy as no mapping had yet been done on the area. In August 1879 field research took him from the area of Dawson Creek in British Columbia to Fort Dunvegan, traversing south-east as far as Fort Edmonton by October, via Fort Assiniboine and Athabasca Landing. He was a meticulous keeper of detail, and tried to record names of features used by the inhabitants of the area, the Cree and the Beaver.

In the 1880s, George Dawson, J.B. Tyrrell and R.G. McConnell conducted research over an area of 259 000 square kilometres, in the western interior of Canada, including what is now northern Alberta. In 1890, Richard George McConnell of the Geological Survey of Canada explored the Peace-Athabasca region, with an emphasis on the oil sands around Fort McMurray. These surveys were conducted to study the feasibility of mineral exploration and transportation routes. For the most part, each was content to record the names as known, rather than provide names of his own.

The pressure on the Dominion Government to have a unified British North America from Atlantic to Pacific, brought it to negotiate with the Hudson's Bay Company. In 1870, the Hudson's Bay Company formally transferred Rupert's Land to the Canadian government, with appropriate compensation, of course. This massive territory took in much of what is now northern Ontario and Québec, Manitoba, much of Saskatchewan, southern Alberta, and part of the Northwest Territories.

In order to prepare this large area for settlement, the land had to be surveyed. To this end, the Dominion Lands Act was brought into force in 1872. The Dominion Lands Surveys, which differed in purpose and scope from the work of the Geological Survey of Canada, were responsible for the next wave of naming in the Canadian west. Using a system similar to one developed in the United States, the surveyors came west as early as 1874 to block the land into the township and range system used to this day. However, it was not until the 1890s that they began systematically surveying north of Edmonton. The baseline surveys were completed between 1905 and 1915. Baselines ran from east to west, 24 miles apart, starting at the Canada-U.S. border. They functioned as starting points for delimiting townships. Names along these lines were reported by local residents, while others were adopted to commemorate members of the survey crews. J.N. Wallace and A.W. Ponton, both Dominion Land Surveyors, for example, had features named after them. Other crew members and their relatives also were commemorated in this way.

In looking at a base map of the province, it is easy to see which areas in northern Alberta have been surveyed. These areas are quickly spotted by the telltale township squares that have been further subdivided into sections. The Peace River Country was first systematically surveyed for settlement in 1909, although baseline surveys were being done in the area as early as 1883. This was the result of pressure to prepare this fertile area for homesteaders. To this day much of northern Alberta has not been surveyed for settlement, because of its unsuitability for farming.

The development of more modern modes of transportation influenced place names. This included the use of steamboats on the major water bodies such as the Peace and Athabasca rivers. A number of steamboat captains have their names on features, including Alexander Island. More influential in modern establishment of northern names has been the railroads. To provide a transportation corridor to exploit the oil sands, and to provide access to the north country, the Alberta and Great Waterways Railway was chartered in 1909. In 1922 the line was completed from Edmonton to Waterways, which is now part of Fort McMurray. The line which served the north-west was the Edmonton, Dunvegan and British Columbia Railway (the E.D.&B.C.R.), which, as the name suggests was to follow a route to the Peace River Country from Edmonton via Dunvegan into British Columbia. It had reached as far as Wembley, just west of Peace River in 1924, and Hythe by 1929. The Central Canada Railway, chartered in 1913, extended north of McLennan in 1916 and as far as Whitelaw by 1924, just west of Peace River. Because of financial difficulties, these three companies, along with a number of other, smaller lines, amalgamated in 1929 to form the Northern Alberta Railways. It was owned jointly by the Canadian National and Canadian Pacific railways. Other lines and branches have been established, such as the Alberta Resources Railway and the Great Slave Lake Railway, all which fall under the jurisdiction of the Canadian National Railway.

Each of these companies named stations after railway employees and families, places in other countries, and nearby geographical features. For example, Aggie was a relative of J.D. McArthur, the general manager of the E.D.&B.C.R. J.B. Prest, an engineer of the E.D.&B.C.R., named a number of stations along the line after places in his home area of Surrey in England. Prestville is in turn named after him.

Another group that had a significant impact on toponymy was the settlers. In the geographical area covered in this volume the largest number of settlers came to the Peace River country. The potential of this area for farming was recognized by some as early as the 1870s. It was not until the 1890s that settlers began trickling in. At the time of the Klondike Gold Rush in 1898, some prospectors ventured no further than the Peace River country, while others stayed on their return journey. Local promoters waged an advertising campaign at the turn of the century, extolling the area's virtues, and lobbied for improved access. Railroad transportation, in the form of the E.D. & B.C.R. line, commenced in 1911. Boosters such as Sheridan Lawrence and James Cornwall, whose names are legend in the north country, were also responsible for getting some federal government money for some roads to be constructed. At the same time survey work was being done in 1909, settlers were arriving to stake claims for land under the homesteading provisions of the Dominion Lands Act. Many left their mark on the names in northern Alberta.

It is in the early established post offices that we find the names of the homesteading pioneers. There were no postal codes in the early days, so post offices needed unique names to ensure delivery to the proper locality. Names chosen were either descriptive, such as Poplar Ridge, or commemorative, after the person on whose land the post office was established, such as DeBolt. If post offices were formed after the communities were established, the post office would take the name of the community. This happened in Slave Lake. Post offices would often change location within a vicinity, but would retain the old name. In this book, the locations listed for the post offices are the first ones. Where the post office name survives only as a locality, it is the current position of the locality that is described.

Some pioneers are commemorated in names of physical features. When people settle in an area, over time, the rivers, lakes, creeks, hills and mountains sometimes become identified with the names of the landowners. Examples of this would be Elford's Hill and Mulligan Creek.

Names have arisen out of the development of industry. The main industries in this area have included forestry, coal mining, oil drilling, tar sands extraction and trapping. Industry also has been closely tied with the development of the railroads. All have had an impact on naming. From the primary resources we get names such as Tar Island, Coalmine Lick Creek and Lignite Creek. Kaybob was named after people involved in oilfield development around Grande Cache. The former Pegasus (now Little McLeod) Lake was named for the activities of the Mobil Oil Company in the area. The winged horse is the symbol of that company. From the time of the fur trade, trappers have been commemorated. Some examples include Furlough Island, French Lake and Eymundson Creek.

Although some casualty naming occurred after World War I, in 1947 the Geographic Board of Alberta began to compile lists of those Albertans who had died during the two world wars. The intention was to use these names when it became necessary to apply a name to a feature. Following World War II there was increased activity in remote parts of Alberta as the result of mineral exploration and forestry. Detailed surveys and mapping of these more remote areas became necessary. Consequently the need arose for reference points and for names to be used on the maps and in reports. As much as possible, the Board tried to use names of those casualties who had been resident in the districts in which features were named. In the northern reaches of the province, this was not always accomplished. In 1947, the Board began to use the casualty names and continued to do so until the early 1970s, which resulted in nearly 50 features being named after war casualties; 11 from World War I, 36 from World War II, and one from the Korean War. These include places such as Lessard Creek, Mearon Creek and Patenaude Lake.

There are a number of features named after bush pilots. This Canadian term, coined in the early days of flight, is defined succinctly, yet poetically, in the *Dictionary of Canadianisms* as "a pilot who flies commercial aircraft (bush planes) over the trackless wilderness of the northern bush and barrens." These aviators were the 20th century explorers of northern Canada, with reputations akin to the swashbuckling heroes of the moving pictures of their day. In Alberta there are ten features named after these pilots, including lakes named after Leigh Brintnell, Wilfrid Reid "Wop" May and Grant McConachie.

Other thematic trends are evident. The most common is descriptive of a feature, or its attributes. There are 11 features with the word "clear" as part of the name and 11 others with the descriptor "long". In the 1950s and 1960s, the Research Council of Alberta (now the Alberta Research Council) submitted nearly 50 names for lakes in the far north, using as inspiration names of prominent geologists. Non-human life forms also provide inspiration for names of features. For example, over 170 places are named after plants, and over 260 features listed in this book are named after animals. As you read the book, more patterns will become apparent.

The foregoing briefly describes the history, patterns and trends in naming in northern Alberta. Many of the names described in the book include in the origin information the phrases "officially approved in...", or "the name was made official...". If you talk to long-time residents in any community, you will likely find many features in the area have names, but these names do not appear on any maps. These are "local" names, for which official status has not been applied. When names are officially approved through the appropriate body, they will have legal status, and will appear on federal and provincial maps. In most cases, it is sufficient for the local population and governmental authorities for names to remain unofficial. Sometimes it is desirable to have official status, especially for legal delineation or directional purposes. The process whereby this is done started nearly a century ago and continues to evolve.

The need to establish a names authority for Canada was recognised in the late 1800s. The catalyst for its creation was the international boundary survey between Canada and the United States. Other reasons for its creation included the work being done on resource mapping beyond the frontiers of settlement in Manitoba, as well as the infrastructure needed for the hoped-for tidal wave of immigration into western Canada. These made it an urgent matter to regulate the country's geographical and place names, and to set standards for feature identification. To meet these needs, the Geographic Board of Canada was created in 1897. Soon after the establishment of the Board, provinces were invited to advise it on spellings and use of names. However, the ultimate authority for naming decisions remained in Ottawa. After 1961, the responsibility was transferred to the provinces, and to the Department of Indian and Northern Affairs for lands within the two territories and Indian Reserves. Since 1979, naming within the Indian and military reserves, and national parks has been done jointly through the provinces and the appropriate federal government department. So this means, for example, names in federal parks must be approved by both the Province of Alberta and Parks Canada.

The Geographic Board of Canada has evolved into the Canadian Permanent Committee on Geographical Names (CPCGN) and currently falls within the jurisdiction of the Natural Resources Canada ministry. It is a joint federal-provincial committee based in Ottawa. Its roles are to foster growth of use in standardisation of policies within Canada for handling of names and terminology, and in co-operation with the United Nations to encourage the development of international standards. Each province and territory in Canada has a member on this committee. The CPCGN also acts as a clearing house and central registry for all approved names in Canada but has no power to accept or reject a given name. The secretariat of this committee maintains the National Toponymic Database, a computer file from which names are drawn for Gazetteers and all federally produced topographic maps. Much gratitude is owed to the CPCGN and its predecessors concerning origins of official names. Because that group was the sole naming authority for so many years, their files contain important background information on Alberta's place names.

It should be noted that responsibility for geographical naming and underlying philosophies vary from province/territory to province/territory. A number of jurisdictions view the process solely as part of surveys, mapping and natural resources. Instances of this are Manitoba's Geographical Names Program which is part of that province's Department of Natural Resources. In Nova Scotia, naming is handled by the Department of Lands and Forests. Other jurisdictions see toponymy as part of heritage and culture.

When Alberta became a province in 1905, it was up to the Provincial Librarian/Archivist to be the geographic names advisor for the province to Ottawa. The first to hold the position was Katherine Hughes who was appointed in 1907. Those who followed her included Provincial Librarians such as J. Ashton Jaffary, Edith Gostick and Eric Holmgren. In 1972, Eric Holmgren published his book on names in Alberta. The third edition, *Over 2000 Place Names of Alberta*, co-authored by Eric and Patricia Holmgren in 1976, became the standard reference work on the subject until the publication of the current expanded series. In 1974, the responsibility for the co-ordination of geographical naming was transferred from the jurisdiction of the Provincial Librarian to the Department of Culture. The Geographical Names Program (GNP) now falls within the Research and Publications Program of Historic Sites Service of the Cultural Facilities and Historical Resources Division within the Department of Community Development.

The responsibilities of the GNP are multifaceted. It maintains and continuously updates the Geographical Names Inventory, which is the data base of nearly 10 000 official names in the Province of Alberta. Included in the Inventory are the geographical and name origin information, along with primary and secondary sources used in gathering evidence on the place names and their origins. The Program works with Alberta Surveys and Mapping, along with other provincial and federal government departments that have interest in naming and mapping. It advises the Director of Historic Sites Service who is the Alberta member on the CPCGN. The GNP provides reference services for anyone wanting toponymic information. It also co-ordinates proceedings between those who want to name features and the body that makes the decisions regarding approval, the Alberta Historical Resources Foundation Board.

The GNP co-ordinates the naming of physical features such as mountains, rivers, lakes and creeks. The responsibility for naming man-made features falls under other jurisdictions. Information on these cultural features such as roads, bridges and campgrounds are most likely to be kept with the responsible jurisdiction. The GNP does keep information in its Inventory on names of municipal governments, national and provincial parks, Indian Reserves, reservoirs and other cultural features.

In Alberta the criteria for making names official have evolved over time, but have remained relatively constant since the transfer of this responsibility from the office of the Legislative Librarian. In Alberta, first consideration is given to names that are well established and in current local use. Unless there are extremely good reasons to the contrary, this principle guides selection of names. For unnamed features, the cardinal rule is that proposed names should have some logical connection with the feature. Commonly, the best name is one that describes the feature itself. Names of early settlers, trappers and explorers are highly appropriate if they had some connection with the area, and the proposed name meets with the approval of the local residents.

The process by which new names are approved has a number of steps and, of necessity, is a lengthy one. Most requests come from the general public but are also received from other departments and levels of governments. If you want more information on naming procedures and principles, please contact the Geographical Names Program at the address given below.

One of the joys of toponymy is that there is always more information to find. Another pleasure is hearing from people who can provide the information. You will notice as you read this book, that the origin of some names is unknown. This is where your help is needed. If you can provide any kind of evidence to fill in the gaps, or if you know of alternate origins, please contact the program at the following address. Geographical Names Program Co-ordinator, Old St. Stephen's College, 8820-112 Street, Edmonton, Alberta T6G 2P8, or telephone (403) 431-2357. If you are interested in joining the Friends of Geographical Names of Alberta Society, information can be obtained at the same address.

Explanatory Notes

Individual place name entries are explained through the following example. Each line in this example has been numbered. Please refer to the appropriate number in the Explanation Section for a description of the type of information found in each line of an entry.

1. Allan Lake (lake)
2. 83 K/16 - Wallace River
3. SE-4-69-14-W5
4. 54°56′20″N 116°03′30″W
5. Approximately 70 km east south-east of Valleyview.

6. This was apparently named by W.T. Green, DLS, after his brother Allan. It was officially approved in 1906.

EXPLANATION:

1. Specialists in geographical nomenclature (i.e., systems used in naming things) see most place names containing two parts. One part is called the *specific*, **Allan**, and the other is referred to as the *generic*, **Lake**. The generic identifies the type of feature, while the specific identifies the name of the feature. Although generics very often form parts of place names, as in Allan Lake, some place names lack them. In this volume, the appropriate generics are always provided in parentheses at the end of the first line. In that way, as an example, Peace River (river) can be differentiated from Peace River (town). The generics used here are consistent with those found in *Generic Terms in Canada's Geographical Names: Terminology Bulletin 176*, Minister of Supply and Services Canada, 1987; Catalogue No. S52-2/176-1987. An asterisk (*) preceding a place name indicates that the name has been rescinded or designates a former locality. A rescinded name is one that has been officially deleted for mapping purposes. This will usually apply to features which not longer exist, such as a dried-up lake; or it will apply to a former name of feature or place which was officially changed. The old name must be officially rescinded before a new name is approved. A square box (■) indicates that a colour photograph of the feature is to be found at the end of the volume.

2. The National Topographic System (NTS) Grid Reference is a mapping system that blocks out the country using map sheets of increasing scales. The second line of each entry identifies the NTS map sheet number and name on which the feature can be found. In this case it is **83 K/16 - Wallace River**. The reference is to maps at a scale of 1:50 000, which means that one centimetre on the map represents 50 000 cm or .5 km on the ground.

3. This line is the legal description. It specifies, where available, the legal subdivision or quarter section, section, township, range and meridian. Originally this system was used to describe only those areas surveyed for settlement. Because of the ease of use for specific identification of a place on a map, this legal description is now used as a grid reference system for the entire province with the exception of the mountains. In our example above, SE-4-69-14-W5, it means the lake can be found in the South-East quarter of Section 4, Township 69, Range 14, West of the 5th Meridian.

When trying to find features on an appropriately gridded map, by custom, the descriptions are usually read from right to left.

W5 – This means the lake is west of the 5th Meridian.

There are three meridians in the province of Alberta, the 4th, 5th, and 6th. They are lines of longitude: 110° (4th Meridian) is the Alberta-Saskatchewan border; 114° (5th Meridian) runs along a line directly through Calgary and Stony Plain; 118° (6th Meridian) runs along a line just east of Jasper and DeBolt.

14 – This means the lake is in the 14th Range west of the meridian given. Ranges run east to west and start numbering from 1 again, west of each meridian. Each range is 9.6 km (6 miles) long.

69 – The lake can be found in Township 69. Townships start numbering from 1 at the Canada-U.S. border, to 126 at the Alberta-Northwest Territories boundary. Each township is 9.6 km (6 miles).

4 – The lake can be found in Section 4 of the township mentioned above. There are 36 sections in each block found in the area described by one township and one range. This 57.6 sq. km (36 sq. mile) area is referred to as a township. Each section is 2.56 sq. km (1 sq. mile). They are numbered consecutively, from 1 starting in the south-east corner of the township, and moving in a snake-like pattern to 36, in the north-east corner of the township.

SE – The lake can be found in the South-East quarter of Section 4. The quarter-section was the standard homestead grant of 64.75 hectares (160 acres). The other quarters would, of course, then be, NE, NW and SW.

Although it does not apply to this entry, the section can be also subdivided into legal subdivisions. A legal subdivision has an area of 16.19 hectares (40 acres). These subdivisions are numbered consecutively, from 1 starting in the south-east corner of the section, and moving, once again, in a snake-like pattern to 16, in the north-east corner of the section. There are a number of entries in the book that give the legal subdivision.

4. This line gives the latitude then the longitude readings.
5. This line gives the approximate distance, as the crow flies, to the nearest larger population centre.
6. This area summarises any available information concerning the feature or its name. Where a name shares a specific with a number of entries, origin information is usually located only under one of the entries. Since the surrounding features are often named as a result of their proximity to the originally named feature, it seems appropriate to present the origin information under one feature. Whenever this is the case, the other entries conclude with a cross-reference.

Photo Credits

ADAH	—	Arwen Aubrey-Hébert
GN	—	Geographical Names Program
PAA	—	Provincial Archives of Alberta

    A   Archives Collection
    B   Ernest Brown Collection
    J   Edmonton Journal Collection
    OB   Oblates of Mary Immaculate Collection
    PA   Public Affairs Bureau Collection
    80.28 Survey trip in northern Alberta, ca. 1913-1914
             (no other details known)
    87.368 Survey crew in Peace River area, ca. 1912-1916
             (albums originally kept by one of the survey crew)

UAA   University of Alberta Archives
    69-160 A.E. Cameron Collection
    72-81   Louis Romanet Collection
    76-50   M. Martin Collection
    77-128 K.A. Clark Collection
    78-45   Julian Mills Collection
    79-21   J.D. Soper Collection

VLDL   Victoria Lemieux and David Leonard
ZJAH   Zyré Aubrey-Hébert

Feature Name/Photo description	Reference number	Location	Page
Albright, W.D., with a sample of produce, 1931	A.6988	PAA	2
Arch Lake, late 1920s	69-160-245	UAA	5
Athabasca Delta, Athabasca River is in centre, Fletcher Channel to the right, 1985	85-2-2	GN	255
Athabasca River, Indian Settlement along, ca. 1914-1918	A.11,532	PAA	7
Athabasca River, 1985	85-5-12	GN	255
Bear Creek stopping house on old Slave Lake-Peace River Trail, n.d.	A.3481	PAA	10
Behan, John (Oblate Brother), ca. 1931-1934	OB.2648	PAA	13
Cascades, 1920s	77-128-26	UAA	36
Cornwall, Jim, on the Athabasca River, ca. 1907-1914	A.1424	PAA	46

Feature Name/Photo description	Reference number	Location	Page
Dog Head, 1985	85-4-19	GN	255
Dunvegan, 1904	B.2828	PAA	61
Dunvegan Bridge over the Peace River from Fort Dunvegan Historic Site, 1995	ADAH		256
East Dollar Lake, looking west, 1995	ADAH		256
Ells, Dr. Sidney, 1928	A.12023	PAA	64
Fairview, 1920s	A.10282	PAA	69
Fort Chipewyan on Athabasca Lake, 1901 (C.W. Mathers photo)	B.2962	PAA	75
Fort Fitzgerald, 1929	69-160-194	UAA	72
Fort MacKay, 1930s	78-45-135	UAA	75
Dr. MacKay and family inside Fort Chipewyan, 1903	B.6988	PAA	76
Gift Lake Metis Settlement, 1974	J.1600/1	PAA	81
Grand Rapids on Athabasca River, ca. 1900	B.2890	PAA	85
Grand Rapids on Athabasca River, ca. 1900, (C.W. Mathers photo)	B.2870	PAA	85
Grand Rapids on Athabasca River, ca. 1900, (C.W. Mathers photo)	B.2899	PAA	85
Grand Rapids on Athabasca River, 1985	85-3-17	GN	256
The Grande Prairie from atop Richmond Hill, 1992	VLDL		257
Grimshaw, Mile Zero, Mackenzie Highway, 1963	A.11179	PAA	88
Guy – Statue of Notre Dame de Fatima, church in background, 1995	MKA 95-2	GN	257
Hay Lakes area, n.d.	B.825	PAA	94
Hines Creek gas pump and flour mill, 1950s	A.6335	PAA	98
John D'Or Prairie, 1985	VLDL		258
Lawrence, Fred, with vegetables from Peace River Crossing, October 1907	B.9047	PAA	119
The Rev. Lucas and family, 1901	B.9591	PAA	131
McConachie, G.W. Grant, ca. 1930	A.13,987	PAA	137
McMillan, Stan, 1937	A.13,989	PAA	139

Feature Name/Photo description	Reference number	Location	Page
Holy Angels Residential School picnic at Fort Chipewyan, near Mission Point, n.d.	OB.734	PAA	143
Mission Point, 1985	85-4-21	GN	257
Moose Portage, Peace River Country, June-July 1913	76-50-14-22	UAA	146
O'Brien Provincial Park and Wapiti River	MKA 95-4	GN	258
Near Peace Point - Gypsum series cliffs on Peace River, late 1920s	69-160-204	UAA	163
Peace River - D.A. Thomas on the Peace River, ca. 1923-1930	72-81-496	UAA	163
Peace River and Smoky River Junction, 1992	VLDL		258
Peace River looking south-west from Peace River (town), 1995	ZJAH		259
Pelican Rapids settlement and trading post near Athabasca River, 1912	A.1938	PAA	166
Pouce Coupé River-Gorge on the river near Imperial Oil Company well location, ca. 1920s	69-160-23	UAA	172
St. Germain, Charles, and Alex McKenzie, n.d.	A.2556	PAA	185
Toward Shaftesbury Settlement, Peace River Bridge at Peace River (town), 1995	ADAH		259
Smith Landing on Slave River, 1901 (C.W. Mathers photo)		PAA	196
Smoky River 9 km south of Guy, 1995	MKA 95-1	GN	259
Smoky River and Peace River Junction, 1961	PA.1616/4	PAA	197
Valhalla, n.d.	A.3935	PAA	218
Vermilion Falls, Peace River, ca.1900	B.3012	PAA	219
Wanham, 1957	A.8978	PAA	223
Waterhole post office and stopping place, 1992	VLDL		Cover
Old Waterways Hotel during a flood, 1936	78-45-163	UAA	225
Watino Bridge opening, 1955	PA.1701/14	PAA	225
West Prairie River Bridge, 1923	A.5072	PAA	227

Feature Name/Photo description	Reference number	Location	Page
Wood Buffalo Park cabin near 27th Baseline at Chenal des Quatre Fourches, n.d.	79-21-35-425	UAA	233
Surveying Photographs			
Getting there:			
Scow loaded with horses, supplies, men, ca. 1915		PAA	246
Surveyor with mosquito netting, on canoe, ca.1915		PAA	246
Everyday duties:			
Dominion Land Survey Party near Peace River, 1915	A.2571	PAA	247
Leveller, northern surveying party, 1917	A.14,216	PAA	247
Testing chains, northern surveying party, 1917	A.14,221	PAA	247
The work of the axemen, survey crew in Peace River area, 1912-1916	87.368	PAA	247
Transit and levelling crew, northern surveying party, 1917	A.14241	PAA	247
Humphrey and Tupper survey party cook making dinner on the raft on the Peace River, 1911	A.7886	PAA	247
Camp life:			
Survey crew in Peace River area, 1912-1916	87.368	PAA	248
Relaxing around the camp fire, survey trip, northern Alberta, ca. 1915	80.28	PAA	248
Bath day, survey trip, northern Alberta, ca. 1915	80.28	PAA	248
Communal grooming, survey crew in Peace River area, ca. 1912-1916	87.368	PAA	248

*M*APS

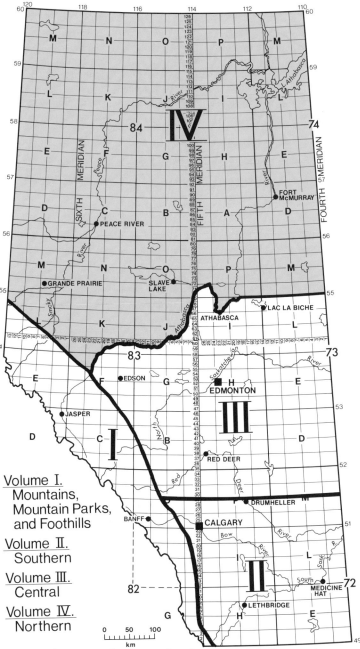

Map showing study areas in the *Place Names of Alberta* series

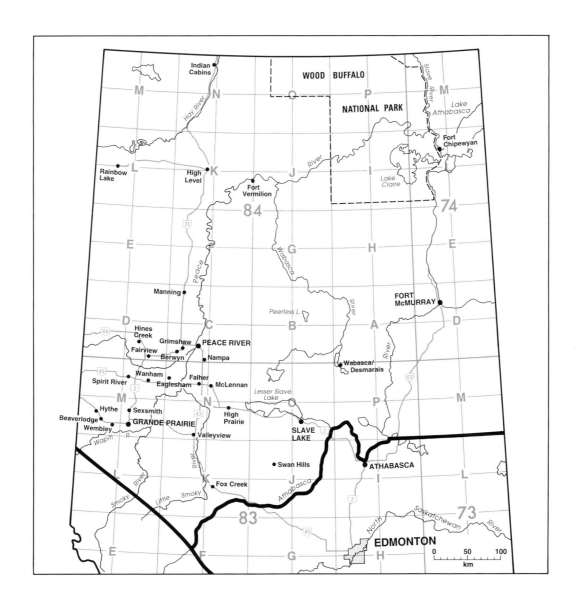

Map showing study area for Volume IV

A~B

3 Channels Area (channel)
74 D/15 - I.D. 18 Alberta
26-89-4-W4
56°45'10"N 110°31'35"W
In the Clearwater River approximately 59 km east of Fort McMurray.

This is a descriptive name given to an area in the Clearwater River where it separates into three channels.

49 Lake (lake)
74 D/7 - Cheecham
21-84-6-W4
56°18'05"N 110°53'05"W
Approximately 57 km south south-east of Fort McMurray.

This lake is called 49 Lake for its location at mile 249 of the Northern Alberta Railways line. It is one of four lakes in the area that takes its name from mileage on the railway tracks. Officially named in 1991 after field research determined the name to be well established and in local use.

51 Lake (lake)
74 D/7 - Cheecham
30-84-6-W4
56°18'55"N 110°56'50"W
Approximately 53 km south-east of Fort McMurray.

This lake is called 51 Lake for its location at mile 251 along the Northern Alberta Railways line. It is one of four lakes in the area that takes its name from mileage on the railway tracks. Officially named in 1991 after field research determined the name to be well established and in local use.

54 Lake (lake)
74 D/7 - Cheecham
2-11-85-7-W4
56°21'01"N 110°59'20"W
Approximately 53 km south-east of Fort McMurray.

*denotes rescinded name or former locality.

This lake is called 54 lake for its location at mile 254 along the Northern Alberta Railways line. It is one of four lakes in the area that takes its name from mileage on the railway tracks. Officially named in 1991 after field research determined the name to be well established and in local use.

55 Lake (lake)
74 D/7 - Cheecham
14-85-7-W4
56°21'59"N 110°60'40"W
Approximately 47 km south-east of Fort McMurray.

This lake is called 55 for its location at mile 255 along the Northern Alberta Railways line. It is one of four lakes in the area that takes its name from mileage on the railway tracks. Officially named in 1991 after field research determined the name to be well established and in local use.

A-H Lake (lake)
84 H/15 - Alberta
17-101-16-W4
57°45'45"N 112°34'45"W
Approximately 135 km north north-west of Fort McMurray.

The most common explanation is that A-H is a symbol on maps used by pilots in this area, especially in the very early days of bush piloting. It was used for navigational purposes.

*****Abasand** (former post office)
74 D/11 - Fort McMurray
17-89-9-W4
56°43'10"N 112°03'40"W
Approximately 2 km west of Fort McMurray.

It is a contraction of **A**th**a**basca tar **sand**s. The post office opened in September, 1937, the first postmaster being Paul Schmidt.

Adair Lake (lake)
84 N/4 - Meander River
18-116-22-W5
59°05'N 117°43'W
Flows east into Hay River approximately 70 km north-west of High Level.

The lake appears on a federal government map as early as 1928; it is not known after whom it is named.

Adams Landing (locality)
84 J/6 - Adams Landing
22-108-7-W5
58°23'N 115°04'W
On the north bank of Peace River approximately 120 km south south-east of High Level.

The precise origin of the name of this locality is unknown. In 1920 surveyor C.P. Hotchkiss reported in his field notes that boats of all sizes could stop at what was known as Adams Landing. A wagon road started out for John D'Or Prairie from this point.

Adskwatim Creek (creek)
84 E/4 - Mearon Creek
12-95-13-W6
57°13'N 119°57'W
Flows south-west into British Columbia approximately 200 km north-west of Peace River (town).

The name was recorded in 1918 by the surveyors on the Alberta-British Columbia Boundary Commission. *Adskwatim* in Cree means "many dams", referring to the abundance of beaver dams on the creek.

Agar Lake (lake)
74 L/1 - Archer Lake
19-106-1-W4
58°13′N 110°09′W
Approximately 173 km north north-east of Fort McMurray.

The name shows on a federal government map as early as 1919; its origin is not precisely known. In botany, agar refers to seaweed of various kinds, and the gelatinous substance extracted from it which is used in food preparation and bacterial cultures. "Agaric" is a fungus which includes the common mushroom. Therefore, when named, there may have been an abundance of mushrooms around the lake.

Aggie (locality)
83 N/7 - Triangle
36-74-18-W5
55°27′N 116°38′W
Approximately 10 km west north-west of High Prairie.

This Edmonton, Dunvegan and British Columbia Railway station was established in 1915, and was named after Agnes McArthur a relative of the general manager of the railway, J.D. McArthur and also J.K. McLennan. (see also Lenarthur and McLennan)

Agnes Lake (lake)
83 J/15 - Upper Saulteaux
26-68-7-W5
54°55′N 114°58′W
Approximately 175 km north-west of Edmonton.

The origin of the name Agnes Lake is not known although there is a suggestion it may have been named by J.N. Wallace, Dominion Land Surveyor, during his survey of the 18th Baseline in 1905. However, it is just one of a number of features in the area that have women's names, all of which were probably named in the 1930s or 1940s. These include the lakes named after Jessie, Jane, Ethel, Kathryn, Edith, Lois, Anna and Sarah. Ethel, Edith and Sarah all have creeks named after them. One man, Archie, is also represented in area lakes. Who these people are is not known.

Agnes Lake (lake)
83 P/15 - Pelican Portage
35-78-17-W4
55°48′N 112°32′W
Approximately 136 km south-west of Fort McMurray.

Officially named in the 1950s; the person after whom this is named is unknown.

Aguhway Lake (lake)
84 A/13 - Liege River
22-91-23-W4
56°54′40″N 113°37′40″W
Approximately 138 km west north-west of Fort McMurray.

This lake takes its name from the many shells to be found in its clear water. *Aguhway* is an aboriginal word, likely Cree, meaning shell.

Akuinu River (river)
83 J/16 - Chisholm
23-68-3-W5
54°53′N 114°21′W
Flows north into Saulteaux River approximately 41 km south-east of Slave Lake.

In 1920, the Dominion Land Surveyor J.N. Wallace wrote: "Akuinu River, name of Indian tribes south of Chipewyans are called Ethinyew or Inenyew." The Cree name for Saulteaux is *Nak-aw-ew-iy-i-new*, which is likely a corruption of this name. The name was recorded by the Geological Survey of Canada in 1892 as the *A-kew-i-new-si-pi*.

W.D. Albright with a sample of produce, 1931

Albright (locality)
83 M/6 - La Glace
NW-29-72-10-W6
55°16′N 119°30′W
Approximately 48 km west north-west of Grande Prairie.

The name for the locality was officially adopted in 1947. It was named for the Albright post office which had been established in 1931. W.D. Albright (1881-1946) came to the Peace River district many years earlier from Ontario. He was an early superintendent of the Beaverlodge Dominion Experimental Farm, and was well known as a promoter of the Peace River Country as a good agricultural district. The post office had originally opened in 1929 under the name of Hommy, after an early settler in the area.

Albright Lake (lake)
83 M/5 - Hythe
NE-8-75-12-W6
55°30′N 119°50′W

Approximately 71 km west north-west of Grande Prairie.

Originally called Goose Lake, this feature was named after W.D. Albright. (see also Albright and Goose Lake)

Albright Creek (creek)
83 M/5 - Hythe
10-7-75-12-W6
55°29′N 120°00′W
Flows west into Tupper Creek, approximately 82 km north north-west of Grande Prairie.

Originally called Goose Creek, this feature was named after W.D. Albright. (see also Albright and Goose Creek)

***Alex Creek** (creek)
83 M/5 - Hythe
5-22-73-11-W6
55°20′N 119°37′W
Flows north-east into Beaverlodge River approximately 50 km north-west of Grande Prairie.

(see Beavertail Creek)

Alex Lake (lake)
84 D/1 - Fairview
14-82-3-W6
56°07′N 118°20′W
Approximately 6 km north north-east of Fairview.

It is not known after whom this feature is named.

Alexander Island (island)
74 E/4 - Fort MacKay
7-94-1-W4
57°09′N 111°37′W
In Athabasca River approximately 50 km north north-west of Fort McMurray.

---

*denotes rescinded name or former locality.

This island was named in 1925 for Captain Alexander, a river pilot on the *Northland Echo*, which plied the Athabasca River. (see also Alexander Lake)

Alexander Lake (lake)
74 M/9 - Colin Lake
29-122-3-W4
59°37′N 110°28′W
Approximately 317 km north of Fort McMurray.

It was named in 1929 after Captain Alexander of the steamer *Northland Echo*, running between Fort McMurray and Fort Fitzgerald. (see also Alexander Island)

Algar Lake (lake)
84 A/8 - Algar Lake
33, 34-84-15-W4
56°18′N 112°18′W
Approximately 70 km south-west of Fort McMurray.

The name was adopted in 1944; it is not known after whom it is named.

Algar River (river)
84 A/9 - Boiler Rapids
17-87-14-W4
56°33′N 112°11′W
Flows north into Athabasca River approximately 50 km west south-west of Fort McMurray.

The name was adopted in 1944; it is not known after whom it is named.

Alice Creek (creek)
84 I/6 - Lake Dene
SW-24-107-20-W4
58°18′N 113°12′W
Flows north into Birch River approximately 195 km north north-west of Fort McMurray.

Originally showing on a map of 1916, it was likely named by F.V. Seibert, DLS, who surveyed this area in August 1915.

Allan Lake (lake)
83 K/16 - Wallace River
SE-4-69-14-W5
54°56′20″N 116°03′30″W
Approximately 70 km east south-east of Valleyview.

This was apparently named by W.T. Green, DLS, after his brother Allan. It was officially approved in 1906.

Allan River (river)
83 J/15 - Upper Saulteaux
24-68-6-W5
54°54′N 114°46′W
Flows east south-east into Saulteaux River approximately 41 km south of Slave Lake.

(see Allan Lake)

Alleman Creek (creek)
84 E/2 - Alleman Creek
5-93-4-W6
57°02′N 118°36′W
Flows south-east into Notikewin River approximately 61 km west north-west of Manning.

This creek was named for Private Martin Alleman, killed in action in August 1943.

Amadou Lake (lake)
83 P/7 - Amadou Lake
16-31-73-19-W4
55°23′N 112°55′W
Approximately 120 km east of Slave Lake.

At one time known locally as Touchwood Lake, the name Amadou Lake was officially adopted in 1955. According to the dictionary, touchwood is a "readily flammable, especially soft substance into which wood is changed by fungi, used as tinder." Amadou is tinder made from fungi. The word amadou comes from its Latin root meaning lover or quickly afire.

Amber River (river)
84 L/15 - Habay
33-113-6-W6
58°52′N 118°56′W
Flows south south-east into Omega River approximately 48 km north north-east of Rainbow Lake.

The descriptive name for this river refers to the colour of the water.

Amber River Indian Reserve #211
(Indian reserve)
84 L/15 - Habay
16-114-6-W6
58°53′N 118°57′W
Approximately 47 km north north-east of Rainbow Lake.

Named for its proximity to Amber River.

Amesbury (locality)
83 P/1 - Wandering River
26-70-17-W4
55°05′N 112°29′W
Approximately 50 km north-west of Lac La Biche.

The post office opened in 1933, with J.T. Smith being the first postmaster. It is possibly named after a place in Wiltshire, England. It combines "Stronghold of a man named Ambre" with "burg," referring to a populated area. It is at the site of Amesbury Abbey where quite some time prior to the establishment of the abbey, Queen Guinevere of Arthurian legend is believed to have died.

Amundson (railway point)
83 L/8 - Simonette River
4-63-3-W6
54°25′N 118°23′W
Approximately 87 km south south-east of Grande Prairie.

*denotes rescinded name or former locality.

The Alberta Resources Railway point was named after Burgo Amundson, killed in action December 1943.

Anderson Lake (lake)
83 M/6 - La Glace
24-73-9-W6
55°20′N 119°15′W
Approximately 33 km north-west of Grande Prairie.

The lake was officially named in the early 1950s; however, the name was well established before then. It was most likely named after Nels J. Anderson and his family who homesteaded on the south-east corner of the lake. Nels Anderson was born in Norway in 1873, and moved with his family to North Dakota, before coming to Canada in 1923. The family settled in the Wembley area in 1928. Local residents also refer to Anderson Lake as Grass Lake because of an abundance of tall grass in and around the lake. (see also Grass Lake)

Andrew Lake (lake)
74 M/16 - Andrew Lake
126-1-W4
59°55′N 110°05′W
Approximately 353 km north north-east of Fort McMurray.

It was named in 1929 after Professor J. Andrew Allan (1884-1855), head of the Department of Geology at the University of Alberta from 1912 to 1929.

Anna Lake (lake)
83 J/11 - Swan Hills
25-66-9-W5
54°44′N 115°14′W
Approximately 12 km south-east of Swan Hills.

Likely named some time in the 1940s, after whom is not known. (see also Agnes Lake)

***Anna Lake** (lake)
83 M/14 - Blueberry Mountain
36-78-10-W6
55°48′N 119°25′W
Approximately 35 km west of Spirit River.

This lake is the source of the Ksituan River, and shows on a 1917 federal government map as Anna Lake. It is now called Ksituan Lake. (see Ksituan Lake)

Ante Creek (creek)
83 K/13 - Long Lake
12-67-25-W5
54°46′N 117°40′W
Flows west into Simonette River approximately 84 km south-east of Grande Prairie.

The name shows as early as 1917 on a federal government map; however, its origin is not known. The noun, ante, refers to the stake put up by a poker player before the cards are drawn. The prefix ante- can mean before, or preceding. Whether there is a connection with any of these meanings is not yet known.

Antler Lake (lake)
84 H/11 - Bergeron Creek
33-98-21-W4
57°32′58″N 113°22′29″W
Approximately 152 km north-west of Fort McMurray.

This remote lake became known as Antler Lake apparently because of a huge antler found there.

Anzac (hamlet)
74 D/6 - Gregoire Lake
7-86-7-W4
56°26′15″N 111°05′15″W
Approximately 36 km south-east of Fort McMurray.

Originally established as a point on the Alberta and Great Waterways Railway line in 1917, the name is commemorative of

World War I's Australia and New Zealand Army Corps. The Anzac post office operated here from 1955-1969. The first postmaster was G. Harrison.

Arcadia (locality)
83 N/8 - High Prairie
9-74-14-W5
55°24′N 116°08′W
Approximately 28 km east of High Prairie.

The Edmonton, Dunvegan and British Columbia Railway station was established here in 1914. The records of the railway state it is named "after the literal meaning of the word *rurally simple*." Arcadia is a mountain district in the Grecian area of Peleponnesus, and is seen as an ideal rustic paradise. The name was likely chosen by the railway as a promotional one extolling the virtues of the farmland to prospective settlers.

Arcadia Creek (creek)
83 N/8 - High Prairie
22-74-14-W5
55°27′N 116°04′W
Flows north into Lesser Slave Lake approximately 28 km east of High Prairie

Named due to its proximity to the locality of Arcadia. (see Arcadia)

Arch Lake (lake)
74 M/15 - Mercredi Lake
21-125-4-W4
59°52′N 110°37′W
Approximately 343 km north of Fort McMurray.

Named in 1929, it describes the feature's shape.

Archer Lake (lake)
74 L/1 - Archer Lake
13-105-2-W4
58°07′N 110°21′W

Luncheon on the Rock, Arch Lake, late 1920s

Approximately 159 km north north-east of Fort McMurray.

Both the lake and the creek were named after W. Archer, a member of the survey crew of F.V. Seibert, DLS, in 1915.

Archer Creek (creek)
74 L/2 - Larocque Lake
16-32-104-4-W4
58°05′N 110°37′W
Flows south-west into Maybelle River approximately 150 km north north-east of Fort McMurray

(see Archer Lake)

Archie Lake (lake)
83 J/11 - Swan Hills
1-66-8-W5
54°41′N 115°04′W
Approximately 22 km east south-east of Swan Hills.

Named before 1940, after whom it is named is not known. (see Agnes Lake)

Ardens Slough (marsh)
74 L/14 - Rivière des Rochers
9-114-9-W4
58°53′N 111°28′W

Approximately 236 km north of Fort McMurray.

Officially named in 1971, it may have been named after D'Arcey Arden, at one time a park ranger in Wood Buffalo National Park. The word *arden* is of Celtic origin and means "high district."

Arrowhead Lake (lake)
84 P/12 - Peace Point
NW-17-123-21-W4
59°41′N 113°38′W
Approximately 235 km east north-east of High Level.

The name was officially adopted in 1955, and is descriptive of its shape.

Ashton Lake (lake)
74 M/16 - Andrew Lake
3-125-3-W4
59°51′N 110°25′W
Approximately 340 km north of Fort McMurray.

The name appears on federal government maps as early as 1930. It was named after J. Ashton Jaffary, Provincial Librarian, who was at that time the Alberta advisor to the Geographic Board of Canada. Ashton is a common word from the old English meaning "where ash [trees] grew."

Asphalt Creek (creek)
74 E/12 - Asphalt Creek
30-98-10-W4
57°32′N 111°38′W
Flows south-east into Eymundson Creek approximately 92 km north north-west of Fort McMurray.

Showing on a federal government map of 1916, the name is probably descriptive, indicating the presence of bitumen impregnated sands exposed along many river banks in the area. The tar sands along the Athabasca and its tributaries are the largest of the four deposits found in north-central Alberta.

*Asplund (former post office)
83 N/3 - Valleyview
SW27-69-22-W5
55°00′N 117°16′W
Approximately 10 km south of Valleyview.

Established here in 1940, the first postmaster was A. Werklund. According to the files of the Geographic Board of Canada Asplund is a descriptive name meaning poplar grove.

Asplund Creek (creek)
83 K/14 - Asplund Creek
3-25-68-22-W5
54°55′N 117°13′W
Flows north-east into Little Smoky River approximately 18 km south south-east of Valleyview.

Officially approved in 1960 it took its name from the nearby post office, which now no longer exists. It was originally recorded as Moose Creek. The name was likely changed due to the large number of features named for the large ruminant. (see also Asplund)

Assineau River Indian Reserve No. 150F
(Indian reserve)
83 O/6 - Kinuso
NE-5-74-8-W5
55°23′N 115°11′W
Approximately 28 km west north-west of Slave Lake.

It was established in 1912 under Treaty No. 8. (see Assineau River)

Assineau River (river)
83 O/6 - Kinuso
8-74-8-W5
55°24′N 115°12′W
Flows north into Lesser Slave Lake approximately 29 km west north-west of Slave Lake.

---
*denotes rescinded name or former locality.

The name for this river was mentioned as early as 1904 by the Dominion Lands Survey which went through the area that year. It has been stated in a number of sources that "Assineau" is a rendering of the Cree word meaning "nobody." Yet another source has translated the word to mean "stony." G.M. Dawson in 1879 transcribed the Cree word for people as *ai-si-ni-wok*. According to another source, the Cree for nobody is *namawiyak*. Other references have been made to it as "Sinew River."

Assineau (locality)
83 O/6 - Kinuso
32-73-8-W5
55°22′N 115°11′W
Approximately 27 km west north-west of Slave Lake.

This Edmonton, Dunvegan and British Columbia Railway station was established in 1914, and was named after the nearby river. (see Assineau River)

Assumption (hamlet)
84 L/10 - Assumption
1-112-5-W6
58°40′N 118°36′W
Approximately 48 km north-east of Rainbow Lake.

When a post office was opened in December 1953 on the North-East quarter of Section 1, Township 112, Range 5, west of the 6th Meridian, it was named Assumption because it was located in the rectory of Our Lady of Assumption Indian School. In 1970 the name of the post office was changed to Chateh at the request of the Band Council, now Dene Tha' Tribal Administration. The name Assumption was retained for a hamlet situated on the reserve. The feast of the Assumption of the Blessed Virgin Mary is celebrated on August 15th, and is a memorial to the day when Mary died and was taken body and soul into heaven.

Athabasca, Lake (lake)
74 M/1 - Winnifred Lake
116-1-W4
59°05′N 110°10′W
Approximately 260 km north north-east of Fort McMurray.

The term "Athabasca" is usually said to be a Cree word, although there is no evidence for this in Father Lacombe's *Dictionnaire de la langue des Cris*, 1874. In 1790, it was referred to as "Lake of the Hills," and the river, the Great Arabuska. Lake of the Hills may have been a more genteel translation of the name for the lake at the time. Peter Fidler recorded the Cree name as *Too-toos Sack-a-ha-gan*, and the Chipewyan name as *Thew Too-ak*. The literal translation of the Cree name is "breast" lake, referring to the north-west shore, which according to Philip Turnor in 1791, came "from their appearing high and rounded at a distance." In 1801 it was called Athapaskow Lake. On maps from the early part of this century, it was recorded as Athabaska. One possibility for the origin of the name is that, since both the lake and river that drains into it were Beaver and Chipewyan territory in the 18th century when the name was first recorded, the name derives from the name of these aboriginal groups' common language, Athapaskan. However, the most commonly accepted version of the origin of the name is from the Cree, where it is said to mean "where there are reeds," referring to the muddy delta of the river where it falls into Lake Athabasca. Of this portion of it, Turner wrote "low swampy ground on the South side with a few willows growing upon it, from which the Lake in general takes its name Athapison in the Southern [Cree] tongue [which] signifies open country such as lakes with willows and grass growing about them." In 1820, George Simpson of the Hudson's Bay Company referred to it as the "Athabasca or Elk River."

Indian settlement along the Athabasca River, ca. 1914-1918

■ **Athabasca River** (river)
74 L/7 - Keane Creek
6-109-6-W4
58°27′N 110°59′W
Flows north-east into Big Channel approximately 35 km south-east of Fort Chipewyan.
(see Lake Athabasca)

*****Athabina Lake** (lake)
83 J/9 - Flatbush
65,66-2-W5
54°41′N 114°17′W
Approximately 8 km west of Flatbush.

The name for this lake was adopted in 1948, and took its name from its proximity to the **Atha**basca and Pem**bina** Rivers. Four years later, the name reverted to its earlier name Deep Lake. (see also Deep Lake)

Atihk Sakahikun (lake)
84 J/11 - Lawrence River
20-112-9-W5
58°44′20″N 115°29′00″W
Approximately 97 km east north-east of High Level.

A Cree phrase meaning elk lake, this name is shared by many features in Northern Alberta where herds of caribou are found.

---

*denotes rescinded name or former locality.

Atikameg (hamlet)
83 O/13 - Atikameg
8-80-11-W5
55°56′N 115°39′W
Approximately 90 km north-west of Slave Lake.

Atikameg is a variation of the Cree word for whitefish. The post office was established here in 1927, with Mrs. Hogue as the first postmaster.

*****Atikamisis Lake Settlement** (settlement)
83 O/13 - Atikameg
80-11-W5
55°55′N 115°40′W
Approximately 90 km north-west of Slave Lake.

Atikamisis is a variation of the Cree word for whitefish. The settlement, first surveyed in 1914, takes its name from the nearby Utikumasis Lake. (see also Utikumasis Lake)

Atikkamek Creek (creek)
83 K/10 - Atikkamek Creek
7-65-19-W5
54°36′N 116°51′W
Flows west into Iosegun River, approximately 140 km south-east of Grande Prairie.

Atikkamek is a variation of a Cree word meaning whitefish. The name shows on maps as early as 1917 and is written "atikameg." Other variations of the word in Alberta place names include *utikuma*, *atikameg*, and *utikoomak*. It is likely descriptive of the abundance of the fish in the creek.

*****Atkinson Lake** (lake)
83 M/6 - La Glace
NW-35-73-8-W6
55°22′N 119°07′W

Approximately 30 km north-west of Grande Prairie.

(see Mulligan Lake)

Audet Lake (lake)
74 E/10 - Audet Lake
4-100-6-W4
57°38′N 110°55′W
Approximately 105 km north north-east of Fort McMurray.

This is a war memorial name. Flight Lieutenant R.J. Audet, DFC (1922-1945), from Coutts, Alberta, enlisted in the RCAF at Calgary in 1941. When he had completed his training course he was commissioned and went overseas. He was awarded the DFC on February 16, 1945. Two weeks later he was reported missing and subsequently presumed dead.

Auger Bay (bay)
83 O/6 - Kinuso
11-74-9-W5
55°24′N 115°16′W
Approximately 30 km west north-west of Slave Lake located in Lesser Slave Lake.

The name was recorded by the Geological Survey of Canada in 1892, and likely refers to the surname of a family in the area.

Avenir (locality)
83 P/1 - Wandering River
6-70-15-W4
55°02′N 112°16′W
Approximately 45 km north north-west of Lac La Biche.

Avenir is the French word for "future" and perhaps indicates the residents' strong belief in their community. It was established as a post office in 1949, the first postmaster being Irene St. Jean.

Bad Rapids (rapids)
84 G/2 - Bad Rapids
30-93-4-W5
57°06′N 114°37′W
In the Wabasca River approximately 182 km east of Manning.

The precise origin of the name of these rapids is unknown; however, it is probably descriptive. According to the 1978 *Canoe Alberta* map these rapids are said to have "obstructed passages, waves high, powerful and irregular, boiling eddies, [and] rocks."

Bad Heart (locality)
83 M/8 - Wembley
17-75-2-W6
55°30′N 118°18′W
Approximately 42 km north-east of Grande Prairie.

The post office of that name was established in July 1929 and closed in June 1968. It takes its name from the nearby river. The first postmaster was R.J. Magee. (see Bad Heart River)

Bad Heart River (river)
83 M/9 - Peoria
2-76-2-W6
55°33′N 118°12′W
Flows south-east into Smoky River approximately 53 km north-east of Grande Prairie.

It is said the name is a translation of the Cree word *maatsiti*, or *missipi*. G.M. Dawson of the Geological Survey of Canada also referred to it in 1879 as Wicked River. Either one of these may refer to the narrow 125-metre-high canyon through which the river flows along its winding route, or the name might have spiritual significance.

---

*denotes rescinded name or former locality.

Bailey Lake (lake)
74 M/16 - Andrew Lake
18-126-1-W4
59°57′N 110°10′W
Approximately 355 km north of Fort McMurray.

The name was submitted in 1958 by the Research Council of Alberta, and is one of a series of features in the area named after prominent geologists. This lake was named in honour of Edward Battersby Bailey, known as Sir Edward Bailey (1881-1968), renowned Scottish geologist, who was Director of the Geological Survey of Great Britain from 1937 to 1945.

Baker Lake (lake)
74 D/8 - Gipsy Lake
5-86-1-W4
56°26′N 110°07′W
Approximately 84 km east south-east of Fort McMurray.

The precise origin of the name of this lake, which has been named since at least 1930, is unknown.

Bald Mountain Creek (creek)
83 L/15 - Big Mountain Creek
10-16-68-5-W6
54°54′N 118°42′W
Flows north-east into Big Mountain Creek approximately 27 km south south-east of Grande Prairie.

Named some time before 1960, although its origin is not precisely known, it might refer to a time when forest fires had burnt the trees off the top of the mountain, rendering it bald. The vegetation has regrown, so the name is no longer descriptive.

*****Ballater** (former locality)
83 N/11 - Donnelly
9-76-21-W5
55°35′N 117°11′W
Approximately 20 km south-west of McLennan.

Likely named after the town of the same name in Scotland, the community grew around the Ballater School District which was established in 1926. The original Ballater in Aberdeen (now Grampian), in east-central Scotland, has at least two meanings. It may mean "broom" land. Broom is a yellow-flowered shrub predominantly associated with Scotland. The name may also mean "village on a sloping hill, or hillside". The post office opened in 1937 with the first postmaster being Fred Caron.

Barber Lake (lake)
74 L/2 - Larocque Lake
11-105-6-W4
58°06′N 110°52′W
Approximately 148 km north of Fort McMurray.

It was named after H.G. Barber, DLS. The name shows as early as 1919 on federal government maps.

Baril Lake (lake)
74 L/12 - Hilda Lake
112-10-W4
58°46′N 111°41′W
Approximately 219 km north of Fort McMurray.

The lake was named in 1916 by J.A. Fletcher, DLS, after M.C.L. Baril of the Surveyor General's staff who was killed in action on November 9, 1915. There is also a mountain peak south-west of Turner Valley named after him. (see also *Place Names of Alberta, Volume I; Mountains, Mountain Parks and Foothills*)

Baril River (river)
74 L/13 - Baril River
11-23-114-11-W4
58°55′N 111°44′W
Flows north into Peace River approximately 50 km north-west of Fort Chipewyan.

(see Baril Lake)

Barr Creek (creek)
83 M/4 - Rio Grande
34-71-13-W6
55°11′N 119°54′W
Flows east into Windsor Creek approximately 63 km west of Grande Prairie.

The name was recorded on the Alberta-British Columbia Boundary Survey map in 1922. Its origin is not known, but a man named Barr was a pioneer in nearby Hythe.

Barrow Lake (lake)
74 M/3 - Ryan Lake
13-118-8-W4
59°15′N 111°13′W
Approximately 273 km north of Fort McMurray.

Name submitted in 1958 by the Alberta Research Council and is derived from the name of a deceased geologist.

Bartsch Creek (creek)
83 N/7 - Triangle
12-74-20-W5
55°24′N 116°56′W
Flows west into Little Smoky River approximately 30 km west of High Prairie.

After field research in the early 1950s showed that the name was well known to residents of the area, it was adopted.

Base Lake (lake)
73 M/12 - Thornbury Lake
8-77-12-W4
55°39′N 111°50′W
Approximately 100 km north of Lac La Biche.

It was known locally as Whitefish. In order to avoid confusion with other locally known Whitefish Lakes, Base was the name

*denotes rescinded name or former locality.

chosen because the 20th Baseline ran just south of it.

Baseline Lake (lake)
84 A/11 - Blanchet Lake
35-88-21-W4
56°41′N 113°13′W
Approximately 119 km west of Fort McMurray.

This lake is descriptively named for its location directly on the 23rd Baseline.

Baseline Lake (lake)
83 J/4 - Whitecourt
3-32-60-13-W5
54°14′N 115°55′W
Approximately 18 km north-west of Whitecourt.

The name for this lake first appears on federal government maps as early as 1917 and refers to its location on the 16th Baseline.

Basse, Pointe (point)
74 L/15 - Burntwood Island
10-113-6-W4
58°48′N 110°54′W
Approximately 226 km north of Fort McMurray.

Probably dating from the time of the fur trade, the name has shown on federal government maps as early as 1917. The origin of the name likely refers to the translation of *basse* which in French means shoal or sandbank.

Basset Lake (lake)
84 L/7 - Zama Lake
30-107-3-W6
58°19′N 118°28′W
Approximately 55 km east south-east of Rainbow Lake.

The precise origin of the name of this lake is unknown. It may have been known originally as Rainbow Lake, named after

Rainbow Fournier, a trapper in the area. The name "Rainbow" was eventually applied to a lake 24 kilometres to the west.

Bat Lake (lake)
84 B/7 - Bat Lake
24-84-7-W5
56°16′N 114°57′W
Approximately 111 km north of Slave Lake.

This name which first appears on a map in 1915, takes its name from the many bats found in the area. In the late 19th century Native people, who had a hunting camp here, encountered a large number of bats nesting in the tall grass. They took sticks to "bat" the disturbed creatures out of the air. The bat is the only true flying mammal, they are nocturnal of order *Chiroptera*. In Canada there are nineteen species ranging in size and weight from 5 to 35 grams. The flying bat hunts using a unique system, echolocation or bisonar. Bats emit a call and then listen. The difference between the original call and the echo contains information about a selected target. Little brown bats, for example, use 50-500 calls per second to detect small insects at a distance of between one and two metres. Some bat calls can be heard, but those that are ultrasonic or of high frequency cannot be heard by the human ear. In Canada bats hibernate or migrate to warmer climes. In summer they roost in trees, cliffs and buildings. Most species mate in fall. Baby bats grow quickly, feeding on their mother's milk until ready to fly and catch insects. In summer the bat consumes 50 percent of its own body weight daily in insects. Bats are known to live as long as 30 years.

***Battle River Prairie** (former post office)
84 C/13 - Manning
15-92-23-W5
56°58′35″N 117°36′40″W
Approximately 6 km north of Manning.

The post office was established here in August, 1919; it was named for its proximity to the Notikewin River. The first postmaster was Charlie N. Brown. (see also Notikewin River)

Bay Tree (locality)
83 M/13 - Bonanza
NE-2-79-13-W6
55°49'N 119°54'W
Approximately 66 km west of Spirit River.

The Bay Tree school was established in 1920, and the Bay Tree post office was established ten years later. The first postmaster was R. Tremblay. Although the precise origin is not known, it may have been named for the presence of mountain ash trees in the area. The mountain ash is a laurel tree, another type of which is the bay.

Bayard Lake (lake)
84 H/16 - Bayard Lake
16-101-15-W4
57°46'N 112°23'W
Approximately 130 km north north-west of Fort McMurray.

The precise origin of the name of this lake is unknown. The lake is also known locally as Burnt Lake.

Bayonet Lake (lake)
74 M/16 - Andrew Lake
8-126-2-W4
59°56'N 110°18'W
Approximately 353 km north of Fort McMurray.

It was named in 1929 and is descriptive of its shape.

Bear Canyon (locality)
84 D/4 - Cherry Point
27-83-12-W6
56°13'N 119°49'W
Approximately 133 km north-west of Grande Prairie.

---

*denotes rescinded name or former locality.

It has been suggested the name came from the number of grizzly bears that used to frequent the area. As this locality is at the head of a canyon running down to Peace River, this explanation may well be true. A post office was established here in 1959, and the first postmaster was Lois Erickson.

Bear Creek stopping house on old Slave Lake-Peace River Trail, n.d.

*Bear Creek (creek)
83 M/6 - La Glace
32-72-7-W6
55°17'N 119°02'W
Flows south-east into Bear Lake approximately 17 km north-west of Grande Prairie.

It is a translation of the Cree word *muskwa*. Many local residents refer to Bear River as Bear Creek. A letter to the Surveyor General from W.G. McFarlane, DLS, dated 1909 referred to this feature as Bear Creek. However, the official name is still Bear River. (see Bear River)

Bear Creek (creek)
83 J/5 - Carson Lake
62-14-W5
54°22'N 115°59'W
Flows south into Sakwatamau River approximately 35 km north-west of Whitecourt.

It shows as early as 1917 on federal government maps and is likely descriptive of the abundance of this animal in the area.

Bear Lake (locality)
83 M/7 - Sexsmith
4-73-7-W6
55°17'N 118°59'W
Approximately 17 km north-west of Grande Prairie.

Named for its proximity to Bear Lake. (see Bear Lake)

Bear Lake (lake)
83 M/7 - Sexsmith
NW-22-72-7-W6
55°19'N 119°00'W
Approximately 9 km north-west of Grande Prairie.

Likely descriptive of the abundance of this animal in the area. The name has been used since the first settlers came into the area; documentation shows name usage in 1910.

*Bear Lake (lake)
83 K/7 - Iosegun Creek
13-63-19-W5
54°27'N 116°44'W
Approximately 155 km south-east of Grande Prairie.

It shows by this name as early as 1916 on federal government maps, and some sources referred to the lake by that name into the 1950s. It was likely descriptive of the prevalence of the animal in the area. However the name that was finally applied to the feature was Raspberry Lake. (see Raspberry Lake)

Bear River (river)
83 M/1 - DeBolt
36-70-4-W6
55°06'N 118°28'W
Flows southeast into Wapiti River approximately 20 km east south-east of Grande Prairie.

The name is likely descriptive of the abundance of this animal in the area.

Bear River (river)
83 M/6 - La Glace
32-72-7-W6
55°17'N 119°02'W
Flows south-east into Bear Lake approximately 17 km north-west of Grande Prairie.

In 1879 George Dawson of the Geological Survey of Canada also referred to the river by its Beaver name, *Sus-za-ka*. However, there is still some discussion whether or not it should be called a river or a creek. The early surveyors did refer to it as a creek, as do local residents today. In 1854, the Fort Dunvegan Hudson's Bay Company post journal refers to it as Bear River.

Bear River (river)
84 J/6 - Adams Landing
34-107-9-W5
58°20'N 115°25'W
Flows east north-east into Wabasca River approximately 101 km east south-east of High Level.

The name was recorded as early as 1890 by the Geological Survey of Canada, and likely refers to the prevalence of the animal in the area.

Bearhead Creek (creek)
84 C/2 - Harmon Valley
18-81-19-W5
56°01'N 116°58'W
Flows north-west into Heart River approximately 30 km south-east of Peace River.

The precise origin of the name of this creek is unknown, however it was referred to by this name by H.W. Selby, DLS, during his survey in 1908.

---
*denotes rescinded name or former locality.

Beaton Creek (creek)
84 C/12 - Dixonville
1-87-24-W5
56°31'N 117°41'W
Flows south-east into Whitemud River approximately 39 km north-west of Peace River.

It was named after A. Beaton, the axeman on the 1913 survey crew of G.A. Tipper, DLS.

Beatty Lake (lake)
84 M/16 - Thurston Lake
14-125-1-W6
59°51'53"N 118°02'50"W
Approximately 153 km north north-west of High Level.

This lake was named by J.R. Akins, DLS, during his 1915 survey of the 6th Meridian. The person for whom the lake was named was not stated in Akins' field correspondence. It was most probably named after one of three colleagues, all called Beatty: James Edward Beatty, of Sarnia, Ontario, commissioned Dominion Land Surveyor on November 18, 1904; Frank Weldon Beatty, of Pembroke, Ontario, or William Benjamin Beatty, both of whom were commissioned Dominion Land Surveyor on May 18, 1914. There is also a possibility that Beatty refers to one of two earlier Dominion Surveyors who received their commission on April 14, 1872, David Beatty and Walter Beatty.

Beaver Creek (creek)
83 J/4 - Whitecourt
35-59-12-W5
54°08'N 115°42'W
Flows north-west into the McLeod River at the town of Whitecourt.

Early settlers called the feature Beaver Creek; however as early as 1917 the name Whitecourt Creek started appearing on maps. It was so named for its proximity to the community of Whitecourt. It never caught on, and during field research in 1982 it was found the local people still referred to it as Beaver Creek. The name was officially changed. The name is descriptive of the beaver dams found on the creek.

Beaver Indian River (river)
84 P/3 - Patenaude Lake
SW-3-116-19-W4
59°03'N 113°09'W
Flows east into Jackfish River approximately 238 km east north-east of High Level.

It was officially named in 1944, and is likely descriptive of the aboriginal people predominant in the area.

Beaver Lake (lake)
74 D/13 - Ruth Lake
18-92-10-W4
56°58'40"N 111°35'40"W
Approximately 30 km north north-west of Fort McMurray.

This man-made lake is called Beaver Lake because of the large beaver population in the vicinity. It was created in a swampy area along the Beaver River west of Ruth Lake when a transformer station was needed for the area.

*Beaver Lake (lake)
84 I/6 - Lake Dene
19-108-20-W4
58°24'N 113°19'W
Approximately 208 km north north-west of Fort McMurray.

The federal government transferred beaver to this lake in the 1940s and they flourished. The name was changed in 1963 to honour an early settler in the area. (see Lake Dene)

*Beaver Lake (lake)
84 H/5 - Burnt Lake
12-98-24-W4
57°29'N 113°46'W
Approximately 165 km north-west of Fort McMurray.

(see Jean Lake)

Beaver Ranch Creek (creek)
84 J/5 - Sled Island
3-109-10-W5
58°26'N 115°34'W
Flows south into Peace River approximately 90 km east south-east of High Level.

The Lawrence family used to live here in the early 1900s and the name comes from the presence of their ranch farmstead. When J.S. Galletly surveyed this area in 1913, he annotated the creek as Beaver Creek, noting a log outbuilding. According to Beaver Ranch residents this area used to be known as *Mostos-Okamik* a Cree name meaning "cow barn." (see also Lawrence River)

Beaver Ranch Indian Reserve No. 163 (Indian reserve)
84 J/5 - Sled Island
3-109-11-W5
58°26'N 115°45'W
Approximately 80 km east of High Level.

Named for its proximity to Beaver Ranch Creek. (see Beaver Ranch Creek)

Beaver River (river)
74 E/4 - Fort MacKay
6-94-10-W4
57°35'N 111°07'W
Flows north north-east into Athabasca River approximately 55 km north of Fort McMurray.

The precise origin of the name of this river is unknown; it probably denotes the presence of the ubiquitous beaver. It was recorded by A.D. Griffin, DLS, in 1915.

*Beaverlodge (locality)
83 M/3 - Wembley
11-72-8-W6
55°14'N 119°07'W
Approximately 35 km west of Grande Prairie.

(see Lake Saskatoon)

Beaverlodge (town)
83 M/3 - Wembley
2-72-10-W6
55°13'N 119°26'W
Approximately 36 km west of Grande Prairie.

The town is named for its proximity to the river of the same name. The first white settlers came to the area in 1908. The first post office was opened in 1910 and named Redwillow since the name Beaverlodge had already been given to the post office at Lake Saskatoon. The name Redwillow is also taken from a nearby river. When the Edmonton, Dunvegan and British Columbia Railway arrived in 1928, the townsite was moved nearly two kilometres to the north-west of the original site and called Beaverlodge, at which time the original Beaverlodge post office was renamed Lake Saskatoon.

Beaverlodge River (river)
83 M/3 - Wembley
18-70-9-W6
55°03'N 119°22'W
Flows south into Redwillow River approximately 35 km west south-west of Grande Prairie.

The name Beaverlodge is from the translation of a Beaver word in which lodge means "temporary dwelling." In 1879, George Dawson of the Geological Survey of Canada refers to it as the Beaver Lodge River, or *Uz-i-pa* in the Beaver language.

Beaverskin Creek (creek)
84 L/4 - Chasm Creek
25-105-13-W6
58°09'N 120°00'W
Flows west north-west into British Columbia approximately 50 km south-west of Rainbow Lake.

Beaverskin Creek is a translation of the Slavey name for this creek, and was adopted in 1952 when a unique name was required by a boundary survey party.

Beavertail Creek (creek)
83 M/5 - Hythe
5-22-73-11-W6
55°20'N 119°37'W
Flows north-east into Beaverlodge River approximately 50 km north-west of Grande Prairie.

Officially named in 1947 at the suggestion of a survey party, for the beaver found on this creek. In 1909, when the Dominion Lands Survey came through the area, the surveyor listed no name for the creek. When the federal government map of 1917 was published, the creek was called Alex Creek.

Bede Creek (creek)
84 K/7 - Child Lake
22-108-18-W5
58°23'N 116°54'W
Flows north-east into Boyer River approximately 19 km south-east of High Level.

The precise origin for the name of this creek is unknown although it may be a surname. The Venerable Bede was an English monk and church historian who lived ca. 673-725. Local Beaver Indians refer to the creek as *Apechi Sake* after one whose trapline cabin was located on the stream.

---
*denotes rescinded name or former locality.

Brother John Behan (Oblate brother), ca. 1931-1934

Behan (locality)
73 M/6 - Winefred Lake
35-72-10-W4
55°17′N 110°26′W
Approximately 70 km north north-east of Lac La Biche.

Originally a stop on the Alberta and Great Waterways Railway line established in 1916, there have been two suggested origins of the name. The 1928 version of *Place-Names of Alberta* stated it was named after the nearby lake which was, in turn, named after the cook on the survey party of G.H. Blanchet, DLS, who worked in the area in 1911. However, another possibility was that it was named after an Oblate missionary, Brother John Behan from Ireland, who worked at the nearby Grouard mission a number of times between 1885 and 1912 before moving to the Wabasca mission in 1912.

*denotes rescinded name or former locality.

Behan Lake (lake)
73 M/5 - Behan Lake
1-73-11-W4
55°18′N 111°34′W
Approximately 63 km north north-east of Lac La Biche.

(see Behan)

Belloy (locality)
83 M/16 - Codesa
4-15-78-2-W6
55°45′N 118°15′W
Approximately 39 km east of Spirit River.

This former Edmonton, Dunvegan and British Columbia Railway station was established in 1916 and was named in honour of Madame Belloy, a Belgian soprano who sang for the Belgian Relief Fund during World War I. Octavie Belloy was born in 1894 in Borgerhout, and made her operatic debut at the Royal Flemish Opera in January 1911. From 1915 to 1918, she performed many concerts in the United States and Canada. After the war she spent a few years as principal singer for a company in New York. She returned to Belgium in 1925 to rejoin the Royal Flemish Opera. The station was likely named by the railway engineer, Maurice Polet, who came from Belgium. In 1916 he also named the Manir station 21 kilometres to the west. At the same site was established the Grizzly Bear Post Office, which opened in December 1916. The name was changed to Belloy in May 1926. Belloy post office closed July 31, 1969. (see also Grizzly Bear)

Belloy Reservoir (reservoir)
83 M/16 - Codesa
2-15-78-2-W6
55°45′N 118°13′W
Approximately 40 km east of Spirit River.

(see Belloy)

Bellrose Lake (lake)
83 N/1 - East Prairie
NE-29-70-15-W5
55°05′N 116°15′W
Approximately 65 km east of Valleyview.

The name was officially approved in 1952 after field research was conducted. It is possibly named after the prominent family who settled in the area.

Belyea Lake (lake)
74 M/9 - Colin Lake
NE-14-121-1-W4
59°31′N 110°03′W
Approximately 310 km north north-east of Fort McMurray.

Named after A.P.C. Belyea, Boundary Commissioner for Alberta and also a director of surveys in Alberta in the 1930s and 1940s.

***Ben Screen's Point** (point)
74 D/11 - Fort McMurray
28-89-9-W4
56°44′55″N 111°22′55″W
Approximately 1 km east of Fort McMurray.

(see Peden's Point)

Benbow (railway point)
83 K/2 - Marsh Head Creek
14-59-18-W5
54°06′N 116°35′W
Approximately 65 km north-west of Whitecourt.

Officially adopted in 1973 for a Canadian National Railways spur line point, it was named after Private William M. Benbow, who had been killed in action in 1945.

Bench Mark Creek (creek)
74 M/13 - Fitzgerald
35-124-12-W4
59°49′N 111°58′W

Flows north into Salt River approximately 335 km north of Fort McMurray.

This name was suggested by Environment Canada as an appropriate name for this feature, for the purposes of identification of a stream gauging station on the creek. It was officially adopted in 1986.

Benjamin Creek (creek)
83 N/15 - Springburn
3-81-19-W5
56°00′N 116°54′W
Flows south-west into Bearhead Creek approximately 40 km south-east of Peace River.

It appears on a federal government map as early as 1915; it is not known after whom it is named.

*****Benville** (village)
83 M/7 - Sexsmith
25-73-6-W6
55°21′N 118°47′W
Approximately 20 km north of Grande Prairie.

This was at one time the proposed name for what became Sexsmith. Benny was the nickname of John Bernard Foster, who came with his family to the area in September 1911. His neighbour to the immediate south was Dave Sexsmith. In 1913, the local papers referred to the coming of the Edmonton, Dunvegan and British Columbia Railway. Mr. Foster was mentioned as the owner of the Foster townsite, and that the likely name for the new town would be Benville. History has decreed otherwise. Benny Foster was active in the activities and politics of the area for many years. (see also Sexsmith)

---

*denotes rescinded name or former locality.

Berdinskies (locality)
74 L/3 - Embarras
16-23-104-9-W4
58°03′N 111°22′W
Approximately 139 km north of Fort McMurray.

Officially approved in 1966, this locality across the Athabasca River from Point Brule, was named after a trapper who, for many years, had his home at this site. This location was originally called Point Brule, but in order to avoid confusion with the community across the river, its current name was chosen.

Bergeron Creek (creek)
84 H/11 - Bergeron Creek
17-100-20-W4
57°41′N 113°15′W
Flows south-west into Birch River 155 km north-west of Fort McMurray.

One source has stated it was named after Jack Bergeron who operated Contact Airways in the 1960s and 70s. However, it is likely named by F.V. Seibert, DLS, while he and his crew surveyed the 27th Baseline in 1914. The baseline crosses the creek. The map compiled from the survey shows the name Bergeron Creek. The name Bergeron has its roots in the work of shepherds, who in French are called *bergers*.

Berland River (river)
83 K/2 - Marsh Head Creek
12-58-20-W5
54°00′N 116°50′W
Flows east into Athabasca River approximately 53 km south of Fox Creek.

At various times it has been called Baptiste River and Baptiste Berland River. The river is named after Baptiste Berland. David Thompson's map of 1813-1814 records the Baptist River. The name Berland River was officially adopted in 1917 to avoid confusion with the Baptiste River that flows into the North Saskatchewan. The Berlands were long involved with the fur trade. The elder Baptiste had his name on a river in the early part of the 19th century. The younger Edward Berland was mentioned by Father de Smet in the 1840s.

Berry Creek (creek)
84 P/5 - Bowhay Lake
25-118-22-W4
59°17′N 113°38′W
Flows east into Jackfish River approximately 216 km east north-east of High Level.

The name, in use since at least the 1940s, is likely descriptive of the vegetation found there.

Berry Lake (lake)
83 O/15 - Brintnell Lake
17-80-5-W5
55°57′N 114°45′W
Approximately 70 km north of Slave Lake.

Named after Matt Berry, a bush pilot. He was born in Ontario in 1888. In World War I, he first enlisted in the Wellington Rifles, later transferred to the Royal Flying Corps, and returned to Canada in 1917. Until 1924 he ranched in the Blindman Valley, but was lured back to aviation as a commercial pilot. In 1934 he took part in a search for lost flyers. He joined Canadian Airways that same year. After retiring from active flying, he became involved in the mining business. This lake is one of an number of lakes in the area named after bush pilots. (see also Brintnell Lake, Calder Lake, Dickins Lake, Farrell Lake, Lake May, McConachie Lake, McMillan Lake, McMullen Lake, Randall Lake and Sawle Lake).

Berwyn (village)
84 C/4 - Grimshaw
31-82-24-W5
56°09′N 117°44′W
Approximately 10 km south-west of Grimshaw.

This new settlement was named in 1922, marking the end of steel for a few years on the Central Canada Railway. The post office was established the same year, with the first postmaster being E.T. Williamson. Before 1922 a settlement was located three miles east and was called Bear Lake. The name Berwyn was suggested by a Welsh railroad official, after the Berwyn Hills or Berwyn Range, a volcanic outcrop of mountains in eastern Wales. The name is apparently derived from the Welsh *bar* (summit) and *gwyn* or *wyn* (white) indicating a snow-covered mountain.

Bethel Lake (lake)
83 M/12 - Boone Creek
4-28-76-13-W6
55°36′N 119°58′W
Approximately 72 km west south-west of Spirit River.

Although the precise origin of this name is unknown, it does have Biblical roots. Bethel comes from the Hebrew and means literally "house of God." It usually refers to a nonconformist church, but it may also have been a surname. It first shows on a map of 1937, and was officially named in 1952.

Betts Creek (creek)
84 D/13 - Betts Creek
6-92-12-W6
56°57′N 119°56′W
Flows west into Doig River approximately 135 km north-west of Fairview.

Named for Private Andrew M. Betts, of the Peace River district, a casualty of World War II.

Bewley Island (island)
84 C/6 - Weberville
6-84-21-W5
56°15′N 117°18′W

*denotes rescinded name or former locality.

Large island in Peace River approximately 3 km north of the town of Peace River.

The precise origin of the name of this island is unknown; the name was recorded by J.S. Galletly, DLS, in 1912.

Bezanson (hamlet)
83 M/1 - DeBolt
NE-10-72-3-W6
55°14′N 118°22′W
Approximately 30 km east north-east of Grande Prairie.

This hamlet was named for one of the pioneers of the Peace River Country, A. Maynard Bezanson (1878-1958), who was born in Halifax, N.S. After working at a number of jobs in the United States, he moved to the Big Smoky area in 1908. From then on he took a leading part in the development of the region and promoted this townsite. In 1913 he and a companion were the first to drive a car into the Peace River Country over the Edson Trail and then back to Edmonton. His reminiscences are recorded in the book *Sodbusters Invade the Peace*. A post office was established here in 1915, with the first postmaster being C. Evans.

Biche, Pointe la (point)
84 A/7 - Livock River
1-86-18-W4
56°26′N 112°42′W
Approximately 87 km south-west of Fort McMurray.

The precise origin of the name of this point is unknown, but is probably descriptive. *Biche* is the French-Canadian term for elk or deer used by fur traders since at least the early 19th century. It was recorded by the Geological Survey of Canada in 1892.

Big Chief Lake (lake)
73 M/4 - Philomena
16-72-11-W4
55°14′N 111°38′W

Approximately 60 km north north-east of Lac La Biche.

Originally known as Little Long Lake; the name was changed to avoid confusion with other Long lakes known locally in the area. A commemorative name was given instead. Solomon "Sam" Cardinal was born at Goodfish Lake on March 18, 1915. He became known as Big Chief. After trapping and hunting for many years, he joined the Canadian Army in 1944 and was killed in the Italian campaign in the same year.

Big Coulee (locality)
83 I/14 - Sawdy
10-68-22-W4
54°53′N 113°17′W
Approximately 20 km north north-east of Athabasca.

Originally established as a post office in 1946, its first postmaster was A. La Porte. The name owes its origin to the local school district that had been established in 1930.

Big Creek (creek)
74 E/11 - Firebag River
31-99-9-W4
57°37′50″N 111°28′24″W
Flows south-east into Athabasca River, 101 km north of Fort McMurray.

This is a descriptive name for this remote creek visited only by trappers.

*****Big Creek** (creek)
74 D/14 - Wood Creek
29-90-9-W4
56°49′N 111°24′W
Flows north-west into Athabasca River approximately 10 km north of Fort McMurray.

(see Donald Creek)

*****Big Eddy** (former locality)
74 L/6 - Richardson Lake
11-109-7-W4
58°27′N 111°04′W

Approximately 186 km north of Fort McMurray.

The locality was named for its proximity to the feature. The community later became known as Jackfish. The name Big Eddy was rescinded for the locality in 1965. (see Big Eddy Bend and Jackfish)

Big Eddy Bend (river bend)
74 L/6 - Richardson Lake
NW-11-109-7-W4
58°27′N 111°03′W
Approximately 184 km north of Fort McMurray.

The name is descriptive of the current at this bend in the Athabasca River.

Big Island (island)
84 I/12 - Buchanan Lake
26-111-23-W4
58°40′N 113°45′W
Approximately 193 km east of High Level in Peace River.

There is a reference to Big Island in the Peace River in the 1823 Hudson's Bay Company post journal for Fort Chipewyan. The name is descriptive.

Big Island (island)
84 H/10 - Alberta
27-99-16-W4
57°37′04″N 112°32′22″W
In Big Island Lake approximately 120 km north-west of Fort McMurray.

A descriptive name for this island in Big Island Lake.

Big Island Lake (lake)
84 H/10 - Alberta
22-99-16-W4
57°36′45″N 112°31′30″W

---

*denotes rescinded name or former locality.

Approximately 116 km north-west of Fort McMurray.

A descriptive name, due to the island in this lake. Locally it is known as both Island Lake and Big Island Lake. (see also Big Island)

***Big Lake** (lake)
84 K/16 - Hotte Lake
3-115-13-W5
58°57′N 116°07′W
Approximately 75 km north-east of High Level.

(see Hotte Lake)

***Big Lake** (lake)
84 H/4 - Osi Lake
25-94-23-W4
57°11′N 113°34′W
Approximately 142 km north north-west of Fort McMurray.

(see Osi Lake)

Big Lakes, Municipal District of, No. 125 (municipal district)
83 O/4 - House Mountain
72-13-W5
From 54°30′N 115°04′W to
55°54′N 116°59′W
North central Alberta.

Established in 1994, this municipal district takes its name from the many large lakes within its boundaries.

Big Mountain Creek (creek)
83 M/2 - Grande Prairie
5-14-70-5-W6
55°04′N 118°40′W
Flows north into Wapiti River approximately 12 km south-east of Grande Prairie.

Origin of the name Big Mountain Creek is not precisely known; however, its source is near the foothills of the Rocky Mountains, so the name may be descriptive. The feature was well known by this name as early as 1905, when it appears on a federal government map. The Hudson's Bay Company had a post at Lake Saskatoon, just north of this feature, and many trails around it are shown in a 1905 map of the area.

Big Muskeg Lake (lake)
83 P/1 - Wandering River
1-29-71-14-W4
55°10′N 112°06′W
Approximately 46 km north north-west of Lac La Biche.

The locally well-established name for this lake is descriptive of the marshy area.

Big Point (point)
83 O/5 - Driftpile
12-75-11-W5
55°29′N 115°34′W
Approximately 45 km west north-west of Slave Lake.

This descriptive name was officially approved in 1945 for the point on the north shore of Lesser Slave Lake.

Big Point (point)
74 L/10 - Big Point
NW-15-111-5-W4
58°38′N 110°46′W
Approximately 208 km north of Fort McMurray.

Shown on federal government maps as early as 1884, the name is descriptive of the feature. The Hudson's Bay Company Fort Chipewyan post journal of 1822 makes reference to Grande Pointe.

Big Point Channel (channel)
74 L/10 - Big Point
16-16-111-5-W4
58°38′N 110°46′W
Flows north-east into Lake Athabasca approximately 206 km north of Fort McMurray.

This name shows on a 1946 map, and is named for the feature by which it flows.

Big Prairie Settlement (settlement)
83 N/9 - Grouard
76-15,16-W5
55°36′N 116°19′W
Approximately 22 km north north-east of High Prairie.

The settlement was first surveyed in 1902, and takes its name from the landscape.

***Big River** (river)
84 N/16 - Alberta-NWT
31-126-12-W5
60°00′N 116°05′W
Flows north-east into the Northwest Territories approximately 175 km north north-east of High Level.

(see Yates River)

Big Slough (marsh)
84 I/14 - Big Slough
30-113-19-W4
58°50′N 113°12′W
Approximately 227 km east north-east of High Level.

This name is descriptive of the backwater on the Peace River. (see also Big Slough).

***Big Slough** (former locality)
84 I/14 - Big Slough
SE-21-113-19-W4
58°50′N 113°09′W
Approximately 231 km east north-east of High Level.

When the name for the locality was officially approved in 1963, Father Vantroys, an Oblate of Mary Immaculate, stated "A small settlement of six cabins is located at the east end of the slough. The name Big Slough was a very old name." He also explained that the name was a translation of the Cree word *Atatchikameg*.

Big Snuff Lake (lake)
74 E/8 - Trout Creek
8-97-2-W4
57°24′20″N 110°17′28″W
Approximately 100 km north-east of Fort McMurray.

This lake takes its name from an incident whereby a trapper lost his can of snuff. His son christened this lake Big Snuff Lake, and the smaller one south of it Little Snuff Lake. These names are used by the families who trap here to identify locations.

Bingo Lake (lake)
84 D/1 - Fairview
1-83-3-W6
56°10′N 118°19′W
Approximately 11 km north north-east of Fairview.

Likely named in the 1950s; the precise origin of the name of this lake is unknown.

Birch Creek (creek)
84 G/14 - Alberta
19-102-9-W5
57°52′N 115°28′W
Flows north into Rat Creek approximately 121 km south-east of High Level.

The precise origin of the name of this creek, which was recorded by the Dominion Lands Survey in 1915, is unknown; it is probably descriptive.

Birch Creek (creek)
73 M/11 - Conklin
32-76-7-W4
55°38′N 111°03′W
Flows east into Christina Lake approximately 105 km north-east of Lac La Biche.

The name was recorded by W.H. Waddell, DLS, when he and his crew were surveying in the area in 1915. The name is likely descriptive of the local flora.

Birch Hills (hills)
83 M/9 - Peoria
77-2,3-W6
55°41′N 118°15′W
Approximately 65 km north-east of Grande Prairie.

The name is apparently a translation of the Cree word *waskwai*. These hills near Wanham were the principal source of birch bark for the fur traders at Dunvegan. The Fort Dunvegan post journal stated under date of June 15, 1806, that two men were sent off to the Birch Hills for bark. In the 1902 Dominion Land Surveyors' field notes it is referred to as Fairchild's Birch Hills, but changed to Birch Hills in the final report.

Birch Hills, Municipal District of, No. 20
(municipal district)
83 M/16 - Codesa
78-1-W6
55°47′N 118°00′W
Above locations delineate the approximate geographical centre of the Municipal District.

The Municipal District, established in 1994, takes its name from the geographic feature that dominates the area. (see Birch Hills)

***Birch Lake** (lake)
73 M/6 - Wiau Lake
2-15-75-9-W4
55°30′N 111°18W
Approximately 90 km north north-east of Lac La Biche.

This is the local name for Glover Lake and is likely descriptive. (see Glover Lake)

---

*denotes rescinded name or former locality.

Birch Lake (lake)
74 D/8 - Gipsy Lake
22-85-3-W4
56°23'N 110°23'W
Approximately 70 km east south-east of Fort McMurray.

The precise origin of the name of this lake is unknown; it is probably descriptive.

Birch Lake (lake)
83 K/14 - Asplund Creek
5-8,9-67-21-W5
54°47'00"N 117°09'20"W
Approximately 115 km south-east of Grande Prairie.

The name was officially approved in 1991 after field research determined it was well established and in local usage. The name was first given to the feature by the aboriginal people, and has been in use since at least 1912. It is descriptive of the trees found around the lake.

Birch Lake (lake)
84 I/13 - Trident Creek
23-114-23-W4
58°55'N 113°45'W
Approximately 196 km east north-east of High Level.

The name was officially approved in 1963 and is descriptive of the flora abundant in the area.

Birch Lakes (lake)
84 H/10 - Alberta
18-99-17-W4
57°35'10"N 112°46'03"W
Approximately 126 km north-west of Fort McMurray.

The precise origin of the name of these lakes is unknown; it is probably descriptive.

Birch Mountains (mountain)
84 H/6 - Alberta
16-98-20-W4
57°30'N 113°10'W
Approximately 138 km north-west of Fort McMurray.

The precise origin of the name is probably descriptive. The name was recorded by A.W. Ponton, DLS, in 1910 and is likely the feature referred to by George Simpson in 1820 as Bark Mountain. Its elevation is 823 metres.

Birch River (river)
84 I/9 - Spruce Point
6-28-110-14-W4
58°35'N 112°17'W
Flows north into Lake Claire approximately 202 km north north-west of Fort McMurray.

It was recorded as early as 1890 by the Geological Survey of Canada, and may have been the one Father Émile Petitot recorded as Pine River in the early 1880s.

Birchwood Creek (creek)
84 A/16 - Birchwood Creek
21-91-14-W4
56°54'N 112°11'W
Flows north-west into MacKay River approximately 51 km north-west of Fort McMurray.

This official name is an English translation of the local Cree name *Waskweyattik*, meaning "birch tree." Birch trees are common along the banks of this creek.

Bird Island (island)
74 E/12 - Asphalt Creek
14-99-10-W4
57°36'N 111°31'W
Island in Athabasca River approximately 97 km north of Fort McMurray.

Joseph Bird, after whom this island was named in 1925, was the son of James Bird, a factor with the Hudson's Bay Company. Joseph came from British Columbia as a riverman and was well known on the Athabasca. He first worked on the upper river at Athabasca Landing, but when steamboat traffic declined he moved to the lower river. He became famous after he and James K. Cornwall piloted the steamer *Northland Echo* through the Grand Rapids to Fort McMurray in 1913, the first time such a feat had been attempted. His son William Bird, continued in his father's footsteps, started on a sternwheel steamer in 1922 at the age of 16, and retired at the end of the shipping season in 1972.

Bisbing Lake (lake)
83 M/5 - Hythe
4-28-72-11-W6
55°15'N 119°38'W
Approximately 50 km west of Grande Prairie.

Named after William and Cornelia Bisbing and family, who came to the Peace River Country in 1918 from Minnesota. They homesteaded on the southwest corner of what is now known as Bisbing Lake. The name for the lake was officially adopted in 1951.

Bison Flats (flats)
83 L/8 - Amundson
NE-10-63-3-W6
54°26'25"N 118°21'10"W
Approximately 85 km south south-east of Grande Prairie.

The name, officially adopted in 1991 after field research was conducted, refers to the buffalo bones found at this site.

Bison Lake (lake)
84 F/1 - Bison Lake
34-94-14-W5
57°13'N 116°10'W
Approximately 94 km east north-east of Manning.

The name is likely descriptive of the fauna found in the area. It is recorded as Buffalo Lake on a 1905 federal government map.

Bison Lake (locality)
84 F/1 - Bison Lake
26-94-14-W5
57°11′N 116°08′W
Approximately 95 km east north-east of Manning.

Named for its proximity to the lake. (see Bison Lake)

Bisset Lake (lake)
83 J/16 - Chisholm
34-68-2-W5
54°56′N 114°13′W
Approximately 48 km south-east of Slave Lake.

It was named before 1914, and likely took its name from survey crew members who surveyed the 18th Baseline in 1905.

Bistcho Lake Indian Reserve No 213
(Indian reserve)
84 M/9 - Pert Lake
33-122-3-W6
59°37′N 118°28′W
Approximately 143 km north-west of High Level.

It is named for its proximity to the feature. (see Bistcho Lake)

Bistcho Lake (lake)
84 M/10 - Jackfish Point
31-123-5-W6
59°44′N 118°51′W
Approximately 144 km north-west of High Level.

The name of this lake is Slavey in origin. The Oblate missionary and linguist, Father Émile Petitot, who visited its shores with a Hudson's Bay Company trading party in 1878, recorded the name as *Bes-Tchonhi*, which he translated as Lac du Gros Ventre or Big Stomach Lake. A decade later, R.G. McConnell of the Geological Survey of Canada recorded Lake Bis-tcho. His translation was Big Knife. It is possible that the discrepancy between Petitot's and McConnell's translations can be explained by the similarity between stomach (*be*) and knife (*beeh*) in contemporary Slavey. Later Dominion Land Surveyors, William Ogilvie in 1891 and J.R. Akins in 1915, both recorded the lake as Bistcho Lake. In 1946 an anthropologist Honigmann, working with the Fort Nelson Slavey, noted a third name, *Betsu*, in addition to Bistcho and Bes-tchonhi. Another interesting point is the Slavey name for the western end of the lake, west of the narrows, *Etthi* or the Head. This name would lend more support to Petitot's translations than that of McConnell.

Bitumount (locality)
74 E/5 - Bitumount
1-97-11-W4
57°23′N 111°38′W
On Athabasca River approximately 73 km north north-west of Fort McMurray.

In 1922 A.W. Wheeler began experimenting with the extraction of oil from the tar sands in a plant at this location, calling the post office after himself and the plant Alcan Oil Co. The company was taken over in 1927 by R.C. Fitzsimmons, who called the operation International Bitumen Co., and renamed the post office Bitumount in 1934.

Bivouac Creek (creek)
84 L/4 - Chasm Creek
24-106-13-W6
58°12′22″N 120°00′00″W
Flows north north-west into British Columbia approximately 50 km south-west of Rainbow Lake.

This name was recorded by the Alberta-British Columbia Boundary Survey in 1950-51. The name bivouac implies that the boundary survey named the creek after camping there for a short while.

Black Duck Lake (lake)
84 D/1 - Fairview
8-83-3-W6
56°11′N 118°27′W
Approximately 12 km north north-west of Fairview.

The name may be descriptive of the bird, a rare visitor to Alberta. Its breeding range is eastern Canada.

Black Fly Creek (creek)
74 E/3 - Hartley Creek
6-95-8-W4
57°09′35″N 111°10′10″W
Flows into Shelley Creek where it meets Green Stockings Creek approximately 48 km north of Fort McMurray.

This creek is named for the abundance of one of the most obnoxious fauna of northern Alberta. There are over a hundred species of these small insects found in Canada. Black fly larvae live in flowing water. The adult females have biting mouthparts with toothed stylets for cutting skin to get the blood they need for development of their eggs. One species, *Simulium arcticum*, secretes a poisonous saliva causing anaphylactic shock, which has resulted in the death of thousands of head of cattle in northern Alberta and Saskatchewan. These flies are so abundant in northern wooded regions that they seriously curtail human activity during summer months. Forestry workers often demand black fly control as part of their work contract.

Blanche Lake (lake)
74 L/6 - Richardson Lake
20-108-8-W4
58°24′N 111°19′W
Approximately 176 km north of Fort McMurray.

It appears on a federal government map as early as 1919. Its origin is not known;

however, it may refer to a woman of that name or to the French word for white.

Blanchet Lake (lake)
84 A/11 - Blanchet Lake
5-89-20-W4
56°41'N 113°09'W
Approximately 107 km west of Fort McMurray.

Named after Guy Haughton Blanchet (1884-1966), DLS, who worked in this area during 1911 and 1912. He had recorded the name for the feature as Island Lake. Blanchet graduated in mining engineering from McGill in 1905 and received his commission from the Dominion Lands Survey in 1910. He had a long career in the Canadian North, running township lines and Baselines, as well as working on a portion of the Alberta-Saskatchewan boundary. In 1929 he was involved in the first search and rescue operation using aircraft in the Arctic, when the C.D.H. MacAlpine party got lost along the coast near Coppermine. Blanchet enlisted in the Royal Canadian Artillery in 1942, but was seconded to work on the Canol pipeline project. Afterwards he spent several years surveying the Mackenzie watershed, before finally retiring. This lake was not officially named until 1974.

***Bloodsucker Lake** (lake)
73 M/5 - Behan Lake
2-2-75-11-W4
55°28N 111°36W
Approximately 81 km north of Lac La Biche.

An unofficial, likely descriptive name, for Little Fish Lake. A bloodsucker is a type of leech found in stagnant lakes. (see Little Fish Lake)

---

*denotes rescinded name or former locality.

Blue Creek (creek)
83 K/16 - Wallace River
2-15-69-16-W5
54°59'08"N 116°27'13"W
Flows east into West Prairie River approximately 157 km south-east of Grande Prairie.

(see Blue Lake)

Blue Lake (lake)
83 K/16 - Wallace River
14-13-69-17-W5
54°58'50"N 116°27'30"W
Approximately 150 km south-east of Grande Prairie.

This lake is named for its proximity to Blue Mountain and is the source for Blue Creek. The name is well established in local usage, and the lake has had this name since at least 1929. It was officially named in 1991 after field research was conducted in the area.

Blue Mountain (hill)
83 N/1 - Bellrose Lake
SW-36-69-17-W5
55°01'N 116°28'W
Approximately 158 km east of Grande Prairie.

Also known as Blue Hill; the origin of the name may refer to the fact that depending on the light and the distance, the hill appears blue. The name has been official since 1952 after research was conducted in the area.

Blueberry Creek (creek)
83 M/15 - Rycroft
11-5-81-6-W6
56°00'N 118°54'W
Flows north into Hamelin Creek approximately 25 km north of Spirit River.

Probably named for its source is in Blueberry Hill. (see Blueberry Hill)

Blueberry Hill (hill)
83 M/14 - Blueberry Mountain
25-79-9,10-W6
55°53'N 119°24'W
Approximately 80 km north-west of Grande Prairie.

Blueberry Mountain was a name well established and in common use when the Dominion Land Surveyors first came through the area in the early 1910s. According to the local history of the area, the name is a translation of the aboriginal name for the feature. It was the aboriginal peoples who first knew the area around the hill to be rich in blueberries. The name which finally given to the feature was Blueberry Hill, since its elevation of 762 metres did not qualify it as a mountain.

Blueberry Mountain (locality)
83 M/14 - Blueberry Mountain
NW-10-80-8-W6
55°56'N 119°09'W
Approximately 25 km north-west of Spirit River.

The post office opened January 1, 1925, and closed November 30, 1945. The first postmaster was George Meldrum. (see Blueberry Hill)

Bluesky (hamlet)
84 D/1 - Fairview
4-82-2-W6
56°04'N 118°14'W
Approximately 8 km due east of Fairview.

The hamlet Bluesky is named for an earlier hamlet it supplanted as a consequence of the extension of the Edmonton, Dunvegan and British Columbia Railway. The descriptive name Bluesky was apparently coined around 1914 by two of the original settlers, a couple called Dodge, for the post office they operated from their homestead approximately five kilometres east of the present Bluesky. When a hamlet grew on the banks of the Burnt River near the Dodge's post office, it too became known as Bluesky. Before the arrival of the railway in 1928, a second hamlet grew up adjacent to the present Bluesky, which was known as Craddock. Curiously, when the Friedenstal post office was moved to Craddock in 1916, it retained the name Friedenstal for the next dozen years. All this changed when the Edmonton, Dunvegan and British Columbia Railway put in a siding adjacent to Craddock. Most of the businesses from the old Bluesky were moved to the new siding, and the post office of Bluesky was closed. The new businesses around the siding, Craddock, and the Friedenstal post office were officially named Bluesky.

Blumenort (locality)
84 K/8 - Fort Vermilion
26-107-14-W5
58°18′42″N 116°13′10″W
Approximately 65 km east south-east of High Level.

Blumenort means "Valley of flowers" and is named after a Mennonite community in Mexico. Blumenort is one of a number of Mennonite localities in the area of La Crete, established during the early 1930s by Mennonite families from Saskatchewan, Mexico and South America.

Bocquene Lake (lake)
74 M/6 - Bocquene Lake
3-121-7-W4
59°28′N 111°06′W
Approximately 298 km north of Fort McMurray.

The name appears on a federal government map as early as 1946; its origin is unknown.

Bocquene River (river)
74 M/11 - Hay Camp
NE-14-121-9-W4
59°31′N 111°26′W

Flows north-west into Slave River approximately 301 km north of Fort McMurray.

The name appears on a federal government map as early as 1946; its origin is unknown.

Bohn Lake (lake)
73 M/15 - Bohn Lake
2-80-5-W4
55°54′N 110°41′W
Approximately 90 km south south-east of Fort McMurray.

The lake was named in 1914 after the explorer on F.V. Seibert's survey crew, F.O. Bohn. This may have been the lake that appears on an earlier sectional map as Sharp-Point Lake.

Boiler Rapids (rapids)
84 A/9 - Boiler Rapids
23-87-14-W4
56°33′N 112°06′W
In Athabasca river approximately 50 km west south-west of Fort McMurray.

Boiler Rapids, previously known as Joe's Rapids, apparently got its name when a boiler being taken for the *Wrigley* – a new steamboat in the process of being built for the Hudson's Bay Company – went down and was lost. This became the stopping place for the boiler, which was travelling by scow. This event occurred in mid-summer 1885, when Captain Smith, who had built the *Grahame*, was taking the boiler and two other scow loads for the *Wrigley* down the Athabasca. The boiler was eventually retrieved. The name Boiler Rapids was recorded by the Geological Survey of Canada in 1892.

Boivin Creek (creek)
84 A/2 - Boivin Creek
26-82-17-W4
56°08′N 112°33′W
Flows north-west into Athabasca River approximately 96 km south-west of Fort McMurray.

The creek was named after E. Boivin, DLS, who worked along Range 17 in 1914.

Bolton Creek (creek)
84 I/5 - Ruis Lake
NW-10-107-23-W4
58°17′N 113°46′W
Flows north into Birch River approximately 195 km east of High Level.

It appears on a federal government map of 1916 and is likely named after a survey crew member.

Bonanza (locality)
83 M/13 - Bonanza
SW-9-8-12-W6
55°55′N 119°49′W
Approximately 35 km west north-west of Spirit River.

The post office established here in 1930 was originally called Kayow. The first postmaster was Anton Kulachkosky. The people in the area decided to change the name. Of the two names submitted, Westview and Bonanza, the latter was finally chosen. According to the local history of the area, Gordon Cameron suggested the name, after the gold bonanza in the Yukon a generation before. This reflected people's confidence in the rich future of the community.

Boone Creek (creek)
83 M/12 - Boone Creek
4-13-77-13-W6
55°40′N 119°53′W
Flows north-west into Pouce Coupé River approximately 66 km west of Spirit River.

Officially named in 1948 this creek, earlier known as Fish Creek, was named after Boone Taylor a hunter and trapper in the Peace River Country from before World War I into the 1940s. Although his home was Swan Lake on the British Columbia side, he was well known and respected throughout the Peace district. He acted as guide to many prospective homesteaders before the arrival of the railway to the area.

Boone Lake (lake)
83 M/11 - Saddle Hills
11-76-10-W6
55°34′N 119°26′W
Approximately 42 km south-west of Spirit River.

(see Boone Creek)

Bootis Hill (hill)
84 M/5 - Bootis Hill
25-120-10-W6
59°27′N 119°34′W
Approximately 116 km north of Rainbow Lake.

Officially approved in 1972, the precise origin of the name of this hill is unknown. Its elevation is 792 metres.

Botha River (river)
84 F/5 - Goffit Creek
29-95-24-W5
57°17′N 117°52′W
Flows south-east into Meikle River, 42 km north north-west of Manning.

This river was named in honour of Louis Botha (1862-1919), South African soldier and statesman. Botha led the Afrikaner forces against the British during the Boer War. Nevertheless, after defeat in 1902, his efforts to reconcile the two colonising peoples in South Africa won him admiration throughout the British Empire. On the unification of South Africa in 1910, Botha became Prime Minister. He led South Africa into World War I. In 1915, on the invitation of the British Government, he commanded the South African forces that captured German Southwest Africa, an exploit that may have prompted the naming of this river in 1916. His name was also given to a community in southern Alberta.

Boucher Creek (creek)
83 M/15 - Rycroft
16-9-80-4-W6
55°56′N 118°33′W
Flows south into Peace River approximately 25 km north-east of Spirit River.

The name for this creek was well established and in local use by the time the Dominion Land Surveyors came through the area in 1908. James and Alphonse Boucher were hired as labourers during that survey season, and they may be related to the family whose name was recorded for this feature on a federal government map in 1905. *Boucher* is the French word for butcher.

Boudin Lake (lake)
74 M/9 - Colin Lake
SE-20-123-2-W4
59°42′N 110°18′W
Approximately 328 km north of Fort McMurray.

The name was submitted in 1965 by the Research Council of Alberta. In French a *boudin* is a blood sausage and the shape of the lake likely reminded the submitter of a sausage.

Boulder Creek (creek)
83 O/3 - Adams Creek
4-34-69-9-W5
55°01′N 115°18′W
Flows north-west into Swan River approximately 45 km south-west of Slave Lake.

Adopted some time between 1922 and 1954, the name is likely descriptive, for there is a stream that flows into the Swan River approximately six kilometres north called Stoney Creek.

Boulder Creek (creek)
83 N/7 - Triangle
7-35-72-20-W5
55°17′N 116°58′W
Flows north into Little Smoky River approximately 35 km south-west of High Prairie.

Adopted in 1954 after field research in the area, the name is likely descriptive.

Boundary Creek (creek)
74 E/8 - Trout Creek
4-97-1-W4
57°23′00″N 110°05′50″W
Flows south south-west into Firebag River approximately 108 km north-east of Fort McMurray.

One possible origin of the name of this remote creek is that it was named by the two partners who operate the trapline and their families in order to easily identify the location. The creek lies on the boundary of the trappers' designated trapping area. The name might also refer to the creek's proximity to the Alberta-Saskatchewan border.

Boundary Lake (lake)
84 D/5 - Boundary Lake
6-85-13-W6
56°20′N 120°00′W
On British Columbia-Alberta border approximately 103 km west north-west of Fairview.

A descriptive name for this lake, which straddles the British Columbia-Alberta border; it appears on a federal government map in 1914.

Bowen Lake (lake)
74 L/1 - Archer Lake
31-106-1-W4
58°14′N 110°10′W
Approximately 175 km north north-east of Fort McMurray.

Officially named in 1916 after Col. R.E. Bowen, who commanded the 202nd Battalion, CEF, Edmonton, during World War I.

Bowesman Lake (lake)
84 C/12 - Dixonville
4-89-24-W5
56°41′N 116°46′W
Approximately 28 km south south-west of Manning.

A survey of 1912 left the lake unnamed, but by 1923, the name began to appear on township plans, which were compiled from the survey of F.V. Seibert in 1921. It was likely named after a survey crew member.

Bowhay Lake (lake)
84 P/5 - Bowhay Lake
13-120-22-W4
59°26′N 113°39′W
Approximately 220 km east north-east of High Level.

The lake was named in 1949 after Flight Lieutenant Sam L. Bowhay, born in Three Hills, Alberta, in 1915. He enlisted in the RCAF in 1940, served as flying instructor in Canada and was killed in a flying accident while stationed at No. 5 Operational Training Unit at Boundary Bay, British Columbia, in January 1945. In 1944 he was awarded a Commendation for valuable services in the air.

Boyer (locality)
84 K/8 - Fort Vermilion
11-109-13-W5
58°28′N 116°04′W
Approximately 56 km east of High Level.

Named for its proximity to Boyer River. (see Boyer River)

Boyer Indian Reserve No. 164 (Indian reserve)
84 K/8 - Fort Vermilion
15-109-14-W5
58°27′N 116°16′W
Approximately 50 km east of High Level.

Named for its proximity to Boyer River, which runs through the reserve. The Boyer River Band occupies two reserve areas. Members of the reserve trace their ancestry to the Beaver Indian Nation. Their name is derived from the word *Tsattine* meaning "dwellers among the beavers." Chief Ambrose Tête Noir entered into Treaty No. 8 on behalf of the band in 1899. (see also Boyer River)

Boyer Rapids (rapids)
84 P/2 - Boyer Rapids
21-117-16-W4
59°10′N 112°40′W
Approximately 262 km east north-east of High Level in Peace River.

May have been named after Charles Boyer, a North West Company trader. The name was recorded by the Geological Survey of Canada in 1875 as Bouille Rapids. (see also Boyer River)

Boyer River (river)
84 J/5 - Sled Island
30-108-12-W5
58°27′N 115°57′W
Flows north-east into Peace River approximately 70 km east south-east of High Level.

This river is said to be named for Charles Boyer, the North West Company trader. Sir Alexander Mackenzie in a letter dated Athabasca, 22 May, 1789, referred to him as "a very fit person for the Peace River." The river appears as Bouille River on the Arrowsmith map of 1854. Boyer sounds close to the infinitive form of the French verb meaning to boil, namely *bouiller*. It may be a reference to the nature of the river. Locally, the portion of the river between Paddle Prairie and the confluence of the Bushe River is called Paddle River, and it is referred to by the Geological Survey of Canada in 1890 as "Paddle or Boyer River."

Boyer Settlement (settlement)
84 K/8 - Fort Vermilion
12-109-13-W5
58°27′N 116°02′W
Approximately 56 km east of High Level.

Originally surveyed in 1906, it was named for its proximity to Boyer River. (see Boyer River)

Braaten (railway point)
83 L/15 - Big Mountain Creek
34-67-5-W6
54°50′N 118°40′W
Approximately 35 km south south-west of Grande Prairie.

This Alberta Resources Railway point was established in 1969 on the industrial spur to serve the Atlantic Richfield plant. It was named after Private Lester L. Braaten, who was killed in action in August, 1944.

Brabant Lake (lake)
84 P/11 - Conibear Lake
NE-23-122-19-W4
59°37′N 113°09′W
Approximately 255 km east north-east of High Level.

It appears on federal government maps as early as 1930; after whom it is named is not known.

Braeburn (locality)
83 M/10 - Woking
29-75-5-W6
55°32′N 118°44′W
Approximately 39 km north of Grande Prairie.

Originally known as Surbiton, this locality was a railway station on the Edmonton, Dunvegan and British Columbia Railway line. The name was officially changed to Braeburn in 1948. *Brae* is a Scottish word meaning "steep bank or hillside" and a *burn* is also Scottish meaning "small stream." (see also Surbiton)

Braeburn Creek (creek)
83 M/10 - Woking
3-77-5-W6
55°37'N 118°42'W
Flows north into Saddle (Burnt) River approximately 16 km south-east of Spirit River.

Name likely approved in 1948 in conjunction with the official renaming of Surbiton. (see Braeburn)

Brainard (locality)
83 M/5 - Hythe
NW-2-74-12-W6
55°23'N 119°44'W
Approximately 61 km west north-west of Grande Prairie.

The locality was originally a post office established in December 1919 and took the name of the first postmaster. The Brainards arrived in the Peace Country a year before, establishing a stopping place along the south-east side of the lake. Lee Brainard first came to southern Alberta from Montana in 1906 to continue his successful career as a rancher. However, he arrived in time for the infamous winter of 1906-1907 during which many ranchers in southern Alberta lost much of their stock due to the severe blizzards. Lee Brainard was no exception. Not only did he lose his livelihood, he lost his son during one of the blizzards. He returned to Canada in 1918 and settled in the Hythe area. Mr. Brainard, born in Minnesota in 1857, died in 1938 after a successful career as a farmer in northern Alberta.

Brainard Lake (lake)
83 M/5 - Hythe
10-74-12-W6
55°24'N 119°45'W
Approximately 65 km north-west of Grande Prairie.

Originally called Sinclair Lake (see Sinclair Creek); officially changed in 1991 because the name Brainard Lake was well established in local usage. (see Brainard)

Brander Lake (lake)
74 L/8 - Brander Lake
2-109-1-W4
58°26'N 110°03'W
Approximately 200 km north north-east of Fort McMurray.

According to one source, it was named in honour of Dr. James F. Brander (1879-1963), a pioneer doctor of Edmonton. He was born at Northport, Nova Scotia, and started a practice in Ponoka in 1909 before moving to Edmonton in 1911. There he gained renown cultivating peonies. Another possible origin of the name is that the lake is part of a group of features surveyed along the 28th Baseline in the mid-1910s, and that it was named after a survey crew member.

Bredin (locality)
83 M/7 - Sexsmith
25-72-7-W6
55°16'N 118°56'W
Approximately 15 km north-west of Grande Prairie.

This was established as a post office in January 1915 on the land of William Fletcher Bredin. His wife, Anna (Marsh) Bredin, was the postmaster until it closed in February 1930. Fletch Bredin was born in 1857 in Stormont, Ontario. In 1882 he began trading furs in what is now Alberta, and by 1896 was operating a trading post in partnership with "Peace River Jim" Cornwall in the Mackenzie River area. In 1906, he became a partner in a trading post on nearby Lake Saskatoon. He was well known in the area, and was elected in 1909 to the Legislative Assembly where he served until 1913. He remained active in local activities until the 1930s when he and his wife moved to Edmonton. He died in 1942.

Bremner Creek (creek)
83 M/16 - Codesa
15-13-78-4-W6
55°46'N 118°29'W
Flows east into Saddle (Burnt) River approximately 10 km east south-east of Spirit River.

Originally called Swamp Creek; the name was changed to Bremner Creek in 1912. The origin of the name is not known; it may have been named after a survey crew member. (see also Swamp Creek)

Breynat (locality)
83 P/1 - Wandering River
13-71-17-W4
55°08'N 112°28'W
Approximately 50 km north-west of Lac La Biche.

This locality was named in honour of Gabriel Breynat (1867-1953). Born in France, he entered the Oblates of Mary Immaculate, a Roman Catholic missionary order, eventually becoming an archbishop. Following his ordination he came to Canada in 1892 to serve at Fort Chipewyan under Bishop Grouard. In 1902 Breynat became Bishop of Mackenzie, an area including almost all the present Northwest Territories and Yukon. By the 1920s he began flying in order to cover the vast area more easily and became known as the "Flying Bishop" that was subsequently used for the title of his autobiography published posthumously in 1955. He visited the area north-west of Lac La Biche in 1933, and when it came time to establish a post office in 1936 the residents asked to have it named after the prominent Oblate. The first postmaster was J.E. Rimeau.

Briant Creek (creek)
73 M/9 - Alberta-Saskatchewan
1-13-77-1-W4
55°40'N 110°00'W
Flows into Saskatchewan approximately 135 km south-east of Fort McMurray.

The creek first appears on federal government maps in 1917. It is likely named after L.D. Briant, a chainman on the J.N. Wallace survey crew in the area in 1909.

Bridgeview (locality)
83 M/10 - Woking
9-77-6-W6
55°40′N 118°51′W
Approximately 14 km south of Spirit River.

The name for this locality originated with the school district established in 1929. Apparently when the local group met to name the district one of them suggested Bridgeview because as he looked out the window of the farmhouse where the meeting was being held, he could see a bridge that crossed a small stream. The Bridgeview post office was established in August 1930 and its first postmaster was A. Drouin.

Bridle Bit Basin (basin)
83 K/13 - Long Lake
14-6-69-25-W5
54°56′55″N 117°48′18″W
Approximately 68 km south-east of Grande Prairie.

(see Bridle Bit Creek)

Bridle Bit Creek (creek)
83 K/13 - Long Lake
7-32-68-25-W5
54°55′26″N 117°46′04″W
Flows south into Spring Creek approximately 72 km south-east of Grande Prairie.

Officially approved in 1991 after field research was conducted, Bridle Bit Creek and Bridle Bit Basin were named after the Brand "A" bridle that was used by Bob Frakes, who homesteaded in the vicinity of these features. Some long-time residents of the area refer to the basin as Willow Flats. (see also Frakes Flat)

---

*denotes rescinded name or former locality.

Brine Creek (creek)
84 P/16 - Brine Creek
NE-13-126-14-W4
59°57′N 112°16′W
Flows north into Salt River approximately 315 km east north-east of High Level.

Officially named in 1949, it is descriptive of the saline nature of the water. This is further evidenced in that it is a tributary of Salt River.

Brintnell Lake (lake)
83 O/15 - Brintnell Lake
33-78-5-W5
55°48′N 114°43′W
Approximately 55 km north of Slave Lake.

This northern lake was named in honour of Leigh Brintnell (1895-1971) of Edmonton. Born in Belleville, Ontario, he served as pilot instructor in the Royal Flying Corps and its successor, the Royal Air Force in 1916-1918. He was pilot for the Ontario Provincial Air Service in 1924-1927. He moved to Winnipeg to become manager of Western Canadian Airways (1928-1931). During the 1930s, as head of Mackenzie Air Service Ltd., he made several pioneering flights into the north including the amazing flight from Winnipeg to Alaska and back via the Northwest Territories crossing the mountains between Aklavik and Dawson, Yukon. During World War II, Brintnell was president of Northwest Industries. In 1946 he was made an officer of the Order of the British Empire. In 1975 he was admitted to the Canadian Aviation Hall of Fame. This is one of a number of lakes in the area named after bush pilots. (see also Berry Lake, Calder Lake, Dickins Lake, Farrell Lake, Lake May, McConachie Lake, McMillan Lake, McMullen Lake, Randall Lake and Sawle Lake)

***British Lake** (lake)
84 D/6 - Many Islands
[31]-84-9-W6
56°19′N 119°24′W

Approximately 70 km west north-west of Fairview.

The name was officially approved in 1956. Apparently, when viewed from the air the lake vaguely resembled the map of Great Britain. Fifteen years later the name was rescinded because the lake had dried up.

Broche Creek (creek)
83 M/13 - Bonanza
16-1-81-13-W6
56°00′N 119°53′W
Flows north-west into Pouce Coupe River approximately 70 km north west of Spirit River.

Although the origin is uncertain, the name was well established and in local use when the Dominion Lands Survey was in the area in 1911. In French, *broche* refers to a spit, meat skewer, peg or pin. A *brochet* is a pike fish. Whether there is some connection with either of these, or if it was a surname, is not known.

Brock Lake (lake)
74 M/16 - Andrew Lake
NW-15-124-3-W4
59°47′N 110°26′W
Approximately 336 km north of Fort McMurray.

Named after Reginald Walter Brock (1874-1935), a Canadian geologist. He held a number of high ranking posts in the field of geology until 1914. During World War I, he joined the Seaforth Highlanders of Canada (72nd Battalion, CEF). By 1915, he had attained the rank of major. Shortly after the war, he resumed his seat as dean of the Faculty of Applied Science at the University of British Columbia. He and his wife died in an airplane crash at Alta Lake, B.C. The name was submitted in 1965 by the Research Council of Alberta, and is one of a series of features in the area named after prominent geologists.

Brousseau Creek (creek)
84 I/12 - Buchanan Lake
4-23-111-22-W4
58°39′N 113°36′W
Flows north into Peace River approximately 202 km east of High Level.

It was officially named in 1949; the name was in use much earlier. According to the files of the Geographic Board of Canada, it was named after an employee of the North West Company who was in the area in the early 1800s.

Brownvale (hamlet)
84 C/4 - Grimshaw
19-82-25-W5
56°08′N 117°53′W
Approximately 20 km west south-west of Grimshaw.

Named after John Brown, who arrived in this district in 1913. When the Central Canada Railway extended west in 1924, a portion of Brown's homestead was subdivided for the new hamlet to be built alongside the line. The suffix "vale" was added as the land on which the hamlet is situated slopes downward in three directions. A post office was established here in 1926, with the first postmaster being F. Algar.

***Bruce Creek** (creek)
83 O/4 - House Mountain
12-72-13-W5
55°13′N 115°51′W
Flows north into Driftpile River approximately 70 km west of Slave Lake (town).

(see Little Driftpile River)

Bruce Creek (creek)
83 N/1 - East Prairie
16-3-70-14-W5
55°02′N 116°02′W
Flows west into East Prairie River approximately 80 km east of Valleyview.

---

*denotes rescinded name or former locality.

This name was adopted in 1952 after field research was conducted in the area. The creek's name was recorded as Bruce River in 1906; after whom it was named is not known. There may be some connection with the lake noted below. (see also Bruce Lake)

Bruce Lake (lake)
83 J/16 - Chisholm
4-69-2-W5
54°57′N 114°14′W
Approximately 51 km south-east of Slave Lake.

It was named before 1914, and took its name from survey crew member Charles Bruce one of the crew which surveyed the 18th Baseline in 1905.

Brule Point (point)
84 A/10 - Brule Point
10-87-17-W4
56°32′N 112°35′W
Approximately 77 km south-west of Fort McMurray.

From the French brûlé meaning "burnt", apparently after stands of burned timber noticed along its shores. The name was recorded in 1892 by the Geological Survey of Canada as Point Brûlée(sic).

Brule, Point (point)
74 L/16 - Stone Point
2-23-114-2-W4
58°55′N 110°13′W
Approximately 245 km north north-east of Fort McMurray.

Brûlé usually refers to an area that has been burnt out by forest fires.

Brulé Rapids (rapids)
84 A/9 - Boiler Rapids
3-87-16-W4
56°31′N 112°27′W
In Athabasca River approximately 70 km south-west of Fort McMurray.

It is most probable that they were named for their proximity to Brule Point. The name was recorded by the Geological Survey of Canada in 1892 as Rapides du Brûlé.

Brush Mountain (mountain)
83 N/2 - Snipe Lake
35-69-18-W5
55°02′N 116°37′W
Approximately 43 km east of Valleyview.

The name was officially adopted in the early 1950s after a field survey was conducted in the area. It is possibly descriptive of the vegetation on the feature, which is fairly visible because of the comparatively flat surrounding terrain. Its elevation is 900 metres.

Bryant Lake (lake)
74 M/8 - Wylie Lake
118,119-2-W4
59°18′N 110°14′W
Approximately 80 km north-east of Fort Chipewyan.

Officially named in 1929 after Corporal Bryant of the RCMP stationed at Fort Chipewyan.

Buchan Lake (lake)
84 O/15 - Vermilion Lake
34-126-6-W5
60°00′N 114°57′W
Approximately 203 km north north-east of High Level.

Officially approved in 1944, it was named by C.B.C. Donnelly, DLS, after an observation plane pilot. In Scotland, Buchan is a region in the north-east of Aberdeenshire (now Grampian). The name comes from the Old Welsh word *Buwch*, with the added suffix *an*, and means "place of cows."

Buchanan Creek (creek)
84 C/14 - Buchanan creek
14-91-21-W5
56°53′N 117°15′W
Flows east into Peace River, 22 km east south-east of Manning.

Named after Dominion Land Surveyor, John Alexander Buchanan. The name shows on a 1919 survey map as Bear Creek.

Buchanan Lake (lake)
84 I/12 - Buchanan Lake
34-110-23-W4
58°36′N 113°45′W
Approximately 193 km east of High Level.

A war casualty commemoration, the lake was named in 1949 after Flight Lieutenant D.S.J. Buchanan of Edmonton. He was born in 1920, and enlisted in the RCAF in Edmonton in 1941. He proceeded overseas in 1942, successfully completing his first tour of operations with 101 Squadron. He began a second tour of operations in 1944 and was reported killed on February 4, 1945. He was awarded the Distinguished Flying Cross on September 1, 1943.

***Buck Lake** (lake)
83 K/7 - Iosegun Lake
19-62-20-W5
54°22′N 116°56′W
Approximately 150 km south-east of Grande Prairie.

The name appears on provincial government maps in the early 1950s and was likely descriptive of the prevalence of male deer in the area. However, the name was officially changed in 1960 in order to avoid duplication with others of the same name in the province. (see Smoke Lake)

---

*denotes rescinded name or former locality.

Buckton Creek (creek)
74 L/5 - Welstead Lake
27-107-12-W4
58°19′N 111°55′W
Flows north-west into Lake Claire approximately 170 km north north-west of Fort McMurray.

Officially named in 1914 after A. Scott Buckton, DLS.

Buffalo Bay (bay)
83 N/9 - Grouard
1-76-14-W5
55°34′N 116°10′W
Approximately 22 km north-east of High Prairie, on Lesser Slave Lake.

For centuries buffalo roamed the area around Lesser Slave Lake and in the marshy meadows by the shore. They were an important source of food for the fur brigades and aboriginal groups passing that way.

***Buffalo Creek** (creek)
83 M/6 - La Glace
10-7-73-7-W6
55°18′N 119°04′W
Flows south into Bear Creek approximately 17 km north-west of Grande Prairie.

Now called Niobe Creek, original settlers in the area referred to this feature as Buffalo Creek and it is noted in the 1909 survey records by that name. It was called this because the path it follows was carved by migration of the bison, and because its water source is the largest of a group of five lakes originally titled Buffalo Lakes. A post office was opened on Buffalo Creek and it was called Niobe. As a result the name of the creek officially changed to Niobe Creek in the early 1950s. (see Niobe Creek)

Buffalo Creek (creek)
84 A/10 - Brule Point
2-87-17-W4
56°32′N 112°36′W
Flows east into Athabasca River approximately 77 km south-west of Fort McMurray.

The precise origin of the name of this creek is unknown, although it likely refers to the presence of the animal in the area.

Buffalo Head Hills (hills)
84 G/5 - Goffit Creek
17-97-12-W5
57°25′N 115°55′W
Approximately 98 km north-east of Manning.

These rugged hills were probably named for the buffalo that roamed extensively over them and whose skulls were still found in there in the 1970s.

Buffalo Head Prairie (hamlet)
84 K/1 - Mustus Lake
26-104-15-W5
58°03′N 116°21′W
Approximately 69 km south-east of High Level.

The precise origin of the name of this hamlet is unknown; it may be taken from the original surrounding topography. A post office was established here in 1976, and the first postmaster was A. Klassen.

Buffalo Hill (hill)
84 F/16 - Buffalo Hill
23-103-14-W5
57°57′N 116°12′W
Approximately 82 km south-east of High Level.

The name shows on a 1916 survey map as Buffalo Head Hills and is part of this set of hills.

Buffalo Lake (lake)
73 M/4 - Philomena
6-71-12-W4
55°07'N 111°50'W
Approximately 40 km north of Lac La Biche.

The well-established name for this lake likely refers to the wood buffalo native to this area.

Buffalo Lake (lake)
83 M/7 - Sexsmith
2-3-74-7-W6
55°23'N 118°58'W
Approximately 22 km north north-west of Grande Prairie.

This lake is one of a group formerly referred to collectively as Buffalo Lakes. The bison were known to use the lakes in the summer as watering holes where they would immerse themselves to cool off and gain some respite from the insects. The name for this lake was made official on January 1, 1952. The other named lakes in the group are Jones Lake and Gummer Lake. At one time one of the lakes was locally known as Spitfire Lake. The Buffalo Lakes School District was established in 1914.

*****Buffalo Lake** (lake)
84 H/7 - Legend Lake
15-97-17-W4
57°25'N 112°40'W
Approximately 108 km north-west of Fort McMurray.

(see Namur Lake)

Buffalo Lake (locality)
83 M/6 - La Glace
4-74-7-W6
55°23'N 119°01'W
Approximately 23 km north-west of Grande Prairie.

---
*denotes rescinded name or former locality.

The post office was opened in October 1917, and took its name from the nearby lake. From 1915 to 1917, the post office operated under the name of Spitfire Lake. John Beattie was the postmaster at the time of the name change. (see also Spitfire Lake)

Buffalo Point (point)
74 L/5 - Welstead Lake
32-108-12-W4
58°25'N 111°58'W
Approximately 182 km north north-west of Fort McMurray.

Officially named in the 1960s, it likely refers to a place where the bison can be seen.

Buffalo River (river)
84 O/16 - Kilome Lake
NE-31-126-3-W5
60°00'N 114°30'W
Flows north-west into NWT approximately 220 km north-east of High Level.

Officially approved in 1946, it is likely descriptive of the animals in the area.

Buffalo River (river)
84 F/14 - Carcajou
21-102-19-W5
57°50'N 117°01'W
Flows north-west into Peace River approximately 76 km south of High Level.

The precise origin of the name of this river is unknown. It may be named for its association with the Buffalo Head Hills in which it has its source.

Buhler Creek (creek)
84 F/7 - Buhler Creek
11-97-18-W5
57°24'N 116°47'W
Flows north-west into Cache Creek approximately 74 km north-east of Manning.

This creek was named for Private Cornelius P. Buhler, a war casualty.

Bulldog Lake (lake)
74 D/3 - I.D. #18
14-83-9-W4
56°12'N 111°19'W
Approximately 57 km south of Fort McMurray.

The descriptive name for this feature apparently derives from the swarms of bulldog flies, alias horseflies, around the lake. The term bulldog is a less widely used name for the horsefly, and provides an apt description of its tenacious nature.

Bunting Bay (bay)
74 D/10 - Hollies Creek
26-87-4-W4
56°34'N 110°31'W
Approximately 57 km east south-east of Fort McMurray.

The precise origin of the name for this large bay on the north arm of Gordon Lake is unknown; Lloyd Bunting worked on a map of the area in 1939, and it may be named after him. It may also have been named after a bird.

Burgess Lake (lake)
83 M/4 - Rio Grande
NW-3-72-11-W6
55°12'N 119°37'W
Approximately 50 km west of Grande Prairie.

Officially named in 1951, this lake was probably named after the Alfred and Arnold Burgess families who arrived in the area to farm in 1930.

*****Burnt Lake** (lake)
84 H/16 - Bayard Lake
16-101-15-W4
57°46'N 112°23'W
Approximately 130 km north north-west of Fort McMurray.

(see Bayard Lake)

Burnt Lakes (lakes)
84 H/5 - Burnt Lakes
26-96-25-W4
57°17′N 113°55′W
Approximately 164 km north of Fort McMurray.

The precise origin of the name of this series of lakes is unknown; the area may have been burned over by a forest fire at the time the name was recorded on a federal government map of 1915.

*****Burnt River** (river)
83 M/16 - Codesa
16-80-1-W6
55°55′N 118°08′W
Flows north into the Peace River.

The origin of the name Burnt River is not known but it is an old name and possibly refers to a time when a fire may have burned on its banks. (see Saddle (Burnt) River)

Burnt River (river)
84 G/9 - Alberta
19-100-3-W5
57°42′N 114°29′W
Flows south-west into Mikkwa River approximately 184 km south-east of High Level.

The precise origin of the name of this river is unknown; it may have been an area burned out by forest fire at the time J.B. St. Cyr, DLS, recorded the name during a survey in 1909.

Burntwood Island (island)
74 L/15 - Burntwood Island
33-114-4-W4
58°56′N 110°37′W
Approximately 242 km north north-east of Fort McMurray in Lake Athabasca.

---
*denotes rescinded name or former locality.

An early name, descriptive of the feature. Burntwood is an English version of the French word *brûlé*.

Burrison Lake (lake)
84 P/4 - Burrison Lake
NW-3-117-22-W4
59°09′N 113°40′W
Approximately 209 km east north-east of High Level.

Named in 1949 after Lance-Sergeant Richard Burrison, MM, who was born in Chauvin and enlisted in Saskatoon in 1942. He was killed in action in Europe in April 1945.

Burstall Lake (lake)
74 M/8 - Wylie Lake
13-119-2-W4
59°20′N 110°12′W
Approximately 290 km north north-east of Fort McMurray.

It was named in 1929 after Constable Burstall of the RCMP in Chipewyan.

Bush Lake (lake)
83 M/6 - La Glace
32-72-9-W6
55°17′N 119°21′W
Approximately 35 km north-west of Grande Prairie.

The name Bush Lake is well established in local usage and is likely a descriptive name. The lake was previously known as Wilkin Lake after Squadron Leader R.P. Wilkin, of Edmonton, who was killed in World War II. The name was changed in 1991 to reflect current local usage of the name Bush Lake. (see also Wilkin Lake)

Bushe River (river)
84 K/7 - Child Lake
6-109-17-W5
58°26′N 116°48′W

Flows east into Boyer River approximately 20 km south-east of High Level.

Local Beaver and Slavey residents refer to this feature as *Kl'o monh Sake* or *Tl'o monh Sake*, which translates into English as "Where the prairie ends creek." The aboriginal name appears to have been in use since the 19th century. A surveyor in the area in 1913 referred to it as Deadhorse Creek. Bushe River is first recorded some time between 1946 and 1958. According to local residents, Bushe refers to shrubs along the sides of the creek.

Bushe River Indian Reserve No. 207
(Indian reserve)
84 K/7 - Child Lake
20-109-18-W5
58°29′N 116°57′W
Approximately 2 km due east of High Level.

Named for its proximity to Bushe River. (see Bushe River)

Bustard Island (island)
74 L/15 - Burntwood Island
2-113-5-W4
58°47′N 110°44′W
Approximately 225 km north north-east of Fort McMurray in Lake Athabasca.

It shows as early as 1823 on a Franklin Expedition map, and in the Fort Chipewyan Hudson's Bay Company 1822 post journal. Bustard, or the French equivalent *outarde*, by which the island was sometimes known, is another name for the Canada goose, *Branta canadensis*. It likely refers to the abundance of the goose on the island at certain times of the year. It is likely the island referred to by George Simpson as Big Island. On Dr. Robert Bell's map of 1884, it is referred to as McFarlane's Island.

Butte, La (hill)
74 M/6 - Bocquene Lake
23-120-9-W4
59°24′N 111°26′W
Approximately 293 km north of Fort McMurray.

The name appears on federal government maps as early as the 1920s, but the name is likely older. Because of its French form, it likely dates from the fur trade days. *Butte*, in French, means hillock or mound. On the banks of the Slave River, it rises 30 metres from the surrounding territory.

Cabin Creek (creek)
83 O/10 - Marten Lakes
3-34-75-6-W5
55°32′N 114°51′W
Flows southwest into Marten Creek approximately 28 km north of Slave Lake.

Although the origin is not known, it may refer to the ranger cabin on the creek at the time the name was adopted in 1954.

Cache Creek (creek)
74 D/13 - Ruth Lake
32-91-10-W4
56°57′N 111°34′W
Flows north-east into Beaver River approximately 26 km north north-west of Fort McMurray.

The precise origin of the name of this creek is unknown; however, it must be linked with a cache once kept here. A cache is defined in the *Dictionary of Canadianisms* as "a storing place where supplies, furs, equipment, and other goods may be deposited for protection from foraging animals and the weather." It comes from the French verb *câcher*, meaning to hide.

Cache Creek (creek)
84 F/10 - Wolverine River
2-100-18-W5
57°39′N 116°50′W
Flows northwest into Wolverine River approximately 94 km north-east of Manning.

The precise origin of the name of this creek is unknown, although it is an indication that someone kept a cache in this area. The name was recorded by J.A. Fletcher, DLS, surveying in the area in 1913. (see also Cache Creek)

Cadotte Lake (hamlet)
84 C/8 - Cadotte Lake
24-86-16-W5
56°28′N 116°22′W
Approximately 61 km north-east of Peace River.

A post office was established here in 1969, with V. Baratto being the first postmaster. (see Cadotte Lake)

Cadotte Lake (lake)
84 C/8 - Cadotte Lake
12-86-16-W5
56°26′N 116°23′W
Approximately 57 km east north-east of Peace River.

This lake and the hamlet of the same name, as well as Cadotte River, are named after Jean Baptiste Cadot (Cadotte) (1723-1803). Cadotte established a reputation as a fur trader, interpreter and British loyalist from his home at Sault Ste. Marie by the mid-eighteenth century. In 1775 Cadot became part of a large group of traders, including Joseph and Thomas Frobisher, Alexander Henry and Peter Pond, who travelled to the North-West from the Sault. Cadot's sons followed him into the fur trade and became partners in the North West Company. Cadotte's River is mentioned in Archibald McDonald's journal under the date August 25, 1828, and later by William Ogilivie, DLS, in 1884.

Cadotte River (river)
84 C/11 - Deadwood
18-89-20-W5
56°43′N 117°10′W
Flows north-west into Peace River approximately 35 km south-east of Manning.

(see Cadotte Lake)

Calahoo Creek (creek)
83 L/13 - Calahoo Creek
27-68-12-W6
54°55′N 119°41′W
Flows east into Wapiti River approximately 36 km south south-west of Beaverlodge.

Both the creek and lake appear on the 1918 federal government map written as Callahoo. They are likely named after early residents and fur traders, trappers or guides in the area. The Calahoo family is descended from Louis L'Iroquois; some members of the family moved to western Canada in the late 18th and early 19th centuries as employees of the Hudson's Bay Company. (see also Iroquois Creek and Sylvester Creek)

Calahoo Lake (lake)
83 L/13 - Calahoo Lake
6-68-13-W6
54°51′N 119°58′W
Approximately 51 km south-west of Beaverlodge.

(see Calahoo Creek)

Calais (hamlet)
83 N/4 - Sturgeon Heights
NE-14-70-24-W55
55°04′N 117°32′W
Approximately 16 km west of Valleyview.

Situated on the Sturgeon Lake Indian Reserve; the name was originally given to the post office in 1911, named after the Reverend Jules Marie Calais, an Oblate of Mary Immaculate (1871-1944). He was the second priest in charge of the old mission on Sturgeon Lake. The first postmaster was T. Jordan.

Calder Lake (lake)
83 O/15 - Brintnell Lake
79-5-W5
55°53′N 114°42′W
Approximately 65 km north of Slave Lake.

Paul B. Calder was born in Beechtown, Nova Scotia, and came west with his parents to Strathcona. He served with the Royal Air Force in World War I. When he returned to Canada he became an aerial photographer with the Royal Canadian Air Force. He later joined Canadian Airways Ltd. and was a pilot on the Edmonton-Calgary-Lethbridge Prairie air-mail run, and later on the northern run. He was killed in 1933 in a flying accident at Rae Lake, NWT. This is one of a number of lakes in the area named after bush pilots. (see also Berry Lake, Brintnell Lake, Dickins Lake, Farrell Lake, Lake May, McConachie Lake, McMillan Lake, McMullen Lake, Randall Lake and Sawle Lake)

Calder River (river)
73 M/8 - Grist Lake
1-73-1-W4
55°18′N 110°00′W
Flows into Saskatchewan approximately 100 km north of Cold Lake.

Although it appears on a federal government map as early as 1913, after whom this lake is named is not known.

Calling Lake (lake)
83 P/3 - Calling Lake
1-16-72-22-W4
55°14′N 113°19′W
Located approximately 100 km north-west of Lac La Biche.

It is a translation of an aboriginal name for the lake the ice on which makes loud noises when freezing up each year. The name was well known and in local use before the arrival of the Dominion Land Surveyors who were in the area in the 1910s. The Geological Survey of Canada recorded the name Island Lake for this feature, and it is under that name it is shown on a federal government map of 1905.

Calling Lake (hamlet)
83 P/3 - Calling Lake
8-72-21-W4
55°15′N 113°12′W
Approximately 95 km north-west of Lac La Biche.

Originally established as a post office in January 1920, it took its name from the nearby lake. The first postmaster was J. Mackintosh. (see Calling Lake)

Calling Lake Provincial Park (provincial park)
83 P/3 - Calling Lake
26-71-21-W4
55°11′N 113°15′W
Approximately 95 km north-west of Lac La Biche.

Established in 1971, this 738-hectare park was named for its proximity to Calling Lake. (see Calling Lake)

Calling River (river)
83 P/3 - Calling Lake
4-35-71-21-W4F
55°11′N 113°12′W
Flows west into Calling Lake approx 67 km north-west of Lac La Biche.

The name was recorded by the Geological Survey of Canada in 1892. (see Calling Lake)

Calling River (locality)
83 P/2 - Calling River
30-70-19-W4
55°05′N 112°54′W
Approximately 60 km of Lac La Biche.

Named for its proximity to the river; the post office was established here in August, 1934. The first postmaster was G. Monson.

Calumet Lake (lake)
74 E/5 - Bitumount
17, 18-97-11-W4
57°25′N 111°46′W
Approximately 75 km north north-west of Fort McMurray.

Originally called Wolf Lake, the name was changed in 1965. (see also Calumet River and Wolf Lake)

Calumet River (river)
74 E/5 - Bitumount
13-97-11-W4
57°25′N 111°39′W
Flows east into Athabasca River approximately 78 km north north-west of Fort McMurray.

This river takes its name from the pipestone cliffs lower down the Athabasca. The calumet or pipe of peace is an ornamented ceremonial pipe traditionally used as a symbol of peace. (see also Pierre au Calumet).

Cameron Creek (creek)
74 D/11 - Fort McMurray
31-88-9-W4
56°40′N 111°25′W
Flows north into Horse River approximately 7 km south south-west of Fort McMurray.

The name appears on a federal government map as early as 1913; after whom it is named is not known.

Cameron Hills (hills)
84 N/13 - Esk Lake
23-125-1-W6
59°48′N 118°00′W
Approximately 153 km north north-east of High Level.

These hills were officially named in 1921 for Maxwell George Cameron, an assistant on a survey crew. He later became chief cartographer of the Surveys and Mapping Branch, Department of Mines and Technical Surveys in Ottawa, 1948-1951. In 1915 J.R. Akins, DLS, had recorded Cutknife Hills as the translation of a name supplied by a group of Behcho Widen- or -chad-Aden Slavey living at Bistcho Lake, whom he met while surveying. In the early 1950s, the Alberta Northwest Territories Boundary Commission mentioned it was formerly known as Eagle Mountain. Today, the west side of the hills is referred to by some trappers in the vicinity of Bistcho Lake as Bistcho Hills. The east side is called *D-agah Zahih* by residents at Indian Cabins and Meander River. This is a descriptive Slavey name that translates as "Hills you can see a long ways from."

Camp Creek (locality)
83 J/7 - Fort Assiniboine
6-61-4-W5
54°15′N 114°35′W
Approximately 20 km north-west of Barrhead.

The name for this locality whose post office opened in August 1934 is taken for its proximity to the creek where it is said that in earlier times the aboriginal people camped. It is on an early trail running from the Pembina River to the Athabasca River.

Camp Island (island)
83 N/13 - Tangent
10-80-26-W5
55°55′N 117°58′W
Approximately 50 km south-west of Peace River (town) situated in the Peace River

The name was in use before 1915, when it first appears on a federal government map. Although the origins are not known, the name is possibly descriptive.

Campbell Creek (creek)
83 L/15 - Big Mountain Creek
14-68-6-W6
54°53′N 118°49′W
Flows south-east into Bald Mountain Creek approximately 22 km south south-west of Grande Prairie.

Lexie Campbell came to Grande Prairie in 1900 at a time when settlers began to move into the area. He and his family eventually settled on what is now called Campbell Creek. The creek was officially named before 1960.

Campbell Lake (lake)
74 D/10 - Hollies Creek
23-88-4-W4
56°39′N 110°32′W
Approximately 58 km east south-east of Fort McMurray.

The precise origin of the name of this lake is unknown.

Campbell Ridge (ridge)
83 L/15 - Big Mountain Creek
32-68-6-W6
54°55′44″N 118°52′28″W
Approximately 29 km south of Grande Prairie.

This ridge takes it name from the creek. (see Campbell Creek)

Camsell Lake (lake)
74 M/16 - Andrew Lake
NE-36-125-2-W4
59°54′N 110°11′W
Approximately 350 km north of Fort McMurray.

After Charles Camsell (1876-1958), prominent geologist. Charles Camsell was born at Fort Liard, N.W.T., the son of a chief factor of the Hudson's Bay Co. He was educated in Manitoba and later at Queen's, Harvard, and the Massachusetts Institute of Technology. In 1900 he was an assistant on a geological survey trip to Great Bear Lake and the Coppermine area. He was geologist in the Geological Survey from 1904 to 1920; Deputy Minister of Mines, 1920-1935, and Deputy Minister of Mines and Natural Resources and Commissioner of the Northwest Territories from 1935 to 1946. He was prominent on the Dominion Fuel Board and the National Research Council and received numerous awards. In 1935 he was created CMG. Holmgren, 1976.

Canoe Lake (lake)
74 D/6 - Gregoire Lake
15-86-7-W4
56°27′50″N 110°31′00″W
Approximately 36 km south-east of Fort McMurray.

This well-established local name is familiar to most residents of the area. The precise origin is unknown; the name may be descriptive of the shape of the lake or it has been suggested that it reflects the sinking of a canoe at some point in the early history of the area.

Canon Smith Lake (lake)
83 M/3 - Wembley
7-28-71-7-W6
55°11′N 119°01′W
Approximately 10 km west of Grande Prairie.

As the name might imply, it was named after a Church of England (Anglican) clergyman, Canon Frederick Charles Smith, who was the overseer of the mission points in the Grande Prairie area in 1911-1914, when he returned to England. Before 1911, he spent time in Africa as a missionary. While in Alberta, he took out a homestead on which the lake was situated, and called it Richmond Hill after a parish he had served in Yorkshire.

Canyon Creek/Widewater/Wagner (hamlet)
83 O/6 - Kinuso
14-36-72-8-W5
55°22′N 115°05′W
Approximately 22 km west north-west of Slave Lake.

Established in 1985, this widespread hamlet is a combination of three hamlets. (see also Canyon Creek, Widewater and Wagner)

Canyon Creek (creek)
83 O/6 - Kinuso
16-36-73-8-W5
55°22′N 115°05′W
Flows north into Lesser Slave Lake approximately 22 km west north-west of Slave Lake.

In the 1920s, the feature was known as Field Canyon Creek after Mr. Field, an employee of a lumber company operating on the steep-banked stream. This was to differentiate it from other Canyon Creeks in the area. The name Canyon Creek was officially adopted in 1967 to coincide with the nearby hamlet.

*Canyon Creek (hamlet)
83 O/6 - Kinuso
36-73-8-W5
54°22′N 115°05′W
Approximately 22 km north-west of Slave Lake.

A post office was established here in March 1928, and was named for the nearby creek. The first postmaster was Mary Potter. In 1985, for economic reasons, it joined with two other hamlets to become Canyon Creek/Widewater/Wagner. (see also Canyon Creek)

Carcajou (hamlet)
84 F/14 - Carcajou
SW-16-101-19-W5
57°46′N 117°02′W
Approximately 80 km south of High Level.

Carcajou is derived from the Algonkian, probably Montagnais, meaning wolverine. In the early records of fur traders it is variously spelled carcajon, carcaseu, casacajou and cacassause. In English the word wolverine is a diminutive of wolf likely referring to its reputation of ferocity. The hamlet of Carcajou is in the vicinity of Wolverine Point which was marked on the David Thompson map of 1814.

Carcajou Settlement (settlement)
84 F/14 - Carcajou
30-101-19-W5
57°48′N 117°07′W
Approximately 84 km south of High Level.

It was first surveyed in 1918 and a post office was established here in 1923. The first postmaster was C. Rankin. (see Carcajou)

Carcajou Settlement No. 187
(Indian reserve)
84 F/14 - Carcajou
30-101-19-W5
57°48′N 117°07′W
Approximately 84 km south of High Level.

(see Carcajou)

Cardinal Creek (creek)
84 C/5 - Chinook Valley
9-86-23-W5
56°27′N 117°33′W
Flows north into Whitemud River 28 km north north-west of Peace River.

(see Cardinal Lake)

Cardinal Lake (lake)
84 C/4 - Grimshaw
21-83-24-W5
56°14′N 117°44′W
Approximately 7 km north-west of Grimshaw.

Named in 1917 for an early settler, Louis Cardinal, who at that time was considered to be the oldest resident on the shores of the lake.

Caribou Creek (creek)
84 K/6 - Parma Creek
23-108-21-W5
58°24′N 117°24′W
Flows north-east into Parma Creek approximately 21 km south-west of High Level.

Local residents suggest that caribou used to frequent this region in the nineteenth century, and the name may be an English translation of the Beaver name *Matchi Sake*. This creek is named for the caribou, a symbol of Canada's North. The caribou belongs to the Deer family (*Cervidae*), species *Rangifer tarandus*. Before settlement, some three million to five million caribou lived in North America; today, there are about one million. Caribou range from forest to tundra habitats, feeding heavily on ground lichens. Biologists believed caribou required lichens and that loss of lichens by fire had caused population declines. It is now recognized that fires are a natural aspect of northern ecosystems and that caribou are adapted to cope with the loss of lichen habitats. One of three sub-species, the woodland caribou inhabits mountains and forests from British Columbia to Newfoundland.

Caribou Horn Lake (lake)
74 D/10 - Hollies Creek
12-87-7-W4
56°31′25″N 110°58′42″W
Approximately 28 km south-east of Fort McMurray.

The precise origin of the long-established name of this lake is unknown. (see also Caribou Creek)

Caribou Islands (island)
74 M/12 - Caribou Islands
NE-29-123-9-W4
59°43′N 111°31′W
Approximately 323 km north of Fort McMurray in Slave River.

---

*denotes rescinded name or former locality.

It is shown on federal government maps as early as the 1920s, and is descriptive of the animal found in the area. (see also Caribou Creek)

Caribou Lake (lake)
83 J/6 - Christmas Creek
31-62-9-W5
54°24′N 115°20′W
Approximately 34 km north of Swan Hills.

The name was recorded as early as 1950 by the Alberta Department of Lands and Surveys, and is likely descriptive. (see also Caribou Creek)

Caribou Lake (lake)
84 N/1 - Steen River
14-116-13-W5
59°03′N 116°05′W
Approximately 84 km north east of High Level.

The precise origin of the name of this lake is unknown; it may be descriptive of the fauna on its shores. It is also known among the Beaver as Little Fish Lake, or *Zlúge Natsútle Minkeh*. This name is used with the locally known Big Fish Lake located approximately 15 km north. (see also Caribou Creek)

Caribou Lake (lake)
73 M/5 - Behan Lake
15-75-13-W4
55°29′N 111°57′W
Approximately 80 km north of Lac La Biche.

The name for this lake is well-established in local usage and is a rough translation from the Cree, *Atikhok Kamusnakasuchik Sagahegan*. The English equivalent is close to "Caribou Sign Lake." (see also Caribou Creek)

---

*denotes rescinded name or former locality.

Caribou Lake (lake)
73 M/2 -
28-70-6-W4
55°04′N 110°52′W
Approximately 90km north north-west of Cold Lake.

Officially approved in 1955, the name is likely descriptive of the local deer population. (see also Caribou Creek)

Caribou Mountains (mountains)
84 O/4 - House Mountain
32-117-10-W5
59°12′N 115°40′W
Approximately 97 km north-east of High Level.

Likely named for the abundance of the animal in the area. (see also Caribou Creek)

Caribou River (river)
84 J/5 - Sled Island
13-109-12-W5
58°28′N 115°51′W
Flows south into Peace River approximately 75 km east south-east of High Level.

The precise origin of the name of this river is unknown; it is probably descriptive of caribou in the vicinity. The name was recorded as early as 1890 by the Geological Survey of Canada. When J.S. Galletly surveyed the area in 1913, he referred to the feature as "Caribou or Deer River." (see also Caribou Creek)

Carl Creek (creek)
84 J/12 - Alberta
24-111-12-W5
58°39′N 115°53′W
Flows south into Caribou River approximately 73 km east north-east of High Level.

Named by J.R. Akins, DLS, during his 1914 survey of the 29th Baseline for Carl Sanderson, a trapper from Fort Vermilion. Sanderson was an axeman on Akins' survey party in 1914 and 1915.

*Carlo Creek (creek)
83 J/6 - Christmas Creek
63-8-W5
54°30′N 115°04′W
Flows north north-east into Freeman River approximately 24 km south south-east of Swan Hills.

This name was first recorded in the 1940s, was rescinded in 1958, then renamed. After whom it was named is not known. (see Morse Lake)

Carlson Landing (locality)
74 L/13 - Baril River
13-9-115-11-W4
58°59′N 111°49′W
Approximately 240 km north of Fort McMurray.

Mr. Carlson worked here as a Technical Officer for the Canadian Northern Affairs and National Resources Department in the 1950s. This "scaler's establishment" in Wood Buffalo National Park originally took the name Point Providence, but this caused confusion with Fort Providence. The federal department wanted to call it Riverside, but it was Carlson Landing which was eventually chosen in 1959.

Carmon Creek (creek)
84 C/6 - Weberville
17-86-20-W5
56°27′N 117°6′W
Flows north-west into Peace River approximately 27 km north north-east of Peace River.

This was named after an early settler in the area. The Dominion Lands Survey at one time recorded a more colourful name for the feature, Rat Root Creek.

Carmon Lake (lake)
84 C/7 - Simon Lakes
8-85-18-W5
56°21'N 116°48'W
Approximately 31 km north-east of Peace River.

(see Carmon Creek)

Carolyn Creek (creek)
84 I/7 - Heron Island
4-7-107-16-W4
58°16'N 112°41'W
Flows west into Swift Current Creek approximately 177 km north north-west of Fort McMurray.

The name shows on federal government maps as early as 1930, but after whom it is named is not known.

Carrot Lake (lake)
84 A/14 - Mink Lake
13-92-22-W4
56°59'N 113°24'W
Approximately 124 km west north-west of Fort McMurray.

It is likely named for an abundance in the area of species of the *Umbelliferae*, or carrot families. It is one of two that are known as Chipewyan Lakes. (see also Chipewyan Lakes)

Carson Creek (creek)
83 J/4 - Whitecourt
36-60-13-W5
54°14'N 115°47'W
South-west into Sakwatamau River approximately 13 km north north-west of Whitecourt.

The name for this creek has appeared on federal government maps as early as 1917, but its precise origin is not known. It may have been named after a survey crew member.

---

*denotes rescinded name or former locality.

***Carson Lake** (lake)
83 J/5 - Carson Lake
24-61-11,12-W5
54°18'N 115°39'W
Approximately 16 km north north-east of Whitecourt.

The feature took this name some time before the 1940s for it is the source of Carson Creek. However, at the request of local residents, the name of this lake, and one to the north-east, were changed in 1986 to reflect local and historical usage. (see also Carson Creek, McLeod Lake and Little McLeod Lake)

Carson-Pegasus Provincial Park (provincial park)
83 J/5 - Carson Lake
61-11,12-W5
54°18'N 115°38'W
Approximately 16 km north north-east of Whitecourt.

This 1210-hectare park was established in the 1980s, and takes its name from former names of two lakes in the park. (see Carson Lake, Pegasus Lake, Little McLeod Lake and Little McLeod Lake)

Cartwright Bay (bay)
74 D/7 - Cheecham
35-86-4-W4
56°29'N 110°30'W
At the south end of Gordon Lake approximately 60 km east south-east of Fort McMurray.

The precise origin of the name of this bay on Gordon Lake is unknown; it is likely named after a person. A cartwright was a person (usually a carpenter) who constructed carts.

Cascade Portage (portage)
74 D/9 - Bunting Bay
8-89-2-W4
56°42'16"N 110°16'42"W

Along the Clearwater River approximately 69 km east of Fort McMurray.

It was recorded by the Geological Survey of Canada in 1892. (see Cascade Rapids)

Running the Cascades, 1920s (On which of the two rivers was not recorded)

Cascade Rapids (rapids)
74 D/9 - Bunting Bay
8-89-2-W4
56°42'08"N 110°16'52"W
Approximately 69 km east of Fort McMurray in the Clearwater River.

These rapids have been known by this name since at least 1888 in which year they appeared in a survey report. Traveller Eden McAdams noted in his diary for May 12, 1889: "Left other side of portage at 12 am and ran down to the head of Cascade Rapids. The portage for these rapids is 1½ miles long and the longest on the Clearwater."

Cascade Rapids (rapids)
74 D/12 - Cascade Rapids
7-88-11-W4
56°37'N 111°44'W
On the Athabasca River approximately 25 km west south-west of Fort McMurray.

These rapids on the Athabasca River are a major obstacle to navigation and were apparently known as *nepe kabatekik* or "where the water falls." The name was recorded by the Geological Survey of Canada in 1892.

Cassette Rapids (rapids)
74 M/13 - Fitzgerald
26-125-10-W4
59°53'N 111°36'W
Approximately 342 km north of Fort McMurray in Slave River.

This name likely dates from the early fur trade days. *Cassette* is a French word meaning small case or chest. It was a strong, light, waterproof box used by fur traders to carry their personal belongings.

Cattail Lake (lake)
74 E/8 - Trout Creek
8-2-97-3-W4
57°23'35"N 110°22'10"W
Approximately 93 km north north-east of Fort McMurray.

This remote lake was named by the partners who have operated a trapline here. They sowed cattail seeds as an experiment in this lake, as well as two others. The name was given for easy identification of the location. (see also Test Lake and Hopeful Lake)

Cattail Lake (lake)
83 N/5 - Puskwaskau River
25-73-25-W5
55°21'N 117°42'W
Approximately 40 km north-west of Valleyview.

Cattail Lake is so named because of the prevalence of the plant around the lake, which lies in a marshy area. This name has been in use since at least the 1930s.

---

*denotes rescinded name or former locality.

Chain Lake (lake)
74 M/9 - Colin Lake
NE-36-122-1-W4
59°38'N 110°01'W4
Approximately 325 km north north-east of Fort McMurray.

The name was submitted in 1961 by the Research Council of Alberta, and is descriptive of the shape of the lake.

Chain Lakes (lakes)
74 D/3 - I.D. #18
27-83-8-W4
56°13'32"N 111°10'32"W
Approximately 50 km south south-east of Fort McMurray.

The name is descriptive of a chain of small lakes, linked by a creek.

Chain Lakes (lakes)
83 M/5 - Hythe
16-74-13-W6
55°24'N 119°55'W
Approximately 72 km west north-west of Grande Prairie.

This descriptive name was adopted in 1952 describing a group of three lakes.

Chain Ponds (ponds)
84 K/4 - Chain Ponds
17-104-24-W5
58°02'N 117°56'W
Approximately 74 km south-west of High Level.

This name is descriptive, as they lie in a north-west south-east direction. The local name for this feature is McKinzie or MacKenzie Lakes, apparently after Alexander McKinzie, a Hudson's Bay Company factor in charge of Fort Vermilion from 1871 to 1876.

Chalifaux Creek (creek)
84 O/12 - Alberta
4-7-122-9-W5
59°35'N 115°33'W
Flows west into Whitesand River approximately 165 km north north-east of High Level.

This was named in 1967 after Lance-Corporal Joseph Chalifaux of Peace River, who was killed in action in World War II.

Chalmers Creek (creek)
83 J/14 - Deer Mountain
27-69-9-W5
55°00'N 115°17'W
Flows north north-west into the Swan River approximately 24 km north-east of Swan Hills.

Likely named after a Dominion Land Surveyor, Thomas Chalmers. (see also Deer Mountain)

*****Chalmers Hill** (mountain)
83 J/14 - Deer Mountain
68-8-W5
54°55'N 115°10'W
Approximately 22 km north-east of Swan Hills.

(see Deer Mountain)

Chalmers Lake (lake)
84 D/8 - Deer Hill
11-84-2-W6
56°16'N 118°12'W
Approximately 26 km north-west of Fairview.

This lake was named for W.C. (Charlie) Chalmers, one of the first settlers in the Waterhole district in 1911. In the spring of 1915 Chalmers purchased a steam-powered sawmill, which he and his sons put to work at their timber berth 20 kilometres north of his homestead near the lake that now bears his name.

Chard (railway point)
73 M/15 - Bohn Lake
17-79-6-W4
55°50′N 110°55′W
Approximately 90 km south south-east of Fort McMurray.

This was originally established in 1925 as a station on the Alberta and Great Waterways Railway line and was named after Alfred Chard, freight and traffic supervisor for the Alberta Government. A post office was established here in 1968, and the first postmaster was Mrs. H. Stepanowich.

Charles Lake (lake)
74 M/15 - Mercredi Lake
25-124-4-W4
59°48′N 110°33′W
Approximately 344 km north of Fort McMurray.

Named in 1929 after "John Charles, a chief factor at Fort Chipewyan, 1830-1833 and 1839." Holmgren, 1976.

Chasm Creek (creek)
84 L/4 - Chasm Creek
36-105-12-W6
58°11′N 120°00′W
Flows west into British Columbia approximately 45 km south-west of Rainbow Lake.

The name originally proposed by the British Columbia-Alberta Boundary Survey in 1950-51 was Canyon Creek. This was rejected as there were already several creeks by that name in Alberta. Later suggestions included Kloof Creek and Cleave Creek, but Chasm Creek was the name finally approved.

Chateh (post office)
84 L/10 - Assumption
1-112-5-W6
58°40′N 118°36′W
Approximately 48 km north-east of Rainbow Lake.

This is a commemorative name in honour of the chief, Chateh, who signed Treaty No. 8 for the Slavey of Upper Hay River in 1900. The post office was called Assumption from 1953 until 1970, when the Band Council requested the change. (see also Assumption)

Checker Lake (lake)
74 D/6 - Gregoire Lake
5-86-7-W4
56°25′45″N 111°03′40″W
Approximately 38 km south-east of Fort McMurray.

This lake was named after Jack Checkers who used to work the trapline surrounding the lake. Checkers remains a mysterious character, and is reputed to be a great storyteller who once rode with Jesse James. No one is sure whether his name was actually Checkers, or whether if the name was given to him because of the checkered shirts he always wore.

Cheecham (locality)
74 D/7 - Clearwater River
15-84-6-W4
56°17′N 110°52′W
Approximately 59 km south-east of Fort McMurray.

First established as a post office in 1913, it was named after the Cheecham family who were well known in the area. It is now also the name of the railway point in the locality. The first postmaster was W. Johnson. (see also Leo's Creek)

Cheecham Creek (creek)
74 D/7 - Cheecham
18-84-5-W4
56°17′00″N 110°46′20″W
Flows north north-west into Gregoire River approximately 62 km south-east of Fort McMurray.

This creek was previously officially known as Georges Creek but the name was changed in 1992 to reflect local usage of the name Cheecham, after the Cheecham family. (see also Leo's Creek)

Cheecham Lake (lake)
74 D/7 - Cheecham
18-84-5-W4
56°17′N 110°47′W
Approximately 60 km south-east of Fort McMurray.

Originally named "Georges Lake"; the name was changed in 1992 to reflect common local usage. The popular usage indicates that most of the people who live in the area call the lake Cheecham after the Cheecham family who lived on the south-west side of the lake. (see also Leo's Creek)

Chelsea Creek (creek)
84 H/7 - Legend Lake
27-95-16-W4
57°16′N 112°32′W
Flows south-west into Ells River approximately 91 km north-west of Fort McMurray.

Why the creek was named this is unknown; it does appear on a federal government map as early as 1916. Chelsea is an area of London, England. It may mean "landing place for chalk or limestone", or it may be from the Old English *cælic*, meaning cup or chalice. Another local name identified for this feature is the Narrows Creek.

Cherry Point (locality)
84 D/4 - Cherry Point
10-83-13-W6
56°11′N 119°57′W
Approximately 99 km west north-west of Fairview.

This name is apparently descriptive of the many pin or choke cherry trees growing in the vicinity.

Cherry Lake (lake)
74 M/16 - Andrew Lake
4-124-1-W4
59°45'N 110°06'W
Approximately 335 km north north-east of Fort McMurray.

The name was submitted in 1958 by the Research Council of Alberta, and was adopted in course of survey work done in 1958. No other explanation was given.

Chester Creek (creek)
84 F/7 - Buhler Creek
1-96-18-W5
57°18'N 116°46'W
Flows north into Cache Creek, 67 km north-east of Manning.

The feature is likely named after Chester Day, a chainman on the J.A. Fletcher survey crew of May 1913. The word chester comes from the Latin word *castra*, meaning military camp.

Chickadee Creek (creek)
83 J/4 - Whitecourt
18-60-13-W5
54°12'N 115°57'W
Flows south-east into Athabasca River approximately 17 km west north-west of Whitecourt.

The name for this creek was mentioned as early as 1912 by J.S. Galletly, DLS, and likely refers to the abundance of the bird in the area. It could either be the black-capped or boreal chickadee, both of which have extensive ranges in the boreal and plains areas of Canada.

Child Lake (lake)
84 K/7 - Child Lake
27-109-16-W5
58°29'N 116°35'W
Approximately 31 km east of High Level.

The name commemorates an accident on the lake around the turn of the century. Two young girls were drowned when they fell through the ice. The Dunne-za or Beaver name for the lake is *Ts'itotu Wonte*.

Child Lake Indian Reserve No. 164A
(Indian reserve)
84 K/7 - Child Lake
15-109-16-W5
58°28'N 116°35'W
Approximately 28 km east of High Level.

Named for its proximity to Child Lake, it is occupied by the Boyer River Band. (see also Boyer River Indian Reserve No. 164)

Chilloneys Creek (creek)
74 L/14 - Rivière des Rochers
15-16-113-8-W4
58°49'N 111°17'W
Flows east into Rivière des Rochers approximately 221 km north of Fort McMurray.

It was officially named in 1971 after a trapper who worked in the area.

Chinchaga River (river)
84 L/16 - Alberta
6-114-2-W6
58°53'N 118°19'W
Flows north into Hay River approximately 75 km north-east of Rainbow Lake.

This name was recorded by Dominion Land Surveyor William Ogilvie in 1891. Ogilvie translated the name to mean beautiful or wonderful. However, according to a later surveyor, J.R. Akins, in 1915, as well as local residents in the 1980s, the name means Big Wood River or Big Timber River, due to the large spruce trees along the river bank - *Chin* (big) *ga* (along). The Slavey at Assumption call the river *Ehchincha Zaheh*, which translates as Big Timber River.

Chinook Valley (locality)
84 C/5 - Chinook Valley
24-86-24-W5
56°29'N 117°39'W
Approximately 32 km north of Grimshaw.

Originally established as a post office in 1931, Chinook Valley is named for the warm dry gusty westerly winds of Alberta experienced in a belt extending some 300 to 400 kilometres east of the slopes of the Rocky Mountains. An aboriginal legend tells of Chinook, a beautiful young woman who wandered away and was lost in the mountains. The bravest warriors searched but failed to find her. Then one day a soft warm wind blew from the west, the spirit of the beautiful Chinook. The Chinook aboriginal group originated on the Pacific Coast. The first postmaster was C.E. Neff.

Chipewyan (settlement)
74 L/11 - Fort Chipewyan
16-112-7-W4
58°44'N 111°08'W
Approximately 215 km north of Fort McMurray.

(see Fort Chipewyan and Chipewyan Indian Reserve No. 201)

Chipewyan Indian Reserve No. 201
(Indian reserve)
74 L/7 - Keane Creek
109-6-W4
58°30'N 110°55'W
Approximately 195 km north of Fort McMurray.

Named for the Chipewyan people who live there. The name for the group is Cree in origin meaning pointed skins, which refers to the way they prepared animal pelts for trade. They call themselves people, or *Dene*. By the end of the 1800s, they occupied what is now the northern portions of the Prairie provinces and the southern part of the Northwest Territories. Their language is a branch of the northeastern Athapaskan, and is closely related to Slavey and Dogrib. (Adapted from *Canadian Encyclopedia, 1988, Vol 1*)

Chipewyan Indian Reserve No. 201A
(Indian reserve)
74 L/10 - Big Point
NW-16-111-4-W4
58°39′N 110°36′W
Approximately 210 km north north-east of Fort McMurray.

(see Chipewyan Indian Reserve No. 201)

Chipewyan Indian Reserve No. 201B
(Indian reserve)
74 L/10 - Big Point
4-4-111-5-W4
58°36′N 110°47′W
Approximately 203 km north of Fort McMurray.

(see Chipewyan Indian Reserve No. 201)

Chipewyan Indian Reserve No. 201C
(Indian reserve)
74 L/7 - Keane Creek
14-34-108-6-W4
58°26′N 110°55′W
Approximately 182 km north of Fort McMurray.

(see Chipewyan Indian Reserve No. 201)

Chipewyan Indian Reserve No. 201D
(Indian reserve)
74 L/7 - Keane Creek
13-27-108-6-W4
58°25′N 110°55′W
Approximately 181 km north of Fort McMurray.

(see Chipewyan Indian Reserve No. 201)

Chipewyan Indian Reserve No. 201E
(Indian reserve)
74 L/7 - Keane Creek
NW-20-108-6-W4
58°24′N 110°58′W
Approximately 178 km north of Fort McMurray.

(see Chipewyan Indian Reserve No. 201)

Chipewyan Indian Reserve No. 201F
(Indian reserve)
74 L/3 - Embarras
13-104-9-W4
58°02′N 111°20′W
Approximately 135 km north of Fort McMurray.

(see Chipewyan Indian Reserve No. 201)

Chipewyan Indian Reserve No. 201G
(Indian reserve)
74 E/14 - Pearson Lake
3-103-9-W4
57°54′N 111°24′W
Approximately 130 km north Fort McMurray.

(see Chipewyan Indian Reserve No. 201)

Chipewyan Lake (lake)
84 A/14 - Mink Lake
3-92-22-W4
56°57′N 113°26′W
Approximately 126 km west north-west of Fort McMurray.

(see Chipewyan Lake)

Chipewyan Lake (locality)
84 A/14 - Mink Lake
33-91-22-W4
56°56′N 113°27′W
Approximately 130 km west north-west of McMurray.

This locality and the lake on whose shore it is situated are named Chipewyan Lake, after a Dene tribe. (see also Chipewyan Indian Reserve No. 201)

Chipewyan Lakes (lakes)
84 A/14 - Mink Lake
11-92-22-W4
56°57′N 113°25′W
Approximately 125 km west north-west of Fort McMurray.

This name refers to a pair of lakes, the larger of which is known as Chipewyan Lake; the smaller lake to the north is called Carrot Lake. (see also Chipewyan Indian Reserve No. 201 and Carrot Lake)

Chipewyan River (river)
84 A/13 - Liége River
4-90-23-W4
56°46′N 113°35′W
Flows south south-west into Wabasca River approximately 134 km west of Ft. McMurray.

(see Chipewyan Indian Reserve No. 201)

Chipewyan Settlement (settlement)
74 L/11 - Fort Chipewyan
17-112-7-W4
58°43′N 111°08′W
Approximately 2 km north of Fort Chipewan.

It was first surveyed in 1911. (see Chipewyan Indian Reserve No. 201)

Chisholm (hamlet)
83 J/16 - Chisholm
26-68-2-W5
54°55′N 114°10′W
Approximately 60 km west south-west of Athabasca.

Originally established in 1914 as an Edmonton, Dunvegan and British Columbia Railway station, it was named after Thomas Chisholm, a local railway contractor. Apparently, Mr. Chisholm ran the Aurora Saloon and Dance Hall in Dawson during the Klondike Gold Rush. He was a colourful character, larger than life, being over six feet tall, 240 pounds, who sported a watch chain made from gold nuggets.

Chisholm Creek (creek)
83 J/16 - Chisholm
26-68-2-W5
54°55′N 114°12′W

Flows north-west into Athabasca River approximately 62 km west north-west of Athabasca.

(see Chisholm)

Chisholm Mills (post office)

83 J/16 - Chisholm
26-68-2-W5
54°55′N 114°10′W
Approximately 61 km west north-west of Athabasca.

This post office opened for the hamlet of Chisholm in July 1923, the first postmaster being J. A. Collins. (see Chisholm)

Christina Crossing (locality)

74 D/8 - Gipsy Lake
6-84-3-W4
56°15′20″N 110°28′00″W
On the Christina River approximately 70 km south-east of Fort McMurray.

This locality, which was once home to 40 families, is named Christina Crossing because it is where people have commonly forded the river. (see Christina Lake and Christina River)

Christina Lake (lake)

73 M/10 - Christina Lake
32-76-6-W4
55°38′N 110°55′W
Approximately 115 km north-east of Lac La Biche.

When William Christie, DLS, surveyed this area in 1910 he referred to it as Narrows Lake. Because the name was duplicated elsewhere, the Surveyor General, Edouard Deville, found the name to be objectionable and ordered Christie to identify this feature as Christina Lake in his final report. The name is apparently in honour of Christine Gordon, a Scotswoman who made her home in Fort McMurray. Miss Gordon came to Canada to join her brother, William Gordon (see Gordon Lake), and according to Agnes Dean Cameron in *The New North* (1909) was "a free trader, if you please, in her own right, operating in opposition to the great and only Hudson's Bay Co...." She was highly respected by everyone in the community. She died in the mid-1940s. (see also Christina River)

Christina River (river)

74 D/11 - Fort McMurray
33-87-7-W4
56°40′N 111°03′W
Flows north-west into Clearwater River approximately 22 km east south-east of Fort McMurray.

The name Christina was chosen to honour Christine Gordon, who in partnership with her brother William, opened a trading post and post office at Fort McMurray in 1905. She remained at Fort McMurray for the rest of her life. In 1911 the name Christina replaced the river's earlier name, Pembina, which was referred to by George Simpson in 1820. Native residents call the river as *Nipnan seepee*, referring to the highbush cranberry, which is a common vegetation in this area. Peter Fidler referred to this river in the 1790s as *mith-quap-pim a seepe*, a Cree name, and also as *ky-goz-zae dez-za*, a Chipewyan name. Both mean red willow.

Christmas Creek (creek)

83 J/3 - Green Court
12-60-10-W5
54°11′N 115°22′W
Flows south into Athabasca River approximately 22 km east of Whitecourt.

The name for this creek shows on a federal government map as early as 1917; its precise origin is unknown. (see also Noel Lake)

*****Christmas Lake** (lake)

73 M/6 - Wiau Lake
6-73-7-W4
55°17′N 111°03′W
Approximately 82 km north-east of Lac La Biche.

(see Ipiatik Lake)

Cinderella Lake (lake)

74 M/16 - Andrew Lake
19-125-1-W4
59°52′N 110°10′W
Approximately 349 km north of Fort McMurray.

The name was submitted in 1958 by the Research Council of Alberta, and is recorded as being descriptive. Of what it is descriptive was not recorded.

Cladonia Lake (lake)

84 O/6 - Kinuso
12-119-7-W5
59°19′N 115°02′W
Approximately 149 km north-east of High Level.

The name Cladonia was chosen for this lake because it is in the centre of the Cladonia Fire Problem Area. The name Cladonia comes from a common species of lichen in the area, *Cladonia rangiferina*, which becomes very dry and thus is susceptible to fires during the summer months.

Claire, Lake (lake)

84 I/9 - Spruce Point
110-13-W4
58°35′N 112°05′W
Approximately 196 km north of Fort McMurray.

Clear Water Lake is referred to in Sir Alexander Mackenzie's journal, October 10, 1792. The Hudson's Bay Company Fort Chipewyan post journal of 1822 refers to it as Clear Lake. Claire is the French word for "clear."

Claire River (river)

74 L/13 - Baril River
8-27-114-12-W4
58°56′N 111°55′W

---

*denotes rescinded name or former locality.

Flows north into Peace River approximately 237 km north north-west of Fort McMurray.

It takes its name from its source. (see Lake Claire)

*Clairmont (hamlet)
83 M/7 - Sexsmith
25-72-6-W6
55°16′N 118°47′W
Approximately 10 km north of Grande Prairie.

The Edmonton, Dunvegan and British Columbia Railway established a station here early in 1916, and named it after the nearby lake. The post office was established on August 15, 1916, with the first postmaster being Mrs. Trout.

Clairmont Lake (lake)
83 M/7 - Sexsmith
30-72-5,6-W6
55°16′N 118°46′W
Approximately 6 km north of Grande Prairie.

Named by the Dominion Land Surveyor Walter McFarlane who surveyed the area first in 1909. It was a variant spelling of his birthplace in Ontario, Claremont. He liked the area so much that he applied for a homestead. (see also Clairmont)

Clark Lake (lake)
83 K/2 - Iosegun Lake
6-61-18-W5
54°15′N 116°41′W
Approximately 16 km south south-east of Fox Creek.

It is noted on a federal government map of 1916. Since it is approximately one kilometre north of the 16th Baseline, it was likely named after a survey crew member.

---

*denotes rescinded name or former locality.

Clarke Creek (creek)
74 D/14 - Wood Creek
5-90-9-W4
56°47′N 111°24′W
Flows west into Athabasca River approximately 6 km north of Fort McMurray.

Named by S.C. Ells in 1925 for Charles Clarke, one of the earliest homesteaders in the Fort McMurray district, who was killed in World War I. (see also Ells River)

Clarkson Valley (locality)
83 N/4 - Sturgeon Heights
3-71-25-W5
55°07′N 117°46′W
Approximately 30 km west north-west of Valleyview.

The post office opened here in September 1937 and closed in August 1968. The name Clarkson Valley was also given to the local school district established in 1935. The origin may refer to the Clarkson brothers who homesteaded in the area around 1920.

Claussen Creek (creek)
74 L/9 - Old Fort Bay
10-36-111-3-W4
58°41′N 110°21′W
Flows south-west into Old Fort Bay approximately 220 km north north-east of Fort McMurray.

Officially named before the 1950s; after whom the creek is named is not known.

Clayton Lake (lake)
84 I/1 - Clayton Lake
9-29-104-14-W4
58°04′N 112°16′W
Approximately 148 km north north-west of Fort McMurray.

The name has appeared on federal government maps since at least 1916, but the origin is unknown.

Clear Hills (locality)
84 C/12 - Dixonville
10-87-25-W5
56°32′N 117°53′W
Approximately 42 km north north-west of Grimshaw.

Named for the nearby hills, a post office was established here in 1921. The first postmaster was C. St. Louis. (see also Clear Hills)

Clear Hills (hills)
84 D/12 - Clear Prairie
34-88-10-W6
56°40′N 119°30′W
Approximately 83 km north-west of Fairview.

The precise origin of the name of these hills is unknown; however, the name appears on a federal government map as early as 1905.

Clear Hills, Municipal District of, No. 22 (municipal district)
84 D/11 - Worsley
82 to 96-1 to 12-W6
From 56°09′N 118°00′W to 57°23′N 120°00′W
Central north-western Alberta.

This municipal district was established in 1994, and takes its name from the most prominent feature within its boundaries. (see also Clear Hills)

Clear Hills Indian Reserve No. 152C (Indian reserve)
84 D/10 - South Whitemud Lake
12-87-5-W6
56°31′N 118°48′W
Approximately 54 km north-west of Fairview.

Named for its proximity to the Clear Hills, this reserve is inhabited by members of the Horse Lake Band, who trace their ancestry to Beaver Indian and Cree origins. (see also Horse Lake Indian Reserve No. 152B)

Clear Lake (lake)
84 H/9 - Alberta
6-101-13-W4
57°44'N 112°07'W
Approximately 119 km north north-west of Fort McMurray.

The precise origin of the name of this lake is unknown; it is probably descriptive. Stoney Lake was the name given by the aboriginal people, because the lake contained a rocky island that had no trees.

Clear Prairie (locality)
84 D/12 - Clear Prairie
28-87-10-W6
56°34'N 119°31'W
Approximately 89 km north-west of Fairview.

The precise origin of the name of this locality is unknown; it is probably descriptive of the open terrain. A post office was established here in 1935, and its first postmaster was M.G. Gunn.

Clear River (river)
84 D/4 - Cherry Point
8-83-11-W6
56°11'N 119°42'W
Flows south south-east into Peace River approximately 69 km north-west of Spirit River.

Likely named after the Clear Hills through which it flows. (see also Clear Hills)

Cleardale (locality)
84 D/5 - Boundary Lake
1-85-11-W6
56°20'N 119°35'W
Approximately 80 km west north-west of Fairview.

---

*denotes rescinded name or former locality.

It is named after the river that runs through it. (see also Clear River)

***Clearview** (post office)
83 M/4 - Rio Grande
16-72-11-W6
55°13'N 119°37'W
Approximately 50 km west of Grande Prairie.

The Clear View (two words) post office opened in October 1920 and the first postmaster was D. Mathe. The name is likely descriptive of its location.

Clearwater Creek (creek)
83 J/7 - Fort Assiniboine
9,10-63-4-W5
54°26'N 114°32'W
Flows east into Athabasca River approximately 28 km south-east of Swan Hills.

The name shows on federal government maps as early as 1917, and is descriptive of the feature.

Clearwater Indian Reserve No. 175 (Indian reserve)
74 D/11 - Fort McMurray
22-88-7-W4
56°39'N 111°01'W
Approximately 23 km east south-east of Fort McMurray near the confluence of Clearwater and Christina Rivers.

Part of the Fort McMurray Bands, they trace their ancestry to the Cree and Chipewyan. The Fort MacKay and Fort McMurray bands used to be one band, but separated in 1949. The reserve takes its name from the nearby river. (see Clearwater River)

Clearwater Lake (lake)
84 A/13 - Liége River
6-91-23-W4
56°52'25"N 113°39'30"W
Approximately 138 km west of Fort McMurray.

The name is likely descriptive of the quality of the water in the lake.

Clearwater River (river)
74 D/11 - Fort McMurray
28-89-9-W4
56°44'N 111°23'W
Flows west into Athabasca River at Fort McMurray.

This largest tributary of the Athabasca from the east is so named from the contrast of its water with that of the muddy Athabasca. It was part of the famous route to the Athabasca via Methy Portage (now in Saskatchewan), and has been referred to by a number of names. Fur trader Peter Pond first travelled the Clearwater River in 1778 in his exploration of the Athabasca country and in 1787 shows it as the Pelican River. David Thompson, in 1798, recorded its name as the Lesser Athabasca River. Philip Turnor, surveyor for the Hudson's Bay Company, noted in his journal for Monday May 14, 1792: "Put up near the old Canadian House below the mouth of the *Wash-a-cum-mow seepe* or clear water river...." The name *Wa-se-ka-mew-see pee* which means "clear water," is apparently in current usage among local residents.

Clements Creek (creek)
84 J/15 - Clements Creek
2-113-4-W5
58°47'N 114°34'W
Flows south-west into Wentzel River approximately 151 km east north-east of High Level.

Clements Creek is named for Clement Paul who logged in the area for forty years. Clement Paul arrived at North Vermilion Settlement with his brothers, Wilfred and Edmond, from Ontario circa 1900. They worked for the Hudson's Bay Company's sawmill operation, cutting logs in the area of La Crete, and floating them downstream to the mill at Vermilion. Later Clement, helped by his wife Eliza (née Chalifoux) and their twelve children, worked his own mill. The mill was at Beaver Ranch. After 1934 he moved it to Fort Vermilion, to supply lumber to the Hudson's Bay Company and the surrounding district.

Clouston Creek (creek)
83 N/6 - Whitemud Creek
9-11-75-22-W5
55°29′N 117°17′W
Flows north into Wabatanisk Creek approximately 50 km north of Valleyview.

For Noel Stewart Clouston, an assistant on the survey crew of L. Brenot in 1920. Clouston apparently rejoined the party at this creek after recovering from an accident. Although this name is official, there was some controversy over it. Since there were other streams called Fish Creek, the Geographic Board of Canada decided to stay with Clouston's name to avoid confusion. (see also *Fish Creek)

Clyde Lake (lake)
84 D/1 - Fairview
24-82-3-W6
56°08′N 118°19′W
Approximately 6 km north-east of Fairview.

Named after Clyde White, a member of a party that surveyed the 19th Baseline in 1912.

Clyde Lake (lake)
73 M/6 - Wiau Lake
9-73-10-W4
55°18′N 111°28′W
Approximately 67 km north north-east of Lac La Biche.

It first appears on a federal government map in 1913 as Cow Lake but by 1921 the name was listed as Clyde Lake. After whom it is named is not recorded.

Clyde River (river)
73 M/4 - Philomena
15-24-71-12-W4
55°10′N 111°42′W
Flows south into Owl River approximately 45 km north north-east of Lac La Biche.

It first appears on a federal government map in 1913 as Cow River but by 1921 the name was listed as Clyde River. After whom it is named is not recorded.

Coal Mine Creek (creek)
83 O/6 - Kinuso
1-73-9-W5
55°18′15″N 115°25′15″W
Flows west into Eula Creek approximately 30 km west of Slave Lake.

It is descriptive of old mine workings in the vicinity.

Coalmine Lick Creek (creek)
83 N/2 - Snipe Lake
2-16-72-17-W5
55°14′N 116°33′W
Flows north-east into West Prairie River approximately 50 km north-east of Valleyview.

Named for a moose lick near an old coal mine. A lick is a place where mineral salts were deposited and animals would lick the salts.

Cockscomb Lake (lake)
74 M/11 - Hay Camp
28-121-7-W4
59°32′N 111°07′W
Approximately 305 km north of Fort McMurray.

It was named in 1929 and is descriptive of its shape.

Codesa (locality)
83 M/16 - Codesa
22-78-1-W6
55°46′N 118°05′W
Approximately 49 km east of Spirit River.

The post office took its name from combined letters of officials' names of the Northern Alberta Railways, Messrs E. <u>Co</u>llins, J. <u>De</u>akin, and W. <u>Sa</u>unders. The post office opened in March 1938. The first postmaster was Charlie Brochu. It was originally known as Rahab. (see also Rahab)

Coffey Creek (creek)
74 E/11 - Myrnam
22-100-9-W4
57°41′N 111°23′W
Flows north into Athabasca River approximately 107 km north of Fort McMurray.

Coffey Creek is named for its proximity to Coffey Lake. (see Coffey Lake)

Coffey Lake (lake)
74 E/11 - Firebag River
4-100-9-W4
57°39′N 111°25′W
Approximately 102 km north of Fort McMurray.

This lake is named in 1925 after Frank L. O'Coffey, a hotelier in Fort McMurray. O'Coffey was involved in the development of the tar sands.

Colin Lake (lake)
74 M/9 - Colin Lake
SW-16-122-1-W4
59°34′N 110°08′W
Approximately 315 km north north-east of Fort McMurray.

The lake was named after Colin Fraser (1849-1941) who was born at Jasper House, the son of Colin Fraser, Sir George Simpson's piper and Hudson's Bay Company servant. Colin Fraser Jr. became a Hudson's Bay factor and later an independent trader and one of Fort Chipewyan's leading citizens. He was in partnership with other traders and established a reputation for the number and excellence of his furs. Holmgren, 1976. It is the source of Colin River.

Colin River (river)
74 M/9 - Colin Lake
NE-13-121-1-W4
59°32'N 110°00'W
Flows east into Saskatchewan approximately 314 km north north-east of Fort McMurray.

(see Colin Lake)

Collins Lake (lake)
74 M/16 - Andrew Lake
30-126-2-W4
59°58'N 110°20'W
Approximately 357 km north of Fort McMurray.

The name was submitted in 1965 by the Research Council of Alberta, and is one of a series of features in the area named after prominent geologists.

***Colquhoun Creek** (creek)
83 M/6 - La Glace
16-2-73-8-W6
55°18'N 119°06'W
Flows east into Bear River approximately 24 km north-west of Grande Prairie.

Flight Lieutenant Ian Colquhoun was born in Edmonton on April 10, 1920, the son of Mr. and Mrs. M.L.B. Colquhoun. He received his education in Edmonton. He enlisted in the RCAF at Edmonton on October 25, 1940. On successful completion of his pilot's training course he was commissioned. He proceeded overseas where he was on operations until he was reported missing, presumed dead, on August 18, 1943. Because the name Colquhoun Creek was never accepted locally, the name was changed back to the original in 1991. (see Fish Creek)

___
*denotes rescinded name or former locality.

Conibear Lake (lake)
84 P/11 - Conibear Lake
7-122-19-W4
59°36'N 113°17'W
Approximately 247 km east north-east of High Level.

Officially named in 1949, after whom it is not known.

Conklin (hamlet)
73 M/11 - Conklin
31-76-7-W4
55°38'N 111°05'W
Approximately 110 km north-east of Lac La Biche.

Originally an Alberta and Great Waterways Railway station, it was named for John Conklin, the timekeeper for J.D. McArthur, a contractor for the Company. The post office was established in May 1924. The first postmaster was W. E. Proctor.

Conn Creek (creek)
74 D/11 - Fort McMurray
29-89-9-W4
56°45'N 111°24'W
Flows east into Athabasca River at Fort McMurray.

The origin of the name of this creek is a matter of some dispute. S.C. Ells, exploring the oil sands around Fort McMurray, presented several features in the area for official naming in 1924. One of them was Conn Creek, apparently after Thomas Conn, one of the oldest inhabitants in Fort McMurray and a fire ranger on the Athabasca River. There is also a local version of the origin of the name, suggesting it was named for one "old Pediconn" who trapped and lived on the creek. (see also Ells River)

Copp River (river)
84 O/16 - Kilome Lake
NW-31-126-1-W5
60°00'N 114°11'W
Flows north-west into the Northwest Territories approximately 232 km north-east of High Level.

The name was officially approved in 1980 based on local usage. It takes its name from Copp Lake into which it flows in the Northwest Territories. The name for Copp Lake arose from the Alberta-Northwest Territories Boundary Commission in 1956.

Corbett Creek (creek)
83 J/6 - Christmas Creek
8-61-7-W5
54°16'N 115°02'W
Flows east into the Athabasca River approximately 34 km north north-east of Mayerthorpe.

The named creek shows as early as 1917 on federal government maps. It may have been named after the early settlers in the area, W. E. Corbett and his family.

Corbett Creek (locality)
83 J/6 - Christmas Creek
7-61-8-W5
54°16'N 115°12'W
Approximately 38 km north of Mayerthorpe.

The post office established here in December 1934 took its name from the nearby creek. The first postmaster was J. Burham. (see Corbett Creek)

Corey Creek (creek)
84 J/15 - Clements Creek
34-112-4-W5
58°46'N 114°34'W
Flows south-west into Wentzel River approximately 150 km east north-east of Peace River.

The precise origin of the name of this creek is unknown.

Corn Lake (lake)
84 A/12 - Woodenhouse River
19-88-25-W4
56°38′N 113°58′W
Approximately 156 km west of Fort McMurray.

The precise origin of the name of this lake is unknown.

Jim Cornwall on the Athabasca River, ca. 1907-1914

Cornwall Creek (creek)
14-2-71-1-W6
55°08′N 118°02′W
Flows south into Simonette River approximately 14 km south of DeBolt.

The name of the creek has been in use since at least the 1940s. The origin of the name is not known, although it may refer to James Cornwall. "Peace River Jim" Cornwall was a well-known Alberta pioneer. He was born in Brantford, Ontario in 1869, and died in Calgary in 1955. He arrived in Alberta in 1896, and settled at Athabasca Landing a year later. There he started a number of businesses including the Northern Transportation Company whose ships plied the waters all over northern Alberta and the Northwest Territories. For a time in the pre-war years, 1908-1912, he was the Liberal MLA for Peace River. He served in World War I as a lieutenant-colonel in the 218th Battalion of the Canadian Expeditionary Force. He was decorated by King George V and the French government for his efforts. Returning to Canada after the war, he continued his life in the Peace River district.

Cornwall Lake (lake)
74 M/10 - Cornwall Lake
14-122-4-W4
59°36′N 110°35′W
Approximately 314 km north of Fort McMurray.

(see Cornwall Creek)

Corrigall Lake (lake)
83 P/2 - Calling River
14-72-18-W4
55°14′N 112°39′W
Approximately 65 km north-west of Lac La Biche.

After whom it was named is not known; the name has been in use since at least the mid-1940s.

Cottonwood Creek (creek)
74 D/2 - Quigley
6-82-4-W4
56°05′N 110°36′W
Flows east south-east into Christina River approximately 86 km south south-east of Fort McMurray.

G.H. Blanchet, DLS, in his report of July 1911 noted there was "dense cottonwood around the river." By 1914 it appears named on the sectional map derived from the surveys done three years before.

Coutts River (river)
83 J/16 - Chisholm
14-68-4-W5
54°53′N 114°30′W
Flows north-east into the Saulteaux River approximately 48 km south south-east of Slave Lake.

It was officially named prior in 1906 after G.M. Coutts, a member of survey party who came from Leith, now a district of Edinburgh, Scotland, and who died around 1911.

Cow Lake (lake)
73 M/4 - Philomena
8-72-11-W4
55°13′N 111°39′W
Approximately 54 km north of Lac La Biche.

The name for this lake is well-established in local usage, and has been associated with the feature since at least 1938. It is a rough translation from the Cree *Paskwaw Moostoos Sagahegan*. (see also Clyde Lake)

Cowper Creek (creek)
74 D/2 - Quigley
11-81-4-W4
56°00′N 110°30′W
Flows north into Winefred River approximately 85 km south-east of Fort McMurray.

Officially approved in 1955, it was named for George Constable Cowper, a Dominion Land Surveyor. The name is listed in the Dominion Land Surveys report of 1913 and is listed as Cowpar Creek and Lake.

Cowper Lake (lake)
73 M/16 - Cowper Lake
6-80-3-W4
55°54′N 110°27′W
Approximately 100 km south-east of Fort McMurray.

(see Cowper Creek)

Cranberry Lake (lake)
74 E/12 - Asphalt Creek
16-99-10-W4
57°35'10"N 111°35'00"W
Approximately 98 km north of Fort McMurray.

This lake takes its name from the abundance of cranberries in the area. (see also Cranberry Lake)

Cranberry Lake (lake)
84 B/3 - Cranberry Lake
32-83-7-W5
56°14'N 115°05'W
Approximately 106 km north of Slave Lake.

The lake is named because of the abundant growth of bog cranberry in the area. Cranberries (genus *Vaccinium*, heath family, *Ericiceae*) are low vine-like perennials that grow in muskeg and peat bogs. Three or four closely related species are identified, one of which is the forerunner of the cultivated cranberry.

Crane Lake (lake)
84 P/1 - Square Lake
5-118-12-W4
59°13'N 112°00'W
Approximately 270 km north of Fort McMurray.

The name appears on provincial government maps as early as 1930 and likely refers to the prevalence of the bird in the area. At one time there was consideration given to naming it D'Aoust Lake after a local park ranger.

Craven Lake (lake)
84 C/5 - Chinook Valley
31-85-23-W5
56°25'N 117°36'W
Approximately 24 km north of Grimshaw.

This lake is named after A. Craven, the cook on the 1913 survey crew of G.A. Tipper, DLS, who were working in the area that year.

Crawford Creek (creek)
83 N/1 - East Prairie
16-7-71-14-W5
55°08'N 116°08'W
Flows north-east into East Prairie approximately 70 km west of Valleyview.

After whom this creek is named is not known; the name was made official in 1952 after field research was conducted.

Crazy Lake (lake)
74 D/6 - Gregoire Lake
4-85-7-W4
56°20'20"N 111°03'30"W
Approximately 47 km south south-east of Fort McMurray.

The name was given to this feature by local trappers, because it is believed to be haunted. People have said they heard voices when no one is around, and these voices apparently terrify dogs. As people approach the lake they get an eerie feeling, it seems to get darker, and the sounds become muffled. It is said the voices are the spirits of people who were killed at the lake.

Crazy Man Creek (creek)
83 N/7 - Triangle
30-73-19-W5
55°21'N 116°54'W
Flows north-west into Stoney Creek approximately 30 km west south-west of High Prairie

When the name was adopted in 1954 it was an old one, well known to residents. It was apparently named after an early homesteader in the area.

Cree Creek (creek)
74 D/10 - Hollies Creek
26-88-6-W4
56°39'55"N 110°50'53"W
Flows west north-west into Clearwater river approximately 35 km east south-east of Fort McMurray.

The Cree were long-time residents of the area and had a cabin by this creek.

Creighton Lake (lake)
84 M/14 - Creighton Lake
13-126-9-W6
59°57'N 119°25'W
Approximately 157 km north of Rainbow Lake.

This a war memorial name commemorating Acting Bombardier Ivan D. Creighton, killed in action in October 1944.

Croker Lakes (lakes)
83 N/7 - Triangle
7-73-17-W5
55°18'N 116°36'W
Approximately 18 km south south-west of High Prairie.

The name was made official in 1954 after field research was conducted. The name was well established and in local use, and is likely a surname; after whom it was named is not known.

Crooked Creek (hamlet)
83 N/4 - Sturgeon Heights
26-71-26-W5
55°10'N 117°52'W
Approximately 75 km east of Grande Prairie.

The name for this hamlet is derived from the descriptive local name of the nearby creek. The post office here opened in December 1930, the first postmaster being P. Thieson.

Crooked Lake (lake)
74 E/8 - Trout Creek
15-98-2-W4
57°30'N 110°14'W
Approximately 112 km north-east of Fort McMurray.

This remote lake was descriptively named by two trappers and their families as a means of identifying locations.

Crooked Lake (lake)

74 E/12 - Asphalt Creek
15-99-11-W4
57°35'12"N 111°43'40"W
Approximately 98 km north of Fort McMurray.

This is a descriptive name.

Crooked Lake (lake)

83 K/6 - Tony Creek
63-22-W5
54°27'N 117°15'W
Approximately 26 km west north-west of Fox Creek.

Officially approved in 1976, the name is descriptive of the feature.

Crooked Rapids (rapids)

74 D/12 - Cascade Rapids
5-88-12-W4
56°36'N 111°52'W
In a bend in the Athabasca River approximately 31 km west south-west of Fort McMurray.

These rapids received their name because of a hairpin turn the river makes around a limestone point at this location. The name was recorded as early as 1914 by A.D. Griffin, DLS.

Crooked River (river)

83 P/14 - Muskeg River
4-28-78-21-W4
55°47'N 113°13'W
Flows north into Pelican River approximately 110 km north-east of Slave Lake.

Likely a descriptive name; it was recorded as early as 1897 on a Geological Survey of Canada map.

---

*denotes rescinded name or former locality.

***Cross, Mount** (mountain)

83 L/4 - Kakwa River
54°05'N 120°00'W
2-59-14-W6
Approximately 61 km west north-west of Grande Cache.

Renamed in 1916 after C. R. Cross, a United States citizen who was a member of exploratory party in the region in 1914. He was killed in France in 1915, while engaged in ambulance work. The name for the feature was recorded in 1924 as Kakwa Mountain by the Alberta and British Columbia Boundary Commission, and that name remains official. (see Kakwa Mountain)

Crow Lake (lake)

83 P/16 - Pelican
32-78-14-W4
55°48'N 112°10'W
Approximately 110 km south south-west of Fort McMurray.

It was learned that Crow Lake was named by the aboriginal peoples of the area and was called that from at least the turn of the century. It is descriptive of the bird found around the lake. Crow Lake was a stopping place for aboriginal people travelling between Cold Lake, Heart Lake, Winefred Lake and Wabasca Lake. Apparently some signs of these trails by way of treaded paths and ruts remained as late as the 1960s.

Crowell (railway point)

83 N/15 - Frank Lake
6-79-20-W5
55°49'N 116°59'W
Approximately 15 km north north-west of McLennan.

This railway point was been named after Frederick Crowell, an employee of Northern Alberta Railways. Mr. Crowell was born in 1887 and was employed by the Edmonton, Dunvegan and British Columbia Railway in 1916 as a fireman. By the time he retired in 1952, he was a well-known and respected engineer from the McLennan area. The name for the railway point was officially adopted in 1980.

Crown Creek (creek)

74 L/9 - Old Fort Bay
6-7-111-3-W4
58°37'N 110°30'W
Flows north into Old Fort Bay approximately 209 km north north-east of Fort McMurray.

It appears on maps as early as 1919; the origin of the name is not known.

Crummy Lake (lake)

84 F/3 - Crummy Lake
19-94-20-W5
57°11'N 117°12'W
Approximately 30 km north-east of Manning.

Named in commemoration of Flying Officer George K. Crummy, of Grande Prairie, killed during World War II.

Crystal Lake (lake)

83 M/2 - Grande Prairie
5-31-71-5-W6
55°11'N 118°46'W
Within the city limits of Grande Prairie.

This name was in local use before it was made official in 1951, and although origin information is not known, it may have referred to the clarity of the water.

Cub Lakes (lake)

84 D/16 - Cub Lakes
34-90-1-W6
56°51'N 118°04'W
Approximately 28 km west south-west of Fairview.

The precise origin of the name of these lakes is unknown.

*Culp (former locality)
83 N/13 - Tangent
17-78-23-W5
55°45′N 117°33′W
Approximately 30 km west of Falher.

This Edmonton, Dunvegan and British Columbia Railway station was established in 1915 and was named after Joseph H. Culp, a conductor for the railroad. A post office was established here in 1931, with the first postmaster being T. Flint.

Currie Lake (lake)
74 L/2 - Larocque Lake
27-104-5-W4
58°03′N 110°44′W
Approximately 144 km north of Fort McMurray.

The name appears on maps as early as 1916, and although the origin is not precisely known the lake may have been named after a survey crew member.

Cut Bank Point (point)
83 O/12 - Salt Creek
SW-23-75-13-W5
55°31′N 115°54′W
Approximately 75 km west north-west of Slave Lake.

The name was adopted in 1954 for the point on the north shore of Lesser Slave Lake and is descriptive of the steep-fronted hill.

Cutbank Lake (lake)
83 M/12 - Boone Creek
9-34-77-12-W6
55°42′N 119°45′W
Approximately 57 km west of Spirit River.

The name for this feature is descriptive. In this case cutbank refers to a hill having a steep front resulting from erosion. The north bank of the lake rises sharply above the lake to a height of approximately fifty metres.

Cutbank Lake (lake)
83 M/6 - La Glace
SW-26-72-8-W6
55°16′N 119°08′W
Approximately 20 km north-west of Grande Prairie.

Cutbank Lake is most likely descriptive because of the sharp bank on the north side of lake. The lake is fed by a spring and has been known officially as this since at least 1940.

Cutbank River (river)
83 L/10 - Cutbank River
16-66-4-W6
54°43′N 118°32′W
Flows north-east into the Smoky River approximately approximately 49 km south south-east of Grande Prairie.

Possibly from the Cree *kiscatinaw sipi* and is descriptive of the banks of the river, which at times rise steeply nearly 150 metres from the river.

Cypress Point (point)
74 M/1 - Winnifred Lake
NW-36-117-2-W4
59°12′N 110°11′W
Approximately 276 km north north-east of Fort McMurray.

Showing on federal government maps as early as 1930, it likely refers to the prevalence of the tree of that name, which in some parts of Canada refers to one of a several species of pine, including the lodgepole pine and jackpine. It shows on Dr. Bell's map of 1884 as Big Fir Point.

---

*denotes rescinded name or former locality.

D~E

D.D.'s Creek (creek)
74 D/9 - Bunting Bay
17-89-1-W4
56°42'45"N 110°07'55"W
Flows south into Clearwater River approximately 78 km east of Fort McMurray.

This creek was named for D.D. Williams, a trapper, who worked a trapline along the creek for over 50 years.

Dagmar Lake (lake)
74 L/6 - Richardson Lake
33-108-9-W4
58°25'N 111°27'W
Approximately 180 km north of Fort McMurray.

The name appears as early as 1919 on a federal government map. The name, Scandinavian in origin, may have been the name of a survey crew member or a relative.

Dalkin Island (island)
74 E/11 - Firebag River
31-99-9-W4
57°38'N 111°28'W
Approximately 100 km north of Fort McMurray.

Named for T. W. Dalkin, an instrument man on a survey in the area, 1922. This island appears to have two official names, Dalkin Island and Lorna Island. (see also Lorna Island)

Daly Lake (lake)
74 M/10 - Cornwall Lake
29-122-5-W4
59°38'N 110°50'W
Approximately 314 km north of Fort McMurray.

The name was submitted in 1958 by the Research Council of Alberta, and is one of a series of features in the area named after deceased prominent geologists. This lake was most likely named after Reginald Aldworth Daly (1871-1957), who had worked for a time with the Geological Survey of Canada and on the International Boundary Survey, 1901-1907. He spent much of his career teaching in American universities including Harvard and the Massachusetts Institute of Technology.

Daphne Island (island)
74 E/5 - Bitumount
25-95-11-W4
57°16'40"N 111°39'30"W
Approximately 65 km north north-west of Fort McMurray.

Named after Daphne, daughter of J.N. Wallace, DLS, in 1925.

Darling Creek (creek)
84 G/7 - Alberta
23-95-5-W5
57°15'N 114°42'W
Flows north-west into Panny River approximately 180 km east north-east of Manning.

This was named after trail locater L. Darling, who worked on the crews of J.S. Fletcher, DLS.

Darough Creek (creek)
74 M/5 - Darough Creek
10-19-119-9-W4
59°21'N 111°32'W
Flows south-east into Murdock Creek approximately 283 km north of Fort McMurray.

The name shows on federal government maps from as early as the 1920s; it was named after a park warden in Wood Buffalo National Park.

Darwin Lake (lake)
74 M/6 - Bocquene Lake
5-119-6-W4
59°18'N 111°01'W
Approximately 280 km north of Fort McMurray.

The name was submitted in 1958 by the Research Council of Alberta, and is one of a series of features in the area named after deceased prominent geologists.

Davidson Lake (lake)
84 I/14 - Big Slough
NE-35-114-20-W4
58°57'N 113°14'W
Approximately 226 km east north-east of High Level.

Named in 1949 after Warrant Officer II William Davidson, MM, of Edmonton, killed in action in Italy in 1944.

Davidson Lake (lake)
83 N/6 - Whitemud Creek
9-36-73-23-W55
55°22'N 117°23'W
Approximately 35 km north north-west of Valleyview.

The name was officially adopted in 1953 after field research was conducted. After whom it is named is not known.

Dawes Lake (lake)
74 D/5 - Alberta
36-84-13-W4
56°19'40"N 111°54'45"W
Approximately 55 km south south-west of Fort McMurray.

This lake is named for Jack Dawes (1935-1985) who trapped in this area for several years. He was born in Ontario and lived in the Fort McMurray region for over 20 years. He owned and operated a roofing company and was in partnership on a trapline for 13 years.

Dawson Lake (lake)
74 M/16 - Andrew Lake
21-125-3-W4
59°52′N 110°28′W
Approximately 344 km north of Fort McMurray.

The name was submitted in 1965 by the Research Council of Alberta, and is one of a series of features in the area named after prominent geologists. Although it was not specifically stated, this was likely named after George Mercer Dawson who became the director of the Geological Survey of Canada and to whom Albertans and Canadians as a whole owe a debt of gratitude for the thorough and painstaking care with which he recorded both "European" and aboriginal names in the latter part of the 19th century. He was better known as a geologist and surveyor. As it states of him in the *Canadian Encyclopedia*, his "brilliance in systematic mapping provided a sound basis for understanding the geology and mineral resources of much of northern and western Canada."

De Manville Lake (lake)
74 M/8 - Wylie Lake
NE-36-119-2-W4
59°23′N 110°11′W
Approximately 296 km north north-east of Fort McMurray.

It was named in 1929 after Mr. De Manville of Fort Chipewyan.

---

*denotes rescinded name or former locality.

Dead Calf Lake (lake)
84 A/14 - Mink Lake
12-90-21-W4
56°47′10″N 113°12′45″W
Approximately 110 km east of Fort McMurray.

This lake received its descriptive name because apparently those who raised cattle in the vicinity once found a dead calf on the lake.

***Dead Man's Creek** (creek)
74 D/8 - Gipsy Lake
26-85-4-W4
56°23′20″N 110°30′01″W
Flows west into Gordon River approximately 65 km south-east of Fort McMurray.

(see Passed Away Creek)

Deadman Creek (creek)
84 A/7 - Livock River
23-84-17-W4
56°18′N 112°35′W
Flows north into Athabasca River approximately 87 km south-west of Fort McMurray.

The precise origin of the name of this creek is unknown, but it is probably descriptive of its potential dangers as a death trap. The water from the creek entering Athabasca River is rough above the nearby Grand Rapids. The name was in use when H.S. Day, DLS, surveyed the area in 1914.

Deadwood (hamlet)
84 C/11 - Deadwood
21-89-22-W5
56°44′N 117°27′W
Approximately 60 km north north-west of Peace River.

A post office was established here in 1930 and the first postmaster was J. Eggenberger. It has been suggested he came from Deadwood, South Dakota, and hence the choice of name. In 1931, when asked about its origin, the postmaster told the Geographic Board of Canada the name referred to the visible remains of a fire that occurred in the area some 30 years before.

Deadwood (station)
84 C/13 - Manning
34-89-23-W5
56°45′N 117°34′W
Approximately 17 km south south-west of Manning.

(see Deadwood)

DeBolt (hamlet)
83 M/1 - DeBolt
SW-12-72-1-W6
55°13′N 118°01′W
Approximately 50 km east north east of Grande Prairie.

Originally a post office which was established in 1923, it was named for H. E. DeBolt (1888-1969) who, with his brother George (1884-1961), came to the Peace River area in 1919 from the State of Washington. Mr. DeBolt was the first postmaster. He also served as Social Credit Member of the Legislative Assembly for the Spirit River constituency from 1940 to 1952.

DeBolt Creek (creek)
83 M/1 - DeBolt
6-23-71-7-W6
55°10′N 118°02′W
Flows south into Harper Creek approximately 10 km west of Grande Prairie.

(see DeBolt)

Decrene (locality/railway station)
83 O/1 - Smith
NE-8-72-2-W5
55° 12′N 114° 10′W
Approximately 40 km east south-east of Slave Lake (town).

This Edmonton, Dunvegan and British Columbia Railway station was established in 1914 and was named after a contractor who constructed a portion of the railway line.

Deep Creek (creek)
83 N/7 - Triangle
NE-23-73-20-W5
55°20′N 116°57′W
Flows east into Little Smoky River approximately 30 km south-west of High Prairie.

The name has been in use since before the turn of the 19th century. The origin is not necessarily descriptive, for the surveyors in the area do not show the creek to be particularly deep.

*Deep Creek (creek)
74 D/11 - Fort McMurray
32-88-8-W4
56°40′N 111°14′W
Flows north-west into Clearwater River approximately 5 km east of Fort McMurray.

(see Saprae Creek)

Deep Creek (creek)
83 I/14 - Sawdy
26-69-22-W4
54°59′N 113°14′W
Flows south-east into Athabasca River approximately 30 km north of Athabasca.

According to the files of the Geographic Board of Canada, this descriptive name for the feature was well known in the area for years before 1931.

Deep Creek (locality)
83 I/14 - Sawdy
17-69-22-W4
54°57′N 113°13′W
Approximately 30 km north of Athabasca.

---

*denotes rescinded name or former locality.

Established as a post office in 1931, it was named for its proximity to the feature. The first postmaster was Dan Bilida. (see also Deep Creek)

Deep Lake (lake)
83 M/3 - Wembley
SE-24-72-8-W6
55°15′N 119°05′W
Approximately 18 km west north-west of Grande Prairie.

Officially named in the early 1950s; the name is likely descriptive.

Deep Lake (lake)
84 D/11 - Worsley
10-89-7-W6
56°42′N 119°01′W
Approximately 80 km north north-west of Fairview.

The precise origin of the name of this lake is unknown; it is probably descriptive.

Deep Lake (lake)
83 J/9 - Flatbush
54°41′N 114°17′W
65,66-2-W5
Approximately 8 km west of Flatbush.

This was the original, descriptive, name of the lake; the name Athabina Lake was adopted in 1948. Four years later the name reverted to the original. (see also Athabina Lake)

*Deep Lake (lake)
84 A/14 - Mink Lake
19-91-20-W4
56°54′N 113°12′W
Approximately 110 km west north-west of Fort McMurray.

Although still referred to locally as Deep Lake, the name was changed in 1953. (see Grew Lake)

*Deep Lake (lake)
84 J/5 - Sled Island
7-109-12-W5
58°27′N 115°59′W
Approximately 66 km south south-east of High Level.

(see Utamik Lake)

Deep Valley Creek (creek)
83 K/12 - Ante Creek
16-20-64-25-W5
54°33′N 117°44′W
Flows north into Simonette River approximately 58 km west north-west of Fox Creek.

It shows as early as 1916 on a federal government map, and is descriptive of the watercourse which has 90-metre-high cliffs where it meets the Simonette River.

Deer Hill (locality)
84 D/8 - Deer Hill
14-84-3-W6
56°17′N 118°20′W
Approximately 24 km north of Fairview.

A post office was established here in 1936, and the name is descriptive of its location. The first postmaster was F. Walsh.

Deer Mountain (mountain)
83 J/14 - Deer Mountain
68-8-W5
54°55′N 115°10′W
Approximately 22 km north-east of Swan Hills.

The name was recorded as Deer Hills by Thomas Chalmers, DLS, in 1897. In that year he surveyed a route through the Swan Hills as a possible overland route to the Klondike. It shows on a map from 1914 as Deer Mountain. For a time in 1922 there was brief consideration given to renaming it Chalmers Hill; the Geographic Board of Canada believed Chalmers too important to be commemorated by such an "unimportant" peak but he never did get anything more prominent named after him in Alberta. The elevation of the feature is 1067 metres. It is one of three features which comprise Swan Hills. (see also Swan Hills and Chalmers Creek)

Delorme Lake (lake)
83 O/1 - Smith
SW-26-70-3-W5
55°05′N 114°21′W
Approximately 35 km south-east of Slave River.

Although the origin of the name is not known, it was given to the lake between 1914 and 1922. It was likely named after V. Delorme who served as a picketman on the crew of H.W. Selby, DLS, 1909.

Demicharge Rapids (rapids)
74 M/6 - Bocquene Lake
NW-11-119-9-W4
59°19′N 111°25′W
Approximately 70 km north of Fort Chipewyan in Slave River.

Demi-charge in Canadian French means literally "half load." It refers to that part of a canoe's contents that was unloaded at a *décharge*, which was a shallow spot or dangerous area where a boat or canoe had to be partly unloaded before it could go on. This name therefore dates from the days of the fur trade, and is at a spot where the rapids were bad enough that the boats had to be lightened.

Demmitt (locality)
83 M/5 - Hythe
35-74-13-W6
55°27′N 119°54′W
Approximately 75 km west north-west of Grande Prairie.

*denotes rescinded name or former locality.

After Chelsea Demmitt, who settled in the area in 1919 following service with the American Expeditionary Force in World War I. The post office was established in November 1929, and first postmaster was Mrs. N. Goodwin.

Dempsey Creek (creek)
74 L/14 - Rivière des Rochers
3-4-115-8-W4
58°57′N 111°18′W
Flows north-east into Rivière des Rochers approximately 236 km north of Fort McMurray.

Officially named in 1971, after whom is not known.

Dene, Lake (lake)
84 I/6 - Lake Dene
19-108-20-W4
58°24′N 113°19′W
Approximately 208 km north north-west of Fort McMurray.

It was renamed in 1963 after the late Adam Dene, one of the early trappers and settlers in the southern portion of Wood Buffalo National Park. It was at one time known as Beaver Lake. (see also Beaver Lake)

*****Desmarais** (hamlet)
83 P/13 - Pelican
14-80-25-W4
55°56′N 113°49′W
Approximately 90 km north-east of Slave Lake.

Formerly Wabasca South, it was named for Father Alphonse Desmarais (1850-1940), an Oblate missionary. He was the first Catholic missionary to visit the Wabasca Settlement in 1891, going there from St. Bernard's Mission at Grouard, where he founded the St Martin Indian Residential School. He was born at St-Damase, Québec and died in Edmonton. The post office was opened in August 1927, its first postmaster

being Father Guimot. In 1982, it amalgamated with the community to the north, and it is now officially called Wabasca-Desmarais. (see also Wabasca-Desmarais)

Devenish (locality)
73 M/11 - Conklin
33-75-8-W4
55°32′N 111°12′W
Approximately 90 km north-east of Lac La Biche.

Originally an Alberta and Great Waterways Railway station, it was established in 1916 and named after Gwen Devenish, a friend of Mrs. Jack Judge, wife of a railroad engineer. Apparently Miss Devenish became a nurse at the Johns Hopkins Hospital in Baltimore.

Devil Creek (creek)
83 N/1 - East Prairie
14-35-71-15-W5
55°12′N 116°12′W
Flows into the East Prairie River approximately 60 km south south-east of High Prairie.

This feature was officially named in 1952 after field research was conducted. It is likely aboriginal in origin.

Devil Lake (lake)
84 K/7 - Child Lake
16-108-17-W5
58°22′N 116°47′W
Approximately 24 km south-east of High Level.

This lake is annotated as Devil's Lake on the survey map drawn in 1914 by P.M.H. LeBlanc, DLS. This is a translation of the Dunne-za or Beaver name *Minke Mets-li*, by which Dunne-za residents refer to the lake. The suggestion from one resident that Bad Lake would be a closer translation, as the lake is very dangerous during stormy weather, is an indication of the descriptive origin of the name.

Devil Rapids (rapids)
83 P/13 - Pelican
4-6-80-23-W4
55°54′N 113°36′W
Approximately 100 km north-east of Slave Lake in the Wabasca River.

Descriptive in nature, the name has been in use since at least 1892.

Devils Elbow (river bend)
74 L/6 - Richardson Lake
4-12-109-8-W4
58°27′N 111°12′W
Approximately 184 km north of Fort McMurray.

It is named for its shape and its temperament.

Devonshire Beach (beach)
83 O/7 - Slave Lake
19-73-5-W5
55°20′N 114°45′W
Approximately 5 km north of Slave Lake.

This beach was locally referred to as Devonshire Beach for a short time during the early 1920s. The name was suggested by a resident of Sawridge (now Slave Lake) to commemorate the visit to northern Alberta of the Duke of Devonshire, then Governor-General of Canada, in September 1920. According to the Governor-General's diary of the trip he actually did some duck hunting in the area. The name was officially approved in 1984.

Diamond Dick Creek (creek)
83 M/4 - Rio Grande
14-20-70-11-W6
55°05′N 119°39′W
Flows north-east into Redwillow River approximately 51 km west of Grande Prairie.

Named after homesteader Dick Harrington who gained a reputation for his ability to tie a diamond hitch on pack horses. Formerly called Sylvester Creek; it had also been known in the area as both Fish Creek and Sheep Creek. The official change from Sylvester Creek to Diamond Dick Creek occurred in 1963.

Dianne Lakes (lakes)
74 E/13 - Ronald Lake
4-103-10-W4
57°54′40″N 111°36′30″W
Approximately 130 km north of Fort McMurray.

These lakes are named for Dianne, daughter of Jack Plewes (possibly spelled Pleures) who trapped in the area.

Diaper Lakes (lake)
84 H/12 - Alberta
20-98-22-W4
57°30′54″N 113°34′51″W
Approximately 157 km north-west of Fort McMurray.

The precise origin of the name of these lakes is unknown.

Diaper Lake (lake)
84 A/6 - Wood Buffalo Lake
12-86-22-W4
56°26′21″N 113°20′46″W
Approximately 123 km west south-west of Fort McMurray.

A story behind the naming of this lake tells how when hide diapers were used years ago, and the people had an abundance of them they decided to see if they would stretch the length of the lake.

Dickins Lake (lake)
84 M/12 - Dickins Lake
24-123-12-W6
59°41′N 119°56′W
Approximately 135 km north north-west of Rainbow Lake.

Named in honour of Clennell Haggerston "Punch" Dickins, OC, OBE, DFC, LLD (1899-1995). Born in Manitoba, he grew up in Edmonton, enlisting in the Canadian Infantry during World War I. He then transferred to the Royal Flying Corps in 1917. Following the war he returned to Canada and joined the Canadian Air Force, becoming one of the original officers of the Royal Canadian Air Force when it was formed in 1924. In 1927 he joined Western Canada Airways and in the following years made many remarkable flights, including landing the first prospectors in the Great Bear Lake area in 1928-29. Later he joined Canadian Pacific Airlines and then, during World War II, was operations manager of Ferry Command, operating six British Commonwealth Training Plan Schools. From 1947 to 1966 he was director and vice-president of De Havilland Aircraft Company of Canada. Dickins was highly honoured for his services to Canadian aviation; he was awarded the McKee Trophy in 1928 and made an Officer of the Order of the British Empire in 1936. In 1967 he received an honorary Doctor of Laws degree from the University of Alberta, and was named an Officer of the Order of Canada in 1968, and a member of Canada's Aviation Hall of Fame in 1973. This is one of a number of lakes in northern Alberta named after bush pilots. (see also Berry Lake, Brintnell Lake, Calder Lake, Farrell Lake, Lake May, McConachie Lake, McMillan Lake, McMullen Lake, Randall Lake and Sawle Lake)

Dickson Lake (lake)
83 M/12 - Boone Creek
NE-24-75-13-W6
55°31′N 119°52′W
Approximately 75 km west north-west of Grande Prairie.

Named in 1952 after Flying Officer C.A. Dickson, AFC. Mr. Dickson who was born in Edmonton on December 17, 1920, the son of Mr. and Mrs. T. A. Dickson. He enlisted in the RCAF in Edmonton in May 1941 and was commissioned in March 1942. He performed ferrying duties in Canada and overseas, until December 15, 1944, when he was reported missing and presumed dead.

Dillon River (river)
73 M/9 - Alberta-Saskatchewan
7-1-78-1-W4
55°44′N 110°00′W
Flows into Saskatchewan approximately 130 km south-east of Fort McMurray.

A local family name submitted by J. N. Wallace, DLS, who surveyed the 4th Meridian in 1909-1910. The 4th Meridian forms the Alberta-Saskatchewan border.

Dimsdale (locality)
83 M/2 - Grande Prairie
15-71-7-W6
55°09′N 118°59′W
Approximately 10 km west of Grande Prairie.

The area was first settled in 1910; when the railroad came through in 1924 a station was established at this spot. It was named after Henry George Dimsdale, a locating engineer on the construction of the Edmonton, Dunvegan and British Columbia Railway. The post office was established here in 1927, the first postmaster being A. Ramsfield.

Dimsdale Lake (lake)
83 M/3 - Wembley
NE-16-71-7-W6
55°09′N 119°00′W
Approximately 10 km west of Grande Prairie.

It was named for its proximity to Dimsdale. The lake was previously named Spring Lake. (see also Dimsdale and Spring Lake)

Dinner Lake (lake)
74 D/7 - Cheecham
15-84-5-W4
56°17′00″N 110°42′15″W
Approximately 64 km south-east of Fort McMurray.

This lake received its name because it was known as a stopping place where people would break their journey to have dinner. It was half-way from Cheecham to the Saskatchewan border or from Cheecham to Christina Crossing, so it provided a good resting place for travellers.

Disappointment Lake (lake)
74 M/7 - Alberta
15-120-5-W4
59°25′N 110°47′W
Approximately 293 km north of Fort McMurray.

This was a name submitted in 1958 by the Alberta Research Council. Although no other explanation was given, it was stated the name was descriptive.

Dixonville (station)
84 C/12 - Dixonville
14-87-23-W5
56°32′N 117°32′W
Approximately 36 km north north-west of Peace River.

(see Dixonville)

Dixonville (hamlet)
84 C/12 - Dixonville
18-87-23-W5
56°32′N 117°40′W
Approximately 39 km north of Grimshaw.

The name Dixonville was coined in honour of Roy "Buster" Dixon who, with his wife Ethel, ran the general store and later the post office during the 1920s and 1930s. The post office was established in October 1930.

Dizzy Creek (creek)
84 N/11 - Steen River
23-122-19-W5
59°37′N 117°09′W
Flows north-west into Hay River approximately 122 km north of High Level.

The precise origin of the name, officially adopted in 1944, is unknown; it may refer to the deep canyon through which the creek leaves the Caribou Mountains, or it may refer to the twisting course it takes as it approaches the Hay River. The local name for the stream is *Wutza Zahéh*, a Slavey term for Muskeg Creek. The name has been used since at least the first part of the century, and refers to the extensive area of muskeg near its mouth.

Doe Creek (creek)
83 M/13 - Bonanza
14-15-1-81-13-W6
56°00′N 119°54′W
Flows north-east into Pouce Coupe River approximately 75 km north-west of Spirit River.

The name was well known and in local use when the Dominion Lands Survey was in the area in 1911. It is likely descriptive of the abundance of deer in the area.

Dog Eating Prairie (flat)
83 K/14 - Asplund Creek
4-24-67-22-W5
54°48′30″N 117°13′30″W
Approximately 110 km south-east of Grande Prairie.

It was officially approved in 1991 after field research determined the name was well established and in local usage. According to the people in the area, the name dates from the early 1900s when a dog was killed and eaten at this location. The name was given to this site by the aboriginal people of the area.

■ **Dog Head** (point)
74 L/11 - Fort Chipewyan
1-112-8-W4
58°42′N 111°12′W
Approximately 211 km north of Fort McMurray.

According to a more modern source Dog Head seems to refer to the double point which, on the map, has the outline of a barking dog's head. However, in his journal of 1800, James Mackenzie refers to it as *Pointe aux chiens*, or Point of the Dogs. Head can refer to a promontory or point of land. Therefore, a more likely explanation would be that Dog Head is a point of land where dogs would gather.

Dog Island (island)
83 O/7 - Slave Lake
14-73-6-W5
55°19′N 114°50′W
Approximately 7 km north east of Slave Lake. It now forms part of the Lesser Slave Lake Provincial Park.

The name for the island was well established and in local use before the Dominion Lands Survey came through in 1913. The name is likely aboriginal and descriptive in origin.

Dog Lake (lake)
84 H/12 - Alberta
15-98-22-W4
57°30′15″N 113°31′45″W
Approximately 156 km north-west of Fort McMurray.

The precise origin of the long-established name of this lake is unknown.

*****Dog Rib Island** (island)
74 D/14 - Wood Creek
31-91-9-W4
56°56′N 111°26′W

---

*denotes rescinded name or former locality.

In Athabasca River approximately 23 km north of Fort McMurray.

This was an earlier name for the feature, the origin of which is unknown. Whether it referred to actual dog ribs found on the island, or whether it referred to the Dogrib aboriginal group is not known. The Dogrib people were much further north in what is now the Northwest Territories. (see Inglis Island)

Dog River (river)
74 M/13 - Fitzgerald
SW-19-125-9-W4
59°52′N 111°34′W
Flows west into Slave River approximately 340 km north of Fort McMurray.

It appears on federal government maps as early as 1930. Although its origin is not precisely known, it may refer to a time when dogs would gather at some point along the river.

Doig River (river)
84 D/13 - Betts Creek
3-92-13-W6
56°57′N 120°00′W
Flows west into British Columbia approximately 139 km north-west of Fairview.

The origin of this name is not known; however, it is likely a surname.

■ **Dollar Lakes** (lakes)
83 N/6 - Whitemud Creek
18-73-21-W5
55°19′N 117°12′W
Approximately 26 km north of Valleyview.

Dollar Lakes were named because of the round shape and small size of the lakes. Local residents and forestry officers refer to the lakes as East Dollar Lake and West Dollar Lake. The lakes have been named since before 1931.

Donald Creek (creek)
74 D/14 - Wood Creek
29-90-9-W4
56°49′N 111°24′W
Flows north-west into Athabasca River approximately 10 km north of Fort McMurray.

Named by S.C. Ells for a son of C.H. Freeman, an instrument man on a survey during 1924. It is also known locally as Big Creek.

Donaldson Lake (lake)
84 F/9 - Donaldson Lake
16-100-14-W5
57°41′N 116°14′W
Approximately 105 km south-east of High Level.

Named for Ordinary Seaman Harold McIntosh Donaldson of the Royal Canadian Naval Volunteer Reserve, who lost his life during World War II.

Donna Creek (creek)
84 M/11 - Donna Creek
14-122-9-W6
59°35′N 119°25′W
Flows north-west into Petitot River approximately 127 km north of Rainbow Lake.

This precise origin of the name of this creek is unknown. The name was submitted by B.M. Rustad of the Alberta Land Survey following his 1964-65 survey of the 31st Baseline.

Donnelly (village)
83 N/11 - Donnelly
1-78-21-W5
55°44′N 117°6′W
Approximately 5 km east of Falher.

The Edmonton, Dunvegan and British Columbia Railway station was established in 1915, and was likely named after an official in the company, although railway records do not list a name of origin. The post office was opened here in April 1917, with A. Côté as first postmaster. Donnelly was incorporated as a village on January 1, 1956.

Donnelly Creek (creek)
83 J/15 - Upper Saulteaux
36-67-7-W5
54°51′N 114°55′W
Flows south-east into Saulteaux River approximately 30 km north-east of Swan Hills.

It shows as early as 1937 on a provincial government map; after whom it is named is not known.

Donnelly Island (island)
84 J/6 - Adams Landing
4-108-8-W5
58°21′N 115°15′W
In Peace River approximately 109 km east south-east of High Level.

The name was applied to this island by C. P. Hotchkiss in 1920 after his First Assistant, Cecil Donnelly (1889-1966), DLS, during survey work in the area. Locally the island is known as *Muskwa Ministik*, which means Bear Island in Cree. It is also known as Drilling Island due to the presence of an old oil well on the south bank of the river opposite the island.

Donovan Lake (lake)
74 M/14 - Tulip Lake
36-126-8-W4
60°00′N 111°14′W
Approximately 355 km north of Fort McMurray on the Alberta-Northwest Territories boundary.

It was named in 1929 after James Donovan, an old-timer of northern Alberta.

---

*denotes rescinded name or former locality.

Doris (locality)
83 J/7 - Fort Assiniboine
10-63-5-W5
54°27′N 114°39′W
Approximately 56 km south-east of Swan Hills.

A post office opened here in April 1931 and according to some sources was named after the daughter of the first postmaster, A. Teha. However, it may also have been named for its proximity to Doris Creek, the name for which predates the post office by at least fourteen years.

Doris Creek (creek)
83 J/7 - Fort Assiniboine
27-63-4-W5
54°29′N 114°31′W
Flows east into Timeu Creek approximately 38 km north north-west of Barrhead.

It appears on federal government maps as early as 1917. (see Doris)

Dorothy Island (island)
74 D/10 - Hollies Creek
2-87-4-W4
56°30′N 110°32′W
Approximately 60 km east south-east of Fort McMurray.

The precise origin of the name of this island in Cartwright Bay on Gordon Lake is unknown.

Dorscheid (railway point)
83 L/15 - Big Mountain Creek
5-67-4-W6
54°46′N 118°35′W
Approximately 41km south-east of Grande Prairie.

This Alberta Resources Railway point was established in 1969. Although its origin is not precisely known, it is likely named after a person since there are members of the Dorscheid family in the Grande Prairie area.

Douglas River (river)
74 L/8 - Brander Lake
10-12-108-1-W4
58°22′N 110°01′W
Flows west into Old Fort River approximately 192 km north north-east of Fort McMurray.

It was named after G. Douglas, the explorer with J.R. Akins, DLS, and his survey crew who were working on the 28th Baseline in 1917. The 28th Baseline falls between townships 108 and 109.

*Doussal (former post office)
83 N/10 - McLennan
35-76-19-W5
53°37′N 116°50′W
Approximately 10 km south south-east of McLennan

The post office operated here from November 1929 to December 1949. The Edmonton, Dunvegan and British Columbia Railway siding was called Kathleen, but the post office was called Doussal to avoid confusion with Kathryn, north of Calgary. Because of the francophone influence in the area, the name chosen was taken from Father Louis Le Doussal. He was a priest of the Oblates of Mary Immaculate who was born in France in 1835. He was ordained in 1860, and first served in Fort Providence in 1876. His final years were spent in Fort Chipewyan, from 1882 to the year of his death, 1923.

Dover River (river)
74 E/4 - Fort MacKay
19-94-11-W4
57°10′N 111°45′W
Flows east into MacKay River approximately 53 km north north-west of Fort McMurray.

The precise origin of the name of this river is unknown, although it is recorded by G.H. Blanchet, DLS, by that name in 1914. A federal government map from earlier that year referred to it as Moose River. The term "dover" is derived from the Welsh Gaelic word *dwfr*, and means "the waters" or "the stream."

Doze Lake (lake)
74 M/16 - Andrew Lake
13-125-1-W4
59°52′N 110°00′W
Approximately 350 km north north-east of Fort McMurray.

The name was adopted in 1939, after J.W. Doze, an assistant on the Saskatchewan-Alberta Boundary Commission's party who surveyed the boundary from Lake Athabasca to the 60th Parallel.

Draper (locality)
74 D/11 - Fort McMurray
31-88-8-W4
56°40′N 111°15′W
Approximately 11 km south-east of Fort McMurray.

This locality was named after Thomas Draper, associated with the exploitation of the Athabasca oil sands. Draper began his career as an oil equipment manufacturer in Petrolia, Ontario. During the 1920s he was involved in mining and extraction research and established the McMurray Asphaltum and Oil Company, of which he was president. Draper supplied oil sands to various investigators, including the Research Council of Alberta. In 1921 he built a small plant to conduct separation research at his company's site southeast of Fort McMurray. In 1925 he began research on oil sands as a paving material. His results were publicized and exhibited at the Edmonton Exhibition. Draper had several paving contracts, including a section of Wellington Street in Ottawa, and 22 blocks of sidewalks in Camrose. The McMurray Asphaltum and Oil company was situated on leased land adjacent to the railway track where it came into the Clearwater Valley at the original Waterways site. When Waterways was relocated this site was named Draper's Landing; now the locality is known simply as Draper. Thomas Draper died at the age of 92 in 1962. (see also Fort McMurray)

Dreamer's Lake (lake)
83 M/9 - Peoria
SE-30-77-3-W6
55°42′N 118°27′W
Approximately 65 km north north-east of Grande Prairie.

According to local stories, an old-timer had a dream to have this lake developed and stocked. It is now being done, and the locally well-established name for the lake has become Dreamer's Lake.

Dreau (locality)
83 N/11 - Donnelly
11-78-22-W5
55°45′N 117°17′W
Approximately 6 km west of Falher.

It was named after Jean-Marie Dreau, a Roman Catholic priest of the Oblates of Mary Immaculate. He was born in France in 1882 and was ordained in 1909. He came to Canada and started at St. Bernard Mission at Grouard in 1910. He served in many communities in Alberta and British Columbia before his death in April 1942. The post office was established here in 1931. The first postmaster was N. Rondelet.

Driftpile (locality)
83 O/5 - Driftpile
22-73-12-W5
55°20′N 115°46′W
Approximately 65 km west of Slave Lake.

Originally established in 1914 as a station of the Edmonton, Dunvegan and British Columbia Railway. The post office opened in May 1919. W. Ashley was the first postmaster. It was named for its proximity to the nearby river. (see Driftpile River)

Driftpile Indian Reserve No. 150
(Indian reserve)
83 O/5 - Driftpile
34-73-12-W5
55°22′N 115°45′W
Approximately 65 km west of Slave Lake.

It is situated on the south shore of Lesser Slave Lake. It was created under Treaty No. 8, 1899, which granted the area around Driftpile and Lesser Slave Lake to five Cree bands who shared the land jointly. (see Driftpile River)

Driftpile Inlet (inlet)
83 O/5 - Driftpile
7-19-73-11-W5
55°20′N 115°40′W
Approximately 55 km west of Slave Lake.

Located on Giroux Bay of Lesser Slave Lake; the name was adopted in the early part of the century and is descriptive. (see Driftpile River)

Driftpile River (river)
83 O/5 - Driftpile
15-32-74-11-W5
55°23′N 115°40′W
Flows north-east into Lesser Slave Lake approximately 58 km west of Slave Lake.

It appears as early as 1892 on a Geological Survey of Canada map. In 1916, James K. Cornwall, in a letter to Dominion Land Surveyor J. N. Wallace, wrote: "...the name Driftpile is a translation of the Cree name of the river, *Mit-tow-et-tocow seepee*, which means drift pile river. As you know having been in that country, that at the mouth of the river, great piles of driftwood have collected.....The name is about 100 years old as near as I can make out. It is about 100 years since that country was first settled by the Cree."

Driftwood Lake (Lake)
84 C/11 - Deadwood
8-88-22-W5
56°37′N 117°27′W
Approximately 35 km south south-west of Manning.

The name was noted in 1919 by J.A. Buchanan, DLS, and is probably descriptive of dead wood on its shores.

Driftwood River (river)
83 O/8 - Driftwood River
16-21-72-2-W5
55°15′N 114°1′W
Flows south into Lesser Slave River approximately 34 km east of Slave Lake.

This descriptive name was well established when the Dominion Land Surveyors first came through the area in 1909.

*Drilling Island (island)
84 J/6 - Adams Landing
4-108-8-W5
58°21′N 115°15′W
In Peace River approximately 109 km east south-east of High Level.

(see Donnelly Island)

Drolet Creek (creek)
84 I/12 - Buchanan Lake
12-3-112-22-W4
58°42′N 113°38′W
Flows south-east into Peace River approximately 200 km east of High Level.

Originally called Swan River, the name was changed in 1920 to honour an employee of the North West Company who worked with the company in the early 1820s.

Dropoff Creek (creek)
83 P/16 - Crow Lake
11-80-16-W4
55°55′N 112°25′W

---

*denotes rescinded name or former locality.

Flows south-west into House River approximately 105 km south-west of Fort McMurray.

Possibly descriptive of the feature which falls over 120 metres from its source to its mouth at the House River. The name has been in use since at least 1914.

Drowned Horse Creek (creek)
83 P/13 - Pelican
8-29-79-24-W4
55°53′N 113°45′W
Flows north-east into South Wabasca Lake approximately 95 km north-east of Slave Lake.

The name appears on federal government maps at least as early as 1897. Although the incident that caused its name is not recorded, it is likely descriptive.

*Dry Stick Lake (lake)
83 M/2 - Grande Prairie
31-71,72-6-W6
55°12′N 118°55′W
Approximately 6 km north-west of Grande Prairie

By 1918, this likely descriptive name for the lake had been changed to Hughes Lake.
(see Hughes Lake)

Dryden Creek (creek)
84 E/8 - Botha River
33-97-1-W6
57°28′N 118°06′W
Flows south into Botha River approximately 65 km north north-west of Manning.

The creek was likely named after J. Dryden, a mounder in the survey crew of J.R. Akins, DLS, in 1915.

Duck Lake (lake)
84 H/3 - Alberta
32-94-19-W4
57°12′N 113°03′W
Approximately 113 km north-west of Fort McMurray.

The precise origin of the name of this lake is unknown. The name Duck Lake has been long used by local people, and one possible explanation lies in its shape, however it is more likely descriptive of the waterfowl found on the lake.

Dugout Creek (creek)
74 D/14 - Wood Creek
32-90-7-W4
56°51′N 111°05′W
Flows south into Steepbank River approximately 29 km north-east of Fort McMurray.

(see North Steepbank River)

Dumbell Lake (lake)
74 M/16 - Andrew Lake
SW-26-126-2-W4
59°58′N 110°14′W
Approximately 358 km north of Fort McMurray.

The name was submitted in 1958 by the Research Council of Alberta, and is descriptive of its shape.

Dummy Creek (creek)
84 J/10 - Wentzel River
2-110-4-W5
58°31′N 114°32′W
Flows south-east into Peace River approximately 152 km east of High Level.

The precise origin of the name of this creek is unknown. The name was supplied in 1946 by local game wardens who said the name was in local use.

Duncan Creek (creek)
83 P/7 - Amadou Lake
2-15-73-18-W4
55°19′N 112°41W
Flows south-west into Athabasca River approximately 75 km north-west of Lac La Biche.

Officially adopted in 1945, the name has appeared on maps as early as 1915. After whom it was named is not known.

Duncan's Indian Reserve No. 151A (Indian reserve)
84 C/4 - Grimshaw
16-82-23-W5
56°06′N 117°51W
Approximately 15 km south-west of Grimshaw

Established in 1907, this reserve was named after Duncan Tustawits, an early chief of the group. At one time it was known as Peace River Crossing Indian Reserve.

Dunkirk River (river)
84 A/15 - Dunkirk River
31-89-16-W4
56°46′N 112°32′W
Flows south-east into MacKay River approximately 70 km west of Fort McMurray.

The name has been in use for this river since at least 1915, therefore it was not named after the famed World War II battle. Dunkirk is a town in northern France on the North Sea founded around the 7th century AD, and often fortified. *Dun* may refer to a hill, fort or castle, and *kirk* comes from the Old Norse meaning "church." According to the *Concise Oxford Dictionary*, *dun* is also a verb meaning to strongly go after a payment of debt, or to pester. It is an abbreviation of the obsolete *dunkirk*, in reference to privateers, which in turn comes

---
*denotes rescinded name or former locality.

from the name of the place in France. So perhaps in centuries long ago, privateers, or royally commissioned armed vessels, would use this Norman port as a base of operations.

■ **Dunvegan** (locality)
83 M/15 - Rycroft
7-80-4-W6
55°55′N 118°36′W
Approximately 85 km north of Grande Prairie.

Evoking romantic images of the 800-year-old castle on Scotland's misty Isle of Skye, the name Dunvegan came from this ancestral home of the person who established this North West Company post in 1805, Archibald Norman McLeod. The post was established on the Peace River. The word itself is derived from *dun*, meaning hill or fort, and *began, bakan*, an old Norse name. In 1772, Samuel Johnson said of the Scottish Dunvegan "To

Dunvegan, 1904

Dunvegan we came, very willing to rest, and found our fatigue amply recompensed by our reception. At Dunvegan I had tasted lotus, and was in danger of forgetting I was ever to depart."

Dunvegan Creek (creek)
83 M/15 - Rycroft
7-80-4-W6
55°54′N 118°38′W
Flows north-east into Peace River approximately 20 km north-east of Spirit River.

The name for this creek which enters the Peace River opposite the locality of Dunvegan was not made official until the early 1950s. It is known by some in the area as Bronco Creek. (see Dunvegan)

*****Dunvegan Settlement** (settlement)
83 M/15 - Rycroft
7-8-80-4-W6
55°54′N 118°35′W
Approximately 20 km north-east of Spirit River.

It was first surveyed in 1910 and was named for its proximity to the old North West Company fort. (see Dunvegan)

Eagle Lake (lake)
74 M/16 - Andrew Lake
1-125-3-W4
59°50′N 110°21′W
Approximately 342 km north of Fort McMurray.

The name was submitted in 1965 by the Research Council of Alberta, because the lake was a prominent nesting site of the bald eagle.

Eaglenest Lake (lake)
84 H/16 - Bayard Lake
13-101-14-W4
57°47′N 112°08′W
Approximately 123 km north north-west of Fort McMurray.

The precise origin of the name Eaglesnest of this lake is unknown, but is most likely descriptive. The name was recorded as early as 1890 by the Geological Survey of Canada. The lake may be also locally known as Old Wives Lake; however, a map from 1897 shows Old Wives Lake to be a bit farther north. (see also Old Wives Lake)

Eaglesham (village)
83 N/13 - Tangent
25-78-26-W5
55°47'N 117°53'W
Approximately 90 km north-east of Grande Prairie.

Originally an Edmonton, Dunvegan and British Columbia Railway station established in 1916, it is possibly named after a village in Renfrewshire (now Strathclyde) in Scotland. The post office opened in February 1929, its first postmaster being Joe McDaid.

Early Gardens (locality)
84 C/14 - Grimshaw
6-82-23-W5
56°05'N 117°36'W
Approximately 12 km south of Grimshaw.

The name Early Gardens commemorates the market gardening operation of J. B. Early who arrived here from Washington State in 1916. Early used half his land to pasture a registered herd of Jersey cows and Belgian horses. He was instrumental in getting the Edmonton City Dairy to set up dairies at Peace River and Berwyn. He irrigated the other half of his land and, in addition to crops of sweet corn, tomatoes, cucumbers and other vegetables, he grew flowers. The gardens were famous for their carnations, hollyhocks, giant delphiniums, petunias and over 175 varieties of gladiolus. The steamer *D.A. Thomas* made sightseeing excursions up the Peace River during the 1920s to see the Early Gardens.

East Chester Creek (creek)
84 F/7 - Buhler Creek
6-96-17-W5
57°18'N 116°44'W
Flows north into Cache Creek approximately 67 km north-east of Manning.

It is likely named for its proximity to Chester Creek. (see Chester Creek)

East Jackpine Creek (creek)
74 E/3 - Hartley Creek
28-94-9-W4
57°05'15"N 111°09'10"W
Flows north-west into Hartley Creek approximately 52 km north of Fort McMurray.

This creek is so named because it is a tributary to Jackpine Creek. (see also Jackpine Creek)

East Peace, Municipal District of, No. 131
(municipal district)
84 C/9 - Golden Lake
77 to 96-7 to 22-W5
From 55°38'N 115°00'W to 57°23'N 117°32'W
North-central Alberta.

This municipal district was created in 1994, and takes its name from the fact it centres on the eastern Peace District of Alberta.

East Prairie Metis Settlement No. 4
(Metis settlement)
83 N/1 - Bellrose Lake
71-15-W5
55°10'N 116°10'W
Approximately 70 km east of Valleyview.

The East Prairie Metis Colony was created in 1939 by an order-in-council. The name was changed in 1990 by an act of the Legislative Assembly. It takes its name from the river that runs through it. (see also East Prairie River)

East Prairie River (river)
83 N/9 - Grouard
2-76-16-W5
55°33'N 116°22'W
Flows north into South Heart River approximately 15 km north of High Prairie.

This descriptive name is mentioned in the field notebook of the Dominion Land Surveyor, J.J. Stock, who went through the area in 1911. He reported that there is "Some good spruce in commercial quantities...along the banks of the East Prairie River."

Eating Creek (creek)
83 O/7 - Slave Lake
34-72-5-W5
55°16'N 114°42'W
Flows north-east into Mitsue Creek approximately 5 km east of Slave Lake.

This area was well known for its abundance of game animals, and it was a place where the aboriginal people would gather to eat. The creek into which it flows is called *Mitsue*, the Cree word for eating. (see also Mitsue Creek)

Economy Creek (creek)
83 M/1 - DeBolt
7-10-71-2-W6
55°08'N 118°13'W
Flows north into Simonette River approximately 15 km south-west of DeBolt.

The name for the creek has appeared on maps since as early as 1918; the origin of the name is not known. Its source is Economy Lake.

Economy Lake (lake)
83 L/16 - Lignite Creek
2-29-68-2-W6
54°54'00"N 118°14'30"W
Approximately 46 km south-east of Grande Prairie.

The origin of the name Economy Lake could not be traced; a 1918 map documents usage of the name. It is the source of Economy Creek.

Edith Creek (creek)
83 J/14 - Deer Mountain
13-67-10-W5
54°49'N 115°23'W
Flows north into the Swan River approximately 4 km north of Swan Hills.

Likely named in the 1930s or 1940s for its source. (see Edith Lake and Agnes Lake)

Edith Lake (lake)
83 J/14 - Deer Mountain
13-67-10-W5
54°48'N 115°23'W
Approximately 9 km north of Swan Hills.

Likely named in the 1930s or 1940s, after whom is not known. (see Agnes Lake)

Edna Lake (lake)
74 D/8 - Gipsy Lake
1-86-3-W4
56°26'N 110°20'W
Approximately 72 km east south-east of Fort McMurray.

After whom this lake is named is not known.

Edra Creek (creek)
84 I/4 - Edra Creek
NE-28-106-23-W4
58°14'N 113°44'W
Flows north-east into Bolton Creek approximately 197 km east of High Level.

The name first appeared on a federal government map in 1916; its origin is not known.

Edward's Lake (lake)
74 E/14 - Pearson Lake
34-103-8-W4
57°59'30"N 111°14'30"W
Approximately 140 km north of Fort McMurray.

This remote lake is named after Edward Cyprien, who trapped the area throughout his lifetime. His father had a trap line here before him and his son, Archie Cyprien, took it over. Edward Cyprien died in 1977.

Edwards Lake (lake)
74 L/7 - Keane Creek
4-107-4-W4
58°15'N 110°37'W
Approximately 170 km north north-east of Fort McMurray.

The name shows as early as 1919 on federal government maps, and although the origin of the name is not precisely known, it may have been named after a member of a survey crew.

Edwards Lake (lake)
73 M/6 - Wiau Lake
10-13-75-9-W4
55°30'N 111°15'W
Approximately 93 km north north-east of Lac La Biche.

This was possibly named after the railroad engineer who drowned here in 1912, during the construction of the Alberta and Great Waterways Railway.

Edwin Creek (creek)
74 D/9 - Bunting Bay
15-89-3-W4
56°43'N 110°23'W
Flows north-west into Clearwater River approximately 62 km east of Fort McMurray.

In correspondence with the Geographic Names Board of Canada, J.N. Wallace stated it was named after Edwin Gay of Lloydminster, a survey crew member. It appears under this name on a federal government map in 1914. The original name of this creek was Swan Lake River, from which the portage found at the mouth of this river, Swan Lake River Portage, took its name.

Egg Island (island)
74 L/16 - Stone Point
NE-9-115-3-W4
58°59'N 110°26'W
Approximately 249 km north of Fort McMurray in Lake Athabasca.

Likely named for its oval shape, the name has been in use since at least the 1950s. There was a navigational light on the feature at one time.

Egg Lake (lake)
74 D/3 - I.D. #18
31-81-9-W4
56°03'55"N 111°24'30"W
Approximately 70 km south of Fort McMurray.

The precise origin of the name of this large lake is unknown; it has been in local usage since the 1930s. One suggestion is that is descriptive of the somewhat egg-shaped outline of the lake.

Egg Lake (lake)
74 L/14 - Rivière des Rochers
15-114-9-W4
58°53'N 111°25'W
Approximately 233 km north of Fort McMurray.

The name was officially approved in 1971, and although the origin is not recorded, it likely refers to an abundance of eggs to be found there, due to waterfowl nesting.

Eight Lake (lake)
74 E/11 - Myrnam
26-98-9-W4
57°32'22"N 111°20'55"W
Approximately 88 km north of Fort McMurray.

This remote lake is shaped like a figure eight. This descriptive name has been used by several generations of trappers in the area.

Eleanor Creek (creek)
74 L/3 - Embarras
2-105-9-W4
58°05′N 111°22′W
Flows north-west into Athabasca River approximately 142 km north of Fort McMurray.

The name first shows on maps as early as 1916; after whom it is named is not known.

Eleske (locality)
84 K/7 - Child Lake
5-11-109-16-W5
58°26′50″N 116°34′00″W
On the Child Lake Indian Reserve approximately 34 km east of High Level.

This name is descriptive, and translated from the Dunne-za or Beaver language means "Dusty Place." Surveyors in 1915 noted the Vermilion Trail branched westwards as the Keg River Trail at an aboriginal village called Aleskay. J.R. Akins, DLS, mentioned Eleske (spelled Aleskay) in a paper to the Association of Dominion Land Surveyors in 1919.

Elford's Field (meadow)
83 L/14 - Wapiti
13-19-68-8-W6
54°54′22″N 119°12′50″W
Approximately 40 km south south-west of Grande Prairie.

(see Elford's Hill)

Elford's Hill (hill)
83 L/14 - Wapiti
10-24-68-9-W6
From 54°54′50″N 119°15′W to
54°54′N 119°14′W
Approximately 40 km south south-west of Grande Prairie.

The Elford family arrived in the area in the late 1920s or early 1930s. Apparently they had one of the best gardens in the country.

Elizabeth Lake (lake)
84 H/4 - Osi Lake
31-94-22-W4
57°12′N 113°31′W
Approximately 140 km west north-west of Fort McMurray.

The origin of the name of this lake is centred in a story related by an elder: "A long time ago our guys were spending the night at that lake and started talking about a woman named Elizabeth and that is how the lake got its name."

Elk Lake (lake)
84 I/2 - Elk Lake
12-34-104-16-W4
58°05′N 112°34′W
Approximately 157 km north north-west of Fort McMurray.

Approved in 1963; it commemorates the 1949 transfer of elk into Wood Buffalo National Park.

Ellazga (locality)
84 K/9 - Ponton River
36-109-15-W5
58°30′N 116°21′W
Approximately 45 km east of High Level.

The precise origins of the name of this village are unknown, but the 1928 *Place-Names of Alberta* refers to it as an aboriginal name meaning "salt place."

Ellenwood Lake (lake)
83 M/1 - DeBolt
14-30-69-2-W6
55°00′N 118°18′W
Approximately 36 km east south-east of Grande Prairie.

This lake was named in 1952 after Corporal R.W. Ellenwood, MM, of Edmonton, born at Cache Creek, Alberta, in 1902. He enlisted in Edmonton in 1939, and was killed in Belgium in September 1944.

Elliott River (river)
84 G/9 - Alberta
11-99-1-W5
57°34′N 114°02′W
Flows south-west into Mikkwa River approximately 185 km north-west of Fort McMurray.

After Lieutenant Elliott Greene, assistant on a survey party in 1913. He joined the 3rd Battalion, Canadian Expeditionary Force, during World War I.

Dr. Sidney Ells, 1928

Ells Lake (lake)
74 M/10 - Cornwall Lake
12-123-4-W4
59°40′N 110°32′W
Approximately 321 km north of Fort McMurray.

Suggested in recognition of the contributions of S.C. Ells, a Canadian geologist, to the knowledge and development to Canada. The name was submitted in 1965 by the Research Council of Alberta, and is one of a series of features in the area named after deceased prominent geologists. (see Ells River)

Ells River (river)
74 E/5 - Bitumount
2-96-11-W4
57°18'N 111°40'W
Flows south-east into Athabasca River approximately 67 km north north-west of Fort McMurray.

After Sidney Clark Ells (1879-1971), a controversial figure in the early period of oil sands research and development. Born in Nova Scotia, he worked as assistant to his father, R.W. Ells, who was with the Geological Survey of Canada. He graduated from McGill in 1908 with a science degree, and in 1912 joined the federal Mines Branch as secretary to the director. In 1913 Ells began surveying the Athabasca country and persuaded the Mines Branch to fund him to conduct a paving experiment with oil sands. A rather high-handed individual, Ells ran afoul of his supervisors on financial issues. In 1915 he began work on the scientific properties of oil sands at the Mellon Institute in Pittsburgh, and produced a report of his findings. Its flaws proved to be the bases of many later discussions. His most important conclusion was that there were methods by which bitumen could be separated from sands, and that only government-sponsored work could solve the economic and technical difficulties before commercial use would be viable. The work of Ells was instrumental in provoking the interest of research scientists and politicians, which bore fruit in the founding of the Research Council of Alberta in 1919 and a second phase of development during the 1920s, which saw provincial sponsoring of industrial research.

---

*denotes rescinded name or former locality.

He was also an illustrator and writer of verse chronicling early life in Alberta. In his poem "Wood Smoke" he commemorated an incident which happened along the shore of Lake Athabasca in 1924, where two men were lost in a snowstorm.

... Just a wisp of smoke! but from sheltering spruce on edge of barrens white,
Its breath spells life to panting men in tempest of winter night;
Just a wisp of smoke! but from lowly cot the scent of its trailing plume,
Gladdens the heart of the settler lone, – wearily plodding home...

In 1922, the Fort McMurray Board of Trade petitioned the Geographic Board of Canada to name this river after S.C. Ells. Like Ells himself, this suggestion caused a certain amount of controversy. The name Moose River was recorded as early as 1890 by the Geological Survey. The 1916 township plans compiled from the Dominion Land Surveys show it as Moose River, and the 1918 sectional map of the area as Namur River. There were those people who wanted to retain the name found on the map. Some of the old-timers in the area wanted to keep the locally well-known name Moose River. After much deliberation, in 1923 the name Ells was chosen, and the name Namur was applied to a river somewhat to the north and east, the river that bears the name today. From a 1986 field survey it was determined there is still controversy over the name. The local people in Fort MacKay know it as Red River.

In December of 1924 Ells himself submitted to the Geographic Board of Canada a list of proposed names for geographical features in the Fort McMurray area, several of which were approved. (see, for example, Haight Island, McClelland Lake, Morton Island, Clarke Creek, Inglis Island, Donald Creek, Conn Creek, Rocke Island)

Elmer's Creek (creek)
74 D/10 - Hollies Creek
31-88-5-W4
56°40'50"N 110°48'08"W
Flows north-west into Clearwater River approximately 37 km east of Fort McMurray.

Named after Elmer Cree, a popular old-timer of the area, whose cabin is located on this creek.

Elmworth (locality)
83 M/4 - Rio Grande
9-70-11-W6
55°03'N 119°37'W
Approximately 50 km west south-west of Grande Prairie.

This is said to be named after a place in Massachusetts. The post office opened in January 1920, the first postmaster being Franklin T. Brewer.

Elsa Lake (lake)
84 M/7 - Elsa Lake
33-120-4-W6
59°28'N 118°37'W
Approximately 115 km north-east of Rainbow Lake.

It was named after Elsa Carter of Fawcett, Alberta, on the suggestion of her husband Cecil Carter, a member of a survey party camping at this lake in 1966. The Slavey refer to it as Running Beaver Lake.

*Embarras (former locality)
74 L/3 - Embarras
9-15-106-9-W4
58°13'N 111°23'W
Approximately 159 km north of Fort McMurray.

Originally established as an airport, likely to serve oil exploration activities, this place was named for its proximity to Embarras Portage approximately 26 kilometres to the north. (see also Embarras Portage and Embarras River)

Embarras Portage (locality)
74 L/6 - Richardson Lake
5-8-109-9-W4
58°27′N 111°29′W
Approximately 187 km north of Fort McMurray.

A post office was established here in 1931 and was named for its proximity to the portage between the Mamawi and Embarras rivers. The first postmaster was E. W. Reed. (see also Embarras River)

Embarras River (river)
74 L/11 - Fort Chipewyan
13-36-111-7-W4
58°30′N 111°03′W
Flows north into Lake Athabasca approximately 207 km north of Fort McMurray.

It is so called due to the great quantities of driftwood that obstructed the stream and rendered it necessary to portage everything. According to *A Dictionary of Canadianisms...*, an embarras is "a tangle of logs and brush obstructing a stream." The word comes from the French and means obstruction or obstacle. The feature is referred to as early as 1820 by George Simpson as Rivière De Embarras, and 1822 in the 1822 Hudson's Bay Company post journal as River d'Embarren.

English Island (island)
74 L/11 - Fort Chipewyan
13-6-112-7-W4
58°42′N 111°11′W
Approximately 210 km north of Fort McMurray in Lake Athabasca.

The name of this island refers to the time that Peter Fidler of the Hudson's Bay Company attempted to establish a post here called Nottingham House.

Engstrom Lake (lake)
74 D/2 - Quigley
17-83-6-W4
56°11′20″N 110°54′20″W
Approximately 60 km south-east of Fort McMurray.

This lake is named for one of the most prominent nature enthusiasts of the McMurray region. Eddy Engstrom immigrated to the Clearwater area near Fort McMurray from Sweden in 1926. Engstrom loved nature and the freedom of the North where he hunted and trapped. Struck by a heart attack in 1973, his body was found, appropriately, in his canoe, floating down the Clearwater River. Shortly before he died he had completed a manuscript of his memoirs, *Clearwater Winter* (1984). In his will, Mr. Engstrom left money to the Boy Scouts and Girl Guides to be used for a camp which was set up on one side of this lake.

Enilda (hamlet)
83 N/8 - High Prairie
NE-13-74-16-W5
55°25′N 116°18′W
Approximately 13 km east of High Prairie.

The post office was opened here in 1913, and took its name from the wife of the first postmaster, J. Tompkins. It is the reversal of her first name, Adline. It is an area referred to by the Cree as *pusto tiwin*, meaning "crossing the tracks" for the old trail that crossed the railway at this point.

Epler Lake (lake)
74 L/8 - Brander Lake
5-109-1-W4
58°26′N 110°08′W
Approximately 195 km north north-east of Fort McMurray.

The name was recorded for this lake in 1917 by J.R. Akins, DLS.

Equisetum Lake (lake)
84 B/10 - Peerless Lake
15-89-5-W5
56°43′N 114°42′W
Approximately 158 km north of Slave Lake.

Equisetum is the Latin word for the reed-like horsetail, a plant that grows in abundance around the lake. It was recorded as early as 1890 by the Geological Survey of Canada.

Eric Creek (creek)
83 P/8 - Pelican
12-16-73-16-W4
55°19′N 112°25′W
Flows south-west into Wandering River approximately 75 km north-west of Lac La Biche.

The name was approved in 1970 upon the suggestion of a provincial mapping official; after whom it is named is not known.

Erickson Lake (lake)
83 J/7 - Timeu Creek
1-63,64-6-W5
54°30′N 114°46′W
Approximately 45 km south-east of Swan Hills.

The name was officially adopted in the 1950s; the person after whom the lake is named is not known.

Erin Lodge (locality)
83 M/16 - Codesa
NW-21-80-2-W6
55°57′N 118°15′W
Approximately 40 km north-east of Spirit River.

The post office was established here in August 1917. The first postmaster was Miss A. Connery and it was apparently named for the poetic name for Ireland, Erin. Lodge was added to distinguish it from the other places in Canada called Erin.

*Esher (former station)
83 M/10 - Woking
NE17-77-5-W6
55°41′N 118°44′W
Approximately 45 km north of Grande Prairie.

This Edmonton, Dunvegan and British Columbia Railway station was named in 1916 for Esher, Surrey, England, where J. B. Prest, engineer of the railway company, lived for a time. Other places named by Mr. Prest are Prestville, Surbiton, Woking and Wanham. From the Old English *esher* can mean ash tree, boundary or ploughshare. From the Old Norse and Gaelic related meanings include a border or a rim.

Esk Lake (Lake)
84 N/13 - Esk Lake
21-126-24-W5
59°58′N 117°57′W
Approximately 166 km north north-west High Level.

The precise origin of the name of this lake is unknown; *eske* in Old Scandinavian means ash trees. There are also four Esk rivers in Great Britain. The British word comes from the Celtic root word meaning "water."

Esmond Creek (creek)
84 M/16 - Thurston Lake
36-125-1-W6
59°54′N 118°01′W
Flows south south-west into Beatty Lake approximately 161 km north north-west of High Level.

This creek was named by Dominion Land Surveyor J.R. Akins during his 1915 survey of the 6th Meridian, as the name is recorded in his field notes. No further data is noted in his field correspondence on the origins of this name, and there is no record of a field crew member of this name.

---

*denotes rescinded name or former locality.

Ess Bend (river bend)
74 L/6 - Richardson Lake
8-109-7-W4
58°27′N 111°08′W
Approximately 184 km north of Fort McMurray.

Descriptive of the shape of the bend in the river.

Ethel Creek (creek)
83 J/14 - Deer Mountain
26-67-7-W5
54°50′N 115°02′W
Flows north-east into Saulteaux River approximately 55 km south-west of Slave Lake.

Reference to it was made as early as 1922. It was officially named in 1960 for its source, Ethel Lake. (see Agnes Lake)

Ethel Lake (lake)
83 J/14 - Deer Mountain
7-67-7-W5
54°47′N 115°03′W
Approximately 25 km east north-east of Swan Hills.

Likely named in the 1930s or 1940s, after whom is not known. (see Agnes Lake)

Eula Creek (creek)
83 O/6 - Kinuso
1-31-73-9-W5
55°22′N 115°22′W
Flows north into Swan River approximately 40 km west north-west of Slave Lake.

The origin of this name is not known, but it was used for the name of the Eula Creek School District when it was established in 1935. The local history for the area stated the name was known in the area well before 1914. The name was officially adopted in 1979.

Eureka River (locality)
84 D/7 - Eureka River
9-86-5-W6
56°27′N 118°44′W
Approximately 47 km north north-west of Fairview.

Named for its proximity to the feature, it was first established as a post office in 1931. The first postmaster was B.W. Basnett. (see Eureka River)

Eureka River (river)
84 D/5 - Boundary Lake
21-85-10-W6
56°23′N 119°30′W
Flows west into Clear River approximately 78 km north-west of Fairview.

The precise origin of the name of this river is unknown. When asked in 1931, a local resident explained the origin of the name in this way. "It is an Indian word meaning a river or creek running in different directions, or a very crooked stream." The name may also have its origins in the Greek word *heurisko*, to find. The exclamation *eureka* ("I have found it") is attributed to Archimedes, mathematician and inventor on his discovery of a method to determine the purity of gold in 212 B.C. J.A. Buchanan referred to it as the West Fork River in his field survey notes compiled in 1915, but by 1931 it was recorded under its current name.

Eva Lake (lake)
84 J/14 - Margaret Lake
24-114-8-W5
58°54′N 115°11′W
Approximately 118 km east north-east of High Level.

This lake is said to be named for the wife of Dominion Land Surveyor James Nevin Wallace. The Cree name for this lake is *Kaministik Sakahikun*, or Island Lake. The name is descriptive of the four islands in the centre of the lake.

Eymundson Creek (creek)
74 E/5 - Asphalt Creek
9-98-10-W4
57°29'30"N 111°34'05"W
Flows south-east into Athabasca River approximately 86 km north of Fort McMurray.

Named after the Eymundson family. Charles Eymundson was an early settler and trapper in the area. Fort MacKay residents call this creek Whitemud, because of the limestone clay bed that leaves the water white, resembling milk.

F~G

Fairview, 1920s

*Fairacres (locality)
84 C/14 - Buchanan Creek
32-89-22-W5
56°46′N 117°27′W
Approximately 20 km south south-east of Manning.

It was established as a post office in 1910, the first postmaster was D.E. Deller. The name owes its origin to the nature of the land.

Fairview (town)
84 D/1 - Fairview
34-81-3-W6
56°04′N 118°23′W
Approximately 71 km west south-west of Peace River.

The descriptive name Fairview was introduced to the district by H.L. Propst, who applied it to his homestead in 1910. When the surrounding community was formally organised as a municipal district in 1914 it appropriated the name to become Fairview Municipal District #858. The Fairview district experienced a sudden change in its status in 1928, when the Edmonton, Dunvegan and British Columbia Railway decided to bypass the existent area centre of Waterhole, 6 kilometres south, and to build a siding at mile 365.8. On the advice of a settler, E.J. Martin, the railroad named the siding Fairview. Most of the buildings at Waterhole were moved north, and by 1949 it had been incorporated as a town. The Fairview post office was established in 1928, and its first postmaster was H. Sigler.

Fairview, Municipal District of, No. 136 (municipal district)
84 D/1 - Fairview
80-2-W6
56°00′N 118°20′W
Centred around the town of Fairview.

Established in 1945, the municipal district was named after one of the main communities in the area.

Falher (town)
83 N/11 - Donnelly
4-78-21-W5
55°44′N 117°12′W
Approximately 20 km west of McLennan.

The Edmonton, Dunvegan and British Columbia Railway Station was established in 1915 and named after Father Constant Falher, a Roman Catholic Oblate missionary who was born in Brittany in 1863. He was ordained in 1889 and was posted to Grouard Mission that year. In 1912, the Mission St-Jean Baptiste de Falher was opened five kilometres from the current site. The post office opened in June 1923 the first postmaster being P.N. Blais.

Fallingsand Point (point)
74 M/8 - Wylie Lake
21-118-1-W4
59°16′N 110°06′W
Approximately 279 km north north-east of Fort McMurray.

This point shows on federal government maps as early as 1884, and is descriptive.

Fallow, Lake (lake)
83 N/5 - Puskwaskau River
31-72-24-W5
55°17′N 117°41′W
Approximately 35 km north-west of Valleyview.

Named after the Honourable William A. Fallow, Minister of Public Works, Railways and Telephones for the Province of Alberta 1935-1948 in the Social Credit governments of William Aberhart and Ernest Manning.

Faria Creek (creek)
84 L/1 - Faria Creek
3-105-1-W6
58°05′N 118°03′W
Flows east into Chinchaga River approximately 73 km south-west of High Level.

It may have been named after a crew member working on the survey of the 27th Baseline, or the Alberta-Saskatchewan Boundary Survey. It appears on a provincial government map of 1930.

---

*denotes rescinded name or former locality.

Farrell Lake (lake)
83 O/15 - Brintnell Lake
30-80-5-W5
55°58′N 114°46′W
Approximately 77 km north of Slave Lake.

This lake was named in 1954 in honour of Conway Farrell, who was born in 1888 and first started flying at Camp Mohawk and Camp Borden in 1917. He was awarded the Distinguished Flying Cross in World War I. He was also a pilot for Canadian Airways. In 1942 he was appointed by Ottawa as manager of northern landing fields on the Canadian portion of the air route to Alaska. There are a number of lakes in this area named after bush pilots. (see also Berry Lake, Brintnell Lake, Calder Lake, Dickins Lake, Lake May, McConachie Lake, McMillan Lake, McMullen Lake, Randall Lake and Sawle Lake)

Farrier Creek (creek)
73 M/1 - Scheltens Lake
8-25-70-1-W4
55°03′N 110°00′W
Flows into Saskatchewan approximately 90 km north of Cold Lake.

Officially adopted in 1950, it is referred to in the 1909 Dominion Lands Survey reports. It was named after W. Farrier, a survey crew member. The word "farrier" refers to a smith whose specialty is shoeing horses.

Faust (hamlet)
83 O/5 - Driftpile
16-73-11-W5
55°19′N 115°38′W
Approximately 56 km west of Slave Lake.

The Edmonton, Dunvegan and British Columbia Railway established a station here in 1914, and named it after E.T. Faust, a locomotive engineer. The post office opened in May 1920 with W. S. Adams as the first postmaster. It is at a site known to the Cree as *akosisi-gunakai-ago*, or fish-drying racks, an old camp for drying fish.

Fawcett Lake (lake)
83 P/5 - Fawcett Lake
73-25,26-W4
55°18′N 113°53′W
Approximately 55 km east of Slave Lake.

This lake was named for Sidney Dawson Fawcett, a Dominion Land Surveyor, who surveyed the 19th Baseline in 1912. It was originally known as Moose Lake. (see also Moose Lake)

Fawcett River (river)
83 O/8 - Driftwood River
6-27-72-2-W5
55°15′N 114°14′W
Flows south-west into Driftwood River approximately 33 km east of Slave Lake.

Referred to as Moose River when the Geological Survey of Canada was first in the area in 1892, the name had changed by 1912. (see Fawcett Lake and Moose River)

Ferguson Lake (lake)
83 M/7 - Sexsmith
26-72-6-W6
55°16′N 118°49′W
Approximately 7 km north of Grande Prairie.

Recorded by the Dominion Lands Survey in 1909, the name had been in use for some years. It was most probably named after the St. Pierre Ferguson family who had been in the area. Mr. Ferguson was born in 1878 in Grouard, the son of an employee of the Hudson's Bay Company. St. Pierre Ferguson was long associated with the area, and had many careers. These included a factor for the Hudson's Bay Company, cattle driver, census taker, farmer, forest ranger, freighter, interpreter, Justice of the Peace, and Municipal Councillor. He is also said to have owned the first pool hall in Grande Prairie. Mr. Ferguson died on January 1, 1972.

Fidler Point (point)
74 M/1 - Winnifred Lake
34-116-3-W4
59°06′N 110°25′W
Approximately 264 km north north-east of Fort McMurray.

Located on the north shore of Lake Athabasca, it was officially named in 1922 in honour of Peter Fidler, of the Hudson's Bay Company, a person who contributed much to the recorded history of Alberta. Fidler was born in England in 1769, and in 1796 he was appointed the chief surveyor and map maker for the Hudson's Bay Company. He established Nottingham House in 1802 to rival the efforts of the North West Company at nearby Fort Chipewyan. During his career, he surveyed and mapped much of western Canada. In 1822, he died in Fort Dauphin in what is now Manitoba. On Dr. Robert Bell's map of 1884, it is shown as Big Point.

Fifth Meridian (hamlet)
84 J/9 - Alberta
24-111-1-W5
58°38′N 114°00′W
Approximately 180 km east north-east of High Level.

This is a descriptive name as the hamlet is situated right on the 5th Meridian or 114 degrees longitude. Dominion Land Surveys of the 1870s and 1880s established six principal meridians; the Prime or 1st Meridian was near Winnipeg. The 4th meridian, 110 degrees, now forms the border between Alberta and Saskatchewan, and the 6th Meridian is 118 degrees longitude.

Fighting Creek (creek)
84 A/12 - Woodenhouse River
33-87-23-W4
56°35′00″N 113°35′20″W
Flows west into Wabasca River approxi-

mately 136 km west of Fort McMurray.

The origin of this name is found in the story of a fight between an old bachelor and an old woman that occurred by this creek. The old woman was the victor. After the fight the creek and nearby lake became known as Fighting Creek and Fighting Lake.

Fighting Lake (lake)
84 A/12 - Woodenhouse River
2-88-23-W4
56°35'45"N 113°33'08"W
Approximately 133 km west of Fort McMurray.

(see Fighting Creek)

Filion Creek (creek)
84 H/11 - Bergeron Creek
20-100-19-W4
57°42'N 113°05'W
Flows south into Birch River approximately 148 km north-west of Fort McMurray.

The precise origin of the name of this creek is unknown; it was referred to by F.V. Seibert, DLS, in 1914.

Fire Creek (creek)
84 L/12 - Fire Creek
9-112-10-W6
58°42'N 119°37'W
Flows north-west into Little Hay River approximately 25 km north north-west of Rainbow Lake.

The precise origin of the name of this creek is unknown.

Fire Point (point)
74 D/8 - Gipsy Lake
34-85-2-W4
56°25'N 110°13'W
On south shore of Gipsy Lake approximately 80 km east south-east of Fort McMurray.

The precise origin of the name of this point is unknown; it is probably an indication of a fire in the area.

Firebag River (river)
74 E/14 - Pearson Lake
11-101-9-W4
57°45'N 111°21'W
Flows north-west into Athabasca River approximately 114 km north of Fort McMurray.

It is not known why this river is named for the firebag. Amerindian ornamented hide bags have been associated with personal medicine powers or sacred smoking for centuries. By the 19th century a man might have one or more bags to carry tobacco, flint and steel for firemaking and, once the muzzle-loader was available, shot and shooting accessories. J.W. Sullivan, secretary on Palliser's expedition, refers to "the bag used by Indians and half-breeds for carrying their flints and steels, touchwood, smoking weed, etc., better known as *sac à commins*." By the end of the 19th century firebags were primarily used for dress occasions. It is possible to trace tribal and regional styles in the form and applied decoration of bags. 18th century geometric patterns in quill and paint gave way to elaborate floral bead designs during the 19th century. By the early nineteenth century two distinct types of firebags were preferred by the Subarctic Algonkians. The first was the panel bag, a pouch from which hung a rectangular panel, and the second, a tagged bag now called an octopus bag, because of the four pairs if tabs hanging at the bottom. These two firebag types were introduced across Canada during the nineteenth century, and regional variations developed as far as the northwest coast. It was the Cree and Cree-Métis styles that exerted the strongest influence on bag designs. The name was recorded as early as 1890 by the Geological Survey of Canada.

First Creek (creek)
74 E/12 - Asphalt Creek
3-100-10-W4
57°39'07"N 111°32'20"W
Flows north into Big Creek approximately 100 km north of Fort McMurray.

The precise origin of the name of this creek is unknown. The name has been used by several generations of trappers.

First Lake (lake)
74 E/14 - Pearson Lake
4-104-8-W4
58°00'00"N 111°16'10"W
Approximately 142 km north north-east of Fort McMurray.

Generations of trappers in this remote area call First Lake by this name because it is the first one on the line.

Fish Creek (creek)
83 M/6 - La Glace
16-2-73-8-W6
55°18'N 119°06'W
Flows east into Bear Creek approximately 24 km north-west of Grande Prairie.

Following World War II, because there was a number of Fish Creeks in Alberta already, it was decided to give this creek a war casualty name, Colquhoun Lake. This reflected naming policy of the time. Since 1974, the main principle guiding naming is that names must be in current local use. The locally well-established descriptive name of Fish Creek has been in use since 1879. Because of this, the name was officially changed back in 1991. George Dawson recorded the Beaver name for the creek as *Klo-[es]-sa-ka*. (see also Colquhoun Creek)

*****Fish Creek** (creek)
83 N/6 - Whitemud Creek
9-11-75-22-W5
55°29N 117°17'W
Flows north into Wabatanisk Creek

*denotes rescinded name or former locality.

approximately 50 km north of Valleyview.

This feature was the scene of a toponymic battle for a number of years. The Geographic Board of Canada favoured Fish Creek as the locally well-known name, but the Geographic Board of Alberta insisted it was better known as Clouston Creek. Unbeknownst to either jurisdiction, each recognised its favourite as the official name. Alberta was able to argue its point more effectively, and Fish Creek was officially rescinded in 1964. (see also Clouston Creek)

Fish Lake (lake)
84 D/11 - Worsley
13-89-10-W6
56°43'N 119°27'W
Approximately 100 km north-west of Fairview.

The precise origin of the name of this lake is unknown; it is probably descriptive.

Fish Lake (lake)
83 J/3 - Green Court
23-60-9-W5
54°12'N 115°15'W
Approximately 30 km east north-east of Whitecourt.

The name for this lake has been official since at least 1950 and is likely descriptive.

***Fish Lake** (lake)
84 J/14 - Margaret Lake
3-115-9-W5
58°57'N 115°25'W
Approximately 112 km east north-east of High Level.

(see Margaret Lake)

Fishing Creek (creek)
74 M/1 - Winnifred Lake
NW-21-117-2-W4

---

*denotes rescinded name or former locality.

59°10'N 110°17'W
Flows south-east into Lake Athabasca approximately 271 km north north-east of Fort McMurray.

It shows on federal government maps as early as 1930, and is descriptive.

Fitz Creek (creek)
84 J/9 - Alberta
34-111-1-W5
58°41'N 114°04'W
Flows south-east into Pakwanutik River approximately 179 km east north-east of High Level.

It appears on a provincial government map as early as 1930; the precise origin of the name of this creek is unknown. According to the Shorter Oxford English Dictionary, "fitz" is an Anglo-French word meaning "son." Later on, the prefix Fitz was used for illegitimate sons of princes and monarchs.

The Moth at [Fort] Fitzgerald, 1929

Fitzgerald (hamlet)
74 M/13 - Fitzgerald
14-125-10-W4
59°52'N 111°36'W
Approximately 339 km north of Fort McMurray.

The name was changed from Smith Landing in 1915, honouring Inspector Francis Joseph Fitzgerald (1867-1911), Royal North-West Mounted Police, who, with Constables Kenny and Taylor and ex-Constable Carter, perished on the Peel River in February, 1911, while on the McPherson-Dawson patrol. The party had left Fort McPherson in December, 1910, on the yearly patrol to Dawson City. When they had not arrived at their destination by mid-February, 1911, concern was aroused. A search was instituted. As they continued they found three camps in 15 miles indicating that Fitzgerald and his party must have been short of food and turned back to Fort McPherson. Thirty miles from Fort McPherson the bodies of Kenny and Taylor were found and 10 miles further on those of Fitzgerald and Carter. A diary found with the bodies told the story and later inquiries revealed that they had insufficient food and the guide had become lost. Full honours were given when they were buried at McPherson. Holmgren, 1976.

Fitzgerald Settlement (settlement)
74 M/14 - Tulip Lake
14-125-10-W4
59°51'N 111°36'W
Approximately 339 km north of Fort McMurray.

On the Slave River; the name was changed from Smith Landing Settlement in 1915. (see Fitzgerald)

Fitzsimmons (locality)
83 M/8 - Smoky Heights
22-73-3-W6
55°20'N 118°22'W
Approximately 30 km north-east of Grande Prairie.

Originally a school district established in 1930, it was named after a homesteader in the district, Scotty Fitzsimmons. The post office was established in 1933, with the first postmaster being C. Milner.

Flagon Lake (lake)
74 M/16 - Andrew Lake
NE-24-125-1-W4
59°53′N 110°00′W
Approximately 350 km north north-east of Fort McMurray on Alberta-Saskatchewan boundary.

The name was submitted in 1958 by the Research Council of Alberta, and is descriptive of its shape.

Flat Cabin Lake (lake)
74 E/15 - I.D. 18
6-103-6-W4
57°54′30″N 110°59′00″W
Approximately 134 km north north-east of Fort McMurray.

This remote lake appears to have got its name from the flat-roofed cabin built on the island by an old-timer in the area.

Flatgrass Lake (lake)
84 P/15 - Flatgrass Lake
NE-24-124-16-W4
59°47′N 112°37′W
Approximately 276 km east north-east of High Level.

Officially named in 1949; the name is descriptive.

Fleming Lake (lake)
84 J/14 - Margaret Lake
34-112-9-W5
58°46′N 115°26′W
Approximately 110 km east north-east of High Level.

It was named by J. R. Akins, DLS, during the 1914 survey after his chainman, Harold N. Fleming, of Grenfell, Saskatchewan. The local name for this lake is *Ehnikinoseh Sakahikun*, which is Cree for Jackfish Lake.

Fletcher Channel (channel)
74 L/10 - Big Point
10-29-111-6-W4
58°40′N 110°58′W
Flows north into Lake Athabasca approximately 207 km north of Fort McMurray.

It was named in 1917 after J.A. Fletcher, DLS.

Fletcher Lake (lake)
74 M/2 - Fletcher Lake
NW-32-116-5-W4
59°07′N 110°49′W
Approximately 260 km north of Fort McMurray.

Officially named in 1962 after J.A. Fletcher, DLS, who in 1916, surveyed the area and the 30th Baseline which runs through the lake.

Flett Lake (lake)
74 L/14 - Rivière des Rochers
33-114-7-W4
58°57′N 111°07′W
Approximately 239 km north of Fort McMurray.

This lake was named after one of the Flett family, well known in the district since the fur trade days. One of the earliest in the area was James Flett (1826-1899), who came from the Orkney Islands, Scotland. The Orkneymen, or Orcadians, were a cheap source of labour, who were often hired by the Hudson's Bay Company as labourers and boatmen. This practice was common in the late 18th and early 19th centuries.

Flood Lake (lake)
84 C/12 - Dixonville
36-86-25-W5
56°30′N 117°48′W
Approximately 36 km north north-west of Grimshaw.

The name was recorded as early as 1913 by G.A. Tipper, DLS, and it suggests a tendency of the lake to overflow.

Florence Creek (creek)
83 J/16 - Chisholm
17-69-3-W5
54°59′N 114°25′W
Flows east into Parker Creek approximately 36 km south south-east of Slave Lake.

Likely named in the 1930s or 1940s; after whom it is named is not known.

Florence Lake (lake)
74 M/8 - Wylie Lake
35-118-3-W4
59°17′N 110°23′W
Approximately 283 km north north-east of Fort McMurray.

It was named in 1929 for the daughter of John Wylie of Fort Chipewyan. (see also Wylie Lake and Winnifred Lake)

Florida Creek (creek)
83 O/2 - Florida Lake
11-13-72-5-W5
55°14′N 114°38′W
Flows north-east into Mitsue Lake approximately 10 km south-east of Slave Lake (town).

It was named some time between 1914 and 1922, but why the name was chosen is not known. *Florida* comes from the Spanish meaning "full of flowers."

Florida Lake (lake)
83 O/2 - Florida Lake
24-71-6-W5
55°10′N 114°47′W
Approximately 15 km south of Slave Lake (town).

(see Florida Creek)

Flowerpot Island (island)
74 D/9 - Bunting Bay
3-89-1-W4
56°41'42"N 110°03'38"W
In Clearwater River approximately 82 km east of Fort McMurray.

This small island received it name because of the colourful vegetation found there. The limestone has been eaten away by the river, which may account for the descriptive "pot."

Flyingshot Lake (lake)
83 M/2 - Grande Prairie
14-9-71-6-W6
55°08'N 118°52'W
Approximately 5 km south-west of Grande Prairie.

The name was established and in local use before 1907, when the first Dominion Land Surveyor came to the district, from the fact that ducks were shot during flight over the lake, which lies between two feeding grounds. According to the local history, an aboriginal people's name for the lake is *kanawaata-hiket*.

Flyingshot Lake Settlement (settlement)
83 M/2 - Grande Prairie
14-9-71-6-W6
55°08'N 118°52'W
Just to the south-west of Grande Prairie.

The first official survey of the settlement was completed in 1907. (see Flyingshot Lake)

Foley Lake (lake)
83 J/10 - Timeu Creek
14-65-6-W5
54°36'N 114°48'W
Approximately 38 km east south-east of Swan Hills.

---

*denotes rescinded name or former locality.

The name appears on provincial government maps as early as 1937; it is not known after whom the lake is named.

Fontas River (river)
84 E/13 - Foulwater Creek
13-103-13-W6
57°57'N 120°00'W
Flows north north-west into British Columbia approximately 75 km south south-west of Rainbow Lake.

The precise origin of the name of this river is unknown.

Footner Lake (lake)
84 K/11 - High Level
8-111-19-W5
58°37'N 117°11'W
Approximately 9 km north of High Level.

This small lake near the head of Meander River was named in 1922 for the writer Hulbert Footner (1879-1944). Footner, a native of Brantford, Ontario, and resident of Maryland, was the author of *New Rivers of the North* (1912), an account of travel through the Peace River Country in 1911. The details of his trip, both overland and in a small craft, the *Blunderbuss*, are also recorded in a number of photographs donated to the University of Alberta Archives. The range of Footner's writings included mysteries, novels, historical studies and biography. At the time of naming in 1922, it was known as Summit Lake. The lake is currently known locally as Loon Lake. It is also called this in the languages of the Cree, Beaver and Slavey. (see also Meander River)

Footner Lake (locality)
84 K/11 - High Level
5-111-19-W5
58°37'N 117°09'W
Approximately 11 km north of High Level.

(see Footner Lake)

Footner Settlement (settlement)
84 K/11 - Footner Lake
111-19-W5
58°37'N 117°12'W
Approximately 10 km north of High Level.

Established in 1968, it was named for the nearby features. (see Footner Lake)

***Forest View** (former locality)
83 N/1 - East Prairie
19-75-20-W5
55°31'N 117°6'W
Approximately 15 km east of Valleyview.

The post office was established here in 1931, the first postmaster being Marc Lambert. The name is descriptive.

Forks, The (confluent)
74 D/11 - Fort McMurray
29-89-9-W4
56°45'N 111°23'W
Confluence of Athabasca and Clearwater Rivers, at Fort McMurray.

This is a descriptive name for the confluence of two rivers, and the feature was known by this name at the time of the establishment of the North West Company's Fort of the Forks in 1790. The Hudson's Bay Company took over the site in 1821, and when it was rebuilt in 1870 it was called Fort McMurray.

Formby Lake (lake)
74 D/1 - Watchusk Lake
2-84-1-W4
56°15'N 110°02'W
Approximately 97 km south-east of Fort McMurray.

This lake on the Alberta-Saskatchewan boundary was named after a suburb of Liverpool, England, by H. Parry, DLS. Formby means "old farmstead" or "farmland of a man called Forni."

Fort Assiniboine (hamlet)
83 J/7 - Fort Assiniboine
1-62-6-W5
54°20'N 114°46'W
Approximately 58 km south-east of Swan Hills.

Located near the Athabasca River. The building of a Hudson's Bay Company post here in 1823 was referred to by John Work in his journal of 24 September 1823: 'About noon arrived at a new house which Mr. McDonald, the gentleman who is superintending the building, calls Fort Assiniboyne. It is situated on the north bank. This is the house that was to have been built at McLeod branch.' It was the northern point on the portage from Fort Edmonton to the Athabasca River en route to Fort Vancouver via Athabasca Pass and Boat Encampment and was in operation the year round, at least in 1827. In 1859 Dr. Hector, of the Palliser Expedition, stated that 'the place consisted of a few ruinous huts on the left bank of the river but it was not then in use the year round.' Holmgren, 1976. The post was likely named after the aboriginal group who were named by the Ojibwa. The name refers to their method of cooking whereby they boiled their food by placing heated rocks into water. At one time their territory was a vast one, ranging from north of the Missouri and Milk rivers in the U.S. to the Assiniboine and Saskatchewan rivers in what is now Canada. Their language is Siouan in origin. A post office was established here in 1913; the first postmaster was J. Walsh.

At one time it was known to the Cree as *Sagawas-kahagnis*, meaning "house in the timber," an old name for the Hudson's Bay Company post at this site.

Fort Chipewyan (hamlet)
74 L/11 - Fort Chipewyan
NW-8-112-7-W4
58°43'N 111°09'W

Fort Chipewyan on Athabasca Lake, 1901

Approximately 213 km north of Fort McMurray.

This North West Company trading post was established on Lake Athabasca in 1788 and was named for the people in the area. The original site for Fort Chipewyan was established on the south side of the lake at Old Fort Point by Roderick Mackenzie at Township 111, Range 3, West of the 4th Meridian. The move in 1804 was most likely the result of a number of factors, including stiff competition from the other fur companies; the Hudson's Bay Company and the XY Company had moved into the area. With the move of the fort north, the North West Company was in a better position to trade with the Chipewyans. Fort Chipewyan is considered to be the first white settlement in what is now Alberta. So important was it to the fur trade, some say second only to Fort William on Lake Superior, that it became known as the "Emporium of the North." A post office opened there in 1912, and the community continues to have an important role in north-eastern Alberta. Other older aboriginal names for this community have been *yatheekwen* in Chipewyan, and *yatseekwen* in Slavey, both of which mean "priest house" (referring to the old Roman Catholic mission there). The name *kaitekum* has also been recorded. It is from the Dogrib language, meaning "willow ground", and is likely descriptive. (see also Old Fort Point)

Fort Creek (creek)
74 E/5 - Bitumount
12-97-11-W4
57°24'30"N 111°38'30"W
Flows north-west into Athabasca River approximately 89 km north north-west of Fort McMurray.

This creek is so named because both the Hudson's Bay Company and the North West Company had trading posts in the vicinity, Berens House and Pierre au Calumet, respectively.

Fort Hills (hills)
74 E/5 - Bitumount
4-97-10-W4
57°23'N 111°34'W
Approximately 75 km north north-west of Fort McMurray.

(see Fort Creek)

Fort MacKay, 1930s

Fort MacKay (hamlet)
74 E/4 - Fort MacKay
25-94-11-W4
57°11'N 111°37'W
Approximately 57 km north north-west of Fort McMurray.

Dr. MacKay and family inside Fort Chipewyan, 1903

Fort MacKay is named for Dr. William Morrison MacKay (1836-1917), of Cambusbarron, Scotland, who came to Canada as a surgeon with the Hudson's Bay Company in 1864. MacKay's practice comprised the entire Canadian Northwest and the Arctic. With the assistance of his wife, Jane Flett of Fort Simpson, he was called in to deal with emergencies throughout this vast area. Simultaneously, MacKay pursued a distinguished career as a fur trader, advancing through the ranks of the HBC, eventually serving as chief trader and factor at Fort Rae, Fort Resolution, Fort Simpson, Dunvegan and Fort Chipewyan. When he retired from the company in 1898 MacKay set up a medical practice in Edmonton, where he helped found the Northern Alberta Medical Association in 1902. MacKay is commemorated in MacKay Avenue and School in Edmonton as well as some of the lakes and rivers of the north. Fort MacKay was known as Red River House until circa 1870, and the nearby Red River was renamed MacKay River in 1912.

Fort MacKay Indian Reserve No. 174
(Indian reserve)
74 E/4 - Fort MacKay
24-94-11-W4
57°10′N 111°37′W
Approximately 56 km north north-west of Fort McMurray.

Named for its proximity to Fort MacKay, the reserve land was allocated under Treaty No. 8. (see Fort MacKay)

Fort MacKay Settlement (settlement)
74 E/4 - Fort MacKay
25-94-11-W4
57°11′N 111°38′W
Approximately 51 km north north-west of Fort McMurray.

First surveyed in 1912, it was named for its proximity to Fort MacKay. (see Fort MacKay)

Fort McMurray (city)
74 D/11 - Fort McMurray
21-89-9-W4
56°44′N 111°23′W
Approximately 378 km north-east of Edmonton.

The city of Fort McMurray takes its name from a Hudson's Bay Company fur trade post established by Factor H. J. Moberly in 1870. The post was built near the confluence of the Athabasca and Clearwater rivers on the site of the old North West Company's Fort of the Forks, which had operated from 1780s until after the amalgamation of the two fur trade companies in 1821. Moberly named the post after his superior Inspecting Chief Factor William McMurray.

Modern Fort McMurray is a combination of the town of Fort McMurray which developed on the site of the post and a separate locality that developed at the mouth of the Hangingstone River about three kilometres south-east, called Waterways. Waterways owed its existence to the Alberta and Great Waterways Railway. Waterways was originally located at the head of navigation of the Athabasca River, on the Clearwater River about 10 kilometres from its mouth, and is now known as Draper. In 1922, the railway was completed from Edmonton to Waterways. In 1925, the terminus was re-established six kilometres farther north, where Waterways became permanently situated. The railhead was established at Waterways, rather than Fort McMurray because the ground surfaces flanking the river lay higher, and were therefore less susceptible to floods and ice jams. The area it occupied is now within the city of Fort McMurray. Fort McMurray developed during the 1920s due to exploration and experimentation with oil recovery from the tar sands. A salt-extraction industry and several fish plants developed in the area. During World War II the town gained importance as a base for the Canol project. In 1964 the modern growth of Fort McMurray began with the development of the Great Canadian Oil Sands project.

Fort Smith Settlement (settlement)
74 M/13 - Fitzgerald
NE-33-126-11-W4
59°59′N 111°50′W
Approximately 354 km north of Fort McMurray on the Alberta-Northwest Territories boundary.

(see Smith Landing)

Fort Vermilion (hamlet)
84 K/8 - Fort Vermilion
24-108-13-W5
58°24′N 116°00′W
Approximately 67 km east south-east of High Level.

(see Fort Vermilion Settlement)

Fort Vermilion Settlement (settlement)
84 J/5 - Sled Island
18-108-12-W5
58°23′N 116°00′W
Approximately 67 km east south-east of High Level.

Fort Vermilion, established in 1788, was the principal post of the North West Company on the Peace River between Fort Chipewyan and Fort Dunvegan. In 1821 Fort Vermilion was taken over by the Hudson's Bay Company. Then, some time before 1831, the post was moved to the site of the present town of Fort Vermilion. The name Vermilion is traditionally said to come from the red ochre deposits in the area. The settlement was first surveyed in 1898.

Foster Creek (creek)
73 M/8 - Winefred Lake
14-12-73-1-W4
55°19′N 110°01′W
Flows east into Saskatchewan approximately 90 km north of Cold Lake.

The name for this creek appears as early as 1913 on a federal government map. After whom it is named is not known.

Foster Lake (lake)
83 O/13 - Atikameg
29-78-13-W5
55°47′N 115°59′W
Approximately 95 km north-west of Slave Lake.

The earliest reference found to this name was in 1922. After whom it is named is not known.

Foulwater Creek (creek)
84 E/13 - Foulwater Creek
23-103-13-W6
57°56′N 120°00′W
Flows north-west into British Columbia approximately 75 km south south-west of Rainbow Lake.

Named by an Alberta-British Columbia Boundary Commission survey party as a result of illness attributed to impurities in the water. The initial suggestion of the name Poison Creek was passed over in favour of Foul Creek, which was finalised in 1951 as Foulwater Creek.

Four Forks Lake (lake)
74 L/12 - Hilda Lake
24-112-10-W4
58°45′N 111°32′W
Approximately 215 km north of Fort McMurray.

Named for its proximity to the Chenal des Quatre Fourches, the name was officially adopted in the 1960s. (see also Quatre Fourches, Chenal des)

Fourth Creek (creek)
84 D/2 - Hines Creek
30-81-6-W6
56°03′N 118°56′W
Flows east into Peace River approximately 33 km east of Fairview.

The precise origin of the name of this creek is unknown; it is likely one of a series of creeks recorded by surveyors, who gave them numbers in order to differentiate one from the other. It was only this one whose name survived.

Fowel Lake (lake)
83 M/4 - Rio Grande
32-71-11-W6
55°12′N 119°39′W
Approximately 52 km west of Grande Prairie.

In 1951 there is a reference to a new name to be added to the map, Ted Fowel Lake. Because of the policy in place at that time not to use compound names, the lake was labelled on the map as Fowel Lake. Although there is no origin information available, it may be some relation to an early trustee of the Hayfield school, Fred Fowl(sic), who is mentioned in the Beaverlodge local history.

Fox Creek (creek)
83 M/16 - Codesa
30-79-1-W6
55°51N 118°09′W
Flows west into Saddle (Burnt) River approximately 65 km south-west of Peace River.

The name was mentioned as early as 1901 in the field notes of the Dominion Land Surveyor working in the area. It is descriptive of the animal found in the area. The name of the creek is noted as Fox Brook on a 1928 federal government map.

Fox Creek (town)
83 K/7 - Iosegun Lake
29-62-19-W5
54°24′N 116°48′W
Approximately 75 km west north-west of Whitecourt.

Officially named in 1967, it took its name from the creek, and took over the nearby hamlet and post office of Iosegun Lake. It was incorporated as a town in 1983. (see also Fox Creek and Iosegun Lake)

Fox Lake (hamlet)
84 J/7 - Vermilion Chutes
14-109-4-W5
58°28′N 114°31′W
Approximately 150 km east of High Level.

This hamlet takes its name from the Indian reserve on which it is situated. The post office was established in 1962, and D. Stevens was the first postmaster.

Fox Lake (lake)
84 J/7 - Vermilion Chutes
3-108-3-W5
58°26′N 114°24′W
Approximately 157 km east south-east of High Level.

The precise origin of the name of this lake is unknown. Some confusion exists as to the exact location of Fox Lake. It is locally held that the real Fox Lake is located in portions of sections 9,10, 16, 17 and 18 of the same township, range and meridian, and is now dried up. However, a 1914 sectional map has Fox Lake annotated in its present position, so if the position of the lake is incorrect, it has been so for over 80 years. Local residents call this lake *Maskiko Sakahikun* meaning Muskeg Lake

Fox Lake Indian Reserve No. 162
(Indian reserve)
84 J/7 - Vermilion Chutes
36-109-4-W5
58°29′N 114°31′W
Approximately 145 km east south-east of High Level.

Named for its proximity to Fox Lake, this reserve is home to the Little Red River Cree Nation, the members of which have ancestral ties to the Woodland and Bigstone Cree at Wabasca. The chief entered into Treaty No. 8 on behalf of his people in 1899. This land was apportioned to the band in 1909 and 1910.

Frakes Flat (flat)
83 K/13 - Long Lake
E-23-68-26-W5
54°54′N 117°51′W
Approximately 70 km south-east of Grande Prairie.

This flat is named for Bob Frakes and his family, who settled on this section of the Simonette River in 1932. Bob Frakes, a respected cowboy, was born in New Mexico in 1889 and came to Alberta in 1902. In 1928 he married Neoma Lambert. Bob continued to live on the Simonette River until his death in 1969. The name was officially approved in 1991 after field research determined the name to be well known and in local use.

Frank Lake (lake)
83 N/15 - Springburn
SE-4-80-19-W5
55°54′N 116°54′W
Approximately 20 km north of McLennan.

The name appears as early as 1914 when the Dominion Land Surveyors were in the area. It is not known after whom the lake is named.

Fraser Bay (bay)
74 L/11 - Fort Chipewyan
NE-16-112-7-W4
58°44′N 111°06′W
Approximately 213 km north of Fort McMurray.

This feature shows on the early maps as Fraser Lake, and is likely named after Colin Fraser, renowned as bagpiper of Sir George Simpson of the Hudson's Bay Company.

Freeman Creek (creek)
83 J/11 - Swan Hills
26-64-10-W5
54°34′N 115°25′W
Flows south-east into Freeman River approximately 5 km south-west of Swan Hills.

According to one version, the river was named first (the other features were named later) for Freeman Dodge, who first came to the Peace River Country in 1900. He was guiding an Indian agent and doctor. When they were crossing the river in the Swan Hills, a packhorse stumbled and fell and would have drowned had not "Free," as he was known, jumped in and held its head up until it was unloaded and could get up. As a result of this experience the doctor suggested naming the river Freeman. When the Dominion Land Surveyors were in the area in the mid-teens they recorded the name of the creek, river and lake as "Freemen," which leads to another and more likely explanation of the origin of the name. It referred to those former employees of fur companies who elected to remain in the interior as free hunters or free trappers. They were also referred to as free fur-traders or free traders. It may be the area was being trapped by these freemen.

Freeman Indian Reserve No. 150B
(Indian reserve)
83 N/9 - Grouard
31-75-14-W5
55°33′N 116°09′W
Approximately 25 km east north-east of High Prairie.

This reserve was established in 1905, and took its name from the prominent family on the reserve, who belonged to the band of Chief Kinoosayo. The Freeman Indian Band is one of the five Cree bands who live around Driftpile and Lesser Slave Lake. Lands were allocated to these bands under Treaty No. 8.

Freeman Lake (lake)
83 J/12 - Swartz Lake
11-66-11-W5
54°42′N 115°32′W m
Approximately 7 km west south-west of Swan Hills.

(see Freeman Creek)

Freeman River (locality)
83 J/7 - Fort Assiniboine
34-62-6-W5
54°24′N 114°49′W
Approximately 40 km north-west of Barrhead.

Established as a post office in September 1912, it took its name from the nearby features. The first postmaster was D. C. Thompson. (see Freeman Creek)

Freeman River (river)
83 J/7 - Fort Assiniboine
35-61-6-W5
54°19′N 114°47′W
Flows south-east into Athabasca River approximately 32 km north-west of Barrhead.

In 1906, Mr. Driscoll, DLS, stated it was known locally as Sa-kwa-ta-mau River, which apparently translates from the Cree as "large sparrow hawk" or "caribou eating bird." (see Freeman Creek and Freeman River)

French Lake (lake)
84 I/10 - French Lake
13-111-17-W4
58°38′N 112°43′W
Approximately 217 km north north-west of Fort McMurray.

The name for this lake was officially approved in 1963. It commemorates a trapper known as "Frenchy" whose cabin was beside by the lake.

Frezie Lake (lake)
74 L/7 - Keane Creek
32-108-6-W4
58°26′N 110°57′W
Approximately 182 km north of Fort McMurray.

It was named after Joseph Frezie, an axeman in the J.R. Akins survey team in the area in 1917.

Friedenstal (locality)
84 D/1 - Fairview
25-81-3-W6
56°03′N 118°20′W
Approximately 4 km south-east of Fairview.

A German Catholic colony was founded here by Peter S. Gans and Lewis Flath in 1910. It was first known as Westphalia, and was then renamed St. Louis in 1911. When a post office was established in 1913, the name Friedenstal was chosen, after Friedensthal, the original home of Peter in Romania. The name is said to mean valley of peace and likely refers to its proximity to the Peace River.

Friock Creek (creek)
84 E/8 - Botha river
1-97-1-W6
57°23′30″N 118°00′15″W
Flows west into Botha River approximately 57 km north north-west of Manning.

W. Friock was an axeman on the crew of H.S. Day, DLS, working in the area in 1913.

Frog Creek (creek)
74 L/5 - Welstead Lake
1-19-108-11-W4
58°23′N 111°49′W
Flows north-west into Lake Claire approximately 176 km north of Fort McMurray.

Officially adopted in the 1970s, the name is likely descriptive of the prevalence of the amphibian in the area.

Frog Lake (lake)
83 K/14 - Asplund Creek
S-10-67-21-W5
54°47′00″N 117°06′50″W
Approximately 120 km south-east of Grande Prairie.

Officially named in 1991, it was given this name by the early aboriginal people in the area and describes the number of frogs in and around the lake.

Funell Lake (lake)
83 M/4 - Rio Grande
2-33-71-11-W6
55°11′N 119°37′W
Approximately 15 km south-west of Beaverlodge.

This lake was officially named in the early 1950s, and although the spelling is slightly different, it may be named after the Funnell family who settled in the vicinity in June 1912. The family came from England, and one of the sons homesteaded in the Nokomis area of Saskatchewan before persuading the rest of his family to move with him to the Beaverlodge area.

Furlough Island (island)
74 E/11 - Firebag River
32-99-9-W4
57°38′N 111°26′W
Approximately 100 km north north-west of Fort McMurray.

Named after Fred Furlough, a well known trapper in the Athabasca district. S.C. Ells named this feature in 1924. A furlough is a leave of absence usually given to armed services personnel. (see also Ells River)

Gage (locality)
84 D/2 - Hines Creek
26-82-4-W6
56°08′N 118°30′W
Approximately 10 km north-west of Fairview.

After a locomotive engineer named Gage, formerly of the Edmonton, Dunvegan and British Columbia Railway; originally Gage Siding, the name was changed to Gage in December 1933. The post office opened in December 1931.

Galoot Lake (lake)
74 L/11 - Fort Chipewyan
28-110-7-W4
58°35′N 111°07′W
Approximately 195 km north of Fort McMurray.

A galoot is a variant name for a Ross's goose (*Chen rosii*), a small white goose that breeds in the far north. It is sometimes referred to as "silly galoot" because of its lack of fear. Galoot is a 19th-century nautical term for a strange or clumsy person.

Gambling Point (point)
84 I/11 - Stovel Lake
SW-12-112-21-W4
58°43′N 113°26′W
Approximately 214 km east of High Level.

Father Vantroys, of the Oblates of Mary Immaculate, provided some information in 1963 on this point on the Peace River. According to him, it was a place where, fifty years earlier or more, the local aboriginal people would gather periodically to gamble.

Garden Creek (creek)
84 I/12 - Buchanan Lake
1-7-112-23-W4
58°42′N 113°52′W
Flows south into Peace River approximately 187 km east of High Level.

Officially approved in 1963, the name may refer to the creek's proximity to Pakwanutik River, which was referred to as Garden River by the Dominion Land Surveyors in 1910. It is an area where cow parsnip was harvested and used as a food source by the local aboriginal people. (see also Pakwanutik River)

Garden Creek (locality)
84 I/12 - Buchanan Lake
13-6-112-23-W4
58°42′N 113°53′W
Approximately 187 km east of High Level.

Officially approved in 1963, the locality was named for the nearby creek. (see Garden Creek)

*Garden River (river)
84 I/12 - Buchanan Lake
10-1-112-24-W4
58°42′N 113°54′W
Flows east into Peace River approximately 184 km east of High Level.

Garden River was the name recorded by the surveyors in 1910. (see Pakwanutik River)

---

*denotes rescinded name or former locality.

Gardiner Lakes (lakes)
84 H/7 - Legend Lake
9-98-16-W4
57°29′N 112°32′W
Approximately 118 km north-west of Fort McMurray.

The precise origin of the name of these trophy fishing lakes is unknown; the name shows on a federal government map of 1916. The two lakes are each known locally by different names, the upper lake as Moose Lake and the lower lake as Willow Lake.

Garfield Lake (lake)
84 C/5 - Chinook Valley
23-85-23-W5
56°23′N 117°31′W
Approximately 22 km north-west of Grimshaw.

The precise origin for the name of this lake is unknown; it is mentioned in the 1913 field notes of G.A. Tipper, DLS.

Garson Lake (lake)
74 D/8 - Gipsy Lake
26-84-1-W4
56°19′N 110°02′W
On the Alberta-Saskatchewan border approximately 92 km east south-east of Fort McMurray.

The name for this lake was changed from "Whitefish Lake" in 1910 to commemorate C.N. Garson, manager of the Hudson's Bay Company post at Onion Lake, Saskatchewan. Peter Fidler referred to this body of water as Swan Lake.

Geikie Lake (lake)
74 M/16 - Andrew Lake
SW-36-125-2-W4
59°54′N 110°12′W
Approximately 351 km north of Fort McMurray.

The name was submitted in 1958 by the Research Council of Alberta, and is one of a series of features in the area named after prominent geologists. It is named "after Sir Archibald Geikie (1835-1924), eminent Scottish geologist, [and] one-time Director of the British Geological Survey." Holmgren, 1976.

George Lake (lake)
84 D/2 - Hines Creek
28-83-4-W6
56°13′N 118°34′W
Approximately 19 km north north-west of Fairview.

The precise origin of the long established name of this lake is unknown. The field notes of G.A. Tipper, DLS, in 1912 describing Township 83, Range 4, West of the 6th Meridian noted "The surface is generally rolling, except in Sections 27, 28 and 29 where Lake George (sometimes called Island Lake) is located, surrounded by hay meadows."

*Georges Creek (creek)
74 D/7 - Cheecham
18-84-5-W4
56°17′00″N 110°46′20″W
Flows north north-west into Gregoire River approximately 62 km south-east of Fort McMurray.

(see Cheecham Creek)

*Georges Lake (lake)
74 D/7 - Cheecham
18-84-5-W4
56°17′N 110°47′W
Approximately 60 km south-east of Fort McMurray.

(see Cheecham Lake)

Gerard Creek (creek)
84 E/8 - Botha River
12-98-1-W6
57°23′N 118°02′W

Flows south into Botha River approximately 57 km north north-west of Manning.

The feature appears named on a federal government map of 1916, and is likely named after a member of the 1915 survey crew of J.R. Akins, DLS, working in the area.

Gerry Lake (lake)
84 D/8 - Deer Hill
20-84-2-W6
56°18'N 118°16'W
Approximately 24 km north north-east of Fairview.

After Pilot Officer R.T. Gerry, who was presumed killed in action in 1940. The 23-year-old Alberta flier was among 47 Canadians who died in the Battle of Britain and were honoured by King George VI in a ceremony at Westminster Abbey in July 1947.

Gift Lake (hamlet)
83 O/13 - Atikameg
28-79-12-W5
55°53'N 115°49'W
Approximately 90km north west of Slave Lake.

The locality name was adopted in 1964, and the post office opened in 1968. Both took their name from the nearby lake. The first postmaster was Mme Alice A. Martineau. (see Gift Lake)

Gift Lake (lake)
83 O/13 - Atikameg
32-79-12-W5
55°53'N 115°51'W
Approximately 95 km north-west of Slave Lake (town).

The name commemorates a local aboriginal tradition of meeting in the locale for feasting and gift exchanging. The Cree name was *Ma-chad-cho-wi-se*, which has been translated to mean "where gifts are exchanged."

Gift Lake Metis Settlement
(Metis settlement)
83 N/16 - Pentland Lake
33-79-12-W5
50°50'N 116°00'W
Approximately 55 km north-east of High Prairie.

The Metis Settlement was established by government statute in 1990. Part of it was formed from the old Utikuma Lake Metis Colony No. 3 established by order-in-council in 1938. It takes its name from the nearby lake. (see Gift Lake)

Entrance to Gift Lake Metis Colony (now Settlement), 1974

Gilmore Lake (lake)
83 N/6 - Whitemud Creek
SW-2-73-22-W5
55°18'N 117°17'W
Approximately 25 km north of Valleyview.

Named for the Sophie and Stanley Gilmore family who homesteaded in the area in 1935. The Gilmore family was one of the first white families to settle in the New Fish Creek area. The family moved to High Prairie in 1944.

Gilwood (locality)
83 N/7 - Triangle
SE-6-74-17-W5
55°23'N 116°36'W
Approximately 10 km south-west of High Prairie.

The post office was established here in January 1931. The first postmaster was O.O. Blackwood. Why it was called Gilwood is not known; it might have been a combination of Mr. Blackwood's last name and something or someone else.

Gipsy Creek (creek)
74 D/9 - Bunting Bay
2-87-3-W4
56°31'N 110°22'W
Flows west north-west into Gordon Lake approximately 67 km east south-east of Fort McMurray.

The precise origin of the name of this creek is unknown. It is some distance north of Gipsy Lake. The source of this creek is Shortt Lake.

Gipsy Lake (lake)
74 D/8 - Gipsy Lake
34-85-2-W4
56°25'N 110°14'W
Approximately 76 km east south-east of Fort McMurray.

The precise origin of the name of this lake is unknown. The name Gipsy Lake was recorded as early as 1910 by J.N. Wallace, DLS. For a period of time this feature was known as Jackfish Lake, but the earlier name was officially adopted in 1955.

Giroux Bay (bay)
83 O/5 - Driftpile
73-11-W5
55°21'N 115°36'W
Approximately 55 km west of Slave Lake.

It was referred to as early as 1892 by the Geological Survey of Canada, possibly after early settlers in the area.

Giroux Lake (lake)
83 K/10 - Atikkamek Creek
9-65-20-W5
54°37'N 116°58'W
Approximately 24 km north-west of Fox Creek.

The name appears on federal government maps as early as 1917. It may have been named after someone in the Giroux family, pioneers in the Peace River Country. Because the lake is just three kilometres north of the 17th Baseline, it was likely named after a survey crew member.

Girouxville (village)
83 N/14 - Lac Magloire
16-78-22-W5
55°45'N 117°20'W
Approximately 9 km west of Falher.

Originally known as Fowler, which was a railway siding of the Edmonton, Dunvegan and British Columbia Railway, the name was changed in 1915 to honour the Giroux family, pioneer settlers in the area. The post office was established in June 1917, with Donat Viens as the first postmaster. The area has been known to the Cree as *umstosee owuskee*, a term that may translate as "Frenchman's Land."

*Glass Lake (lake)
83 M/6 - La Glace
3-74-10-W6
55°23'N 119°27'W

---
*denotes rescinded name or former locality.

Approximately 45 km west north-west of Grande Prairie.

The name is possibly descriptive. It was renamed Valhalla some time after 1917 possibly to avoid confusion with nearby La Glace Lake. (see Valhalla Lake)

Glen Leslie (locality)
83 M/1 - DeBolt
4-1-72-4-W6
55°12'N 118°29'W
Approximately 20 km east north-east of Grande Prairie.

Originally established as a post office, it was probably named after the Thomas Leslie family who arrived in the district in 1912 to homestead. Thomas and Margaret Leslie married in 1887, and settled on a farm in Roslin, Ontario. It wasn't until their son Edward came west that they decided to start a new life. Glen is from the Gaelic meaning narrow valley. The first post office opened on July 1, 1914. The postmaster was Thomas Leslie.

Glover Lake (lake)
73 M/6 - Wiau Lake
2-15-75-9-W4
55°30'N 111°18'W
Approximately 90 km north north-east of Lac La Biche.

It was named after the Dominion Land Surveyor A.E. Glover, working in the area in 1918. It is known locally by another name. (see also Birch Lake)

Godin Lake (lake)
84 B/1 - Pastecho River
11-82-1-W4
56°07'N 114°03'W
Approximately 100 km north north-east of Slave Lake.

It appears on maps as early as 1944. After whom it is named is not known.

Gods Lake (lake)
84 B/16 - Goosegrass Lake
20-90-2-W5
56°49'N 114°17'W
Approximately 171 km north north-east of Slave lake.

The name Gods Lake was proposed for this designated trophy lake, which requires a special licence to fish there. The origin is not known.

Goffit Creek (creek)
84 F/5 - Goffit Creek
29-95-23-W5
57°16'N 117°42'W
Flows south into Meikle River approximately 39 km north of Manning.

The precise origin of the name of this creek is unknown; it appears on maps as early as 1930.

Gold Creek (creek)
83 L/15 - Big Mountain Creek
12-31-67-5-W6
54°51'30"N 118°44'30"W
Flows north into Big Mountain Creek approximately 32 km south of Grande Prairie.

Gold Creek was named some time before the 1960s because of the yellow colour on the bottom of the creek. Except for local legend, there is no evidence that the colour is a result of real gold.

Golden Creek (creek)
83 N/2 - Snipe Lake
12-14-71-17-W5
55°09'N 116°31'W
Flows north into McGowan Creek approximately 50 km east north-east of Valleyview.

Golden Creek may have been named for the reflection in the water of poplar trees in their autumn colours. The name was approved in 1952 after field research in the area found the name well established and in local use.

Golden Lake (lake)
84 C/9 - Golden Lake
30-87-15-W5
56°33′N 116°23′W
Approximately 65 km north-west of Peace river.

It shows on a 1915 federal government map as Good Lake, but by 1930, it was appearing as Golden Lake. The origin is not known.

*Goldschidt Lake (lake)
74 M/16 - Andrew Lake
NE-36-125-1-W4
59°55′N 110°01′W
Approximately 353 km north north-east of Fort McMurray.

(see Inkster Lake)

Goldschmidt Lake (lake)
74 M/15 - Mercredi Lake
NW-26-125-5-W4
59°54′N 110°45′W
Approximately 345 km north of Fort McMurray.

The name was submitted in 1958 by the Research Council of Alberta, and is one of a series of features in the area named after deceased prominent geologists.

Goldsmith Creek (creek)
83 J/13 - Wallace Mountain
9-68-12-W5
54°54′N 115°47′W
Flows north-west into Driftpile River approximately 31 km north-west of Swan Hills.

It wa officially named in 1906 after Sandy Goldsmith of Edmonton, a member of a survey party.

*denotes rescinded name or former locality.

Goodfare (locality)
83 M/5 - Hythe
4-25-72-12-W6
55°16′N 119°43′W
Approximately 55 km west of Grande Prairie.

Established as a post office in April 1919, after the residents petitioned for postal service, the name Goodfair was chosen, being descriptive of the area, the name was changed to the current spelling since there was already a Goodfair post office in Saskatchewan. John Third was the first postmaster. The area was originally known as Kempton.

Goodfish Lake (lake)
84 B/10 - Peerless Lake
9-89-5-W5
56°42′N 114°44′W
Approximately 156 km north of Slave Lake.

It is recorded on federal government maps as early as 1905, and is descriptive.

Goodwin (locality)
83 M/1 - DeBolt
4-12-72-2-W6
55°13′N 118°11′W
Approximately 40 km east north-east of Grande Prairie.

Originally established as a post office in 1923, it took its name from an earlier time. The Goodwin brothers, who were ranchers in the area, had a camp where the Edson-Grande Prairie Trail crossed the Simonette River. It was known as Goodwin's Crossing.

Goodwin Lake (lake)
73 M/5 - Behan Lake
20-74-11-W4
55°26′N 111°39′W
Approximately 75 km North of Lac La Biche.

Possibly named after Frank Goodwin, the chief packer on the 1912 party surveying the 19th Baseline 15 kilometres south of the lake.

Goose Creek (creek)
83 N/4 - Sturgeon Heights
15-13-70-24-W5
55°04′N 117°31′N
Flows north into Sturgeon Lake approximately 80 km east of Grande Prairie.

Officially named in 1952 after field research was conducted in the area. It likely refers to the abundance of the birds in the area.

Goose Creek (creek)
83 J/7 - Fort Assiniboine
32-61-6-W5
54°19′N 114°52′W
Flows east into Athabasca River approximately 37 km north-west of Barrhead.

It shows on federal government maps as early as 1917, and is likely descriptive of the abundance of the birds in the area.

*Goose Creek (creek)
83 M/5 - Hythe
10-7-75-12-W6
55°29′00″N 120°00′50″W
Flows west into British Columbia.

The name, likely descriptive, was changed to Albright Creek. (see Albright Creek)

Goose Island (island)
74 L/10 - Big Point
23-111-6-W4
58°39′N 110°54′W
Approximately 208 km north of Fort McMurray in Lake Athabasca.

This island north of the Peace-Athabasca Delta was at one time a favourite spot for hunting geese in the autumn. Philip Turnor noted in his journal for July 2, 1791, that he and a companion went across "to an island called the Goose Island."

Goose Island Channel (channel)
74 L/10 - Big Point
16-17-111-5-W4
58°38′N 110°48′W
Flows north into Lake Athabasca approximately 207 km north of Fort McMurray.

Officially named in the 1940s, it takes its name from the adjacent island. (see Goose Island)

Goose Lake (lake)
83 J/6 - Christmas Creek
33-61-8-W5
54°20′N 115°08′W
Approximately 39 km north-east of Whitecourt.

It shows on federal government maps as early as 1917, and is likely descriptive of the abundance of the birds in the area. It is the source of Goose Creek.

Goose Lake (lake)
83 K/13 - Long Lake
14-69-24-W5
54°59′N 117°33′W
Approximately 83 km east south-east of Grande Prairie.

The name appears on provincial government maps as early as 1937 and was in use long before that. It is descriptive of the bird found at the lake.

***Goose Lake** (lake)
83 M/5 - Hythe
NE-8-75-12-W6
55°29′30″N 119°49′30″W
Approximately 71 km north-west of Grande Prairie.

The name, likely descriptive, was changed to Albright Lake before the 1930s. (see Albright Lake)

_____
*denotes rescinded name or former locality.

Goose River (river)
83 K/14 - Asplund Creek
7-69-21-W5
54°58′N 117°11′W
Flows north-west into Little Smoky River approximately 12 km south-east of Valleyview.

Origin of the name Goose River is probably related to the large number of geese in the area. The name appears on a federal government map dated 1917.

Goosegrass Lake (lake)
84 B/16 - Goosegrass Lake
9-91-3-W5
56°52′N 114°24′W
Approximately 176 km north of Slave Lake.

Officially named some time after the 1930s, it is likely descriptive of the abundance of "any of several herbs supposedly eaten by geese, especially silverweed, _Polygonum aviculare_, and horsetail, _Equisetum_." _Dictionary of Canadianisms_. Both of these are found in Alberta. (see also Equisetum Lake)

Gordon Creek (creek)
74 D/16 - High Hill River
27-90-1-W4
56°50′N 110°03′W
Flows south into Sutton Creek approximately 83 km east of Fort McMurray.

In correspondence with the Geographic Board of Canada, J.N. Wallace, DLS, said he named the feature after Gordon Sutton, a survey party member.

Gordon Lake (lake)
74 D/8 - Gipsy Lake
33-86-3-W4
56°30′N 110°25′W
Approximately 55 km east south-east of Fort McMurray.

Named after William Gordon, a Scot who came first to Athabasca with his sister, Christine, in 1900. At Athabasca they operated a restaurant, while William also worked as a free trader. In 1905 William moved the base of his fur trading operations to Fort McMurray, where he and Christine operated a trading post and post office for many years. The pair became well known in the district and several other geographical features were named for one or other or both of them. Gordon Lake was known as Swan Lake before it was officially named for Gordon. The name Swan Lake is apparently still in use among some in the area. (see also Christina River, Gordon River, Gordon Creek)

Gordon River (river)
74 D/7 - Cheecham
17-85-4-W4
56°22′N 110°35′W
Flows south south-west from Gordon Lake into Christina River approximately 63 km south of Fort McMurray.

(see Gordon Lake)

Gordondale (locality)
83 M/13 - Bonanza
SW-17-79-10-W6
55°50′N 119°33′W
Approximately 40 km west of Spirit River.

The Gordondale post office opened in December 1930. The first postmaster was F. G. Stewart. According to the local history for the area it was named after the son of the owner of a nearby stopping house, F. G. Kirkness. The Kirknesses were known for their hospitality, and their home was the venue for local dances.

Governor Lake (lake)
74 M/9 - Colin Lake
32-122-1-W4
59°38′N 110°08′W
Approximately 324 km north north-east of Fort McMurray.

Officially named in 1961 in honour of J.J. Bowlen, the Lieutenant Governor of Alberta from 1950-1959.

Graham Creek (creek)
83 M/4 - Rio Grande
SW-25-71-13-W6
55°10'N 119°52'W
Flows east into Windsor Creek approximately 68 km west of Grande Prairie.

It appears on a boundary survey map of 1922, and may be named after a survey crew member working in the area in the mid-1910s.

Graham Creek (creek)
73 M/16 - Cowper Lake
4-9-80-1-W4
55°54'N 110°07'W
Flows west into Landels River approximately 120 km south-east of Fort McMurray.

This creek was named after Graham Davies of Lloydminster, a member of a survey party. The name was recorded in the 1910 notes of J.N. Wallace, DLS.

Graham Lake (lake)
84 B/10 - Peerless Lake
22-87-4-W5
56°34'N 114°33'W
Approximately 136 km north of Slave Lake.

This lake, halfway between Peace River and Fort McMurray, is named for a factor of the Hudson's Bay Company who was in the area for many years. At one time the name Perfection Lake was also suggested for the feature due to its proximity to Peerless Lake.

Grand Island (island)
84 A/7 - Livock River
34-84-17-W4
56°20'N 112°36'W

Grand Rapids on the Athabasca River, ca.1900

Grand Rapids on the Athabasca River, ca.1900

Grand Rapids on the Athabasca River, ca.1900

In Athabasca River approximately 86 km south-west of Fort McMurray.

The name is a descriptive one for this island in the middle of the Athabasca River, which is named for its proximity to the Grand Rapids. The name appears on a federal government map as early as 1915. The island is known in Cree as *kitchi powistik*, "Great Rapids."

Grand Rapids (rapids)
84 A/7 - Livock River
33-84-17-W4
56°20'N 112°36'W
In Athabasca River approximately 87 km south-west of Fort McMurray.

This is a descriptive name. The name "Grand" was applied to these rapids because they were the most formidable and spectacular rapids on the lower part of the Athabasca River. It is one of the few rapids in the province that on a 1974 Alberta government canoeing map is given a rating of VI. This means "extremely obstructed passages, waves continuous, long and very violent, rocks and boiling eddies unavoidable." Canoeists are warned to avoid the rapids for there is, according to the map, "DEFINITE RISK OF LIFE." The name was recorded by the Geological Survey of Canada in 1892.

Grande Prairie (city)
83 M/2 - Grande Prairie
23-71-6-W6
55°10'N 118°48'W
Approximately 150 km south-west of Peace River.

Established as a post office in 1911, the community grew as a hub for the surrounding territory, and on January 1, 1958, it incorporated as a city. (see Grande Prairie)

■ **Grande Prairie** (prairie)
83 M/2 - Grande Prairie
71-5-6-W6
55°12′N 118°48′W
Just north-west of the city of Grande Prairie.

One thing is certain about the origin of the name, it is a French term meaning "large plain." One source has stated that the name was given to the feature in 1912 by Bishop Grouard, the Roman Catholic Oblate missionary who described the area as "la grande prairie." According to the 1879 field notes of George Dawson, of the Geological Survey of Canada, the area was known as the Grande Prairie. It was referred to even earlier in the Hudson's Bay Company Fort Dunvegan post journal of 1854 as "the Grande prairie." The area was also referred to by North West Company traders as Buffalo Plains. The Cree have known it as *mistahay-muskotoyew*, which means big prairie.

Grande Prairie County No. 1 (county)
83 M/2 - Grande Prairie
55°15′N 119°00′W

The County of Grande Prairie was established 1950. (see Grande Prairie)

Grande Prairie Creek (creek)
83 M/7 - Sexsmith
10-19-72-6-W6
55°15′N 118°54′W
Flows south into Bear River approximately 8 km north-west of Grande Prairie.

When the Dominion Lands Survey went through the area in 1909, the name was recorded as Pine Creek. This was corroborated by Provincial Archivist Katherine Hughes when she went on a trip to the north country the same year. When the first detailed federal map of the area was produced in 1912, the name was shown as

---

*denotes rescinded name or former locality.

Spruce Creek. In the 1950s it was not the policy to have the same name on more than one feature. Since there was another Spruce Creek nearby, it was decided to change the name. In 1952 the name Grande Prairie Creek was adopted because it flows through the area known as the Grande Prairie. (see Grande Prairie)

Grant Island (island)
74 D/14 - Wood Creek
32-89-9-W4
56°45′55″N 111°24′00″W
In the Athabasca River approximately 13 km north of Fort McMurray.

This is a commemorative name; Tom Grant lived on the island for many years.

*****Grant Lake** (lake)
84 F/1 - Bison Lake
27, 28-94-15-W4
57°15′N 116°23′W
Approximately 75 km north-west of Fort McMurray.

It appears on federal government maps as early as 1918. In 1955, the name was rescinded for it had become an indefinite lake, possibly only an area of exceptionally wet muskeg. It is not known after whom the lake is named.

Grass Creek (creek)
74 L/9 - Old Fort Bay
3-33-110-1-W4
58°35′N 110°06′W
Flows west into Harrison River approximately 210 km north north-east of Fort McMurray.

Officially named in 1955, it is descriptive of the vegetation near the creek.

*****Grass Lake** (lake)
83 M/6 - La Glace
24-73-9-W6
55°30′N 119°15′W

Approximately 33 km north-west of Grande Prairie.

Local name describing the abundance of grass around the shores of the lake. (see Anderson Lake)

Grassy Lake (lake)
83 K/13 - Long Lake
24-67-23,24-W5
54°49′N 117°31′W
Approximately 30 km south-west of Valleyview.

The name shows as early as 1917 on federal government maps, and is descriptive of the flora growing around the lake.

Gravel Creek (creek)
84 P/4 - Burrison Lake
NE-31-117-21-W4
59°13′N 113°34′W
Flows east into Jackfish River approximately 216 km east north-east of High Level.

Likely descriptive, the name shows on a federal government map as early as 1929.

Gravina Creek (creek)
84 F/3 - Crummy Lake
30-94-21-W5
57°12′N 117°22′W
Flows south-east into Notikewin River approximately 33 km north north-east of Manning.

It appears on federal government maps as early as 1930; the precise reason for the naming of the creek is unknown. There is a town in south-east Italy by this name where Frederick II built a castle.

Grayling Creek (creek)
74 L/3 - Embarras
10-12-104-9-W4
58°01′N 111°21′W
Flows north into Athabasca River approximately 134 km north of Fort McMurray.

The name was officially approved in 1966, and may refer to the presence of a silver-grey freshwater fish, *Thymallus arcticus*, of the trout family, found in northern waters. (see also Grayling Lake)

Grayling Lake (lake)
74 E/15 - I.D. 18
3-103-6-W4
57°54'40"N 110°54'00"W
Approximately 135 km north of Fort McMurray.

This lake is named for a fish common to northern Alberta's lakes and streams, the Arctic Grayling. The grayling is a member of the salmon family. The Grayling spawns in spring and raises its young in warm streams. In fall the fish migrate to larger streams or lakes to over-winter. The grayling is a prized sport fish among anglers. It is highly susceptible to overfishing, and populations have declined dramatically in some more accessible areas.

Green Lake (lake)
83 K/15 - Sweathouse Creek
N-16-68-17-W5
54°53'25"N 116°31'50"W
Approximately 148 km south-east of Grande Prairie.

The name for this lake describes the colour of the water in the lake. It was officially approved in 1991 after field research in the area established the name was well established and in local use.

Green Stockings Creek (creek)
74 E/3 - Hartley Creek
6-95-8-W4
57°12'40"N 111°18'05"W
Flows north into Black Fly Creek approximately 48 km north of Fort McMurray.

---
*denotes rescinded name or former locality.

According to an unsubstantiated source, Green Stockings was the name of a young aboriginal woman with whom Sir George Back (1796-1878), explorer with the Franklin Expedition, and Robert Hood (1797-1821), surveyor and draughtsman with the Franklin Expedition, were alleged to have had a romantic liaison.

Greenview, Municipal District of, No. 16
(municipal district)
83 L/9 - Latornell
53-77-14-14-W5-6
From 53°35'N 116°00'W
to 55°40'N 118°00'W
South and east of Grande Prairie.

A "Name the Improvement District" contest was run through the local schools in 1993, and these suggestions were taken to public information meetings where the ratepayers were requested to vote on the names provided by the children. The name Greenview was chosen as it received the most votes from the ratepayers. The Municipal District was subsequently established in 1994.

*Gregoire Lake (lake)
74 D/6 - Gregoire Lake
14-86-8-W4
56°27'30"N 111°08'30"W
Approximately 30 km south-east of Fort McMurray.

(see Willow Lake)

Gregoire Lake Indian Reserve No. 176
(Indian reserve)
74 D/6 - Gregoire Lake
35-85-8-W4
56°25'N 111°09'W
Approximately 35 km south south-east Fort McMurray.

Named for its proximity to Gregoire Lake, officially known as Willow Lake since 1988. Located near the community of Anzac, this is the largest and most heavily populated of the four which comprise the Fort McMurray Reserves which fall under Treaty No. 8. They trace their roots back to the Chipewyan and Cree. (see also Willow Lake)

Gregoire Lake Indian Reserve No.176A
(Indian reserve)
74 D/6 - Gregoire Lake
10-86-8-W4
56°26'N 111°11'W
Approximately 33 km south south of Fort McMurray.

(see Gregoire Lake Indian Reserve No. 176)

Gregoire Lake Indian Reserve No. 176B
(Indian reserve)
74 D/6 - Gregoire Lake
24-86-10-W4
56°28'N 111°07'W
Approximately 32 km south south-east of Fort McMurray.

(see Gregoire Lake Indian Reserve No. 176)

Gregoire Lake Provincial Park
(provincial park)
74 D/6 - Gregoire Lake
27-86-8-W4
56°29'N 111°11'W
Approximately 27 km south south-east of Fort McMurray.

Established in 1969, it was named for its proximity to Gregoire Lake, known as Willow Lake since 1988.

Gregoire River (river)
74 D/7 - Cheecham
25-86-6-W4
56°29'N 110°48'W
Flows east north-east into Christina River approximately 45 km south-east of Fort McMurray.

This river was named along with Gregoire Lake (now Willow Lake) after an early settler. (see also Willow Lake)

Grew Lake (lake)
84 A/14 - Mink Lake
19-91-20-W4
56°54′N 113°12′W
Approximately 110 km west north-west of Fort McMurray.

Named after J. Grew, of the Indian Affairs Branch, Department of Mines and Resources, who originally reported the name as Deep Lake. In 1944 the name was changed to Grew Lake, but is still also known as Deep Lake.

Greywillow Point (point)
74 M/8 - Wylie Lake
35-118-1-W4
59°17′N 110°02′W
Approximately 288 km north north-east of Fort McMurray.

The name shows on federal government maps as early as 1884, and is likely descriptive of the plant found on the point.

Griffin Creek (creek)
83 N/13 - Tangent
2-81-25-W5
55°59′N 117°48′W
Flows south into Peace River approximately 40 km south-west of Peace River (town).

According to the local history of the area, this creek was named in 1912 after Thomas Griffin, born in Uttoxeter, Staffordshire. After spending some time in the United States, he moved to Innisfail, Alberta, then settled in the Peace River area in 1904. He constantly promoted the Peace River Country as prime agricultural land. According to Katherine Hughes in her diary of the journey to the North country in 1909, she noted that Mr. Griffin was already successfully growing wheat and barley. He died at a young 39 years of age in 1919.

Griffin Creek (locality)
84 C/4 - Grimshaw
16-81-25-W5
56°01′N 117°51′W
Approximately 25 km south-west of Grimshaw.

Established as a post office in 1912, it was named after a settler of the district, Thomas Griffin, who died in 1919. The first postmaster was Mrs. B. Eaton. (see Griffin Creek)

Griffiths Creek (creek)
74 M/8 - Wylie Lake
NE-1-120-1-W4
59°24′N 110°00′W
Flows south-east into Saskatchewan approximately 300 km north north-east of Fort McMurray.

Officially named in 1953, after World War II casualty Flight Sergeant Robert Thomas Griffiths.

Grimshaw, Mile Zero, Mackenzie Highway, 1963

Grimshaw (town)
84 C/4 - Grimshaw
17-83-23-W5
56°11′N 117°36′W
Approximately 20 km west of Peace River.

Grimshaw was established as a post office in 1923 and was named in honour of Dr. M.E. Grimshaw, a native of Kingston, Ontario, who was the medical officer for the Central Canada Railway. He practised medicine at Innisfail in 1912 and at Medicine Hat in 1913, then moved to the Peace River district to establish a practice in 1914. He was Mayor of Peace River in 1922 and in 1929 started a medical practice at Fairview, where he died in November the same year. The town of Grimshaw owes its origin to the Edmonton, Dunvegan and British Columbia Railway. In September 1921 the line was extended west of Peace River and two sidings were built in the Bear Lake district, west of Peace River. One of them was called Miller's Crossing and the other Berwyn. Buildings from Bear Lake were moved to Miller's Crossing, forming a new settlement. When the postal authorities requested an official name for Miller's Crossing the choice made was Grimshaw. It was created a village in 1930, and a town in 1953. (see also Berwyn)

Grist Lake (lake)
73 M/8 - Grist Lake
1-74-4-W4
55°22′N 110°28′W
Approximately 105 km north of Cold Lake.

Officially adopted in 1945, the name appears on maps as early as 1913. The origin is not known; it may be a surname, or may refer to grain ready for grinding.

Grizzly (railway point)
83 K/3 - Tony Creek
10-61-22-W5
54°15′N 117°12′W
Approximately 100 km west of Whitecourt.

Officially named in 1974, it was a point on the spur track off the Sangudo subdivision of Canadian National Railways. It is likely descriptive of the animal in the area.

*Grizzly Bear (former post office)
83 M/16 - Codesa
22-78-1-W6
55°45′N 118°15′W
Approximately 39 km east of Spirit River.

Originally established in December 1916, the name for this post office probably referred to the prevalence of the animal in the area. The name was changed to Belloy in 1926. (see Belloy)

*Gros Cape (cape)
74 L/11 - Fort Chipewyan
15-112-7-W4
58°43′N 111°06′W
Approximately 214 km north of Fort McMurray.

(see Grouse Cape)

Gross Creek (creek)
74 L/2 - Larocque Lake
10-8-105-4-W4
58°06′N 110°37′W
Flows south-west into Maybelle River approximately 150 km north north-east of Fort McMurray.

The name appears on maps as early as 1919, and although the origin of the name is not precisely known, it may have been the surname of a survey crew member working for F.V. Seibert, DLS, in 1915.

Grouard (hamlet)
83 N/9 - Grouard
19-75-14-W5
55°31′N 116°09′W
Approximately 24 km north-east of High Prairie.

This locality was originally known as Stoney Point, but when the post office was first established in 1903 it was called Lesser Slave Lake post office. The name was changed in 1909 to Grouard. The name for this area in Cree is *asinskow-newatin*, which means "stony point." (see Grouard Mission, Lesser Slave Lake and Stoney Point)

Grouard Mission (locality)
83 N/9 - Grouard
1-75-14-W5
55°33′N 116°09′W
Approximately 25 km east north-east of High Prairie.

Émile-Jean-Marie Grouard was born in Brûlon, France in 1840, and was ordained a priest in 1862. He served continuously and faithfully in the Northwest from 1862-1931 except for a two-year leave in 1874-1876. He was consecrated bishop in 1891. He ranks as one of the most prominent figures in Alberta history. Originally the Grouard Mission was known as St. Bernard's Mission. There are references to it as early as 1845 in the Fort Dunvegan journal of the Hudson's Bay Company, in which is mentioned that Father Bourassa was visiting from the mission in the Lesser Slave Lake area.

Grouroches Chere (hill)
74 L/11 - Fort Chipewyan
10-111-8-W4
58°38′N 111°15′W
Approximately 204 km north of Fort McMurray.

The name for this hill was officially adopted in 1971 and is likely a corruption of the French for large rock, or *gros rocher*. In the 1822 Hudson's Bay Company Fort Chipewyan post journal, there is mention of a feature called Gros Rocher.

Grouse Cape (cape)
74 L/11 - Fort Chipewyan
15-112-7-W4
58°43′N 111°06′W
Approximately 214 km north of Fort McMurray.

It was officially named in the late 1950s, but it appeared on federal government maps as early as 1917. Recent research has shown this is likely an incorrect name for the feature and has nothing to do with the bird. Today local residents have no name for this location, but do refer to a feature just north and east of this as Gros Cape, which is descriptive of the steep rocky point of land jutting into Lake Athabasca. There is also a reference to Gros Cape in the 1822 Fort Chipewyan Hudson's Bay Company post journal. *Gros* is the French word for large.

Grovedale (hamlet)
83 M/2 - Grande Prairie
SW-4-70-6-W6
55°02′N 118°52′W
Approximately 17 km south south-west of Grande Prairie.

The descriptive name for this hamlet whose post office opened in October 1939, refers to the grove of trees near the post office. The first postmaster was Mrs H. Bain.

Gull Creek (creek)
84 K/8 - Fort Vermilion
25-108-13-W5
58°24′N 116°01′W
Flows south-east into Peace River approximately 65 km east of High Level.

(see Gull Lake)

Gull Lake (lake)
84 K/8 - Fort Vermilion
5-109-13-W5
58°26′N 116°07′W
Approximately 58 km east of High Level.

A descriptive name due to the large number of gulls found there. This name was apparently in use at the turn of the century as it was recorded by A.W. Ponton during the 1910 Dominion Survey of Township 108, Range 13, west of the 5th Meridian. J.B. St. Cyr DLS, during the survey of the

---
*denotes rescinded name or former locality.

North Vermilion settlement, recorded the stream draining this lake as Gull Creek.

Gumboot Lake (lake)
73 M/5 - Behan Lake
3-24-73-13-W4
55°20′N 111°52′W
Approximately 63 km north of Lac La Biche.

The precise origin for the locally well-established name for this feature is unknown. The name is intriguing.

Gummer Lake (lake)
83 M/7 - Sexsmith
34-73-7-W6
55°22′N 119°00′W
Approximately 21 km north-west of Grande Prairie.

Although not officially named until the 1950s, the name for this lake probably refers to Ed and Eva (Laver) Gummer who homesteaded on land nearby. Mr. Gummer was born in 1889 in Norham, Ontario. He moved to the Peace River Country in 1912 and filed for land about 15 kilometres west of Sexsmith. In the early years he worked on the Dominion Lands Survey as a chainman. This lake is one of a group of lakes that were known collectively as Buffalo Lakes. (see also Buffalo Lake and Jones Lake)

*****Gun Creek** (creek)
84 L/15 - Habay
15-113-5-W6
58°58′N 118°45′W
Flows north into Hay River approximately 51 km north-east of Rainbow Lake.

(see Sousa Creek)

Gunner's Lake (lake)
74 D/16 - Gregoire Lake
10-86-8-W4
56°26′20″N 111°11′20″W
Approximately 34 km south south-east of Fort McMurray.

(see Milton's Lake)

Gunns Creek (creek)
83 N/6 - Whitemud Creek
12-21-74-20-W5
55°26′N 117°01′W
Flows south-west into Little Smoky River approximately 42 km north-east of Valleyview.

Gunns Creek was named after Charles T. and Mabel (Largrock) Gunn and family who moved to the area from Sounding Lake in 1931. They homesteaded nearby from 1931 to 1936, after which they moved to the New Fish Creek area. Mr. Gunn was born in Rapid City, South Dakota. During World War I he spent time in the RNWMP.

■ **Guy** (hamlet)
83 N/11 - Donnelly
1-76-21-W5
55°33′N 117°07′W
Approximately 23 km south-west of McLennan.

The post office opened here in April 1930 and was named for Bishop Joseph Guy, a Roman Catholic Oblate missionary. He was born in Montreal in 1883, and ordained a priest in 1906. He was elevated to the office of bishop in 1930, and was Vicar Apostolic of Grouard from 1932 to 1938.

---

*denotes rescinded name or former locality.

Habay (hamlet)
84 L/15 - Habay
14-113-5-W6
58°48'40"N 118°42'30"W
Approximately 53 km north-east of Rainbow Lake.

Established as a post office in 1951, it was named after Father Joseph Charles Leon Marie Habay, OMI. R. Smith was the first postmaster. Habay, who was born in Tarbes, France in 1875 and came to Canada in 1903, spent his first year at Grouard. From there he went to Fort Vermilion (1904-1912), and then to other missions in northern Alberta, including Wabasca and Sturgeon Lake. Father Habay first visited this Meander River area in 1908 with Father Joussard. From 1951 to 1955 he was the director of the Indian Residential School of Our Lady of Assumption at Hay Lakes. He died on August 31, 1965, in Edmonton.

Hackmatack Lake (lake)
83 M/4 - Rio Grande
32-71-11-W6
55°11'N 119°40'W
Approximately 52 km west of Grande Prairie.

From an Algonkian word *akemantak* meaning wood for snowshoes. It is one of the variations of the word tamarack. It is a member of the larch family, the botanical name for which is *Larix laricina*. Larches are best known for their soft needles which they lose every fall and regrow every spring. Tamarack grow best around muskeg. The name hackmatack is used primarily in the Maritimes. This lake was originally known as Tamarack Lake, but at the time the name was made official there was a Tamarack Lake near St. Paul, so it was decided to use Hackmatack in order to avoid duplication.

Haig Lake (lake)
84 C/16 - Haig Lake
13-91-14-W5
56°54'N 116°06'W
Approximately 90 km east of Manning.

Named some time after 1930, the precise origin of the name is unknown.

Haig River (river)
84 E/16 - Haro River
1-104-1-W6
58°00'N 118°00'W
Flows east into Chinchaga River approximately 77 km south-west of High Level.

Haig Lake is named for Sir Douglas Haig (1861-1928), who had a distinguished career with the British armed forces from 1885 to 1918. Of the famous family of distillers, Haig fought in the Boer War, served in India, and was British commander-in-chief on the western front during World War I. After the war he became interested in the welfare of the soldiers in his former command. He organised the British Legion and the British Empire Service League to assist veterans. One of Haig's enduring contributions is Poppy Day or Remembrance Day, November 11, which he first organised as a means of funding the legions. He was created Earl Haig in 1919. The name first appears on federal government maps as early as 1916.

Haight Island (island)
74 E/4 - Fort MacKay
36-94-11-W4
57°12'N 111°37'W
In Athabasca river approximately 55 km north north-west of Fort McMurray.

This island was named by S.C. Ells in 1925 for Captain E.B. Haight, one of the best known steamboat captains on the river. Before arriving in the Athabasca district Haight had been on the Nile Expedition in 1884 and had served during the Northwest Rebellion of 1885. He was well known on the run from Athabasca Landing to Fort McMurray. In 1921 he assumed command of the newly constructed sternwheeler *Athabasca River*.

Hair Lake (lake)
74 M/9 - Colin Lake
NE-16-123-1-W4
59°42'N 110°07'W
Approximately 330 km north north-east of Fort McMurray.

Officially named in 1961, its shape apparently looked like a head of hair to the person who submitted the name.

Halcourt (locality)
83 M/4 - Rio Grande
6-71-10-W6
55°07'N 119°31'W
Approximately 40 km west of Grande Prairie.

According to one source, this locality was named after an early settler in the area, H. Halcourt Walker. The Halcourt School District was established in 1912; the post office was opened in May 1913. It is one of the earliest settled communities in the area. The Dominion Land Surveyors first surveyed the land in 1910.

Halcro Indian Reserve No.150C
(Indian reserve)
83 N/9 - Grouard
24-76-15-W5
55°35'N 116°11'W
Approximately 25 km north-east of High Prairie.

Established in 1905, it was named after Thomas Halcro, who obtained severalty under Treaty No. 8. (see also Drift Pile Indian Reserve No. 150)

Halfway Creek (creek)

74 D/6 - Gregoire Lake
13-86-8-W4
57°27′25″N 111°16′45″W
Flows north into a small unnamed lake approximately 31 km south south-east of Fort McMurray.

The well-established name for this creek is descriptive of its location halfway between Highway 63 and Willow Lake (formerly Gregoire Lake). It is locally well known for its clear drinking water.

Halfway Lake (lake)

83 N/7 - Triangle
1-74-19-W5
55°23′N 116°47′W
Approximately 20 km west south-west of High Prairie.

One source has stated that Halfway Lake was named by the aboriginal people who lived in the area. It was named before 1898. This small lake is halfway between Grouard and Sturgeon Lake. People travelling between the two destinations would camp at this spot. The name was officially adopted in the early 1950s.

Halfway Lake (lake)

74 D/13 - Ruth Lake
2-90-12-W4
56°46′30″N 111°47′20″W
Approximately 24 km west north-west of Fort McMurray.

The name for this lake comes from its location halfway between the Thickwood Hills fire road which runs west along Conn Creek, and a large lake locally known as Birch Lake.

---

*denotes rescinded name or former locality.

Halverson Ridge (ridge)

84 E/3 - Halverson Ridge
10-93-9-W6
57°03′N 119°21′W
Approximately 115 km west north-west of Manning.

This ridge was named in commemoration of Rifleman Sigvard O. Halverson, killed in action on February 27, 1945.

Hamelin Creek (creek)

84 D/2 - Hines Creek
16-81-6-W6
56°02′20″N 118°52′30″W
Flows east north-east into Peace River approximately 30 km west south-west of Fairview.

It first shows on federal government maps as early as 1918, and is likely named after a survey crew member.

Hammer Creek (creek)

83 L/13 - Calahoo Creek
5-1-67-11-W6
54°45′30″N 119°23′30″W
Flows south-west into Nose Creek approximately 66 km south south-west of Grande Prairie.

This creek is named for Ted Hammer, an early Timber Inspector of the area.

Hangingstone River (river)

74 D/11 - Fort McMurray
10-89-9-W4
56°43′N 111°20′W
Flows north into Clearwater River, at Fort McMurray.

This descriptive name, noted by A.J. Tremblay during his survey in 1912, comes from a big rock that hung out over the edge of the river bank. On hot days the oil sands used to seep through fissures in the rock. The Cree name *assnew seepee* correlates with the English meaning of the name Hangingstone River.

Harker Lake (lake)

74 M/16 - Andrew Lake
34-126-2-W4
59°59′N 110°15′W
Approximately 359 km north of Fort McMurray.

The name was submitted in 1958 by the Research Council of Alberta, and is one of a series of features in the area named after prominent geologists. The lake was named for the British geologist, Alfred Harker (1859-1939).

*Harmon River (river)

84 C/3 - Peace River
29-83-21-W5
56°14′N 117°17′W
Flows north-west into Peace River, through the town of Peace River.

(see Heart River)

Harmon Valley (locality)

84 C/2 - Harmon Valley
12-82-19-W5
56°07′N 116°50′W
Approximately 22 km south-east of Peace River.

Harmon Valley is named after Daniel Williams Harmon (1778-1843), fur trader and diarist. Harmon is best known for his *Journals of Voyages and Travels in the Interior of North America* (1820). Born in Vermont, Harmon entered the service of the North West Company in Montreal in 1800 and spent the next 19 years at trading posts in the Northwest. In 1805 he was posted to South Branch House, near present-day Batoche, on the North Saskatchewan River. Here he married Lizette Duval, a young Métis with whom he had a large family. In 1808-1810, he was in charge at Fort Dunvegan on the Peace River, and then moved to Fort St. James, in the New Caledonia district. His last posting was in the east at Fort William, where he lived with his wife and children until 1819, when he left the company. He returned to Vermont where he set up a store and sawmill, and developed a small settlement, known as Harmonville. A post office was established here in 1931, and the first postmaster was L.B. Hilliard.

*Hartley Creek (creek)
74 E/6 - Kearl Lake
24-95-10-W4
57°15'40"N 111°28'15"W
Flows north-west into Muskeg river approximately 60 km north of Fort McMurray.

(see Jackpine Creek)

Haro River (river)
84 E/16 - Haro river
30-103-2-W6
57°55'N 118°13'W
Flows north-east into Chinchaga River approximately 94 km south-east of Rainbow Lake.

The precise origin of the name of this river is unknown, although it does appear on federal government maps as early as 1930.

Harold Creek (creek)
83 M/3 - Wembley
SE-18-71-9-W6
55°09'N 119°22'W
Flows south-east into Beaverlodge Creek approximately 33 km west of Grande Prairie.

Named in 1951 after Lance-Sergeant Raymond Alexander Harold born in North Dakota in 1922. He enlisted in Calgary in 1943 and was killed in action in continental Europe in 1944. He was mentioned in despatches.

---

*denotes rescinded name or former locality.

Harper Creek (creek)
83 M/1 - DeBolt
15-14-71-1-W6
55°08'N 118°02'W
Flows south west into Cornwall Creek approximately 45 km east of Grande Prairie.

The local people remember Danny Harper, who operated a stopping place along the creek at approximately Section 1, Township 71, Range 1, west of the 6th Meridian. He may have been a member of the survey crew although his name was not mentioned in any of the extant Dominion Land Surveys records of the time.

Harper Creek (creek)
84 I/4 - Edra Creek
SW-32-106-24-W4
58°14'N 113°56'W
Flows east into Birch River approximately 189 km east of High Level.

It has appeared on federal government maps as early as 1916, and was named after C.H. Harper, Dominion Land Surveyor, a leveller on the survey crew of T.H. Plunkett, DLS.

Harrison River (river)
74 L/9 - Old Fort Bay
10-36-111-3-W4
58°41'N 110°21'W
Flows west into Old Fort Bay approximately 218 km north north-east of Fort McMurray.

It appears on maps as early as 1919. According to the files of the Geographic Board of Canada, it was named by J.B. McFarlane, DLS, after his friend Mr. Harrison from Toronto who was interested in hunting and exploration.

Harry's Snye (river)
74 E/11 - Firebag River
22-100-9-W4
57°41'40"N 111°23'20"W

Approximately 104 km north of Fort McMurray.

Harry's Snye is named after Harry MacDonald, an early trapper of the area. A snye usually refers to a narrow, meandering, sluggish side channel of a river. It may be a corruption of the Canadian French *chenal*, meaning channel. An older spelling of snye makes the connection clearer, i.e., "shnye."

*Hartley Creek (creek)
74 E/6 - Kearl Lake
24-95-10-W4
57°15'40"N 111°28'15"W
Flows north-west into Muskeg river approximately 60 km north of Fort McMurray.

(see Jackpine Creek)

*Harvey Creek (creek)
83 N/7 - Triangle
13-74-18-W5
55°25'N 116°38'W
Flows north-east into Iroquois River 10 km west of High Prairie.

The name is shown on maps from the 1940s as Harvey Creek; after field research was conducted in the area the name Shadow Creek was make official in 1957. (see Shadow Creek)

Harwood Lake (lake)
74 L/1 - Archer Lake
SE-35-104-3-W4
58°04'N 110°22'W
Approximately 151 km north north-east of Fort McMurray.

Colonel Reginald de Lotbinière Harwood (1871-1955) was born in Vaudreuil, Quebec. He received his medical degree from McGill University. He practised medicine in St. Lambert, just outside Montreal, and Chicago, following which he moved to Pincher Creek, Alberta. Later he came to Edmonton where he built up a large surgical practice. He joined the 101st Regiment and in 1914 when it was reorganized he became commander of the 51st (Edmonton) Battalion, CEF. Harwood took his unit to England in 1916. Because of his medical background, he was later transferred to the Canadian Army Medical Corps and served in different senior administrative posts. In 1919 he was appointed officer commanding the military hospital in Edmonton. Holmgren, 1976. In later years, he practised in Vancouver.

*Hash River (river)
83 K/11 - Waskahigan River
30-66-21-W5
54°44′N 117°11′W
Flows north-west into Smoky River approximately 6 km north of Fox Creek.

(see Iosegun River)

Hat Lake (lake)
74 E/8 - Trout Creek
24-97-3-W4
57°25′N 110°20′W
Approximately 105 km north-east of Fort McMurray.

The precise origin of the name of this lake is unknown. It is one of several landmarks named by local trappers to identify locations for themselves and their families.

Hatcher Lake (lake)
83 J/16 - Chisholm
33-67-3-W5
54°51′N 114°25′W
Approximately 54 km south south-east of Slave Lake.

Officially named in 1950; the origin of the name is unknown.

---

*denotes rescinded name or former locality.

Havet Creek (creek)
84 F/5 - Goffit Creek
22-96-25-W5
57°21′N 117°57′W
Flows south-west into Botha River approximately 51 km north north-west of Manning.

The origin of the name of this creek is unknown.

Hawk Hills (locality)
84 F/3 - Crummy Lake
13-95-22-W5
57°14′N 117°25′W
Approximately 39 km north of Manning.

It is named for its proximity to the hills of the same name. (see Hawk Hills)

Hawk Hills (hills)
84 F/5 - Goffit Creek
33-98-24-W5
57°30′N 117°38′W
Approximately 60 km north of Manning.

The precise origin of the name of these hills is unknown; the name is likely descriptive.

Hawkins Lake (lake)
83 O/13 - Atikameg
3-81-12-W5
56°59′N 115°47′W
Approximately 100 km north-west of Slave Lake.

This lake was named after a Dominion Land Surveyor, A. H. Hawkins, who was working in the area in 1910. The name was officially adopted in 1971.

Hay Camp (hamlet)
74 M/11 - Hay Camp
SW-22-121-9-W4
59°31′N 111°28′W
Approximately 302 km north of Fort McMurray.

Established before the 1950s, this was a place where hay was cut for horses.

Hay Creek (creek)
83 M/3 - Wembley
NW-16-72-10-W6
55°14′N 119°29′W
Flows south-west into Beaverlodge River approximately 41 km west of Grande Prairie.

It was known as Hay Creek by the late 1940s. Although the origin of the name is not precisely known, it may be due to the prevalence of natural hay lands in the area.

Hay Lake area, n.d.

Hay Lake (lake)
84 L/15 - Habay
29-113-5-W6
58°50′N 118°47′W
Approximately 50 km north-east of Rainbow Lake.

This name is descriptive of the plant life found there. It is locally known as either *Hátl'ode* or *Hátl'oin Mieh* in the Slavey language. These names translate as Habay's Hay Lake after Father Habay, OMI. He first visited the Hay Lake area in 1917 while stationed at Fort Vermilion. He was later stationed at Assumption in the 1950s. Another Slavey name for the lake is *Kutlowklay*, meaning "plenty of hay." (see also Habay)

Hay Lake (lake)
84 D/2 - Hines Creek
35-82-4-W6
56°09′N 118°31′W
Approximately 12 km north north-west of Fairview.

The origin of the name of this lake is probably descriptive.

Hay Lake (lake)
83 M/6 - La Glace
32-72-10-W6
55°17′N 119°25′W
Approximately 39 km north-west of Grande Prairie.

The locally well-established name is descriptive of the slough grass that surrounds the lake. The name has been in use since approximately 1913. The name was changed in the 1950s to McNeill Lake since there were already a number of Hay Lakes in Alberta. After field research was conducted in the area, it was determined the name Hay Lake was still in local usage, so in 1991 the name was changed back. (see also McNeill Lake)

*__Hay Lake__ (lake)
83 M/5 - Hythe
3-75-13-W6
55°28′N 119°56W
Approximately 75 km west north-west of Grande Prairie.

Likely a descriptive name, it was changed some time in the 1950s, probably to avoid confusion with the other Hay Lakes in Alberta. (see Keeping Lake)

Hay Lake Indian Reserve No. 209
(Indian reserve)
84 L/15 - Habay
112-5-W6
58°45′N 118°42′W

---

*denotes rescinded name or former locality.

Approximately 95 km west north-west of High Level.

Named for its proximity to the lake. (see Hay Lake)

Hay River (river)
84 N/15 - Lessard Creek
6-126-17-W5
60°00′N 116°56′W
Flows north north-east into the Northwest Territories approximately 165 km north of High Level.

The river, from which other features are named, was so called because it traverses a broad plain that produced good crops of prairie hay.

*__Hay River__ (river)
74 L/12 - Hilda Lake
6-14-111-10-W4
58°38′N 111°34′W
Flows east into Mamawi Lake approximately 204 km north of Fort McMurray.

Officially named some time in the 1950s as Prairie River. (see Prairie River)

Hayfield (locality)
83 M/4 - Rio Grande
SW-27-71-11-W6
55°10′N 119°36′W
Approximately 50 km west of Grande Prairie.

The locality was added to the federal government maps in the early 1950s; however there is evidence of the name as early as 1934, when the Hayfield School District was established. The origin of the name is not known; it may be descriptive.

Hazelmere (locality)
83 M/4 - Rio Grande
16-3-70-12-W6
55°02′N 119°44′W
Approximately 58 km west south-west of Grande Prairie.

The post office was established here in 1930, and H. Jordan was the first postmaster. Mr. Jordan named it after a town in England, where he was stationed at the Canadian training camp in Bramshott.

Hazelnut Hill (hill)
83 N/1 - Bellrose Lake
E -8-71-14-W5
55°08′N 116°07′W
Approximately 169 km east of Grande Prairie.

The locally well-established name has been in use since the early part of the 20th century, and is likely descriptive of the hazel bush which in Alberta grows to a height of one to three metres, and can be found in woods and thickets.

Heart Lake (lake)
73 M/3 - Logan Lake
4-9-70-10-W4
55°02′25″N 111°28′23″W
Approximately 41 km north-east of Lac La Biche.

According to the records of the Oblates of Mary Immaculate, this Lac des Cœurs was a mistranslation by the French speakers. The word for "heart" in Chipewyan is *miteh*, which is close to the word for sorcerer/medicine man, *mitew*. The name therefore should more properly have been translated as Medicine Lake. The lake must have had some magical or healing significance. The English translation from the French was well established when the name was put on federal government maps in the early 1900s.

Heart Lake Indian Reserve No. 167
(Indian reserve)
73 M/3 - Logan Lake
17-70-10-W4
55°04′N 111°30′W
Approximately 40 km north-east of lac La Biche.

It is named for its proximity to Heart Lake. Many of the band members are Chipewyan from the Cold Lake area. The reserve was established in 1915, under the provisions of Treaty No. 8.

Heart River (locality)

83 N/10 - McLennan
13-76-17-W5
55°35′N 116°30′W
Approximately 18 km north of High Prairie.

It is named for its proximity to the nearby South Heart River. The post office was established in October 1930, the first postmaster being J. Anderson.

Heart River (river)

84 C/3 - Peace River
29-83-21-W5
56°14′N 117°17′W
Flows north-west into Peace River, through the town of Peace River.

The precise origin of the name of this river is likely aboriginal and was recorded as early as 1804. In a source from 1828 it is referred to by its French translation, Rivière la Cœur. In 1917 the name was changed to Harmon River after Daniel Williams Harmon. By 1950 the name Heart River had been restored to the feature. (see also Harmon Valley)

Heart River Settlement (settlement)

83 N/9 - Grouard
23-76-15-W5
55°36′N 116°13′W
Approximately 25 km north-east of High Prairie.

It is named for its proximity to the South Heart River.

Heart Valley (locality)

83 M/9 - Peoria
16-76-3-W6
55°34′N 118°24′W
Approximately 45 km north north-east of Grande Prairie.

The post office opened here in August 1923. Apparently Jessie McLean, the first postmaster, chose the name for the post office, but exactly why is not known. Perhaps it is due to the fact Mrs. McLean lived near the Bad Heart River, and she used a more positive rendition of the name.

Heavysound Creek (creek)

83 K/7 - Iosegun Lake
29-62-18-W5
54°24′N 116°40′W
Flows west into the Iosegun River approximately 8 km east of Fox Creek.

Likely aboriginal in origin, it appears on federal government maps as early as 1916. The reason for naming it Heavysound is unknown.

Helen Lake (lake)

84 C/12 - Dixonville
18-87-24-W5
56°32′N 117°49′W
Approximately 41 km north north-west of Grimshaw.

After whom this is named is not known; the name first appears in the notes of G.A. Tipper, DLS, in 1913. The lake may also have been known as Slimson Lake before that.

Helene Lake (lake)

74 L/1 - Archer Lake
3-106-1-W4
58°10′N 110°04′W
Approximately 170 km north north-east of Fort McMurray.

After whom it is named is not known; the name appears on maps as early as 1916.

Henderson Creek (creek)

83 M/13 - Bonanza
17-79-13-W6
55°51′N 120°00′W
Flows west into British Columbia approximately 71 km west of Spirit River.

It was named after Robert (Jock) Henderson, a picketman on the Alberta and British Columbia Boundary Commission survey in 1919. Henderson, a lance-sergeant of the 49th Battalion, Canadian Expeditionary Force, won the Military Medal and Bar, and the Distinguished Conduct Medal for conspicuous bravery in World War I.

Henderson Creek (creek)

84 K/13 - Henderson Creek
15-115-23-W5
59°00′N 117°50′W
Flows north north-east into Hay River approximately 66 km north-west of High Level.

Named by J. R. Akins, DLS, during the 1914 survey season. It was named after Francis Dillon Henderson, also a surveyor, who at the time this was named was Secretary of the Board of Examiners for the Dominion Land Surveyors. The creek is known locally as *Tunachade Zahéh*, a Slavey name meaning Swift, or Strong Current Creek.

Henderson Lake (lake)

83 M/6 - La Glace
NW-24-73-8-W6
55°21′N 119°06′W
Approximately 25 km north-west of Grande Prairie.

Henderson Lake may be named after the Henderson family who homesteaded the land to the north-west of the corner of the lake. Locally the name has been in use since

1911. In the fall of 1915, Henry Henderson moved from Port Arthur (later Thunder Bay) Ontario with some of his family to join his sons who were already in the area. There he farmed until his death 10 years later.

Henrietta Lake (lake)

74 L/7 - Keane Creek
1-7-108-5-W4
58°22′N 110°49′W
Approximately 177 km north of Fort McMurray.

The name appears on federal government maps as early as 1930; after whom it is named is not known.

Henry Creek (creek)

83 J/14 - Deer Mountain
16-69-9-W5
54°58′N 115°18′W
Flows north-east into the Swan River approximately 28 km north north-west of Swan Hills.

Likely named in the 1930s or 1940s; after whom is not known.

Henson Lake (lake)

74 M/16 - Andrew Lake
NW-2-126-2-W4
59°56′N 110°14′W
Approximately 353 km north of Fort McMurray.

The name was submitted in 1958 by the Research Council of Alberta, and is one of a series of features in the area named after prominent geologists. Henson was a pioneer in the field of geophysical exploration.

Hermit Lake (lake)

83 M/2 - Grande Prairie
6-2-72-7-W6
55°12′N 118°58′W

---

*denotes rescinded name or former locality.

Approximately 9 km north-west of Grande Prairie.

According to local stories, it is named for a tall, eccentric recluse who settled on a quarter-section which he tried to cultivate by hand. As he walked away from the local store in Grande Prairie one day with a bundle over his shoulder and a blanket trailing behind, someone remarked that he looked like a hermit and the nickname stuck. Holmgren, 1976. It has appeared on maps since at least 1918.

Hermit Lake (locality)

83 M/3 - Wembley
16-32-71-7-W6
55°12′N 119°02′W
Approximately 15 km west of Grande Prairie.

The post office was established there on May 1, 1915, and it closed on October 31, 1919. The first postmaster was Mrs. Braybrook. (see also Hermit Lake)

Heron Island (island)

84 I/7 - Heron Island
13-108-17-W4
58°22′N 112°42′W
Approximately 189 km north north-west of Fort McMurray in Birch River.

The name for this island was officially approved in 1963 and commemorates F.J. Heron, a trapper from Fort Smith, Northwest Territories. He made this his trapping headquarters for many years.

Hidden Lake (lake)

84 E/5 - Tanghe Creek
2-98-13-W6
57°28′N 120°00′W
On the Alberta-British Columbia border approximately 156 km west north-west of Manning.

The precise origin of the name of this lake is unknown, but the name is likely descriptive.

Hiding Creek (creek)

83 L/13 - Calahoo Creek
36-67-14-W6
54°50′N 120°00′W
Flows west into British Columbia approximately 82 km south-west of Grande Prairie.

Recorded by the Alberta-British Columbia Boundary Commission in 1924, the name is descriptive of its location for it traverses very difficult country and at one time provided safe haven for moose.

*****High Bank** (rock)

74 L/14 - Rivière des Rochers
SW-28-114-9-W4
58°55′N 111°27′W
Approximately 236 km north of Fort McMurray.

(see High Rock)

High Hill Lake (lake)

74 D/15 - I.D. 18
8-91-4-W4
56°52′58″N 110°37′00″W
Approximately 49 km east north-east of Fort McMurray.

The lake probably takes its name from its proximity to High Hill River.

High Hill River (river)

74 D/10 - Hollies Creek
26-89-4-W4
56°45′N 110°30′W
Flows south-west into Clearwater River approximately 59 km east of Fort McMurray.

It has been suggested the name High Hill was given to this river because it lies in very high country. The name was recorded by the Geological Survey of Canada in 1892.

High Island (island)
74 L/11 - Fort Chipewyan
7-9-112-7-W4
58°43′N 111°07′W
Approximately 212 km north of Fort McMurray in Lake Athabasca.

Named in the 1960, the name is likely descriptive of its elevation.

High Level (town)
84 K/11 - High Level
32-110-19-W5
58°31′N 117°08′W
Approximately 253 km north of Peace River.

This descriptive name was given to the new town incorporated in 1965, due to the height of land that separates the Peace River and the Hay River. The High Level post office was established there seven years earlier. The first postmaster was Jesse Matheson. It was previously called *Tloc-Moi*, which translates from Slavey as Hay Meadow. It was a stopping place for trappers between Hay Lakes and Fort Vermilion. The area has also been referred to by the Beaver Indians as *Tlowma* and by the Slavey as *Tlowmeh*.

High Prairie (town)
83 N/8 - High Prairie
23-74-17-W5
55°26′N 116°29′W
Approximately 100 km south-east of Peace River.

It is descriptive of the surrounding country. The aboriginal people named the High Prairie region *muskatayosipi* or "prairie river," after the main watercourse in the district. Prairie River was the earliest name for the community. The Edmonton, Dunvegan and British Columbia Railway established a station there in 1915. High Prairie post office was opened in 1910, the first postmaster being W. McCue. The area prospered and the community grew so that it was able to incorporate as a town on January 10, 1950.

High Rock (hill)
74 L/14 - Rivière des Rochers
SW-28-114-9-W4
58°55′N 111°27′W
Approximately 236 km north of Fort McMurray.

The name was officially approved in 1971, and is descriptive of the high rock formation.

Highland Park (locality)
84 D/2 - Hines Creek
16-82-6-W6
56°06′N 118°52′W
Approximately 30 km west of Fairview.

The precise origin of the name of this locality is unknown; it is likely to be descriptive as the locality is on the plain above a steep bank down to the Peace River. A post office was established here in 1932, and J. Uhryn was the first postmaster.

Hilda Lake (lake)
74 L/12 - Hilda Lake
22-110-11-W4
58°34′N 111°45′W
Approximately 196 km north of Fort McMurray.

The name is found on maps as early as 1919, and is likely named after a relative of a survey crew member.

Hilliard's Bay Provincial Park (provincial park)
83 O/12 - Salt Creek
19-24-75-13-W5
55°31′N 115°56′W
Approximately 72 km west north-west of Slave Lake.

Established in 1978, the 2329-hectare park was named after the homesteader who owned the land against the bay on Slave Lake.

Hines Creek (creek)
83 M/15 - Rycroft
13-7-80-4-W6
55°55′N 118°37′W
Flows south into Peace River approximately 20 km north-east of Spirit River.

Possibly named after an Anglican missionary who, according to *Crockford's Clerical Directory*, served at Sandy Lake (Asessipi) Mission in what was then known as the North-West Territories. He was there for the years 1875-1888. The surveyor in the area in 1908 recorded it as Muddy Creek. In 1912, the surveyor G.A. Tipper referred to it as Hines Creek, but also noted it was at one time called Island Creek.

Hines Creek gas pump and flour mill, 1950s

Hines Creek (village)
84 D/2 - Hines Creek
31-83-4-W6
56°14′55″N 119°08′50″W
Approximately 25 km north north-west of Fairview.

It was named for its proximity to the creek. Originally established as a post office in

October 1928, the first postmaster was Carol Leonard. (see also Hines Creek)

Hinton Trail (locality)
83 M/4 - Rio Grande
SW-13-70-11-W6
55°03′N 119°32′W
Approximately 46 km west south-west of Grande Prairie.

The post office opened in August 1923. This was apparently the end of the trail from Hinton to Grande Prairie at the time it was named. The trail came north along Nose Creek, then followed the Wapiti River for a bit, went overland to the Redwillow River, crossed the Redwillow River going north until it joined up with a surveyed road approximately five kilometres north of the original site of the Hinton Trail Post Office. The first postmaster was S. Ronksley. The town of Hinton was named for William P. Hinton who was an official for the Grand Trunk Pacific. The word *hinton* has at least two meanings in Old English, "town situated in high land" or "the monk's or nun's town."

Hodgins Creek (creek)
83 K/12 - Ante Creek
6-32-64-25-W5
54°34′30″N 117°44′55″W
Flows east into Simonette River approximately 95 km south south-east of Grande Prairie.

This creek is named after one of the men who first logged in the area. He built the first bridge across the creek in the 1940s. The name was officially approved in 1991 after field research determined the name was well known and in local use.

Hollies Creek (creek)
74 D/10 - Hollies Creek
30-88-6-W4
56°40′N 110°57′W

Flows south-west into Clearwater River approximately 28 km east south-east of Fort McMurray.

Named in 1925 for R.T. Hollies, an instrument man, on a survey of the area in 1914-1915.

Holmes Crossing (locality)
83 J/7 - Fort Assiniboine
31-61-5-W5
54°19′N 114°44′W
Approximately 32 km north-west of Barrhead.

William Holmes arrived in the area in 1905. An unmanned ferry was established at this point on the Athabasca River in 1906 and was therefore consistently on the wrong side of the river when needed. Mr. Holmes became the ferryman as a result, and remained in that capacity until 1913. The post office opened in 1908, with Mr. Holmes as its first postmaster.

Holmes Lake (lake)
74 M/16 - Andrew Lake
35-125-2-W4
59°54′N 110°13′W
Approximately 350 km north of Fort McMurray.

The name was submitted in 1958 by the Research Council of Alberta, and is one of a series of features in the area named after deceased prominent geologists. "It was named after the English geologist, Sir Arthur Holmes. He was one of the first to promote the idea of continental drift." Holmgren, 1976.

Homestead (locality)
83 M/11 - Saddle Hills
20-75-9-W6
55°31′N 119°22′W
Approximately 48 km north-west of Grande Prairie.

The post office was established here in November 1930. The first postmaster was C. Nordhagen. The name is descriptive of the way in which the land was obtained by the farmers. Homesteads were a land grant obtained under the Dominion Lands Act whereby for a fee of $10, the prospective homesteader would file for a quarter-section of land (160 acres). Then, within a set period of time, usually three years, after a prescribed number of improvements had been made, the homesteader would gain free and clear title to the land.

***Hommy** (former post office)
83 M/6 - La Glace
NW-29-72-10-W6
55°16′N 119°30′W
Approximately 48 km west north-west of Grande Prairie.

(see Albright and Hommy Provincial Park)

***Hommy Provincial Park** (provincial park)
83 M/5 - Hythe
16-30-72-10-W6
55°16′N 119°31′W
Approximately 42 km west of Grande Prairie.

The park was named after early settlers in the area, Hans and Sidsel Hommy, who came to the Grande Prairie area in 1916 from Norway via Minnesota. It was originally established in 1932, and was eventually closed some time in the 1960s.

Hondo (locality)
83 O/1 - Smith
23-70-1-W5
55°04′N 114°02′W
Approximately 53 km south-east of Slave Lake.

It may be named after a town in Texas. *Hondo* is a Spanish word meaning deep. The post office opened in November 1930, the first postmaster being Ole Finstad.

---
*denotes rescinded name or former locality.

Hoohey Creek (creek)
84 O/13 - Alberta-Northwest Territories
11-18-125-10-W5
59°52′N 115°44′W
Flows east into Whitesand River approximately 166 km north north-east of High Level.

Joe Hoohey was a local Slavey trapper along this creek. He lived at Indian Cabins, Alberta, where he was known as "The Little Chief." The name was officially adopted in 1963.

Hook Lake (lake)
74 D/2 - Quigley
23-81-4-W4
56°02′18″N 110°30′10″W
Approximately 93 km south-east of Fort McMurray.

The descriptive name for this lake resembling a fish hook is well established in local usage.

Hooker Lake (lake)
74 M/10 - Cornwall Lake
31-121-5-W4
59°33′N 110°52′W
Approximately 306 km north of Fort McMurray.

It was named in 1929 after Mr. Hooker, a storekeeper for the Hudson's Bay Company at Fort Chipewyan.

Hoole Creek (creek)
83 P/13 - Pelican
4-19-80-24-W4
55°57′N 113°46′W
Flows south-west into South Wabasca Lake approximately 95 km north-east of Slave Lake.

Likely named after a pioneer in the area; the name appears on federal government maps at least as early as 1918. The word *hoole* comes from the Old English and refers to the land formation "hollow."

Hope Creek (creek)
83 J/5 - Carson Lake
24-62-14-W5
54°23′N 116°00′W
Flows south-west into Sakwatamau River approximately 36 km north-west of Whitecourt.

It shows in federal government maps as early as 1917; its origin is unknown.

Hopeful Lake (lake)
74 E/8 - Trout Creek
6-97-1-W4
57°23′45″N 110°09′15″W
Approximately 105 km north-east of Fort McMurray.

One of three lakes in which trappers have planted cattails as an experiment. (see also Cattail Lake, Test Lake)

Horberg Lake (lake)
74 M/16 - Andrew Lake
SW-1-126-1-W4
59°55′N 110°02′W
Approximately 355 km north of Fort McMurray.

The name was submitted in 1958 by the Research Council of Alberta, and is one of a series of features in the area named after prominent geologists. It was named after the American geomorphologist Leland Horberg (1910-1955).

Hornaday River (river)
74 M/6 - Bocquene Lake
5-21-120-9-W4
59°26′N 111°28′W
Flows east through Wood Buffalo National Park into Slave River approximately 292 km north of Fort McMurray.

The name has appeared on federal government maps since at least 1946. The precise origin of the name is not known. It has been speculated it may have been named after the renowned American zoologist, William Temple Hornaday (1854-1937). He was a pioneer in world wildlife conservation, and was a founder of the New York Zoological Park, the Bronx Zoo. He was no stranger to Canadian wildlife concerns, for in 1906 he published *Camp-Fires in the Canadian Rockies*. He had an interest in bison and because of this he set up the Montana Bison Range. It is possible that when the time came to name this river flowing through Wood Buffalo National Park, it was thought a fitting tribute to William Hornaday.

Horse Creek (creek)
74 D/5 - Alberta
31-84-10-W4
56°19′40″N 111°35′00″W
Flows north-east into Little Horse Creek approximately 48 km south south-west of Fort McMurray.

The exact origin for the name of this creek is unknown.

Horse Creek (creek)
83 J/7 - Fort Assiniboine
33-61-5-W5
54°20′N 114°41′W
Flows south-east into the Athabasca River approximately 47 km south-east of Swan Hills.
It shows on federal government maps as early as 1917, but its precise origin is not known.

Horse Island Creek (creek)
74 L/14 - Rivière des Rochers
13-26-112-9-W4
58°46′N 111°24′W
Flows west into Quatre Fourches Channel approximately 215 km north of Fort McMurray.

Officially named in 1971; its origin is not known.

Horse Lake (lake)
84 A/13 - Liége River
28-90-23-W4
56°50′00″N 113°36′40″W
Approximately 135 km west of Fort McMurray.

This lake takes its name from the horses grazed there by local residents.

Horse Lake (lake)
74 D/4 - Horse River
27-82-13-W4
56°08′32″N 111°56′44″W
Approximately 46 km south-west of Fort McMurray.

Horse Lake is so named as it is the source for Horse River.

Horse Lake (lake)
74 D/7 - Cheecham
30-84-6-W4
56°18′30″N 110°56′02″W
Approximately 55 km south-east of Fort McMurray.

The precise origin of the name of this lake is unknown, although it has been said the shape of the lake resembles a horse; it may alternatively be due to its proximity to the Horse River.

Horse Lake (lake)
83 M/5 - Hythe
24-73-12-W6
55°20′N 119°42′W
Approximately 65 km west north-west of Grande Prairie.

Origin of the name is unknown although it may refer to a time when horses were seen at the lake. A federal government map shows the name was in use as early as 1917.

Horse Lakes Indian Reserve No.152B (Indian reserve)
83 M/5 - Hythe
73-12-W6
55°21′N 119°42′W
Approximately 60 km west north-west of Grande Prairie.

It is named for its proximity to Horse Lake. The group of Beaver Indians of the Dunvegan Band petitioned the Federal Government for reserve land in 1911. In was not until April 29, 1920, that the reserve was established.

Horse River (river)
74 D/11 - Fort McMurray
17-89-9-W4
56°43′N 111°23′W
Flows north-east into Athabasca River at Fort McMurray.

The origin of the name Horse River is unclear. It has been suggested that the river received its name because a horse fell through ice into the river, or because packhorses were able to ford this river in two places. A.J. Tremblay, DLS, referred to it as Horse Creek in 1912.

Horseshoe Lake (lake)
74 D/10 - Hollies Creek
26-88-7-W4
56°39′50″N 110°59′30″W
Approximately 18 km east south-east of Fort McMurray.

This is a descriptive name. The lake is an oxbow and therefore its shape resembles a horseshoe. A great variety of vegetation, shore birds and aquatic life is found in the area of the lake.

Horseshoe Slough (slough-marsh)
74 L/13 - Baril River
2-114-10-W4
58°52′N 111°34′W
Approximately 229 km north of Fort McMurray.

The name is descriptive of the shape of a small lake found within it. It was officially named in 1971.

Horsetail Lake (lake)
84 A/3 - Horsetail Lake
32-81-22-W4
56°04′N 113°24′W
Approximately 142 km south-west of Fort McMurray.

It may be a translation from the Cree *kanes-ka-was-kos-kak* or "place where the horsetail grows."

Hospital Creek (creek)
84 B/8 - Hospital Creek
14-84-3-W5
56°17′N 114°20′W
Flows south into Trout River, 115 km north north-east of Slave Lake.

The precise origin of the name of this creek is unknown; it does appear on a federal government map as early as 1915.

Hotchkiss (hamlet)
84 F/4 - Hotchkiss
13-93-23-W5
57°04′N 117°33′W
Approximately 16 km north of Manning.

A post office was established here in 1930, and the first postmaster was G.C. Hartt. (see Hotchkiss)

Hotchkiss (station)
84 F/4 - Hotchkiss
26-93-23-W5
57°06′N 117°34′W
Approximately 19 km north of Manning.

The station, hamlet and river were all named in 1915 in honour of C. P. Hotchkiss, DLS, who worked with J. R. Akins on the survey of the 93rd township in 1915-1916.

Hotchkiss River (river)
84 F/3 - Crummy Lake
5-93-22-W5
57°02′N 117°28′W
Flows south-east into Notikewin River approximately 16 km north north-east of Manning.

This was formerly known as the Second Battle River. (see Hotchkiss and Notikewin)

Hotte Lake (lake)
84 K/16 - Hotte Lake
3-115-13-W5
58°57′N 116°07′W
Approximately 75 km north-east of High Level.

This is a war memorial name to commemorate Lance Corporal Alfred Hotte, who was killed March 6, 1945. The local Beaver name for this feature is *minkechok*, which means "big lake." The name is descriptive as the lake is the largest in the immediate area.

House Creek (creek)
84 A/13 - Liége River
26-91-25-W4
56°55′N 113°54′W
Flows south-east into Liége River approximately 158 km west of Fort McMurray.

The precise origin of the name of this creek is unknown; it appears on federal government maps as early as 1915.

House Mountain (mountain)
83 O/4 - House Mountain
10-70-11-W5
55°03′N 115°36′W
Approximately 60 km west south-west of Slave Lake (town).

According to J.N. Wallace, DLS, in correspondence to the Geographic Board of Canada it is a "translation of Waskahigan Watchee, so called from the resemblance of its profile to the roof of a house which is very marked from a certain direction." *Waskahegan* is the Cree word meaning house or lodge. The name was officially approved in 1906. It is one of three features which comprise Swan Hills. (see also Swan Hills)

House River (river)
84 A/2 - Boivin Creek
18-83-16-W4
56°12′N 112°30′W
Flows north-west into Athabasca River approximately 89 km south-west of Fort McMurray.

The precise origin of the name of this river is unknown. The early route from Edson to Grande Prairie followed this river from Lac Ste. Anne to Sturgeon Lake. The aboriginal name name for the river is *Waskahegan*, meaning house or lodge. The name was recorded in the 1912 field notes of G. McMillan, DLS.

*****House River** (river)
83 K/14 - Waskahigan River
35-66-22-W5
54°45′N 117°13′W
Flows north-east into Little Smoky River approximately 115 km south-east of Grande Prairie.

(see Waskahigan River)

House River Indian Cemetery No.178 (Indian reserve)
84 A/2 - Boivin Creek
16-18-83-16-W4
56°12′6″N 112°30′31″W
Approximately 89 km south-west of Fort McMurray.

Named for its proximity to House River, this reserve of approximately two acres for a cemetery was established by order-in-council on July 25, 1918.

---

*denotes rescinded name or former locality.

Howard Creek (creek)
83 M/15 - Rycroft
11-19-79-5-W6
55°51′N 118°46′W
Flows north into Ksituan River approximately 10 km north north-east of Spirit River.

Because of the numbers of muskrats in the creek, it is known locally as Rat Creek. A 1917 federal map of the area shows it as Rat Creek, but by the late 1920s the maps show the name as Howard Creek. It is not known after whom it is named.

Howard Creek (creek)
83 P/5 - Fawcett Lake
6-22-73-1-W5
55°20′N 113°20′W
Flows south-east into Fawcett River approximately 55 km east of Slave Lake.

(see Howard Lake)

Howard Lake (lake)
83 O/8 - Driftwood River
25-73-1-W5
55°21′N 114°01′W
Approximately 45 km east of Slave Lake.

It shows on maps as early as 1914, and is the source of Howard Creek; after whom it is named is not known.

Huallen (locality)
83 M/3 - Wembley
22-71-9-W6
55°10′N 119°17′W
Approximately 28 km west of Grande Prairie.

Originally a post office, it was established in May 1929, and was named after Hugh Allen (1889-1972), United Farmers of Alberta MLA for Peace River and Grande Prairie 1926-1935. In 1934, he became Minister of Municipal Affairs and Lands and Mines and held the posts until his defeat in 1935. The first postmaster was Mrs. C. Clow.

Huggard Creek (creek)
83 K/14 - Asplund Creek
9-23-69-22-W5
54°59'20"N 117°13'48"W
Flows north into Little Smoky River approximately 102 km south-east of Grande Prairie.

Officially named in 1991 after field research found the name to be well established and in local use. It is named for Ed Huggard and his family who lived on the creek from 1927 to1945. Before living near the creek, Mr. Huggard had been the first fire ranger north-west of Edmonton. He died in 1965, at the age of 94.

Hughes Lake (lake)
83 M/2 - Grande Prairie
31-71,72-6-W6
55°12'N 118°55'W
Approximately 6 km north-west of Grande Prairie.

According to the 1928 publication, *Place-Names of Alberta*, this feature was named after the father and brother of Katherine Hughes. Katherine Hughes was Alberta's first Provincial Archivist; she was also the Alberta advisor to the Geographic Board of Canada. In 1909 she took a trip to the Lesser Slave Lake and Peace River areas. In her diary of the trip she mentioned passing "the old fort at which Hughes was killed." Whether there is some connection between the two is not known. It was once called Dry Stick Lake. (see also Dry Stick Lake)

Hume Creek (creek)
83 M/4 - Rio Grande
4-22-72-13-W6
55°15'N 119°55'W
Flows south into Steeprock Creek approximately 70 km west of Grande Prairie.

It was named after E. Hume, a returned soldier from World War I who settled here. The name appears on the map in the early 1950s.

Hump, The (hill)
83 L/11 - Alberta
2-21-65-10-W6
From 54°37'30"N 119°25'00"W
Approximately 73 km south south-west of Grande Prairie.

This hill was descriptively named in 1985 as the result of a need to name a landmark in this area. The name was officially approved in 1991. Its elevation is 1265 m.

Hunt Creek (creek)
84 G/3 - Lafond Creek
16-93-7-W5
57°04'N 115°04'W
Flows north-west into Loon River approximately 155 km east north-east of Manning.

The precise origin of the name of this creek is unknown; it is said to have been named after a local resident.

Hunting Creek (creek)
83 N/13 - Tangent
8-4-79-23-W5
55°49'N 117°32'W
Flows north-west into Smoky River approximately 40 km west north-west of McLennan.

The name was recorded by a surveyor in 1909. The origin of the name is not known; however, it may be descriptive of activities carried on near the watercourse. When it was being surveyed, a portion of it was labelled as Racing Creek.

Hunts Lake (lake)
83 O/3 - Adams Creek
NW-32-70-9-W5
55°07'N 115°21'W
Approximately 40 km south-west of Slave Lake (town).

It was officially named some time between 1922 and 1954; the origin of the name is not known.

Hurdy (railway point)
83 K/1 - Windfall Creek
19-60-14-W5
54°12'N 116°06'W
Approximately 32 km north-west of Whitecourt.

Officially adopted in 1973 for a Canadian National Railways spur line point, it was named after Private John Hurdy [Hrudy] of the 1st Battalion of the Canadian Scottish Regiment, killed in action in 1944. He was born in Andrew, Alberta in 1922.

Hutch Lake (locality)
84 K/11 - High Level
23-112-20-W5
58°44'N 117°15'W
Approximately 26 km north north-east of High Level.

It took its name from the nearby lake. (see Hutch Lake)

Hutch Lake (lake)
84 K/14 - Hutch Lake
29-112-20-W5
58°46'N 117°20'W
Approximately 28 km north of High Level.

The precise origin of the name of this lake is unknown. It may be a surname, or it may be descriptive. The Concise Oxford Dictionary defines hutch as a boxlike pen for rabbits, etc., or a derogatory term for a hut, cabin or small house.

Hutton Lake (lake)
74 M/16 - Andrew Lake
SE-13-125-2-W4
59°51'N 110°11'W
Approximately 345 km north of Fort McMurray.

The name was submitted in 1958 by the Research Council of Alberta, and is one of a series of features in the area named after prominent geologists. It was named after a pioneer Scottish geologist, James Hutton (1726-1797). He was the first to theorise on the subject of the earth's crust.

Hythe (village)
83 M/5 - Hythe
NW-13-73-11-W6
55°20′N 119°33′W
Approximately 50 km west north-west of Grande Prairie.

The post office opened in October 1914, and was named after the home town in Kent, in south-east England of the first postmaster, H. Harley. The name comes from the Old English meaning "landing place or harbour."

Indian Cabins (hamlet)
84 N/14 - Indian Cabins
15-125-18-W5
59°52′N 117°02′W
Approximately 151 km north of High Level.

The name likely attests to the existence of cabins that were in the area. A post office was established here in 1953 with the first postmaster being E. Bourassa, and it is situated on the Great Slave Lake Railway line. The old Slavey name for this locality is *Tsentu*, which means "dirty water" referring to the high silt content of the Hay River on which it is situated.

*****Indiana** (former railway station)
83 O/5 - Driftpile
NW34-73-13-W5
55°22′N 115°57′W
Approximately 72 km west of Slave Lake.

An Edmonton, Dunvegan and British Columbia Railway station was established

---
*denotes rescinded name or former locality.

here in 1914. According to railway records, the name referred to an old aboriginal settlement there. The name was later changed to Joussard Station. (see Joussard Station)

Inglis Island (island)
74 D/14 - Wood Creek
31-91-9-W4
56°56′N 111°26′W
In Athabasca River, 23 km north of Fort McMurray.

Named by S.C. Ells in 1924, after Inglis McDonald, son of Constable John McDonald, a member of the Alberta Provincial Police Force. The island used to be known as Dog Rib Island. (see also Dog Rib Island)

Ings Island (island)
74 E/4 - Fort MacKay
13-95-11-W4
57°15′N 111°39′W
Island in Athabasca River, 59 km north of Fort McMurray.

The island was named after Major George A. Ings, a well-known physician.

Inkster Lake (lake)
74 M/16 - Andrew Lake
NE-36-125-1-W4
59°55′N 110°01′W
Approximately 353 km north north-east of Fort McMurray on the Alberta-Saskatchewan boundary.

Records indicate that the name was included in a list of additional names dated November 28, 1938, after the members of the Saskatchewan-Alberta Boundary Commission and the survey party who made the survey of the boundary from Lake Athabasca to the 60th Parallel. The lake was named after O. Inkster, the assistant on the survey.

Inverness River (river)
83 O/3 - Adams Creek
3-21-70-9-W5
55°04′N 115°18′W
Flows north-east into Swan River approximately 40 km south-west of Slave Lake (town).

Likely named after the northern city of Inverness in Scotland. From the Scots Gaelic *inbhir-nis* literally meaning "mouth of the (river) Ness." It was officially approved in 1906.

*****Iosegun Lake** (hamlet)
83 K/7 - Iosegun Lake
29-62-19-W5
54°24′N 116°48′W
Approximately 75 km west north-west of Whitecourt.

It was established as a post office in 1958, and the name changed 10 years later to Fox Creek. The first postmaster was E.W. MacKain. (see also Fox Creek)

Iosegun Lake (lake)
83 K/7 - Iosegun Lake
19-63-19,20-W5
54°29′N 116°52′W
Approximately 8 km north of Fox Creek.

It is the source of the Iosegun River. (see Iosegun River)

Iosegun River (river)
83 K/11 - Waskahigan River
30-66-21-W5
54°44′N 117°11′W
Flows north-west into Smoky River approximately 6 km north of Fox Creek.

There have been a number of interpretations of this name. One source states that it is an aboriginal word meaning "tail." Some people have stated that it had something to do with sulphur. The most commonly accepted meaning is that it is a translation from the Cree, and means "Hash." In fact both the river and the lake were known by the name Hash in the early years. Why hash? The meaning itself causes some confusion. It may mean "all mixed up" or "undecided" as one source mentioned. However, some have speculated it may also relate to a story in which someone cut up some food on the shore and made a stew of it. Further details may shed more light on its origin. Hash River was actually a variation of the older Rivière la Hache. *Hache* can be translated from the French to mean hatchet or axe. George Dawson in 1879 recorded the Cree word for axe as *x - ga-h -gun*. Therefore, the French fur traders may have taken the earlier aboriginal word and translated it to their own language. Why it was called this is not known.

Ipiatik Lake (lake)
73 M/6 - Wiau Lake
6-73-7-W4
55°17′N 111°03′W
Approximately 82 km north-east of Lac La Biche.

It is a Cree word for "look out", but why it is called that is not precisely known. It appears on maps as early as 1913. It was at one time known as Christmas Lake.

Ipiatik River (river)
73 M/3 - Winefred Lake
5-5-71-7-W4
55°07′N 111°03′W
Flows south-east into Sand River approximately 60 km east north-east of Lac La Biche.

(see Ipiatik Lake)

Irma Island (island)
74 D/10 - Hollies Creek
1-87-4-W4
56°31′N 110°30′W

In Gordon Lake approximately 60 km east south-east of Fort McMurray.

It is not known after whom this feature is named.

Iron Point (point)
83 P/7 - Amadou Lake
NE-6-75-18-W4
55°28′N 112°47′W
Approximately 80 km north-west of Lac La Biche in the Athabasca River

It first appears on a map in 1949, and may refer to evidence of iron oxide in the river bank.

Iroquois Creek (creek)
83 N/7 - Triangle
14-14-75-17-W5
55°29′N 116°32′W
Flows north-east into West Prairie River approximately 8 km west of High Prairie.

In his field notes of 1911, Arthur St. Cyr, DLS, records, "*nat-sho-e* or Iroquois Creek." (see Iroquois Lakes)

Iroquois Creek (creek)
83 M/3 - Wembley
12-33-69-9-W6
55°01′N 119°19′W
Flows north-west into Wapiti River approximately 30 km west south-west of Grande Prairie.

The name appears as early as 1918 on a federal government map. It likely refers to the aboriginal people from the east who were employed in the fur trade to act as guides and emissaries for the bateaux brigades of the Hudson's Bay Company.

Iroquois Lakes (lakes)
83 N/7 - Triangle
35-74,75-18-W5
55°28′N 116°40′W
Immediately north-west of High Prairie.

They were known as Iroquois Lakes when the surveyors came through the area in 1911. It likely refers to the time when the Iroquois may have camped there when in the employ of the fur trading companies. They acted as guides, interpreters and emissaries for the traders.

Isadore's Lake (lake)
74 E/4 - Fort MacKay
8-95-10-W4
57°14′00″N 111°36′10″W
Approximately 58 km north north-west of Fort McMurray.

Isadore Lacorde lived and trapped on this lake many years ago. Local residents of Fort MacKay have continued to refer to it as Isadore's Lake.

Isidore Lake (lake)
84 P/5 - Bowhay Lake
NW-28-119-22-W4
59°22′N 113°45′W
Approximately 213 km east north-east of High Level.

This lake was named after Isidore Mercredi, a former park warden of Wood Buffalo National Park who later moved to Fort Smith.

Island Creek (creek)
83 O/3 - Adams Creek
16-8-71-9-W5
55°09′N 115°20′W
Flows north-west into Swan River approximately 40 km south-west of Slave Lake (town).

Adopted some time between 1922 and 1943; the name is likely descriptive.

Island Creek (creek)
84 D/2 - Hines Creek
18-81-4-W6
56°01′N 118°37′W

Flows south into Hines Creek approximately 15 km west south-west of Fairview.

The name is likely descriptive of the feature and was noted by J.B. St. Cyr, DLS, in 1908.

Island Lake (lake)
84 A/14 - Mink Lake
34-89-21-W4
56°46'55"N 113°15'40"W
Approximately 124 km west of Fort McMurray.

A descriptive name, because of the small island in the centre of the lake. It was recorded by G.H. Blanchet, DLS in 1912.

Island Lake (lake)
74 D/6 - Gregoire Lake
21-84-8-W4
56°17'30"N 111°12'15"W
Approximately 48 km south south-east of Fort McMurray.

This name is descriptive of the small island in the south end of the lake.

Island Lake (lake)
83 J/11 - Swan Hills
9-65-7-W5
54°36'N 115°00'W
Approximately 26 km east south-east of Swan Hills.

The name was recorded as early as 1950, and is descriptive.

Island Lake (lake)
83 P/14 - Muskeg River
35-79-22-W4
55°53'N 113°30'W
Approximately 105 km north-east of Slave Lake.

The name appears as early as 1905 on a federal government map, and is descriptive of the island in the lake.

*Island Lake (lake)
83 P/3 - Calling Lake
1-16-72-22-W4
55°14'N 113°19'W
Approximately 100 km north-west of Lac La Biche.

(see Calling Lake)

*Island Lake (lake)
84 J/14 - Margaret Lake
24-114-8-W5
58°54'N 115°11'W
Approximately 118 km east north-east of High Level.

(see Eva Lake)

*Island Lake (lake)
73 M/6 - Wiau Lake
30-74-9-W4
55°26'N 111°23'W
Approximately 84 km north north-east of Lac La Biche.

(see Rat Lake)

Iyinimin Creek (creek)
74 E/6 - Kearl Lake
28-95-8-W4
57°16'45"N 111°13'57"W
Flows north-west into Kearl Lake approximately 61 km north of Fort McMurray.

Iyinimin is the Cree word for blueberries. This area is known for an abundance of blueberries. The blueberry, *Vaccinium myrtilloides*, is one of many species of wild shrubs producing edible fruit generally found in thickets and dry bogs.

---

*denotes rescinded name or former locality.

J~K

Jack Creek (creek)
84 D/2 - Hines Creek
23-83-5-W6
56°12′N 118°41′W
Flows south south-west into Hines Creek approximately 24 km north-west of Fairview.

The precise origin of the name of this creek is unknown; it appears on a map by G.A. Tipper, DLS, as the result of his 1912 survey.

Jackfish (locality)
74 L/7 - Keane Creek
5-34-108-6-W4
58°25′N 110°55′W
Approximately 182 km north of Fort McMurray.

Officially approved in 1946 it was named for its proximity to Jackfish Creek. On some early maps, it was shown as Big Eddy. (see also Big Eddy)

Jackfish Creek (creek)
74 L/16 - Stone Point
1-1-115-1-W4
58°58′N 110°00′W
Flows east into Saskatchewan approximately 253 km north north-east of Fort McMurray.

Officially named in 1946, the name is descriptive of the fish found in the creek.

Jackfish Creek (creek)
74 L/7 - Keane Creek
5-34-108-6-W4
58°25′N 110°55′W
Flows north-east into Athabasca River approximately 182 km north of Fort McMurray.

The name was well established and in local use by the 1940s, and refers to the prevalence of the fish in the creek.

Jackfish Lake (lake)
83 M/12 - Boone Creek
4-14-76-11-W6
55°34′N 119°36′W
Approximately 70 km north-west of Grande Prairie.

The well-established name for this lake is descriptive of the large number of jackfish found in the lake.

Jackfish Lake (lake)
83 K/12 - Ante Creek
25-66-27-W5
54°44′35″N 117°56′00″W
Approximately 73 km south-east of Grande Prairie.

This descriptive name was officially adopted in 1991 after field research determined the name had long been in local use.

Jackfish Lakes (lakes)
84 P/5 - Bowhay Lake
31-120-22-W4
59°28′N 113°46′W
Approximately 216 km east north-east of High Level.

Officially named in the 1944, the name is descriptive of the fish found in them.

Jackfish Point (point)
84 M/10 - Jackfish Point
15-123-4-W6
59°41′N 118°35′W
Approximately 139 km north north-east of Fort McMurray.

The precise origin of the name of this point is unknown; it may be descriptive.

Jackfish Point Indian Reserve No. 214
(Indian reserve)
84 M/10 - Jackfish Point
10-123-4-W6
59°41′N 118°35′W
Approximately 137 km north north-east of Rainbow Lake.

Named for its proximity to Jackfish Point.

Jackfish River (locality)
84 I/15 - Jackfish River
11-18-115-17-W4
59°00′N 112°53′W
Approximately 256 km north north-west of Fort McMurray.

Named for its proximity to the river.

Jackfish River (river)
84 P/2 - Boyer Rapids
SW-8-116-17-W4
59°04′N 112°53′W
Flows east into Peace River approximately 249 km east north-east of High Level.

Named for the abundance of the fish in the river; the name was recorded as early as 1890 by the Geological Survey of Canada.

Jackfish River (river)
73 M/11 - Conklin
31-77-7-W4
55°42′N 111°06′W
Flows north into Christina River approximately 120 km north-east of Lac La Biche.

This name which, has been in use since 1915, is descriptive of the large number of jackfish in the lake.

Jackpine Creek (creek)
84 C/15 - Jackpine Creek
14-90-18-W5
56°48′N 116°45′W
Flows south-west into Little Cadotte River

approximately 55 km east south-east of Manning.

The origin of the name of this creek, which has its source in Jackpine Lake, likely refers to an abundance of the tree in the area. Jackpine, or *Pinus banksiana*, is a small tree, ranging from five to ten metres in height, and is found predominantly in central and northern Alberta.

Jackpine Creek (creek)
74 E/6 - Kearl Lake
24-95-10-W4
57°15'40"N 111°28'15"W
Flows north-west into Muskeg River approximately 60 km north of Fort McMurray.

This creek takes its name from the jackpine trees found in this area. The local name was officially adopted in 1991, and replaced the former official name Hartley Creek. Although Fort MacKay residents call this creek Jackpine, Fort McMurray residents continue to call it Hartley Creek. The name Hartley is for John Stephen Hartley, Stoker First Class, of Ashmont, Alberta. He was killed in World War II.

Jackpine Lake (lake)
84 C/15 - Jackpine Creek
19-91-16-W5
56°55'N 116°34'W
Approximately 63 km east of Manning.

Found on federal government maps as early as 1930, the name is likely descriptive of the flora in the area.

Jackpot Creek (Creek)
84 N/14 - Indian Cabins
15-125-18-W5
59°52'N 117°02'W
Flows north-east into Hay River approximately 149 km north of High Level.

The name was officially adopted in 1963 when it was determined the name had long been in local usage. Although the origin of the name is not known, there may be at least two explanations. The *Dictionary of Canadianisms* defines jackpot to mean "a difficult or embarrassing situation, a predicament." Whether the creek was the site of an embarrassing incident, or of something more positive is not recorded. The more widely known meaning of the word comes from games of chance, meaning to have great luck.

Jaillante, La Petite Rivière (river)
83 P/2 - Calling River
SW-35-71-19-W4
55°11'N 112°49'W
Flows south-east into the Athabasca River approximately 65 km north-west of Lac La Biche.

Although not officially adopted until 1954, the name for this river was noted on a map as early as 1884. In English the name translates to "little gushing/spouting river" and likely refers to the flow of water along the narrow 61-metre-high canyon on its way to the Athabasca River.

James Creek (creek)
84 N/15 - Lessard Creek
25-124-18-W5
59°48'N 116°58'W
Flows north-east into Hay River approximately 142 km north of High Level.

It is not known after whom this creek is named.

Jane Lake (lake)
83 J/14 - Deer Mountain
11-68-8-W5
54°53'N 115°06'W
Approximately 25 km north-east of Swan Hills.

Likely named in the 1930s or 1940s, after whom is not known. (see Agnes Lake)

Janvier Indian Reserve No. 194
(Indian reserve)
73 M/15 - Bohn Lake
80-5-W4
55°56'N 110°43'W
Approximately 90 km south south-east of Fort McMurray.

This was named after the Paul Janvier family, part of the Chipewyan Band who hunted in what is now western Saskatchewan and eastern Alberta. Part of Treaty No. 8, the land was not surveyed until 1922. The reserve is known locally as Chipewyan Prairie.

Jean Baptiste Gambler Indian Reserve No. 183 (Indian reserve)
83 P/6 - Pelican
30-72-21-W4
55°16'N 113°13'W
Approximately 100 km east of Slave Lake.

This was named after an early chief or elder of the group.

Jean Côté (hamlet)
83 N/14 - Lac Magloire
36-79-22-W5
55°54'N 117°19'W
Approximately 20 km north north-west of Falher.

Senator Jean Léon Côté was born in Quebec in 1867 and became a Dominion Land Surveyor, a civil engineer and a mining engineer. He worked for the Canadian Department of the Interior as a land surveyor in Alberta from 1893 until 1900. He also ran a number of resource and land-based companies. In 1909, Côté tried his hand at politics and was elected as a Liberal member of the Alberta Legislative Assembly. He was re-elected for Grouard in subsequent elections, and was appointed

Provincial Secretary in 1918, a post he held until 1921. He was appointed to the Senate of Canada in 1923, and died a year later.

Jean Lake (lake)
84 H/5 - Burnt Lake
12-98-24-W4
57°29′N 113°46′W
Approximately 165 km north-west of Fort McMurray.

The precise origin of the name of this lake is unknown; it appears on federal government maps as early as 1916. There was a settlement by the lake that at one time was referred to by local people as Beaver Lake.

Jemis Lake (lake)
74 L/11 - Fort Chipewyan
28-111-9-W4
58°40′N 111°27′W
Approximately 207 km north of Fort McMurray.

It was named after trapper who worked in this area at one time.

Jerry Creek (creek)
83 O/3 - Adams Creek
2-33-70-9-W5
55°06′N 115°18′W
Flows north-west into Swan River approximately 40 km south-west of Slave Lake (town).

The origin of this name is not known; it was recorded some time between 1914 and 1922.

Jessie Lake (lake)
83 J/15 - Upper Saulteaux River
68-7-5-W5
54°53′N 114°58′W
Approximately 33 km north-east of Swan Hills.

Situated on the 18th Baseline; it was likely named in the 1930s or 1940s, but after whom it is named is not known. (see Agnes Lake)

Jim Creek (creek)
84 C/13 - Manning
15-91-24-W5
56°53′N 117°45′W
Flows north into Notikewin River 8 km south-west of Manning.

The creek was named in 1920 after Jim Durocher, a trapper who lived on the bank of the creek near the junction of Notikewin River. He died of influenza during the 1918 epidemic.

Jimmys Slough (marsh)
74 L/13 - Baril River
NW-9-113-10-W4
58°48′N 111°38′W
Approximately 222 km north of Fort McMurray.

Officially named in 1971 after a trapper who worked in the area.

Jodoin Creek (creek)
84 P/2 - Boyer Rapids
NW-21-116-17-W4
59°06′N 112°50′W
Flows south-east into Peace River approximately 251 km east north-east of High Level.

Named in 1950 after Able Seaman Lawrence James Jodoin, born in Edmonton in 1925. He enlisted as soon as he was old enough in March 1943. He died 15 months later during the invasion of Normandy.

Joe's Lake (lake)
74 D/7 - Cheecham
21-85-5-W4
56°23′03″N 110°43′15″W
Approximately 56 km south-east of Fort McMurray.

Joe's Lake was named after Joe Desjarlais, who lived and trapped in the area at one time.

John Bull Slough (marsh)
74 L/11 - Fort Chipewyan
21-112-9-W4
58°44′N 111°27′W
Approximately 214 km north of Fort McMurray.

The name is that of an old respected trapper who had this as his muskrat trapping area. It is a landmark for those travelling to Fort Chipewyan from the eastern trapping grounds.

■ **John D'Or Prairie** (locality)
84 J/6 - Adams Landing
30-109-7-W5
58°29′N 115°08′W
On John D'Or Prairie Indian Reserve approximately 115 km east of High Level.

The post office was established here in 1971, with the first postmaster being John St. Arnault. (see also John D'Or Prairie Indian Reserve)

John D'Or Prairie Indian Reserve No. 215 (Indian reserve)
84 J/6 - Adams Landing
15-110-7-W5
58°33′N 115°05′W
Approximately 111 km east of High Level.

Named after a Cree called Weskwatemapow. The English translation of this name is "someone who sits by the door." Weskwatemapow was an orphan and raised by a Cree family. He received his name from his habit of sitting beside the opening of his step-parents' tepee. He was also known as Grandfather in Cree. John D'Or is apparently the result of the transliteration of the English word *door* into the French *d'or*. The reserve is locally called Johnny D'Or Prairie. Surveyor C.P. Hotchkiss in his survey notes for 1920 referred to Adams Landing on the Peace River from "where a wagon road starts for Johnny Dores Prairie." In 1909 and 1910, more land was set aside for this band in response to migration of people from the Wabasca area.

Johnson Lake (lake)
74 E/9 - Johnson Lake
10-100-3-W4
57°39′N 110°23′W
Approximately 119 km north-east of Fort McMurray.

Named in 1950 for Sergeant Gordon Fraser Johnson who was born in Leader, Saskatchewan in 1919 and enlisted in Calgary in 1941. He was killed in action in continental Europe in 1944 and was mentioned in despatches.

Johnson Lake (lake)
74 M/16 - Andrew Lake
SE-14-124-1-W4
59°46′N 110°03′W
Approximately 338 km north north-east of Fort McMurray.

This was named after P.N. Johnson, a Director of Surveys of Alberta.

Johnson Lake (lake)
84 I/7 - Heron Island
3-1-108-18-W4
58°21′N 112°52′W
Approximately 190 km north north-west of Fort McMurray.

Officially named in 1963 after a trapper called Johnson who made his headquarters on the banks of this small lake.

Joli Fou, Rapides du (rapids)
84 A/2 - Boivin Creek
5-82-17-W4
56°04′N 112°37′W
In the Athabasca River approximately 105 km south-west of Fort McMurray.

This long-established name marks the death of an unskilled steersman who died trying to run these rapids. The name was recorded by the Geological Survey of Canada in 1892. J.W. Tyrrell notes in *Across the Sub-Arctic of Canada* (1897): "....we reached a place known as the Rapid of the Jolly Fool. It is said to have received its name from the fact that at one time an awkward canoeman lost his life by allowing his canoe to be smashed upon the most conspicuous rock in the rapids." The question remains as to why "jolly fool." The translation of joli is usually pretty or nice, and sometimes, ironically, piquant. A possible explanation is that the "jolly fool" was one Chalifoux whose name could easily have been corrupted to joli fou.

Jones Lake (lake)
83 M/6 - La Glace
9-74-7-W6
55°23′N 119°00′W
Approximately 24 km north north-west of Grande Prairie.

The lake became known as Jones Lake some time after 1927 when Rhys Jones and family bought adjoining land from Bill Turner. Jones Lake is one of a group of lakes that were known collectively as Buffalo Lakes. (see also Buffalo Lake)

Josephine Creek (creek)
83 M/15 - Rycroft
3-81-7-W6
56°00′N 119°00′W
Flows east into Hamelin Creek approximately 25 km north north-west of Spirit River.

Although pure speculation, this creek may have been named after Josephine Hamelin. According to the Métis Land Scrip files and records of the Oblates of Mary Immaculate, there was a woman named Josephine Hamelin in Alberta in the late 19th century.

Joslyn Creek (creek)
74 E/5 - Bitumount
34-95-11-W4
57°17′N 111°42′W
Flows south-east into Ells River approximately 65 km north north-west of Fort McMurray.

It was named by G.H. Blanchet, DLS, during his survey in 1914; the origin is unknown.

Joussard (hamlet)
83 O/5 - Driftpile
8,9-74-13-W5
55°24′N 115°57′W
Approximately 75 km west of Slave Lake.

According to one source, this was named after an early settler in the area. Katherine Hughes in her diary of a trip to northern Alberta in 1909 refers to a Father Jussard (sic) being stationed at Fort Vermilion. Another source has stated it was named after Bishop Henri Célestin Joussard (1851-1932). He was born in France, joined the Oblates of Mary Immaculate in 1873, and served as a missionary in various northern posts. He became auxiliary bishop of Athabasca in 1909. The post office was established in June 1928. The first postmaster was Joe Turner.

Joussard Station (railway point)
83 O/5 - Driftpile
NW-34-73-13-W5
55°22′N 115°55′W
Approximately 72 km west of Slave Lake.

An Edmonton, Dunvegan and British Columbia Railway station, originally called Indiana, was established here in 1914. (see also Joussard and Indiana)

Judah (locality)
84 C/3 - Peace River
35-82-22-W5
56°09′N 117°19′W
Approximately 5 km south of Peace River.

Named after Noel Fulton Judah, former auditor of the Edmonton, Dunvegan and British Columbia Railway. The name was first applied in 1916 to the station in the area. The post office was established here in 1928, with Mrs. M.A. Mills as first postmaster.

Judy Creek (creek)
83 J/11 - Swan Hills
25-64-10-W5
54°33′N 115°23′W
Flows north-east into Freeman River approximately 16 km north of Swan Hills.

Officially adopted in 1957; it is not known after whom this creek is named.

Kakenokamaksik Lake (lake)
84 H/11 - Bergeron Creek
24-99-22-W4
57°36′33″N 113°27′59″W
Approximately 161 km north-west of Fort McMurray.

This well-established descriptive name has been in use for many years and translates from Cree as "long" lake.

Kakisa River (river)
84 M/13 - Lake May
25-126-11-W6
59°59′N 119°46′W
Flows north-west into the Northwest Territories approximately 220 km north-west of High Level.

The name was officially approved in 1962. Although likely aboriginal in origin, the meaning of the word is not yet known.

Kakut Creek (creek)
83 M/9 - Peoria
9-76-2-W6
55°34′N 118°15′W
Flows south-east into Heart River approximately 55 km north-east of Grande Prairie.

(see Kakut Lake)

Kakut Lake (lake)
83 M/10 - Woking
34-76-4-W6
55°37′N 118°32′W
Approximately 25 km south-east of Spirit River.

This name is possibly Beaver or Cree in origin and has been translated to mean "Mud Lake." The name was recorded when J.H. Smith, DLS, surveyed the area in 1911. It was also recorded on an earlier Geological Survey of Canada map as Ka-kout Lake.

Kakwa Mountain (mountain)
83 L/4 - Kakwa River
2-59-14-W6
54°05′N 120°00′W
Approximately 61 km west north-west of Grande Cache.

For a short period of time, this feature, 2295 metres in altitude, was known as Mount Cross. The Alberta-British Columbia Interprovincial Boundary Commission recorded the name Kakwa Mountain in 1924. The name already had been suggested about a decade before by S. Prescott Fay, who spent three seasons in the Canadian Rockies, determining the ranges of the big game between Lake Louise and the Peace River. It takes its name from the nearby river. (see also Kakwa River and Cross, Mount)

Kakwa River (river)
83 L/9 - Latornell River
64-4-W6
54°37′N 118°27′W
Flows north-east into Smoky River approximately 140 km west south-west of Grande Prairie.

Kakwa is the Cree word for porcupine, and it is the name Porcupine River that was recorded by the Dominion Land Surveyors when they were through the area around 1910. By 1924, the Cree name was applied to the river.

Kamisak Lake (lake)
83 M/4 - Rio Grande
22-71-12-W6
55°10′N 119°45′W
Approximately 57 km west of Grande Prairie.

Although the name is likely First Nations in origin, the meaning is unknown.

Kamistikowik Lake (lake)
84 A/4 - North Wabasca Lake
34-82-23-W4
56°09′N 113°31′W
Approximately 144 km south-west of Fort McMurray.

Approved in 1975, it is a descriptive Cree name that means "that which is in a wooded area" or "that which is surrounded by bush or trees." The name which was once suggested for the lake was Gocan, an abbreviation of **G**ulf **O**il **Can**ada.

Karr Creek (creek)
83 L/9 - Latornell River
2,5-64-2-W6
54°34′20″N 118°10′00″W
Flows north-east into Latornell River approximately 80 km south south-east of Grande Prairie.

Officially approved in the 1980s, the creek takes its name from its source. (see also Karr Lake)

Karr Lake (lake)
83 L/9 - Latornell River
9-17-64-2-W6
54°32′N 118°15′W
Approximately 80 km south south-east of Grande Prairie.

Origin of the name Karr Lake is not known. The name has been in use since at least 1915 at the time it was surveyed.

Kathleen (hamlet)
83 N/10 - McLennan
35-76-19-W5
55°37′N 116°50′W
Approximately 10 km south south-east of McLennan.

Established as a station in 1915, it was named after a relative of W. R. Smith, at one time general manager of the Edmonton, Dunvegan and British Columbia Railway. In order to avoid confusion with Kathyrn near Calgary, the post office at this spot was called Doussal. (see also Doussal)

Kathryn Lake (lake)
83 J/10 - Timeu Creek
30-66-6,7-W5
54°44′N 114°55′W
Approximately 65 km south south-west of Slave Lake.

Likely named in the 1940s, after whom it is named is not known. (see Agnes Lake)

Kaybob (railway point)
83 K/7 - Iosegun Lake
1-62-20-W5
54°20′N 116°51′W
Approximately 6 km south south-west of Fox Creek.

Early in 1941, a committee including John Harvie, Deputy Minister of Lands and Mines and Robert Ethan Allen, chairman of the Petroleum and Natural Gas Conservation Board, recommended some 15 areas where half the lands should be withdrawn from disposal under the normal lease and natural gas rights. One of these areas was called the Kaybob oil field. It is likely a combination of the name of Mr. Allen's mother and wife who shared the same name, Kathryn, and his first name, Robert. The name for this station was officially approved on January 18, 1974.

---

*denotes rescinded name or former locality.

*****Kayow** (former post office)
83 M/13 - Bonanza
SW-9-8-12-W6
55°55′N 119°49′W
Approximately 35 km west north-west of Spirit River.

(see Bonanza)

Keane Creek (creek)
74 L/7 - Keane Creek
5-2-109-6-W4
58°26′N 110°54′W
Flows north-west into Athabasca River approximately 182 km north of Fort McMurray.

It was named after Jason Keane, an explorer who accompanied J.R. Akins during the survey of this area in 1917.

Kearl Lake (lake)
74 E/6 - Kearl Lake
33-95-8-W4
57°17′N 111°14′W
Approximately 62 km north north-east of Fort McMurray.

This lake is named after Flight Lieutenant E.E. Kearl, DFC, (1920-1945), born in Cardston, Alberta. He enlisted in the RCAF at Edmonton in 1941 and was awarded the DFC on January 26, 1945. The following day he was reported missing and subsequently presumed dead. The lake was at one time known as Muskeg Lake.

Keeblo Hill (hill)
83 L/10 - Cutbank River
12-66-6-W6
54°41′20″N 118°45′00″W
Approximately 53 km south of Grande Prairie.

This feature is named after Pete Keeblo, who set up a camp for his portable sawmill at this location some time around the early 1940s. It was officially named in 1991 after field research was conducted in the area.

Keeping Lake (lake)
83 M/5 - Hythe
3-75-13-W6
55°28′N 119°56′W
Approximately 75 km west north-west of Grande Prairie.

Keeping Lake is named after Minter Keeping, who came to the Grande Prairie area in 1919 from Prince Edward Island. Mr. Keeping had planned to raise cattle, so this lake with hay, water, and grazing was ideal. He stayed as a squatter on the land until it was surveyed in 1920 at which time he applied for a homestead grant. Originally it was called Hay Lake but likely due to the abundance of Hay Lakes, the surveyor used the name of the homesteader. (see also Hay Lake)

Keg River (railway point)
84 F/13 - Keg River
23-101-23-W5
57°47′N 117°40′W
Approximately 87 km south south-west of High Level.

(see Keg River)

Keg River (hamlet)
84 F/13 - Keg River
21-101-24-W5
57°48′N 117°52′W
Approximately 91 km south-west of High Level.

Established as a post office in 1932, it takes its name from the nearby feature. The first postmaster was L.G. Harrington. (see Keg River)

Keg River (locality)
84 F/12 - Kemp River
9-101-23-W5
57°45'N 117°38'W
Approximately 90 km south south-west of Manning.

Named for its proximity to the Keg River. This locality was formerly known as Keg River Cabin, as it was the site of the stopover cabin on the old Dominion Telegraph Line, which passed through here. (see Keg River)

Keg River (river)
84 F/14 - Carcajou
25-102-20-W5
57°53'N 117°07'W
Flows west north-west into Peace River approximately 69 km south of High Level.

The origin of this name is obscure but it has been in use since 1828 as it was mentioned by Chief Factor Archibald McDonald of the Hudson's Bay Company who accompanied Sir George Simpson on his journey to the Pacific that year. The river is also mentioned by Charles Mair in *Through the Mackenzie Basin*, (1908) as "the keg" or "Keg of Rum," which would suggest some incident involving a keg of rum. Holmgren, 1976. However, Dr. Mary Percy Jackson of Keg River has stated the name is a translation of the Cree *markak seepee*, meaning "something narrow and deep like a keg."

Kelly Lake (lake)
74 E/12 - Asphalt Creek
27-100-10-W4
57°42'20"N 111°32'30"W
Approximately 110 km north of Fort McMurray.

The precise origin for the name of this lake is unknown. The name has been used by several generations of trappers.

---
*denotes rescinded name or former locality.

Kemp River (locality)
84 F/11 - Scully Creek
34-98-22-W5
57°33'N 117°30'W
Approximately 69 km north of Manning.

The precise origin of the name of this creek is unknown.

Kemp River (river)
84 F/12 - Kemp River
8-101-22-W5
57°45'N 117°35'W
Flows north into Keg River approximately 90 km south south-west of High Level.

The precise origin of the name of this river is unknown; it appears on a federal government map as early as 1919.

***Kempton** (former locality)
83 M/5 - Hythe
25-72-12-W6
55°16'N 119°43'W
Approximately 56 km west of Grande Prairie.

Origin information is not known for this locality. Kempton comes from the Old English and means warriors' town, village or homestead. (see Goodfare)

Kenee Island (island)
74 D/8 - Gipsy Lake
32-86-3-W4
56°30'N 110°27'W
In Gordon Lake approximately 63 km east south-east Fort McMurray.

The precise origin of the name of this island is unknown.

Kennedy Lake (lake)
84P/6 - Merryweather Lake
21, 30-120-19-W4
59°27'N 113°15'W
Approximately 140 km north-west of Fort Chipewyan.

The lake was named in 1928 after Alexander Kennedy, a trapper who worked out of Fort Smith.

Kenny Woods (locality)
74 L/3 - Embarras
2-14-105-9-W4
58°07'N 111°23'W
Approximately 146 km north of Fort McMurray.

Listed on a map as early as 1956; it is not known after whom this locality was named.

Kenzie (locality)
83 N/10 - McLennan
29-75-18-W5
55°31'N 116°45'W
Approximately 20 km west north-west of High Prairie.

This Edmonton, Dunvegan and British Columbia Railway station was opened in 1915. The origin of the name is not known, but it likely refers to an individual.

Keppler Creek (creek)
84 F/3 - Crummy Creek
35-94-20-W5
57°11'45"N 117°05'50"W
Flows north-west into Peace River approximately 44 km north-west of Manning.

A local name that has been officially adopted to honour Henry Keppler (1898-1959), who lived and trapped on this stream from 1913 to 1938. Keppler, a German merchant seaman, jumped ship in New York in 1913 to avoid compulsory military service. He made his way to Alberta, and walked over the Edson Trail to the Peace River Country, where he established himself as a trapper. He hauled freight and passengers in the summer months from Peace River to Vermilion. By the late 1930s increased settlement for farming, brush and forest fires, and depressed prices of fur caused Keppler to leave the area. In the spring of 1940 he built a scow on which he departed with a load of lumber for Yellowknife, where he pursued the blacksmith and machine shop trades he had learnt as a boy in Germany.

*Kerndale (former locality)
84 C/2 - Harmon Valley
83-18-W5
56°12′N 116°48′W
Approximately 25 km east of Peace River (town).

Established as a post office in November 1917, it was named, after a fashion, for the applicant for the post office, Herbert Kiernen. The first and only postmaster was L. Larson.

*Ketchum (former post office)
84 D/1 - Fairview
24-82-1-W6
56°07′35″N 118°01′45″W
Approximately 23 km east north-east of Fairview.

The post office opened in September 1919, likely taking its name from the nearby lake. The first postmaster was Miss H. Maring. The name was changed in 1924. (see also Liliendale)

Ketchum Lake (lake)
84 D/1 - Fairview
13-82-3-W6
56°06′N 118°19′W
Approximately 6 km north-east of Fairview.

The origin of the name of this lake is unknown.

Kettle River (river)
73 M/15 - Bohn Lake
28-80-5-W4
55°58′N 110°42′W

---
*denotes rescinded name or former locality.

Flows east into Christina River approximately 90 km south south-east of Fort McMurray.

Officially approved in 1945; the origin of the name is not known.

Khahago Creek (creek)
74 E/6 - Kearl Lake
36-95-9-W4
57°17′02″N 111°18′41″W
Flows north into Muskeg Creek approximately 58 km north of Fort McMurray.

Khahago is the Cree word for raven. There is a story that a raven bit someone and this creek became associated with the incident.

Kidney Lake (lake)
84 B/15 - Kidney Lake
2-90-4-W5
56°47′N 114°31′W
Approximately 166 km north of Slave Lake.

The name, which was recorded as early as 1905, may be descriptive of its shape, which has some resemblance to a kidney.

Kidney Pond (lake)
84 K/5 - Kidney Pond
6-109-23-W5
58°26′18″N 117°50′40″W
Approximately 43 km west south-west of High Level.

This lake was once a part of the hunting and trapping area of Dunne-za or Beaver families by the name of Kidney. A member of the Kidney family is buried to the east of the lake.

Kilome Lake (lake)
84 O/16 - Kilome Lake
SW-6-126-1-W5
59°55′N 114°10′W
Approximately 226 km north-east of High Level.

Approved in 1967, it was named after Adam Kilome (1896-1962), a trapper in Wood Buffalo National Park.

Kilpatrick Creek (creek)
84 P/2 - Boyer Rapids
27-116-18-W4
59°06′N 112°58′W
Flows east into Knights Creek approximately 245 km east north-east of High Level.

Named in 1950 after Pilot Officer Vernon Francis Kilpatrick, of Calgary, who was mentioned in despatches. He was killed in action in Continental Europe in July 1944.

Kimiwan Lake (lake)
83 N/15 - Springburn
14-8-78-19-W5
55°45′N 116°55′W
Immediately to the north of McLennan.

This name was in use when the surveyors came through the area in 1914 and at the time of the survey, there was heavy flooding on the creek. It is a form of a Cree word meaning rain. The Dominion Lands Survey makes reference to its being known originally as Round Lake.

Kimowin Lake (lake)
74 D/1 - Watchusk Lake
16-83-1-W4
56°12′00″N 110°05′50″W
Approximately 98 km south-east of Fort McMurray.

Named for its proximity to the Kimowin River which runs into Saskatchewan. (see also Kimowin River)

Kimowin River (river)
74 D/1 - Watchusk Lake
24-83-1-W4
56°13′N 110°00′W
Flows into Saskatchewan approximately 104 km east south-east of Fort McMurray.

The precise origin of the name of this river is unknown; it may be a transliteration of the Cree word meaning rain. In 1791 Peter Fidler referred to it in Cree as *Wa-pe-sue a seepe*, and in Chipewyan as *Caw-coos a Dez-za*. Both mean "Swan River."

Kinosis (locality)
74 D/7 - Cheecham
1-85-7-W4
56°20′N 110°57′W
Approximately 50 km south-west of Fort McMurray.

Translated from Cree the name means Little Fish. The name Kinosis was originally applied to an Alberta and Great Waterways Railway station in this location in 1917. It is probable that the name was taken from the nearby Kinosis Lake.

Kinosis Creek (creek)
74 D/7 - Cheecham
8-85-6-W4
56°21′39″N 110°55′20″W
Flows north-east into Gregoire River approximately 49 km south-east of Fort McMurray.

Kinosis Creek is the major creek draining from Kinosis Lake. (see also Kinosis)

Kinosis Lake (lake)
74 D/6 - Gregoire Lake
36-84-7-W4
56°20′N 111°01′W
Approximately 59 km south south-east of Fort McMurray.

As the English translation of Kinosis suggests, there are a number of small fish in this deep lake. However, not all the fish are so little, at least one 35-pound jackfish has been caught in the lake. (see Kinosis)

Kinuso (village)
83 O/6 - Kinuso
23-73-10-W5
55°20′N 115°25′W
Approximately 40 km west of Slave Lake.

This is a rendering of the Cree word meaning "fish." It is likely descriptive of the prevalence of fish in the nearby lake. The post office was opened in May 1915 and an Edmonton, Dunvegan and British Columbia Railway station was established there in 1921. The first postmaster was W. L. McKillop. The area was originally known as Swan River. (see also Swan River)

Kipeecheechagum Lake (lake)
84 A/14 - Mink Lake
36-91-22-W4
56°56′15″N 113°23′30″W
Approximately 122 km west north-west of Fort McMurray.

The name for this lake comes from the Woods Cree and means "a place to stop for a while on a portage."

Kirby Lake (lake)
73 M/7 - Kirby Lake
6-74-5-W4
52°28′N 110°46′W
Approximately 110 km north-east of Lac La Biche.

Named after Flight Sergeant Erlyn E. Kirby of Waskatenau, Alberta, who died in World War II. (see also Sterner Lake)

Kirkness Island (island)
84 M/15 - Kirkness Lake
21-124-5-W6
59°47′N 118°48′W
Approximately 144 km north of Rainbow Lake.

The precise origin of the name of this island is unknown. Kirkness comes from the Scots Gaelic and means "church point."

Kiskatinaw Lake (lake)
74 D/11 - Fort McMurray
14-87-7-W4
56°33′N 111°00′W
Approximately 32 km south-east of Fort McMurray.

Kiskatinaw is Cree word for "down in a valley" or "deep in a bank." This lake has very high banks so the name is indeed descriptive.

Kleskun Creek (creek)
83 M/8 - Smoky Heights
NE-28-73-2-W6
55°21′N 118°14′W
Flows east into Smoky River approximately 40 km north-east of Grande Prairie.

Its source is in the hill of the same name. (see Kleskun Hill)

Kleskun Hill (hill)
83 M/7 - Sexsmith
28-72-4-W6
55°15′N 118°32′W
Approximately 7 km north-east of Grande Prairie.

This name, likely Beaver in origin, means "white mud." It was well established by the time G.M. Dawson's geological survey crew were in the area in 1879. It is an area of interesting geological formations and in a modest way the area mimics the more famous badlands features to the south. There even are some fossilized dinosaur remains in the area. The elevation of the hill is 732 metres.

Kleskun Hill (locality)
83 M/8 - Smoky Heights
24-72-4-W6
55°15′N 118°29′W
Approximately 20 km north-east of Grande Prairie.

The post office was established in May 1913 and closed in May 1940. The first postmaster was J. A. Brims. (see Kleskun Hill)

Knight (railway point)
83 K/2 - Marsh Head Creek
1-60-18-W5
54°09′N 116°33′W
Approximately 65 km northwest of Whitecourt.

Officially adopted in 1973 for a Canadian National Railways spur line point, the origin of the name is not precisely known, although it likely refers to a surname.

Knights Creek (creek)
84 P/2 - Boyer Rapids
SW-7-116-17-W4
59°03′N 112°53′W
Flows south into Jackfish River approximately 248 km east north-east of High Level.

Named in 1950 after Flight Lieutenant J.K. Knights, who was born in Strathmore in 1916 and enlisted in Calgary in 1940. He proceeded overseas and in 1943 received the Distinguished Flying Cross. During his second tour of operations he was reported missing, presumed dead, in February 1945.

Krause Lake (lake)
83 J/11 - Swan Hills
3-66-10-W5
54°41′N 115°26′W
Approximately 3 km south-west of Swan Hills.

Named in the late 1940s or early 1950s, after whom is not known.

Kress Lake (lake)
74 E/14 - Pearson Lake
31-103-7-W4
57°58′50″N 111°08′40″W
Approximately 145 km north of Fort McMurray.

This lake was named locally for Gerry Kress, a forest ranger at Fort McMurray. Gerry Kress was born in Kendall, Saskatchewan in 1959. He came to Alberta in 1979 and joined Alberta Forestry at Fort MacKay in 1981. That same year he suffered injuries in a local hockey tournament that left him a paraplegic.

Ksituan (locality)
83 M/14 - Blueberry Mountain
NW-34-79-7-W6
55°54′N 119°01′W
Approximately 25 km north north-west of Spirit River.

The post office was established here in 1935. The first postmaster was J. Waknuk. Named after the nearby Ksituan River, which flows into the Peace River. (see Ksituan River)

Ksituan Lake (lake)
83 M/14 - Blueberry Mountain
36-78-10-W6
55°48′N 119°25′W
Approximately 35 km west of Spirit River.

The lake is the source of the Ksituan River and is shown on a 1917 federal government as Anna Lake. (see Ksituan River)

Ksituan River (river)
83 M/15 - Rycroft
14-11-80-5-W6
55°56′N 118°40′W
Flows north into Peace River approximately 20 km north north-east of Sexsmith.

This is another rendering of a Cree word which is recorded elsewhere as "saskatchewan" and means "swift current." It was well known and in use when the Dominion Lands Survey came through in 1909.

L

La Biche River (river)
83 P/2 - Calling River
28-69-17-W4
55°00'15"N 112°31'30"W
Flows south-west into the Athabasca River approximately 60 km north-east of Athabasca.

Well known and in use before the Dominion Lands Survey surveyed the area in 1910, the name probably refers to the abundance of deer or elk in the area.

La Butte (hill)
74 M/6 - Bocquene Lake
23-120-9-W4
59°24'N 111°26'W
Approximately 293 km north of Fort McMurray.

(see under Butte, La)

La Butte Creek (creek)
74 M/6 - Bocquene Lake
6-15-120-9-W4
59°25'N 111°27'W
Flows north-west into Slave River approximately 290 km north of Fort McMurray.

The creek appears on the federal government maps from as early as 1930, and is named for its proximity to the hill. (see Butte, La)

La Crête (hamlet)
84 K/1 - Mustus Lake
9-106-15-W5
58°11'N 116°24'W
Approximately 56 km south-west of High Level.

The Rivard brothers came to Alberta from Quebec during World War I. They filed for land at the mouth of a small creek that flows into the Peace River. At that point there was a ridge of land they thought resembled a rooster's comb which in French is *la crête*, and thus the name of the landing was recorded. *Crête* is also the French word for the topographical feature known as a ridge or crest. The hamlet, created in 1955, took its name from the nearby feature. The post office was established in 1956 with Mrs. S. Knelson as the first postmaster.

La Glace (hamlet)
83 M/6 - La Glace
10-74-8-W6
55°24'N 119°09'W
Approximately 32 km north-west of Grande Prairie.

It was named after Charles La Glace, settler in Section 7, who was drowned in Valhalla Lake, aged 62, around 1909. He was chief of the Beaver Indians and restrained his tribe from force against white settlers who were invading tribal lands. For this he won the respect of both tribesmen and settlers. Originally the name of the post office. (1917). Holmgren, 1976. The first postmaster was F.G. Weber.

La Glace Lake (lake)
83 M/6 - La Glace
15-1-74-9-W6
55°2'N 119°14'W
Approximately 33 km north-west of Grande Prairie.

It was unofficially known as Rat Lake for many years, due to the prevalence of muskrat in the area. The name was changed to La Glace Lake in the early 1950s due to its proximity to the hamlet. (see La Glace)

***Lac Cardinal** (former locality)
84 C/5 - Chinook Valley
12-84-25-W5
56°17'N 117°46'N
Approximately 17 km north-west of Grimshaw.

It was named after the nearby lake. The post office opened in December 1923, the first postmaster being R. Cadmus.

***Lac Magloire** (former locality)
83 N/14 - Lac Magloire
9-79-21-W5
55°50'N 117°12'W
Approximately 12 km north of Falher.

The post office was established here in 1929, with A. Poirier the first postmaster. It was named for its proximity to the lake. (see Magloire, Lac)

Lafond Creek (creek)
84 G/3 - Lafond Creek
17-93-7-W5
57°03'N 115°05'W
Flows east south-east into Loon River approximately 155 km east north-east of Manning.

It was likely named after Joe Lafond, a packer for many survey crews who worked in this area. It appears on a map as early as 1915.

Lafont Island (island)
74 E/5 - Bitumount
12-97-11-W4
57°23'N 111°39'W
Island in Athabasca River, 76 km north north-west of Fort McMurray.

This island, spelled incorrectly Lafont, is named after Father Laffont, an Oblate priest. Adolphe Laffont was born in France in 1876, and came to western Canada as an ordained priest in 1902. He served at Fort Chipewyan, Fond du Lac (Saskatchewan), Fitzgerald, and then in the Northwest

---
*denotes rescinded name or former locality.

Territories before returning to Fort Chipewyan in 1909. In 1914 he was transferred to the area of Fort McMurray, where he built a mission and remained until 1929. He spent the remainder of all but the last year of his life at Fort Smith, and died in Montreal in 1943.

Lake Saskatoon (locality)
83 M/3 - Wembley
13-11-72-8-W6
55°14′N 119°07′W
Approximately 18 km west north-west of Grande Prairie.

The post office was established here in 1912 and was named for its proximity to the lake. It was previously called Beaverlodge, before that community moved. The first postmaster was W. H. Lowe. (see also Beaverlodge and Saskatoon Lake)

Lalby Creek (creek)
83 N/14 - Lac Magloire
15-20-78-22-W5
55°47′N 117°22′W
Flows south-west into Hunting Creek approximately 12 km west north-west of Falher.

It shows as early as 1914 on the federal government maps; the origin of the name is not known. The surveyor first in the area was H.W. Selby, and whether there is any connection with the last three letters of his name and the name of the creek is not known.

Lambert Creek (creek)
84 J/1 - Harper Creek
6-106-2-W5
58°11′N 114°19′W
Flows north-west into Harper Creek approximately 168 km east south east of Peace River.

After whom this feature is named is not known.

Landels River (river)
73 M/16 - Cowper Lake
10-28-80-2-W4
55°58′N 110°15′W
Flows north-west into Winefred River approximately 100 km south-east of Fort McMurray.

The feature was named in 1909 after A.F. Landels of Calgary.

Landry Heights (hamlet)
83 M/2 - Grande Prairie
S -15-70-6-W6
55°03′N 118°49′W
Approximately 12 km south of Grande Prairie.

The name for this hamlet first came into use in 1976. The land was subdivided in 1977 and the hamlet was established in 1980. The name was taken after the previous owner of the land, Dale Landry.

Lane Lake (lake)
84 P/8 - Pierre Lake
3-121-13-W4
59°28′N 112°08′W
Approximately 300 km north of Fort McMurray.

It was named in 1951 after Brigadier John Lane, DSO, of Edmonton, who commanded the divisional artillery for the 4th Canadian Armoured Division. He was killed in action in the Netherlands in November 1944.

Lapworth Point (point)
74 M/1 - Winnifred Lake
NW-32-116-3-W4
59°07′N 110°29′W
Approximately 264 km north north-east of Fort McMurray.

This was named after the British geologist Charles Lapworth (1842-1920), who in 1879 proposed the name Ordovician for a geological period known previously as Cambro-Silurian. Lapworth's name was suggested in 1958 by the Alberta Research Council.

Larne Creek (creek)
84 N/5 - Russet Creek
8-119-23-W5
59°19′N 117°54′W
Flows south-east into Steen River approximately 102 km north north-west of High Level.

The precise origin of the name of this creek is unknown; it may be after Larne, Co. Antrim, Northern Ireland. It was first noted by J.R. Akins, DLS, during his survey of September 1915.

Larocque Lake (lake)
74 L/2 - Larocque Lake
7-105-5-W4
58°06′N 110°49′W
Approximately 148 km north of Fort McMurray.

The lake was named after E. Larocque, an axeman for F.V. Seibert, DLS, who surveyed this area as early as 1915.

Last Lake (lake)
84 D/1 - Fairview
36-83-1-W6
56°14′N 118°01′W
Approximately 29 km north-east of Fairview.

Last Lake was recorded as early as 1911, and is descriptive of its position as the last lake in a series of lakes before the large Cardinal Lake on the old trail north-west to Peace River.

Last Lake (locality)
84 C/4 - Grimshaw
25-83-26-W5
56°13′N 117°58′W
Approximately 24 km north-west of Grimshaw.

Named for its proximity to Last Lake, a post office was established here in 1917. The first postmaster was J. Thompson.

Lathrop Creek (creek)
84 D/5 - Boundary Lake
28-86-10-W6
56°29'N 119°31'W
Flows south into Little Clear River approximately 83 km north-west of Fairview.

The precise origin of the name of this creek is unknown.

Latornell (railway point)
83 L/9 - Latornell River
14-65-3-W6
54°37'N 118°19'W
Approximately 65 km south south-east of Grande Prairie.

A point on the Alberta Resources Railway, established in 1969, it was named for the nearby feature. (see Latornell River)

Latornell River (river)
83 K/13 - Long Lake
14-69-27-W5
54°58'N 118°00'W
Flows east into Simonette River approximately 55 km east south-east of Grande Prairie.

Originally known as Moose River; the name was changed around 1920 to honour Lieutenant-Colonel A.J. Latornell, Edmonton City Engineer and Dominion Land Surveyor, killed in World War I. (see also Moose River)

Lattice Creek (creek)
83 M/4 - Rio Grande
NW-10-70-13-W6
55°03'N 119°54'W
Flows north-east into Redwillow River approximately 70 km west south-west of Grande Prairie.

The name was recorded by boundary survey crews in 1922; no origin information is known.

Laura Lake (lake)
83 J/5 - Carson Lake
32-61-11-W5
54°18'N 115°36'40"W
Approximately 10 miles north of Whitecourt.

The name was officially adopted in 1978 after it was determined the name had long been in local use. After whom it is named is not known.

Fred Lawrence with vegetables from Peace River Crossing, October 1907

Lawrence River (river)
84 J/6 - Adams
24-108-7-W5
58°23'N 115°01'W
Flows south-east into Peace River approximately 123 km east south-east of High Level.

The name of this river derives from the influential Lawrence family who lived in northern Alberta. In 1885, Henry H. Lawrence moved from Kingston, Ontario, to become the manager and instructor at the Anglican mission farm at Fort Vermilion which had been started by his father, Erastus Lawrence. It was called the Irene Training School. Henry's wife, Margaret, followed in 1886 with their eight children, the eldest of whom, Sheridan (1870-1952), was to become a well-known pioneer in the area. Sheridan, his wife and 15 children operated a large farm at Fort Vermilion, as well as stores at Fort Vermilion and Hay Lakes. By 1900 Sheridan had imported a turbine water wheel, which he used to power a threshing machine, flour mill and sawmill to serve the Fort Vermilion area. Erastus' son Fred became an ardent promoter of the Peace River country to the south. The name was first applied to the stream by C.P. Hotchkiss, DLS in 1920. In 1914, the name for the stream was recorded as Horse Creek. Horse Creek is now locally known as the next stream to the east. The Lawrence River is known as *Mistahe Sepe* by the Cree residents of John D'Or Prairie, and means Big River.

Lazar Lake (lake)
84 H/5 - Burnt Lakes
10-98-25-W4
57°29'20"N 113°58'13"W
Approximately 177 km north-west of Fort McMurray.

This well-established local name is apparently for a man called Lazar Merrier, who at one time lived in Wabasca.

Leddy (railway point)
84 C/5 - Chinook Valley
11-85-23-W5
56°22'N 117°31'W
Approximately 19 km north-west of Peace River.

The railway point was officially named in 1962 after the nearby lake. (see Leddy Lake)

Leddy Lake (lake)
84 C/6 - Weberville
30-85-22-W5
56°24'N 117°28'W
Approximately 20 km north-west of Peace River.

The lake was officially named in 1949 commemorating Flight Lieutenant G.B. Leddy originally from La Fleche, Saskatchewan, later of Edmonton. He lost his life in World War II. At the time of the survey in 1914, it was one of a pair of lakes labelled Germain Lakes. (see also St. Germain Lake)

Legend Lake (lake)
84 H/7 - Legend Lake
7-97-18-W4
57°24'N 112°55'W
Approximately 118 km north-west of Fort McMurray.

The precise origin of the name of this lake is unknown; it was recorded as early as 1914 by G.H. Blanchet, DLS. According to the files of the Geographic Board of Canada, it was named for the Chipewyan legend that said the lake sometimes swallowed canoes. Residents of Fort MacKay know this lake by another name, Red Water Lake.

Leggett Creek (creek)
74 D/14 - Wood Creek
31-91-9-W4
56°56'N 111°26'W
Flows west north-west into Athabasca River approximately 28 km north of Fort McMurray.

S.C. Ells submitted this name which is after a merchant, Mr. Leggett of the Paul & Leggett store in Fort McMurray. Mr. Leggett died in 1945.

Leggo Lake (lake)
74 M/10 - Cornwall Lake
SW-4-124-4-W4
59°45'N 110°38'W
Approximately 330 km north of Fort McMurray.

It was named in 1929 after Mr. Leggo, for years the Hudson's Bay Company storekeeper at Fitzgerald.

Leicester (locality)
83 N/9 - Grouard
SW-3-78-16-W5
55°43'N 116°24'W
Approximately 30 km north or High Prairie.

The post office opened here in December 1930, and may have been named after the English city of Leicester. Leicester is the administrative centre for Leicestershire in the English Midlands. It means "Roman town of the people named Ligore [tribal name of unknown origin.]" The first postmaster was C. C. Porter.

Leighmore (locality)
83 M/4 - Rio Grande
12-5-71-11-W6
55°07'N 119°40'W
Approximately 52 km west of Grande Prairie.

The post office was opened in July of 1922 and was apparently named, with a spelling error, after Teighmore, Channel Islands, the former home of the first postmaster, A. Beadle.

Leismer (locality)
73 M/14 - Waddell Creek
17-78-7-W4
55°45'N 111°03'W
Approximately 100 km south of Fort McMurray.

The Alberta and Great Waterways Railway station was established in 1916; the origin of the name was not recorded.

Leith (Little Burnt) River (river)
83 M/16 - Codesa
5-7-80-1-W6
55°55'N 118°09'W
Flows south into Peace River approximately 43 km north north-east of Spirit River.

When the Dominion Land Surveyors came to the area in the early 1910s, this river was known as the Little Burnt River, because this shorter river entered the Peace River just opposite the mouth of the Burnt River. In 1925, the name of Burnt River was changed to Saddle River, probably to avoid confusion with another Burnt River to the north. This river was given the name of an early fur trader at Fort Dunvegan. However, the earlier name of the river was still in use years later so in 1948, the Geographic Board of Canada decided to give the river a dual name. Leith, meaning "grey", or if it has a Welsh/Celtic root possibly meaning "moist", is the port of Edinburgh on the Firth of Forth in Scotland.

Leland Lakes (lakes)
74 M/14 - Tulip Lake
126-6-W4
59°55'N 111°02'W
Approximately 338 km north of Fort McMurray.

These have shown on federal government maps since at least 1930, but after whom they are named is not known.

Lemiseau Lake (lake)
83 P/1 - Wandering River
35-70-17-W4
55°07'N 112°29'W
Approximately 45 km north-west of Lac La Biche.

The origin is not known, but this name has been in use since the 1920s. The lake may have been named after an early resident in the area.

Lemon Island (island)
74 M/12 - Caribou Islands
NW-21-123-9-W4
59°42′N 111°31′W
Approximately 322 km north of Fort McMurray in Slave River.

The name was submitted in 1958 by the Research Council of Alberta, and was apparently descriptive of the feature. In what way it was descriptive was not recorded.

Lenarthur (locality)
74 D/11 - Fort McMurray
9-87-7-W4
56°31′N 111°03′W
Approximately 31 km south-west of Fort McMurray.

This name is a compound of the names of Dr. J.K. McLennan and J.D. McArthur, vice-president and president, respectively, of the Alberta and Great Waterways Railway. The name was originally given to a station in this location in 1917. (see also Aggie and McLennan)

Lennard Creek (creek)
84 E/5 - Tanghe Creek
22-96-12-W6
57°20′30″N 119°51′30″W
Flows south into Chinchaga River approximately 142 km west north-west of Manning.

The creek is named for Carl Lennard, who had a trapline along it during the 1930s. Lennard operated a string of trading posts on various lakes north-west of the locality of Eureka.

Leo's Creek (creek)
74 D/10 - Hollies Creek
25-89-5-W4
56°44′55″N 110°39′02″W

---
*denotes rescinded name or former locality.

Flows south into Clearwater River approximately 44 km north-east of Fort McMurray.

Leo's Creek is named after a trapper Leo Cheecham. (see also entries under Cheecham)

Lessard Creek (creek)
84 N/15 - Lessard Creek
28-124-17-W5
59°48′N 116°53′W
Flows south-west into James Creek approximately 142 km north of High Level.

Named after Orel Lessard, of the Royal Canadian Air Force, from Peace River, who lost his life during World War II.

Lesser Slave Lake (lake)
83 O/6 - Kinuso
75-14-W5
55°27′N 115°45′W
Approximately 23 km east of High Prairie.

Fur trader and explorer Alexander Mackenzie recorded the name "Slave Lake" in his journal in 1792, while he was somewhat to the north of Lesser Slave Lake on the Peace River, preparing for his trip the next year as the first Canadian overland expedition to the Pacific. He reported that the Cree spoke of hunting at Slave Lake, named for the original inhabitants, whom the Cree called by a term translated into English as "Slaves." The Cree did not mean the people further north known as "Slavey" Indians. For the Cree, the same term that indicated slaves also evidently meant strangers or outsiders. So the Cree were probably using the term to refer to the Beaver Indians driven out when the Cree advanced into the Lesser Slave Lake region; although some have argued that the people driven out in front of the Cree may have been Blackfoot. In any case, when the Cree named the lake that would later become Lesser Slave Lake, the term "slave" may have meant "stranger" in reference to the strangers who occupied the lake's region before the Cree. In 1927, R. Douglas, the Secretary of the Geographic Board of Canada wrote: "Both lakes [Lesser Slave Lake and Great Slave Lake] are named after a tribe who received the name *Awonak*, or Slaves from the Crees, and have always been known by it to the white men....The Slave Indians own name [for themselves] *Etchareottine* means 'people dwelling in the shelter' of the Rocky Mountains, according to [Émile] Petitot."

*****Lesser Slave Lake** (post office)
83 N/9 - Grouard
19-75-14-W5
55°31′N 116°09′W
Approximately 23 km east of High Prairie.

Named for its proximity to the lake, the post office was established in June 1903. Six years later the name was changed to Grouard. (see also Grouard and Lesser Slave Lake)

Lesser Slave Lake Provincial Park (provincial park)
83 O/7 - Slave Lake
74,75-6-W5
55°26′N 114°49′W
Approximately 10 km north of Slave Lake.

This nearly 7600-hectare. park was established in 1966, and was named for its proximity to the lake. (see Lesser Slave Lake)

Lesser Slave Lake Settlement (settlement)
83 N/9 - Grouard
21-75-14-W5
55°31′N 116°07′W
Approximately 25 km east north-east of High Prairie.

First surveyed in 1901, this settlement was named for its proximity to the lake. (see Lesser Slave Lake)

Lesser Slave River (river)
83 O/1 - Smith
NE-22-71-1-W5
55°10′N 114°03′W
Flows south-east into Athabasca River approximately 48 km east south-east of Slave Lake.

(see Lesser Slave Lake)

Lesser Slave River, Municipal District of, No. 124 (municipal district)
83 O/1 - Smith
65 to 80-25 to 6-W5 and 6
From 54°36′N 113°32′W to
55°58′N 115°23′W
Central north-west Alberta.

Created in 1994, this municipal district takes its name from the predominant feature within its boundaries.

Levellers Creek (creek)
84 E/13 - Foulwater Creek
25-103-13-W6
57°58′N 120°00′W
Flows south-west into British Columbia approximately 70 km south south-west of Rainbow Lake.

The name Levellers Creek was recorded by the Alberta-British Columbia Boundary Survey of 1951-52, due to an accident that resulted in the levellers of the party getting a dunking.

*L'Hirondelle (hamlet)
84 C/8 - Cadotte Lake
11-86-14-W5
56°26′10″N 116°06′30″W
Approximately 75 km north-east of Peace River.

The post office was established here in 1956 with the Rev. R. Smith as the first postmaster. It was named after a well-known family in the area. (see also Little Buffalo)

---
*denotes rescinded name or former locality.

Liége River (river)
84 A/13 - Liége River
30-90-24-W4
56°50′N 113°49′W
Flows south into Wabasca River, 148 km west of Fort McMurray.

Named after Liège, Belgium, an important industrial centre which suffered heavily during both World Wars because of its strategic position on the Meuse River. The name was recorded by the surveyor in the area in 1915, and likely is commemorative of activities there during World War I. The official spelling for the Alberta river used an acute accent (Liége). The Belgian city uses the grave accent (Liège). This river is also locally known as Prairie River because Prairie Creek drains into it.

Lightbulb Lake (intermittent lake)
83 K/16 - Wallace River
7-11-68-16-W5
54°52′10″N 116°19′25″W
Approximately 161 km east of Grande Prairie.

The descriptive name for the shape of this lake was first applied when Forestry officials began to use helicopters to survey the area. From the air the lake looks like a big lightbulb. It was officially named in 1991 after field research determined the name was well established and in local use.

Lightning Creek (creek)
84 D/9 - Sulphur Creek
34-87-2-W6
56°35′N 118°14′W
Flows south into Whitemud River approximately 58 km north of Fairview.

The precise origin of the name of this creek is unknown.

Lignite Creek (creek)
83 L/16 - Lignite Creek
28-69-3-W6
55°00′N 118°24′W
Flows north into Smoky River approximately 30 km south-east of Grande Prairie.

Lignite Creek is named for the seam of this low grade coal at the mouth of the river. Documentation shows name was in use in 1918.

*Liliendale (former locality)
84 D/1 - Fairview
24-82-1-W6
56°07′35″N 118°01′45″W
Approximately 23 km east north-east of Fairview.

Originally called Ketchum, the name was changed in 1924 to reflect that of the new postmaster, C. Lilienskold. (see also Ketchum)

Lillabo Lake (lake)
74 L/16 - Stone Point
1-114-1-W4
58°53′N 110°01′W
Approximately 245 km north north-east of Fort McMurray on the Alberta-Saskatchewan boundary.

Officially named in 1944; the origin of the name is not known.

Lillian Lake (lake)
74 E/5 - Bitumount
21-97-11-W4
57°26′N 111°44′W
Approximately 80 km north north-west of Fort McMurray.

This lake is named after Lillian Berryman of Fort McMurray. The name had been submitted by S.C. Ells.

Lily Creek (creek)
83 O/7 - Slave Lake
14-14-74-6-W5
55°24′N 114°47′W

Flows south-west into Lesser Slave Lake approximately 15 km north of Slave Lake. (see Lily Lake)

Lily Lake (lake)
83 O/7 - Slave Lake
11-7-75-5-W5
55°29′N 114°46′W
Approximately 20 km north of Slave Lake.

The origin of the name, which has been in use since at least 1912, is not known; the name may refer to the prevalence of the flower in the area. There are a number of varieties of lily common to the province.

Limon Lake (lake)
74 L/6 - Richardson Lake
31-108-8-W4
58°26′N 111°20′W
Approximately 180 km north of Fort McMurray.

This descriptive name was noted as early as 1917 by J.R. Akins, DLS. Limon, is the French translation of its earlier name, Mud Lake.

Lindgren Lake (lake)
74 M/16 - Andrew Lake
35-126-2-W4
59°59′N 110°13′W
Approximately 360 km north of Fort McMurray.

The name was submitted in 1958 by the Research Council of Alberta, and is one of a series of features in the area named after prominent geologists. It is named "for Waldemar Lindgren (1860-1939), [Swedish-born chief geologist of the United States Geological Survey], who was noted for his petrological and mineralogical work on ore deposits." Holmgren, 1976.

Line Lake (lake)
74 E/9 - Johnson Lake
34-100-3-W4
57°44′N 110°24′W
Approximately 128 km north-east of Fort McMurray.

This is a descriptive name as the lake is situated on the 26th Baseline. It was apparently called Reid Lake until it was officially named Line Lake. It is the source of Reid Creek.

Linton Lake (lake)
84 K/1 - Mustus Lake
6-106-15-W5
58°10′N 116°29′W
Approximately 52 km south-east of High Level.

The precise origin of the name of this lake is unknown, but is likely named after a person. This lake has been locally known as Long Lake since the 19th century and was probably a literal translation from the Cree. The surveyor working in the area in 1914 recorded the name as Long Lake.

Lister Lake (lake)
74 M/9 - Colin Lake
30-123-1-W4
59°43′N 110°09′W
Approximately 330 km north north-east of Fort McMurray.

The name was submitted in 1965 by the Research Council of Alberta, in honour of the University of Alberta official. "This lake in the north-east corner of Alberta was named for Reginald 'Reg' Lister (1891-1960), a native of England who came to Canada in 1909. In 1911 he came to Edmonton where he worked for the University of Alberta. After serving in World War I he returned to Edmonton and to the university and for the next 40 years was superintendent of the student residences. The main student dining complex on the campus is also named for him." Holmgren, 1976.

Little Bear Lake (lake)
73 M/3 - Logan Lake
6-34-70-10-W4
55°06′30″N 111°26′58″W
Approximately 49 km north north-east of Lac La Biche.

The well-established local name for this lake may be descriptive.

Little Beaver Lake (lake)
83 P/1 - Wandering River
13-24-71-14-W4
55°10′N 112°02′W
Approximately 44 km north of Lac La Biche.

The name for this lake is well established in local usage and was applied in 1938 by Magloire Cardinal. The name refers to a story told to him by his father, dating to an event in the early 19th century when a man spotted a beaver pinned under a tree that he had been felling. The beaver starved to death. Fish and Wildlife officers refer to this lake also as Little Sandy Lake. The Cree name is *Amskaat Sagahegan*.

Little Blue Lake (lake)
83 K/16 - Wallace River
5-18-69-16-W5
54°58′18″N 116°26′20″W
Approximately 152 km south-east of Grande Prairie.

This lake was named for its proximity to the locally named Blue Lake which in turn was named after the mountain. It was officially named in 1991 after field research determined the name was well established and in local use. (see Blue Mountain)

Little Buffalo (hamlet)
84 C/8 - Cadotte Lake
11-86-14-W5
56°26′10″N 116°06′30″W
Approximately 75 km north-east of Peace River.

The hamlet is on the north shore of Little Buffalo Lake, from which it takes its name. The community was formerly known as L'Hirondelle, after Joseph L'Hirondelle who settled with his family on the north shore of Little Buffalo Lake in 1913. L'Hirondelle post office was closed in 1957, and the name of the hamlet was changed to Little Buffalo in September 1981. The L'Hirondelle family is of Iroquois descent and had come west with the fur traders. *Hirondelle* is the French word for the bird, swallow.

Little Buffalo Lake (lake)
84 C/8 - Cadotte Lake
3-86-14-W5
56°26′N 116°08′W
Approximately 73 km north-east of Peace River.

The precise origin of the name of this lake is unknown.

Little Buffalo River (river)
84 P/15 - Flatgrass Lake
NW-34-126-17-W4
60°00′N 112°53′W
Flows north into the Northwest Territories approximately 290 km north-east of High Level.

It is a tributary of the Buffalo River.

Little Buffalo River (river)
84 L/5 - Little Buffalo River
7-107-12-W6
58°16′15″N 120°00′00″W

---
*denotes rescinded name or former locality.

Flows north-west into British Columbia approximately 49 km south-west of Rainbow Lake.

The name Little Buffalo was applied to this tributary of Hay River, because Hay River, from its headwaters to Buffalo Forks, was called Buffalo River or *Puskwa Mostos Sakakikun*.

*Little Buffalo River (river)
84 A/7 - Livock River
12-86-18-W4
56°27′N 112°43′W
Flows east into Athabasca River approximately 87 km west south-west of Fort McMurray.

(see Livock River)

Little Cadotte River (river)
84 C/11 - Deadwood
34-88-20-W5
56°41′N 117°06′W
Flows west into Cadotte River approximately 41 km south-east of Manning.

This river takes its name from its status as a tributary of the Cadotte River. (see Cadotte River)

Little Cascade Rapids (rapids)
74 D/12 - Cascade Rapids
35-87-12-W4
56°36′N 111°47′W
In Athabasca River approximately 28 km south-west of Fort McMurray.

Named to distinguish them from the larger Cascade Rapids farther along the river to the north-west. The name was recorded by the Geological Survey of Canada in 1892. (see also Cascade Rapids)

Little Clear River (river)
84 D/5 - Boundary Lake
21-85-10-W6
56°29′N 119°33′W

Flows east into Clear River approximately 69 km north-west of Fairview.

So named because it is a tributary of the Clear River. (see Clear River)

Little Driftpile River (river)
83 O/4 - House Mountain
12-72-13-W5
55°13′N 115°51′W
Flows north into Driftpile River approximately 70 km west of Slave Lake (town).

In the 1920s it was known as Bruce Creek; however, since the name was duplicated nearby, Little Driftpile River was adopted in 1952. It is named such because it is a tributary of Driftpile River. (see also Driftpile River)

Little Fish Lake (lake)
73 M/5 - Behan Lake
2-2-75-11-W4
55°28′N 111°36′W
Approximately 81 km north of Lac La Biche.

The name for this lake is well established in local usage and is likely descriptive. It is also referred to as Bloodsucker Lake. (see also Bloodsucker Lake)

Little Fishery (locality)
84 I/12 - Buchanan Lake
NE-1-112-22-W4
58°42′N 113°33′W
Approximately 205 km east of High Level.

The name was officially approved in 1963 and referred to a group of five cabins which, during the winter season, were occupied by 15 to 25 people. It was likely at a place where fish were caught to supply the fur trade posts.

Little Fishery River (river)
74 D/11 - Fort McMurray
18-89-9-W4
56°43′N 111°26′W

Flows east south-east into Athabasca River, at Fort McMurray.

Several fish plants were established in the area in the 1920s; however, the name was well known and in use in 1892 when it was recorded by the Geological Survey of Canada. It was likely a spot where fish were caught to supply nearby Fort McMurray. Before 1955 Little Fishery River was known as Potts Creek after Cyril Potts, Fort McMurray's first lawyer. Potts lived on the west side of the Athabasca River near Moberly Falls. Here he kept the meteorological records for the Dominion Government and cultivated a beautiful garden. His garden was famous throughout the Northwest and featured sweetpeas, honeysuckle, hops, pansies, roses, poppies and herbs.

Little Goose Lake (lake)
83 K/13 - Long Lake
W-17-69-24-W5
54°58'25"N 117°37'00"W
Approximately 80 km south-east of Grande Prairie.

Officially named in 1991 after field research was conducted in the area, the locally well-established name for this lake is taken from its proximity to Goose Lake. (see Goose Lake)

Little Hay River (river)
84 L/14 - Vardie River
28-112-9-W6
58°46'N 119°28'W
Flows east north-east into Hay River approximately 28 km north of Rainbow Lake.

The name is probably descriptive of its status as a tributary of the Hay River.

---
*denotes rescinded name or former locality.

Little Horse Creek (creek)
83 O/13 - Atikameg
27-79-12-W5
55°53'N 115°47'W
Approximately 90 km north-west of Slave Lake.

The origin of the name is not known, but after field research in 1960 it was determined that the name was well established and in local use.

Little Horse Lake (lake)
83 O/13 - Atikameg
13-79-12-W5
55°51'N 115°45'W
Approximately 85 km north-west of Slave Lake.

(see Little Horse Creek)

Little Island Lake (lake)
84 H/5 - Burnt Lakes
24-95-25-W4
57°15'30"N 113°55'00"W
Approximately 164 km west north-west of Fort McMurray.

The locally established name for this lake is descriptive of a small island at its south-west extremity. It is one of the Burnt Lakes. (see also Burnt Lakes)

Little Lake (lake)
83 M/3 - Wembley
36-71-8-W6
55°12'N 119°05'W
Approximately 15 km west of Grande Prairie.

Although origin information is not precisely known, it may be descriptive due to its proximity to the much larger Saskatoon Lake to the north. It has been known by this name at least since the 1950s.

*Little Long Lake (lake)
73 M/4 - Philomena
16-72-11-W4
55°14'N 111°38'W
Approximately 60 km north north-east of Lac La Biche.

This was a local name for the feature, but in order to avoid confusion with similar names of lakes in the area another name was officially adopted. (see Big Chief Lake)

Little McLeod Lake (lake)
83 J/5 - Carson Lake
31-61-11-W5
54°19'N 115°38'W
Approximately 20 km north of Whitecourt.

Although never made official before 1986, the name has been known and in use since the 1850s. In 1961 Mobil Oil of Canada requested to name the lake after its symbol, the Pegasus. However, in the 1980s, residents requested to have the name of the lake reflect historical and local usage. Because of this, the name was changed to Little McLeod Lake in 1986. (see also McLeod Lake, Carson Lake and Pegasus Lake)

Little Mountain (hill)
83 N/8 - High Prairie
12-29-72-16-W5
55°16'N 116°26'W
Approximately 18 km south of High Prairie.

The name is likely descriptive of its elevation of 686 metres. It is used for navigational purposes.

Little Muskeg Lake (lake)
83 P/1 - Wandering River
5-27-71-14-W4
55°10'39"N 112°04'42"W
Approximately 46 km north of Lac La Biche.

The descriptive name for this lake is well established in local usage, and refers to its proximity to Big Muskeg Lake.

Little Musreau Lake (lake)
83 L/10 - Cutbank River
3-22-64-5-W6
54°32'45"N 118°40'10"W
Approximately 70 km south of Grande Prairie.

This lake was named for its proximity to Musreau Lake. (see Musreau Lake)

Little Poplar Island (island)
74 L/10 - Big Point
SW-21-111-4-W4
58°39'N 110°37'W
Approximately 207 km north north-east of Fort McMurray in Lake Athabasca.

Officially named in the 1950s, but appearing on federal government maps since 1923; the name is descriptive.

Little Prairie Creek (creek)
83 N/1 - East Prairie
4-23-70-16-W5
55°04'N 116°20'W
Flows west into West Prairie River approximately 60 km east of Valleyview.

It may take its name from the fact it flows into the West Prairie River. It was made official in 1952 after field research was conducted.

*****Little Prairie Creek** (creek)
83 O/7 - Slave Lake
11-5-73-5-W5
55°18'N 114°44'W
Flows north-east into Lesser Slave River approximately 10 km east of Slave Lake.

---

*denotes rescinded name or former locality.

Shown in a 1914 map as Little Prairie Creek, it was descriptive of the local terrain. By 1922 it had changed to Sawridge Creek. (see Sawridge Creek)

Little Puskwaskau Lake (lake)
83 N/3 - Valleyview
NW 11-71-22-W5
55°08'N 117°17'W
Approximately 10 km north of Valleyview.

Puskwaskau is a Cree word meaning dry grass. It is descriptive of the area.

Little Puskwaskau River (river)
83 M/8 - Smoky Heights
12-25-74-1-W6
55°26'N 118°01'W
Flows west into Puskwaskau River approximately 55 km north-east of Grande Prairie.

It is a tributary of the Puskwaskau River. (see Puskwaskau Lake)

Little Rapids (rapids)
74 L/14 - Rivière des Rochers
13-19-114-7-W4
58°55'N 111°11'W
Approximately 236 km north of Fort McMurray in Rivière des Rochers.

Officially named in 1971; the name is descriptive of the feature.

Little Rapids Creek (creek)
84 N/6 - Lutose Creek
21-120-19-W5
59°26'N 117°13'W
Flows north-west into Hay River approximately 112 km north of High Level.

The precise origin of the name of this creek is unknown, but it is likely descriptive. The local name for the stream is *Tsunaga Zahéh*, which in Slavey means standing black spruce creek, which is also descriptive.

Little Rat Lake (lake)
83 K/16 - Wallace River
W-11-69-17-W5
54°57'35"N 116°29'10"W
Approximately 151 km south-east of Grande Prairie.

The name describes its size and the large muskrat population around the lake. The name has been in use since the late 1920s. It was officially named in 1991 after field research in the area determined the name was well established and in local use.

Little Red River (locality)
84 J/7 - Vermilion Chutes
28-108-5-W5
58°24'N 114°46'W
Approximately 138 km east south-east of High Level.

This locality takes its name from the old North West Company fur trading post which once was located in this area from 1798 to circa 1803. David Thompson noted in his journal for the season 1798-99 that the post was called Fort de la Rivière Rouge or Grand Marais. Fur-trade historian A.M. Voorhis suggests that this post was at the junction of Little Red River (now Mikkwa) and Peace River. It was called Fort de la Rivière Rouge and was known as Little Red River Fort to distinguish it from Old Red River Fort on the Athabasca River. Another historian, Terry Smythe, notes that the name Rivière Rouge applied to this post refers not to the Mikkwa, or Vermilion River, but to a small stream called the Little Vermilion, just above this area. The name is now used by the John D'Or, Garden Creek and Fox Lake Cree as their band name, Little Red River Band.

Little Rocky Point (point)
74 D/9 - Bunting Bay
20-87-3-W4
56°33'35"N 110°26'58"W
Approximately 60 km south-east of Fort McMurray.

This is a descriptive name given to an area in Bunting Bay on Gordon Lake. It identifies the only spot on the north shore solid enough to land a boat.

Little Smoky (locality)
83 K/11 - Waskahigan River
25-66-21,22-W5
54°44′N 117°11′W
Approximately 35 km south of Valleyview.

It came into existence some time before 1955 and was named for its proximity to the Little Smoky River. (see also Little Smoky River)

Little Smoky (hamlet)
83 N/7 - Triangle
SE-29-74-19-W5
55°26′N 116°52′W
Approximately 25 km west of High Prairie.

It was named for its proximity to the Little Smoky River. The area is likely the remnants of population surrounding the Little Smoky School District established in 1931. A post office was established there in 1975, and Mrs. D. Blower was the first postmaster. (see Little Smoky River)

Little Smoky River (river)
83 N/12 - Watino
15-77-24-W5
55°40′N 117°38′W
Flows west into Smoky River approximately 45 km west of McLennan.

Referred to in 1879 by George Dawson of the Geological Survey of Canada, this is one of the "Smoky" rivers found in northwestern Canada. The names usually derive from coal beds that have become ignited and sometimes burn for many years.

Little Snuff Lake (lake)
74 E/8 - Trout Creek
5-97-2-W4
57°23′47″N 110°17′32″W

Approximately 100 km north-east of Fort McMurray.

(see Big Snuff Lake)

Livock River (river)
84 A/7 - Livock River
12-86-18-W4
56°27′N 112°43′W
Flows east into Athabasca River approximately 87 km west south-west of Fort McMurray.

Officially named in 1922 after Chief Factor W.T. Livock, Hudson's Bay Company, in charge of all transport down the Athabasca River from 1890 to 1911. The feature was originally called Little Buffalo River; since there were other rivers of similar name it was decided to honour Mr. Livock.

Lobe Lake (lake)
74 E/8 - Trout Creek
14-97-3-W4
57°24′45″N 110°22′20″W
Approximately 100 km north-east of Fort McMurray.

This is descriptively named by local trappers for its likeness to an ear lobe in shape.

Lobstick Creek (creek)
74 D/10 - Hollies Creek
16-89-5-W4
56°42′45″N 110°44′30″W
Flows east into Clearwater River approximately 36 km east of Fort McMurray.

This creek received its name because a man named Rapheal (sic) Cree made a lobstick on a big spruce tree on the prairie here. (see also Lobstick Island)

Lobstick Island (island)
74 L/11 - Fort Chipewyan
16-5-112-7-W4
58°42′N 111°08′W

Approximately 212 km north of Fort McMurray in Lake Athabasca.

Likely named for the abundance of the trees on the island that were commonly used as lobsticks. Lobsticks (or lopsticks) were pine or spruce trees which had their lower branches removed and served as a landmark, and were used by some aboriginal peoples as a monument, or a living symbol of the person for whom it was made. The island is in Lake Athabasca, opposite the old Chipewyan Settlement. It appears on federal government maps as early as 1919.

Logan Lake
74 M/16 - Andrew Lake
23-126-3-W4
59°58′N 110°24′W
Approximately 355 km north of Fort McMurray.

The name was submitted in 1965 by the Research Council of Alberta, and is one of a series of features in the area named after geologists. Sir William Logan (1798-1875), born in Montreal was the first director of the Geological Survey of Canada (1842-1869). Mount Logan, the highest mountain in Canada, also bears his name.

Logan Lake (lake)
73 M/3 - Logan Lake
70-9-W4
55°05′N 111°23′W
Approximately 52 km north-east of Lac La Biche.

The name has been on the maps since at least 1918, and was likely named after the Dominion Land Surveyor. (see Logan River)

Logan River (river)
73 M/4 - Philomena
15-13-71-12-W4
55°09′N 111°42′W

Flows south-east into Owl River approximately 45 km north north-east of Lac La Biche.

A native of Nova Scotia, Robert Archibald Logan decided to follow in the footsteps of his grandfather, a land surveyor in that province. After a number of years of apprenticeship working on survey crews in the Canadian West, he received his commission as Dominion Land Surveyor in 1914. Shortly after this he enlisted and served in the Royal Flying Corps until being taken prisoner of war in 1917. After the war, he returned to Canada. In 1922 he was the pilot on a government mission to establish police posts in the North and while there, explored the area. His subsequent career was devoted to promoting the use of aerial photography for surveying. He was an authority on the Cree language and published a dictionary on the subject. Holmgren, 1976.

Lois Lake (lake)
83 J/11 - Swan Hills
9-66-9-W5
54°42'N 115°17'W
Approximately 4 km east of Swan Hills.

Likely named some time in the 1930s or 1940s, after whom is not known. (see Agnes Lake)

Lone Pine (locality)
83 J/6 - Christmas Creek
27-61-8-W5
54°18'N 115°07'W
Approximately 40 km north of Mayerthorpe.

Originally established as a post office in July 1930, it was apparently named for a solitary pine tree recognisable in the area. The first postmaster was G. Davidson.

---

*denotes rescinded name or former locality.

*Lone Star (locality)
84 C/12 - Dixonville
29-89-23-W5
56°43'N 117°39'W
Approximately 21 km south of Manning.

Established as a post office in 1930, the first post master was J. Pollon. It has not been recorded why the name was chosen, but there are at least two possibilities. The person who first suggested the name might have been from Texas, the "Lone Star State." It may also have been named for its proximity to the North Star post office 10 kilometres south of it, which had been established a year earlier.

Long End Lake (lake)
83 J/9 - Flatbush
34-64,65-3-W5
54°35'N 114°23'W
Approximately 50 km north of Barrhead.

Officially named in 1953 and is descriptive of the feature.

Long Island (island)
83 M/16 - Codesa
1, 12-80-1-W6
55°55'N 118°01'W
Approximately 54 km north north-east of Spirit River in the Peace River.

The name for this feature is descriptive, and has been in use since 1924.

Long Lake (lake)
84 B/10 - Peerless Lake
18-89-4-W5
56°43'N 114°39'W
Approximately 160 km north of Slave Lake.

The name is descriptive of the shape of the lake. The basin in which it lies was probably formed during the last ice age some 20,000 years ago. The ice left a glacially streamlined or fluted terrain of alternate elongated ridges and depressions. The lakes formed in these depressions are all long and narrow. There are numerous other lakes in the province with this descriptive name.

Long Lake (lake)
83 K/13 - Long Lake
22-68-24-W5
54°54'N 117°33'W
Approximately 85 km east south-east of Grande Prairie.

The name appears on federal government maps as early as 1917 and is descriptive of the shape of the lake.

Long Lake (lake)
74 D/7 - Cheecham
36-85-7-W4
56°24'50"N 110°58'30"W
Approximately 47 km south-east of Fort McMurray.

The name is descriptive. Many local residents agree that it is not as long as some of the other lakes of the area, but the name still enjoys wide usage.

Long Lake (lake)
74 E/14 - Pearson Lake
26-103-7-W4
57°58'00"N 111°01'55"W
Approximately 140 km north north-east of Fort McMurray.

This is a descriptive name first recorded by the surveyors in the area in 1905.

Long Lake (lake)
74 D/7 - Cheecham
27-84-6-W4
56°18'40"N 110°51'40"W
Approximately 56 km south-east of Fort McMurray.

This feature is so named because it is reputed to be the longest lake in the area.

Long Lake (lake)
83 L/7 - Prairie Creek
6-34-62-6-W6
54°24'20"N 118°48'55"W
Approximately 85 km south of Grande Prairie.

The locally well-established name for this lake is descriptive of its shape. The name was officially adopted in 1991 after field research was conducted.

Long Lake (lake)
83 P/14 - Muskeg River
20-78-20-W4
55°46'N 113°05'W
Approximately 120 km north-east of Slave Lake.

The name is descriptive of the feature, and was referred to as early as 1897 on a federal government map.

***Long Lake** (lake)
83 J/6 - Christmas Creek
36-61-8-W5
54°19'N 115°05'W
Approximately 47 km north-east of Whitecourt.

This descriptive local name was eventually replaced by another in 1976. (see Schuman Lake)

***Long Lake** (lake)
84 K/1 - Mustus Lake
6-106-15-W5
58°10'N 116°29'W
Approximately 52 km south-east of High Level.
(see Linton Lake)

***Long Lake** (lake)
84 L/6 - Rainbow Lake
16-107-8-W6
58°17'N 119°16'W

---

*denotes rescinded name or former locality.

Approximately 21 km south of the town of Rainbow Lake.
(see Rainbow Lake)

Long Rapids (rapids)
74 D/12 - Cascade Rapids
34-87-13-W4
56°36'N 111°59'W
In Athabasca River approximately 38 km west south-west of McMurray.

A series of rapids in the Athabasca River are closely grouped together and called by the Cree *kaukinwauk pastiche* or rapids without end. William Ogilvie's geological report of 1884 refers to the Long Rapids. They are either the Noyé or Brulé Rapids noted on Father Petitot's map of 1883.

Loon Creek (creek)
84 A/7 - Livock River
33-84-17-W4
56°19'N 112°37'W
Flows north into Athabasca River approximately 87 km south-west of Fort McMurray.

The precise origin of the name of this creek is unknown; it is probably named for the common loon, *Gavia immer*. Summer plumage is black or grey streaked and spotted in bold patterns with white. Loons eat mainly fish, diving to depths of 7.5 metres, usually for less than a minute. The loon, known for its unique cries, has become a Canadian symbol, and is featured on the $1 coins affectionately known as "loonies." The name was recorded in the 1914 field notes of H.S. Day.

Loon Lake (hamlet)
84 B/11 - Loon Lake
17-87-9-W5
56°33'N 115°24'W
Approximately 145 km north north-west of Slave Lake.

Named for its proximity to Loon Lake. (see Loon Creek)

Loon Lake (lake)
84 P/11 - Conibear Lake
SE-21-122-19-W4
59°37'N 113°12'W
Approximately 255 km east north-east of High Level.

The name appears on federal government maps as early as 1929, and is likely descriptive of the types of birds found on the lake. (see Loon Creek)

Loon Lake (lake)
84 B/11 - Loon Lake
7-87-9-W5
56°33'N 115°26'W
Approximately 140 km north north-west of Slave Lake.

Named for the bird for whom this lake is a favourite nesting place. (see also Loon Creek)

Loon River (river)
84 G/3 - Lafond Creek
3-94-7-W5
57°08'N 115°03'W
Flows north-east into Wabasca River approximately 158 km east north-east of Peace River.

Named for the common loon, it was noted in the 1912 field notes of A.H. Hawkins. (see also Loon Creek)

Loop Creek (creek)
74 M/12 - Caribou Islands
NE-2-123-12-W4
59°39'N 111°51'W
Flows east into Salt River approximately 318 km north of Fort McMurray.

Officially named in the early 1970s, it is descriptive of the course of the creek.

Lorna Island (island)
74 E/11 - Firebag River
31-99-9-W4
57°38′N 111°28′W
In Athabasca River approximately 76 km north north-west of Fort McMurray.

The precise origin of the name of this island is unknown. It appears to have two names, Lorna Island and Dalkin Island. (see also Dalkin Island)

Lost Creek (creek)
83 N/13 - Tangent
12-79-26-W5
55°50′N 117°56′W
Flows west into Fox Creek approximately 60 km south-west of Peace River.

Named after Miss Maclean and Miss Ellis, after they were lost one day while out on a horseback trip to Peace River. Both women were nurses from Nova Scotia who had worked with the American Expeditionary Force travelling overseas in 1917 to help American wounded in World War I. After the war, they came to the Peace River area and filed for a homestead near Eaglesham.

Lost Hope Creek (creek)
83 N/1 - East Prairie
16-2-70-16-W5
55°02′N 116°19′W
Flows north-west into West Prairie River approximately 60 km east of Valleyview.

The origin of the name Lost Hope Creek is not known although there is likely a good story behind it. The name was well established and in local use when is was recorded during field research in 1952.

Lothrop (locality)
83 M/16 - Codesa
SW-29-80-1-W6
55°57′N 118°08′W
Approximately 48 km north-east of Spirit River.

The post office established here in July 1927 was apparently named after the first settler in the area, Herb Lothrop. Both Mr. Lothrop and the first postmaster, Rémi Fortin, had travelled the Klondike Trail.

Louise Creek (creek)
6-64-11-W5
54°35′N 115°34′W
Flows north-east into Freeman River approximately 15 km south-west of Swan Hills.

Adopted in the 1940s; after whom it is named is not known.

Louise River (river)
84 H/10 - Alberta
21-100-18-W4
57°42′N 112°53′W
Flows south-west into Birch River approximately 141 km north-west of Fort McMurray.

The precise origin of the name of this river is unknown; it is noted in the survey of 1914.

Loutit Lake (lake)
74 L/15 - Burntwood Island
18-115-5-W4
58°59′N 110°52′W
Approximately 245 km north of Fort McMurray.

This lake commemorates the Loutit family, an old family of Fort Chipewyan. J.J. Loutit was the factor at Fort Chipewyan around the turn of the century, a post he held for a number of years. Agnes Dean Cameron in The New North (1909) notes: "...there were Loutits in Fort Chipewyan as far back as the old Journals reach." Holmgren, 1976.

Lovet Creek (creek)
84 D/16 - Cub Lakes
21-91-2-W6
56°54′N 118°15′W
Flows south into Notikewin River approximately 93 km north of Fairview.

The precise origin of the name of this creek is unknown.

Lowe Lake (lake)
83 M/6 - La Glace
12-16-73-8-W6
55°20′N 119°11′W
Approximately 27 km north-west of Grande Prairie.

This was named after James and Margaret (McCracken) Lowe and family, original settlers in the area who came up from Grand Forks, North Dakota, and homesteaded around 1911.

Lowen Lake (lake)
83 M/4 - Rio Grande
10-33-71-11-W6
55°12′N 119°37′W
Approximately 50 km west of Grande Prairie.

This was likely named for the John and Justina Lowen family who moved into the area in the late 1920s. John Lowen's ancestors were Dutch, but his family came from Russia. The name was approved for the lake in 1951.

Lubicon Lake (hamlet)
84 B/5 - Lubicon Lake
17-85-12-W5
56°22′N 115°52′W
Approximately 89 km east north-east of Peace River.

It was named for its proximity to the lake. (see Lubicon Lake)

Lubicon Lake (lake)
84 B/5 - Lubicon Lake
22-85-13-W5
56°23′N 115°56′W
Approximately 78 km east north-east of Peace River.

This lake and the river that flows into it received their name in 1911 after a Métis family who lived near the lake in autumn and winter. The name may be a variation of another family name Laboucane. According to *A Dictionary of Canadianisms* the word boucan comes from the Canadian French meaning place or device for smoking meat.

Lubicon River (river)
84 B/11 - Loon Lake
2-87-10-W5
56°31′N 115°28′W
Flows north into Loon Lake approximately 118 km east north-east of Peace River.

(see Lubicon Lake)

Lucas Island (island)
74 L/15 - Burntwood Island
23-113-5-W4
58°49′N 110°43′W
Approximately 227 km north north-east of Fort McMurray in Lake Athabasca.

The Rev. Lucas and family, 1901

The feature was named after the Right Reverend James Richard Lucas who, during his early career as a minister, was the resident Anglican priest at Fort Chipewyan (1892-1899). He served many years in the north, and in 1913 was consecrated Lord Bishop of the Diocese of Mackenzie River.

Lucky Lake (lake)
83 J/6 - Christmas Creek
20-61-7-W5
54°17′N 115°00′W
Approximately 42 km west north-west of Barrhead.

The name is recorded on a federal government map as early as 1910; its origin is unknown.

Lutose (locality)
84 N/6 - Lutose Creek
18-120-19,20-W5
59°25′N 117°16′W
Approximately 113 km north of High Level.

Established as a Great Slave Lake Railway station in 1962, it was named for the nearby creek. (see Lutose Creek)

Lutose Creek (creek)
84 N/6 - Lutose Creek
6-120-19-W5
59°24′N 117°16′W
Flows north-east into Hay River approximately 98 km north of High Level.

Lutose means covered in mud and is likely descriptive. The local name for this stream, which has been in use since the early 1900s, is Thenaka Zahéh which is Slavey for "creek that flows parallel" [to the Hay River].

Lyle Lake (lake)
83 P/1 - Wandering River
9-11-72-17-W4
55°13′N 112°30′W
Located approximately 61 km north north-west of Lac La Biche.

The name has been in use since the late 1920s; after whom it is named is not known.

Lylich Lake (lake)
83 O/10 - Marten Lakes
5-78-4-W5
55°44′N 114°35′W
Approximately 50 km north north-east of Slave Lake.

The name received official approval in 1970; after whom it is named is not known.

Lymburn (locality)
83 M/5 - Hythe
28-73-12-W6
55°21′N 119°47′W
Approximately 62 km west north-west of Grande Prairie.

This Northern Alberta Railways station was established in 1930, and was named after John Farquhar Lymburn, a Member of the Legislative Assembly and Attorney General in the United Farmers of Alberta Government. He was first elected in 1926, and was defeated in 1935. Born in Ayr, Scotland, in 1880, he was educated in law at the University of Glasgow and set up his law practice in Edmonton in 1911. He died at the age of 89 in 1969. A post office was established here in 1932 with G.A. Pollock as the first postmaster.

Lynton (railway point)
74 D/11 - Fort McMurray
8-88-7-W4
56°37′N 111°06′W
Approximately 22 km east south-east of Fort McMurray.

The precise origin of the name of this railway point is unknown although it may have been named after a place in England. When it was the terminus of the Alberta and Great Waterways Railway it was known as Cache 23. In 1917 the name

Lynton was applied to the station at this location.

Lynx Lake (lake)
84 P/8 - Pierre Lake
NW-7-119-12-W4
59°19′N 112°04′W
Approximately 283 km north of Fort McMurray.

Officially named in 1949; it is likely descriptive of the animal in the area.

M~N~O

Mabel Creek (creek)
83 O/4 - House Mountain
6-7-71-11-W5
55°08'N 115°41'W
Flows north into Driftpile River approximately 60 km south-west of Slave Lake (town).

The name was adopted some time between 1914 and 1922; it is not known after whom it is named.

MacIntosh Lake (lake)
83 J/6 - Christmas Creek
30-61-7-W5
54°18'N 115°02'W
Approximately 45 km west north-west of Barrhead.

It shows on federal government maps as early as 1910; it is not known after whom it is named.

MacKay River (river)
74 E/4 - Fort MacKay
24-94-11-W4
57°10'N 111°38'W
Flows north-east into Athabasca River approximately 53 km north north-west of Fort McMurray.

It is named for its proximity to Fort MacKay. Residents in the area also know the river as Red River which was a name in use during the early 1800s. It is also apparently known by a Chipewyan word meaning deep valley. (see also Fort MacKay)

Mackenzie, Municipal District of, No. 23 (municipal district)
84 K/11 - High Level
90 to 128-1 to 12-W5 to 6
From 57°20'45"N 114°00'00"W to 60°00'00"N 120°00'00"W
North-western Alberta.

Taking up a large portion of north-western Alberta, this Municipal District was established in 1994, and took its name from the explorer, Alexander Mackenzie.

Magloire, Lac (lake)
83 N/14 - Lac Magloire
26-79-21-W5
55°52'N 117°10'W
Approximately 12 km north of Falher.

The name was well established when the Dominion Lands Survey came through the area in 1915, although the survey of 1909 recorded the name of the feature as Reed Lake. Although the precise origin of the name is not known, a local history of the area makes reference to a man named Magloire Onyandé whose death is recorded at the nearby Spirit River Mission of St. Joseph in 1911.

Magnussen Lake (lake)
74 D/14 - Wood Creek
30-91-9-W4
56°00'N 111°26'W
Approximately 19 km north of Fort McMurray.

This lake is named after the Magnussen family who lived in the area.

Mahigun Lake (lake)
84 H/6 - Alberta
20-97-20-W4
57°26'14"N 113°13'33"W
Approximately 135 km north-west of Fort McMurray.

Mahigun Lake takes its name from the Cree word for wolf and is likely descriptive.

Main Point (point)
74 D/9 - Bunting Bay
7-87-3-W4
56°32'N 110°28'W
West shore of Gordon Lake approximately 60 km east south-east of Fort McMurray.

The name is descriptive.

Mamawi Creek (creek)
74 L/11 - Fort Chipewyan
2-30-110-9-W4
58°34'N 111°30'W
Flows north into Mamawi Lake approximately 194 km north of Fort McMurray.

It is apparently a rendition of the Cree word *mamiwiw* which according to Father Lacombe's Cree dictionary, means "the river flows this way."

Mamawi Lake (lake)
74 L/11 - Fort Chipewyan
4-111-9-W4
58°37'N 111°28'W
Approximately 200 km north of Fort McMurray.

(see Mamawi Creek)

Manir (station)
83 M/10 - Woking
4-78-4-W6
55°44'N 118°33'W
Approximately 20 km south south east of Spirit River.

This was an Edmonton, Dunvegan and British Columbia Railway station named after Mme Manir (Boulanger) Polet, a Belgian painter of note, who was for 15 years a resident of Alberta. Manir Boulanger came to Canada in 1906 with her mother and her sister to join her brother Pierre who was farming close to Villeneuve near St. Albert. There she met and married Eugène Polet. Mme Polet's brother-in-law, Maurice Polet, was a civil engineer for the railway. It was he who suggested the name for the station. Manir and Eugène Polet farmed for a number of years, but returned to Belgium around 1921.

Manning (town)
84 C/13 - Manning
28-91-23-W5
56°55'N 117°37'W
Approximately 73 km north north-west of Peace River.

Named in honour of Ernest Charles Manning (1908-1996), radio evangelist and politician. The name Manning was chosen by public meeting in 1947, after the original name of the settlement, Aurora, had been rejected by the postal authorities because of possible confusion with Aurora in Ontario. The town's original name is perpetuated in various businesses such as the Aurora Hotel and Theatre.

Manning began his career as a student of William Aberhart at the Calgary Prophetic Bible Institute and became involved with the Social Credit Party, joining Aberhart's first cabinet as Provincial Secretary in 1935. On Aberhart's death in 1943 Manning became Premier leading the Social Credit Party to power through seven elections until his retirement in 1968. Throughout his tenure his weekly broadcast "Canada's National Back to the Bible Hour" went on the air. Manning's claims of using Alberta's oil riches after the Leduc strike in 1947 to finance corruption-free government, attract capital and maximize oil exploitation and development made him and Social Credit invincible for 25 years. Ernest Manning served as an Alberta Senator (1970-83), received several honorary degrees, and was made a Companion of the Order of Canada. In 1981, he was the first recipient of the Alberta Order of Excellence.

Many Creeks (creek)
73 M/5 - Behan Lake
5-29-73-12-W4
55°12'N 111°50'W
Flows south-east into Logan River approximately 66 km north of Lac La Biche.

The descriptive name for this creek is well established in local usage.

Many Islands (islands)
84 D/6 - Many Islands
27-84-8-W6
56°19'N 119°10'W
In bend of Peace River approximately 55 km north-west of Peace River.

This is a descriptive name for this group of islands in the Peace River.

Margaret Lake (lake)
84 J/14 - Margaret Lake
3-115-9-W5
58°57'N 115°25'W
Approximately 112 km east north-east of High Level.

It was named by J. R. Akins, DLS, in 1914 after his first wife Margaret (Grass) Akins. Akins notes this lake was called Fish Lake at the time, and was an important source for fish at Fort Vermilion. There is some suggestion that the lake may also have been known as *Kaska Minke* in Beaver. *Kaska Sakeh* is the Beaver name for Ponton River. Locally the lake is known among the Cree as *Kinosayo Sakahikun*, or Fish Lake. The Slavey refer to it as *Minkeshok*, or Big Lake.

Margie (locality)
73 M/6 - Winefred Lake
33-74-9-W4
55°27'N 111°20'W
Approximately 85 km north-east of Lac La Biche.

This Alberta and Great Waterways Railway station was established in 1916 and was likely named after the wife of J. W. Judge, assistant superintendent of the railway.

Marguerite River (river)
74 E/11 - Firebag River
16-99-7-W4
57°36'N 111°06'W
Flows south-east into Firebag River approximately 99 km north north-east of Fort McMurray.

This river is named after Marguerite, sister of F.V. Seibert, a Dominion Land Surveyor.

Maria Lake (lake)
84 B/7 - Bat Lake
21-86-4-W5
56°28'N 114°34'W
Approximately 117 km due north of Slave lake.

The precise origin of the name of this lake is unknown. It is one of a pair of lakes labelled in 1905 as Trout Lakes. (see also Peerless Lake)

Mariana Lake (lake)
83 P/16 - Crow Lake
19-80-13-W4
55°57'N 112°01'W
Approximately 100 km south south-west of Fort McMurray.

The name, which was adopted in 1966, is taken from the botanical name for the black spruce common to the area, *Picea mariana*. It was the centre of a large forest fire in June 1995.

Mariana Lake (locality)
83 P/16 - Crow Lake
19-80-13-W4
55°47'15"N 112°01'05"W
Approximately 100 km south south-west of Fort McMurray.

The name is derived from the nearby body of water. (see Mariana Lake)

Mariana Settlement (settlement)
73 M/13 - Winefred Lake
80-13-W4
55°58'N 111°59'W
Approximately 90 km south south-west of Fort McMurray.

First surveyed in 1966, it was named for the nearby lake. (see Mariana Lake)

Marie Reine (hamlet)
84 C/3 - Peace River
6-82-21-W5
56°04′N 117°17′W
Approximately 28 km south of Peace River. The precise origin of the name of this hamlet is unknown.

This refers to Mary, the mother of Christ. In the Roman Catholic Litany of the Blessed Virgin Mary, she is referred to as "Queen of Angels, Queen of Patriarchs,...Queen assumed unto heaven...." There is a significant francophone population in the area. A post office was established here in 1955, the first postmaster being A. MacKell.

Marigold Lake (lake)
83 J/12 - Swartz Lake
32-65-11-W5
54°40′N 115°37′W
Approximately 9 km south-east of Swan Hills.

Officially named in 1977; the name refers to the abundance of marsh marigolds around the lake. Of the genus *Caltha*, they can be found in forested areas in marshy ground.

Marina (locality)
84 D/11 - Worsley
2-87-8-W6
56°30′N 119°10′W
Approximately 72 km north-west of Fairview.

Established as a post office in November 1935, the origin of the name is not precisely known. One explanation has been that it was named after Princess Marina Hellenes, daughter of Prince Nicholas of Greece. In November 1934 she married Prince George, Duke of Kent. Princess Marina, the Duchess of Kent, was by all accounts a popular figure, so perhaps she was the inspiration for the name. The first postmaster was C. Robinson.

Marlow Creek (creek)
84 M/16 - Thurston Lake
1-125-1-W6
59°50′N 118°02′W
Flows west north-west into Beatty Lake approximately 154 km north north-west of High Level.

Named by J.R. Akins, DLS, during his 1915 survey of the 6th Meridian. His field correspondence gives no clues as to the identity of Marlow.

Marsh Head Creek (creek)
83 K/2 - Marsh Head Creek
35-59-18-W5
54°09′N 116°36′W
Flows south-east into Athabasca River approximately 30 km south south-east of Fox Creek.

It shows as early as 1916 on federal government maps, and is likely descriptive.

Marten Creek (creek)
83 O/7 - Slave Lake
18-75-6-W5
55°30′N 114°55′W
Flows south-west into Lesser Slave Lake approximately 25 km north of Slave Lake.

It shows on a Geological Survey of Canada map of 1892 as Martin River. (see Marten Mountain)

Marten Lakes (lakes)
83 O/10 - Marten Lakes
28-76-4-W5
55°37′N 114°35′W
Approximately 35 km north north-east of Slave Lake.

(see Marten Mountain)

Marten Mountain (mountain)
83 O/7 - Slave Lake
8-75-5-W5
55°28′N 114°43′W
Approximately 20 km north of Slave Lake.

Some sources have stated this set of features, including the creek and lakes, was named after an old-timer in the area. Because the name predates organised settlement, it might also refer to the prevalence of the member of the weasel family, also known as sable, which was highly prized for its fur. A local wildlife biologist stated the mountain was perfect marten habitat and well within marten range. It shows on a Geological Survey of Canada map of 1892 as Martin Mountain.

Marten River (locality)
84 C/9 - Golden Lake
33-86-14-W5
56°30′N 116°10′W
Approximately 75 km north-east of Peace River.

It likely takes its name from its proximity to the river.

Marten River (river)
84 C/8 - Cadotte River
13-86-16-W5
56°28′N 116°23′W
Flows south-west into Cadotte Lake approximately 62 km north-east of Peace River.

The precise origin of the name of this river is unknown; it may named for the marten. The marten (*Martes americana*) is a slender weasel that inhabits the northern coniferous forests. The marten is trapped for its soft luxurious fur, which is shades of brown. The marten has a yellow spot on its chest, white ears, and blackish legs and tail. The tail is bushy and half the body length. Big feet and sharp climbing claws allow the marten to hunt in trees for squirrels and birds' nests. On the ground marten hunt for mice, voles, hares and birds, and also eat insects, berries and carrion.

Martin Lake (lake)
83 M/5 - Hythe
26-74-11-W6
55°26′N 119°34′W
Approximately 56 km north-west of Grande Prairie.

This lake was named in 1947 after Pilot Officer S.S. Martin, killed in World War II. He was born in Toronto on September 14, 1920, the son of Mr. and Mrs. W.G. Martin and was educated in Edmonton. He enlisted in Calgary in September 1940 and went overseas after receiving his pilots's flying badge. On June 1, 1942, he was reported missing, and subsequently presumed dead.

Mary Lake (lake)
74 D/8 - Gipsy Lake
13-86-2-W4
56°28′N 110°11′W
Approximately 79 km east south-east of Fort McMurray.

It is not known after whom this lake is named.

Maurice Lake (lake)
83 N/7 - Triangle
SE-36-74-19-W5
55°27′N 116°46′W
Approximately 18 km west of High Prairie.

The lake was named in 1949 after a former mayor of High Prairie, Verner (Barney) Maurice. He was born in Sweden in 1875, and was a blacksmith. He first emigrated to the United States where he stayed a couple of years before coming to Canada in 1898. He started for the Klondike, but like many others, he didn't quite make it. He returned to Edmonton to work before moving to Grouard in 1905. There he was the local smith and some time operator of a steamer on Lesser Slave Lake. He moved to High Prairie during World War II, and was elected its first mayor in 1945. He wrote two books – one on the life of Peace River Jim Cornwall and one titled *Fifty Years in Peace River*. Mr. Maurice died in 1959 after having spent many years in the Peace River Country.

Maxwell Lake (lake)
74 E/13 - Ronald Lake
19-102-12-W4
57°52′N 111°58′W
Approximately 130 km north north-west of Fort McMurray.

The precise origin of the name of this lake is unknown; it appears on a federal government map as early as 1916.

May Hill (hill)
83 P/9 - Pelican
NW-3-76-16-W4
55°34′N 112°24′W
Approximately 70 km west north-west of Lac La Biche.

The name for the hill was officially adopted in 1973, after a suggestion from the Alberta Surveys Branch. The hill took its name from the forestry lookout tower on the hill. This in turn possibly took its name for its relative proximity to the May River, the source of which is 38 kilometres directly east. (see also May River)

May, Lake (lake)
84 M/13 - Lake May
3-126-12-W6
59°55′N 119°59′W
Approximately 159 km north north-west of Rainbow Lake.

Named in honour of Captain Wilfrid Reid "Wop" May, DFC (1896-1952). May joined the Royal Flying Corps in 1918 and had a brief but distinguished career. He was awarded the Distinguished Flying Cross for his exploits, which included an encounter with the celebrated Manfred von Richthofen, the "Red Baron," on the day the German ace was shot down. After the war May returned to Edmonton where he was a pioneer in flying mail and passengers to the North. In 1929 he founded Commercial Airways, which received the mail contract from Edmonton to the Mackenzie River district. His gruelling mercy flight in sub-zero temperatures to the Little Red River Settlement on the Peace River in January 1929, to carry diphtheria serum there to fight an epidemic became legend. During World War II, May was involved in setting up the Commonwealth Air Training Plan. Wop May was admitted to Canada's Aviation Hall of Fame in 1973. This is one of a number of lakes in northern Alberta named after bush pilots. (see also Berry Lake, Brintnell Lake, Calder Lake, Dickins Lake, Farrell Lake, McConachie Lake, McMillan Lake, McMullen Lake, Randall Lake and Sawle Lake)

May River (river)
73 M/11 - Conklin
29-77-9-W4
55°42′N 111°22′W
Flows north into Christina River approximately 110 km south of Fort McMurray.

This name was in use at least as early as 1912. The origin of the name is not known. There is speculation that since the river flows into the Christina River, it also could have been named after a woman.

Maybelle River (river)
74 L/7 - Keane Creek
16-19-108-6-W4
58°24′N 110°59′W
Flows north-west into Richardson Lake approximately 178 km north of Fort McMurray.

Named around 1915 after the wife of F.V. Seibert, DLS.

McAllister Creek (creek)
84 C/3 - Peace River
23-82-23-W5
56°07'N 117°30'W
Flows south-east into Peace River approximately 5 km south-east of Grimshaw.

The precise origin of the name of this creek is unknown, although it may refer to the McAllister/McCorrister family who were involved with Fort Dunvegan.

McClelland Creek (creek)
74 E/11 - Firebag River
1-99-8-W4
57°34'00"N 111°09'45"W
Flows into Moose Creek approximately 90 km north north-east of Fort McMurray.

The precise origin of the name of this creek is unknown. It may be after Tom McLelland (sic). This creek has been known by this name for at least three generations of trappers. (see McClelland Lake)

McClelland Lake (lake)
74 E/11 - Firebag River
12-98-9-W4
57°29'00"N 111°19'30"W
Approximately 83 km north of Fort McMurray.

S.C. Ells apparently suggested this name, and submitted the spelling McLelland, after Tom McLelland, trader in the district. The spelling McClelland; went into use. When the issue of its incorrect spelling arose during the 1960s, it was decided to maintain the spelling McClelland to avoid duplication with another McLelland Lake in Townships 123 and 124, Range 8, West of the 4th Meridian. McClelland Lake may have been the one known as Thirty Minute Lake by early bush pilots.

McConachie Lake (lake)
83 O/15 - Brintnell
7-79-5-W5
55°50'N 114°45'W

G.W. Grant McConachie, ca. 1930

Approximately 60 km north of Slave Lake.

George William Grant McConachie was born in Hamilton, Ontario, in 1909. As a young boy he moved with his parents to Edmonton where he received his education. In 1930 he began his career as chief pilot with Independent Airways Limited. After serving in various capacities with a number of companies, he formed Yukon Southern Airlines in 1937. From 1939 to 1941, he was in charge of the Portage Air Observer School. In 1947 he became president of Canadian Pacific Airlines Limited. Grant McConachie was named a member of Canada's Aviation Hall of Fame in 1973. This is one of a number of lakes in the area named after bush pilots. (see also Berry Lake, Brintnell Lake, Calder Lake, Dickins Lake, Farrell Lake, Lake May, McMillan Lake, McMullen Lake, Randall Lake and Sawle Lake)

McCowan Lake (lake)
74 M/16 - Andrew Lake
18-126-1-W4
59°57'N 110°10'W
Approximately 355 km north of Fort McMurray.

This lake was named after Dan McCowan (1882-1956) who was a writer of natural history, with a specialization in northwestern Canada.

McDermott Island (island)
74 E/5 - Bitumount
0-23-96-11-W4
57°21'N 111°40'W
Island in Athabasca River approximately 71 km north north-west of Fort McMurray.

Andrew Miles McDermot (not McDermott) began with the Hudson's Bay Company in 1885 as clerk at the Assiniboine Lake post in the English River District. From 1920 to 1928, he was post manager at Fort McMurray. He had worked with the Company for 40 years at the time this feature was named in 1925.

McDonald Island (island)
74 D/11 - Fort McMurray
21-89-9-W4
56°44'N 111°22'W
At the confluence of the Athabasca and Clearwater Rivers, at Fort McMurray.

The precise origin of the name of this island is unknown. It may be named for John McDonald, a servant of the Hudson's Bay Company who came to the area in 1872. According to field notes of the Dominion Lands Survey, the feature was not named until after 1913.

McGowan Creek (creek)
83 N/2 - Snipe Lake
6-10-72-17-W5
55°13'N 116°32'W
Flows north into West Prairie River approximately 50 km east north-east of Valleyview.

The name was adopted some time before 1954; after whom this creek is named is not known.

McInnes Lake (lake)
74 M/9 - Colin Lake
SE-27-123-3-W4
59°42'N 110°25'W
Approximately 327 km north of Fort McMurray.

The name was submitted in 1965 by the Research Council of Alberta, and is one of a series of features in the area named after prominent geologists. William McInnes (1858-1925), born in Fredericton, New Brunswick, joined the Geological Survey of Canada in 1882 as a geologist. He became director of the GSC (1914-1920), and finally director of the Victoria Memorial Museum in Ottawa (1920-1925). That museum housed the Geological Survey and its collections.

McIvor River (river)
84 I/8 - Pointe de Roche
12-25-107-13-W4
58°19′N 112°02′W
Flows north into Lake Claire approximately 171 km north north-west of Fort McMurray.

It was named in 1915 after Dan McIvor, an axeman on a Dominion Lands Survey party working in the area that year.

McKinley Creek (creek)
83 N/1 - East Prairie
1-34-70-14-W5
55°06′N 116°02′W
Flows east into East Prairie River approximately 80 km east of Valleyview.

The name was adopted some time before 1954; it is not known after whom this creek is named.

McLean Creek (creek)
74 D/14 - Wood Creek
91-9-W4
56°53′N 111°25′W
Flows north-west into Athabasca River approximately 15 km north of Fort McMurray.

The creek was officially named in 1925 after M.C. McLean, an instrument man on a 1914-1915 survey crew. The name was submitted by S.C. Ells.

McLean Creek (creek)
84 D/5 - Boundary Lake
13-86-12-W6
56°27′N 119°46′W
Flows south-east into Little Clear River approximately 92 km north-west of Spirit River.

Although the origin of the name is not precisely known, it may have been named after the McLean family. Alexander McLean was employed at Fort Dunvegan in the 1860s.

McLeans Creek (creek)
83 N/7 - Triangle
16-22-74-20-W5
55°26′N 116°59′W
Flows west into Little Smoky River approximately 30 km west of High Prairie.

It is named after the McLean family who settled along the creek in 1925.

McLelland Lake (lake)
74 M/11 - Hay Camp
26-123-8-W4
59°43′N 111°16′W
Approximately 325 km north of Fort McMurray.

It was officially named in 1929 after the engineer on the *Athabasca River*.

McLennan (town)
83 N/10 - McLennan
32-77-19-W5
55°42′N 116°54′W
Approximately 135 km north-east of Grande Prairie.

This town located in the Peace River District was named after Dr. J.K. McLennan. He was then Secretary and later Vice-President of the Edmonton, Dunvegan, and British Columbia Railway when it reached this site in 1915. The post office opened here the same year, and E.E. Appleton was the first postmaster. The town was incorporated in 1948. (see also Aggie and Lenarthur)

McLennan Lake (lake)
74 L/1 - Archer Lake
NE-23-106-1-W4
58°13′N 110°03′W
Approximately 170 km north north-east of Fort McMurray.

The origin of the name is not known; the name appears on maps as early as 1919.

McLeod Lake (lake)
74 L/4 - Buckton Creek
NE-7-104-10-W4
58°01′N 111°39′W
Approximately 136 km north of Fort McMurray.

The lake was named in 1916 after Captain G. McLeod, DLS.

McLeod Lake (lake)
83 J/5 - Carson Lake
24-61-11,12-W5
54°18′N 115°39′W
Approximately 16 km north north-east of Whitecourt.

The name McLeod Lake likely takes its name from the nearby McLeod River, a name that dates from the time of the fur trade. David Thompson showed it on a map in 1814. It may refer to Archibald Norman McLeod (fl. 1796-1837), a North West Company fur trader who became a partner before 1799, and ventured to the Athabasca Country in 1802. Paul Kane referred to the lake in the 1850s as being a great source of whitefish. For a time from before 1940 to 1986, the lake was known as Carson Lake, for it is the source of Carson Creek. In the 1980s, local residents requested to have the name return to its historical and local usage. The name was officially changed to McLeod Lake in 1986. At the same time the name of the lake to the north-east had its name changed from Pegasus Lake to Little

McLeod Lake. (see also Carson Creek, Carson Lake and Pegasus Lake)

McLeod Lake (lake)
83 O/16 - Mistehae Lake
32-80-1-W5
55°59′N 114°07′W
Approximately 90 km north-west of Slave Lake.

The name has appeared on maps as early as 1918. The origin of the name is not known, but the person after whom it was named may have worked on a survey crew. J. Burns was a chainman in A.H. Hawkins' survey crew. On a map dated to April 1914, this lake appears as Long Lake, connected by Burns Creek to Weaver Lake.

McLeod River (river)
83 J/4 - Whitecourt
27-59-12-W5
54°08′N 115°43′W
Flows north-east into the Athabasca River at Whitecourt.

(see McLeod Lake)

McMillan Lake (lake)
83 P/7 - Amadou Lake
23-74-18-W4
55°26′N 112°40′W
Approximately 80 km north-west of Lac La Biche.

The name has appeared on maps as early as 1918. The origin of the name is not known, but the person after whom it was named may have worked on a survey crew.

McMillan Lake (lake)
83 O/16 - Mistehae Lake
24-78-3-W5
55°47′N 114°28′W
Approximately 55 km north north-east of Slave Lake.

Stanley Ransome McMillan was born in Dryden, Ontario, but moved to Edmonton

Stan McMillan, 1937

with his parents as a boy. He attended the University of Alberta before he joined the Royal Canadian Air Force in 1927. He worked with a number of airlines that held mail and passenger contracts in the North. He served as an instructor in World War II, and after the war, worked for a time as a test pilot. This is one of a number of lakes in the area named for bush pilots. (see also Berry Lake, Brintnell Lake, Calder Lake, Dickins Lake, Farrell Lake, Lake May, McConachie Lake, McMullen Lake, Randall Lake and Sawle Lake)

McMillar Creek (creek)
83 L/15 - Big Mountain Creek
10-30-67-4-W6
54°49′50″N 118°35′28″W
Flows north-east into Smoky River approximately 40 km south of Grande Prairie.

This creek was named after Dan McMillar, who camped here and was one of the first forest rangers in the area. He may have been in the area as early as 1919.

McMullen Lake (lake)
83 O/16 - Mistehae
16-79-1-W5
55°50′N 114°05′W
Approximately 75 km north-west of Slave Lake.

Archie McMullen was born in 1906 at Gilbert Plains, Manitoba. He moved with his parents to Alberta as a young boy, and received his education in Alberta. He started flying in 1927 and flew the first air mail out of Fort McMurray on December 10, 1929. He worked as a northern pilot until the start of World War II. He was a test pilot during the war. For a year he worked in the United States, then returned to Edmonton to join Canadian Pacific Airlines as a transport captain, remaining there until his retirement in 1963. He was inducted into the Canadian Aviation Hall of Fame in 1973. This is one of a number of lakes in the area named after bush pilots. (see also Berry Lake, Brintnell Lake, Calder Lake, Dickins Lake, Farrell Lake, Lake May, McConachie Lake, McMillan Lake, Randall Lake and Sawle Lake)

McMurray Settlement (settlement)
74 D/11 - Fort McMurray
89-9-W4
56°43′N 112°22′W
Located in the city of Fort McMurray.

First surveyed in 1911, it was named for the nearby community. (see Fort McMurray)

McNaught Lake (lake)
83 M/3 - Wembley
S -15-71-10-W6
55°09′N 119°27′W
Approximately 38 km west of Grande Prairie.

The lake was named for the first settlers in the area. Eliza Jane McNaught applied for a homestead under a South African Volunteer grant in 1911, and John McNaught was granted land in 1919 through the Soldier Settlement Board.

McNeil Lake (lake)
84 P/9 - Peace Point
SE-36-121-15-W4
59°33'N 112°25'W
Approximately 290 km east north-east of High Level.

This is named for one of the first buffalo rangers in Wood Buffalo National Park, where the lake is situated.

*McNeill Lake (lake)
83 M/6 - La Glace
35-72-10-W6
55°17'N 119°25'W
Approximately 39 km north-west of Grande Prairie.

Wing Commander J.G. McNeill was born in Calgary on April 15, 1919, the son of Mr. & Mrs. J.A. McNeill. He received his early education in Alberta. He enlisted in the RCAF for aircrew duties at Kingston, Ontario, on June 10, 1940, completed his flying training and was commissioned. He proceeded overseas, where he was an outstanding pilot. He was awarded the Distinguished Flying Cross in August 1943, and was killed in a flying accident on August 21, 1944. A field survey established that the local usage was still Hay Lake, so in 1991 the name was officially changed back to its original name. (see Hay Lake)

Meadow Creek (creek)
74 D/2 - Quigley
4-84-6-W4
56°15'N 110°53'W
Flows north-east into Cheecham Lake approximately 55 km south-east of Fort McMurray.

---

*denotes rescinded name or former locality.

Likely descriptive of the terrain through which it flows, the name appears on federal government maps as early as 1917.

Meander River (hamlet)
84 N/4 - Meander River
5-116-22-W5
59°02'N 117°42'W
Approximately 67 km north north-west of High Level.

It is named for its proximity to Meander River. The Slavey name for this locality is *Tahcheh*, which translates as "meeting place" and has two local interpretations. It may have been the meeting place where people would gather at certain times of the year, or it may refer to the confluence of the Hay and Meander rivers. A post office was established here in 1954, and the first postmaster was Mme M. Lizotte. It is located on the Great Slave Lake Railway line.

Meander River (river)
84 N/4 - Meander River
32-115-22-W5
59°02'N 117°42'W
Approximately 66 km north north-west of High Level.

This river may have been named by Hulbert Footner for he mentions it in his book *New Rivers of the North* (1912). "On the third day (out from Fort Vermilion) we crossed the imperceptible divide and thereafter the streams flowed westward. The ground was stonier and less fertile on the side. We passed two pretty lakes drained by a smoothly flowing river that wound its crooked way through meadows of grass waist height. We christened it the Meander." However, J. R. Akins, DLS, reported in 1914 that the stream was called locally the Meander. If this was the case, Footner may have obtained the name from his guide. (see also Footner Lake)

Meander River Station (station)
84 K/13 - Henderson Creek
14-115-22-W5
58°59'N 117°37'W
Approximately 60 km north north-west of High Level.

This station was established in 1962 on the Great Slave Lake Railway line. (see Meander River)

Mearon Creek (creek)
84 D/13 - Betts Creek
1-92-13-W6
56°57'N 119°58'W
Flows south-west into Doig River approximately 137 km north-west of Fairview.

It was named after Private Sidney Mearon, killed in action on December 27, 1943.

Meekwap Lake (lake)
83 K/10 - Atikkamek Creek
34-65-18-W5
54°40'N 116°38'W
Approximately 150 km east south-east of Grande Prairie.

Aboriginal in origin, the name was officially adopted in the late 1950s. Its meaning is not yet known.

Mega River (river)
84 L/14 - Vardie River
22-113-7-W6
58°50'N 119°09'W
Flows south-east into Zama Lake approximately 41 km north north-east of Rainbow Lake.

Officially named in 1957, its origin is not precisely known. Mega denotes large; the name may have been conferred to distinguish this river from another smaller one in the area.

Meikle River (river)
84 F/3 - Crummy Lake
19-94-21-W5
57°10′N 117°22′W
Flows south-east into Notikewin River approximately 29 km north north-east of Manning.

It was named after McKay Meikle, bookkeeper and timekeeper for the survey party of J.R. Akins, 1915-16. Meikle apparently fell into the river and had to be fished out by the crew who named the river for him. This river was formerly known as the Third Battle River. (see also Battle River, Notikewin, Second Battle River and Third Battle River)

Melito Creek (creek)
84 K/6 - Parma Creek
11-108-19-W5
58°21′N 117°03′W
Flows south-east into Bede Creek approximately 18 km south of High Level.

The precise origin of the name of this creek is unknown; the name appears on a provincial government map as early as 1930.

Melvin River (river)
84 N/4 - Meander River
28-117-21-W5
59°11′N 117°31′W
Flows north-west into Hay River approximately 77 km north north-west of High Level.

It was apparently named by J. R. Akins, DLS, during his 1914 survey of the 30th Baseline, as this name was recorded in his field correspondence. The local name for the stream is *Xatloh Chateh Zahéh* which in Slavey means the First Slavey River. Chateh was the Slavey Chief who signed Treaty No. 8. The name has been in use since the late 19th century. (see also Slavey Creek)

Mercredi Lake (lake)
74 M/15 - Mercredi Lake
18-126-4-W4
59°56′N 110°42′W
Approximately 351 km north of Fort McMurray.

It was named in 1929 after Pierre Mercredi, Hudson's Bay Company trader at Resolution and for many years a trader at Fort Chipewyan. *Mercredi* is a corruption of the name MacCready.

Merganser Bay (bay)
74 D/8 - Gipsy Lake
14-86-2-W4
56°27′N 110°12′W
North-east bay on Gipsy Lake approximately 77 km east south-east Fort McMurray.

It is likely descriptive of the fish-eating diving duck, *Mergus merganser*, found in the area. Like many other Canadian residents, these birds like to winter in the southern United States and Northern Mexico. Mergansers return in summer and fly northward to enjoy northern climes, including the Lake Athabasca region.

Meridian Lakes (lakes)
84 O/10 - Meridian Lakes
SW-17-122-5-W5
59°35′N 114°50′W
Approximately 178 km north-east of High Level.

The name for these lakes was officially approved in 1967 and describes their location on the 5th Meridian. (see also Fifth Meridian)

Merlin Creek (creek)
84 D/4 - Cherry Point
21-82-13-W6
56°08′N 119°58′W
Flows north into Peace River approximately 75 km west north-west of Spirit River.

The name was submitted by R.W. Cautley, DLS, after having been asked by the Surveyor General to provide a name for the creek. The significance of the name is not precisely known. It may refer to the small falcon *Falco columbarius*, known in Canada as the pigeon hawk. Its breeding distribution in Canada includes all but the high Arctic.

Merryweather Lake (lake)
84 P/6 - Merryweather Lake
22-119-20-W4
59°21′N 113°21′W
Approximately 232 km east north-east of High Level.

It was named in 1949 after Coder Hugh Merryweather of Fallis, Alberta, who was mentioned in despatches and killed in World War II.

Metis (station)
84 K/3 - Metis
11-106-21-W5
58°12′N 117°21′W
Approximately 38 km south south-west of High Level.

The precise origin of the name of this station is unknown, although it likely refers to the people living in the area. A Great Slave Lake Railway station was established here in 1962.

Michael Lake (lake)
84 H/16 - Bayard Lake
22-101-15-W4
57°47′N 112°22′W
Approximately 132 km north north-west of Fort McMurray.

Likely named in the late 1940s or early 1950s; after whom this lake is named is not known.

Middle Rapids (rapids)
84 A/9 - Boiler Rapids
30-87-13-W4
56°34′N 112°03′W
In thrAthabasca River approximately 45 km west south-west of Fort McMurray.

A descriptive name the rapids are midway between the Boiler Rapids and the Long Rapids. *Tuwao pastiche* is the Cree name for this feature. The name was recorded by the Geological Survey of Canada in 1892.

Mikkwa River (river)
84 J/7 - Vermilion Chutes
28-108-5-W5
58°25′N 114°46′W
Flows north-west into Peace River approximately 138 km east south-east of High Level.

The Cree name for this river is descriptive of the reddish-brown colour of the water. It was known either as the Red or Little Red River until 1914, when it was changed to Mikkwa, as there were other rivers of the same name in Alberta. The source of this river is a lake in the Birch Mountains and it enters the Peace several miles below the Vermilion Falls.

Mildred Lake (lake)
74 E/4 - Fort MacKay
8-93-10-W4
57°03′N 111°35′W
Approximately 37 km north north-west of Fort McMurray.

This lake was named after Mildred Tarpenny, daughter of the caretaker of the Hudson's Bay Company shipyards. The name was recorded by A.D. Griffin, DLS, during his survey of the area in 1914.

---
*denotes rescinded name or former locality.

Mildred Lake (locality)
74 E/4 - Fort MacKay
6-93-10-W4
57°02′N 111°36′W
Approximately 37 km north north-west of Fort McMurray.

It was named for its proximity to Mildred Lake. The post office was established here in 1975, with Randy Harris as postmaster. (see Mildred Lake)

Miller Creek (creek)
74 D/11 - Fort McMurray
28-89-9-W4
56°45′N 111°23′W
Flows west north-west into Athabasca River at Fort McMurray.

This was named after Paul Miller, one of the first homesteaders in the Fort McMurray district.

***Miller's Crossing** (former locality)
84 C/4 - Grimshaw
17-83-23-W5
56°11′N 117°36′W
Approximately 20 km west of Peace River.

(see Grimshaw)

Mills Island (island)
74 E/4 - Fort MacKay
18-95-10-W4
57°14′N 111°37′W
In Athabasca River approximately 62 km north north-west of Fort McMurray.

Named for Captain James William Mills (1859-1933), a Nova Scotian who sailed in the West Indies, then came in 1885 to the Canadian Northwest where he joined the Hudson's Bay Company to work on the fleet of river steamers. By 1893 he had become master of the *Wrigley*. Mills was appointed naval designer of other steamers that plied the northern rivers, and was responsible for the building of the first *Athabasca River* and the *Slave River*, which operated around Fort McMurray. He also built and skippered the *Fort McMurray* which was constructed in the Snye. In 1921 he retired but four years later superintended the establishment of the wireless station at Aklavik, N.W.T., as well as the store there.

Milne Lake (lake)
83 O/12 - Salt Creek
21-77-13-W5
55°41′N 115°47′W
Approximately 85 km north west of Slave Lake.

The lake appears as early as 1922 on a township plan; it is not known after whom it was named.

Milton's Creek (creek)
74 D/6 - Gregoire Lake
10-86-8-W4
56°26′05″N 111°10′30″W
Flows north-east into an unnamed creek flowing into Gregoire Lake approximately 34 km south south-east of Fort McMurray.

This creek was named because of its proximity to Milton's Lake. The lake was named for Johnny Milton who ran a trap line through the area.

Milton's Lake (lake)
74 D/16 - Gregoire Lake
10-86-8-W4
56°26′20″N 111°11′20″W
Approximately 34 km south south-east of Fort McMurray.

It is the source of Milton's Creek. In popular local usage this lake has several other names, including Gunner's Lake after Gunner Brody, a forester who had a cabin near the lake, and Mud Lake, descriptive of the muddiness of the lake bottom. (see also Milton's Creek)

Mink Lake (lake)
84 B/4 - Mink River
14-81-11-W5
56°01′N 115°35′W
Approximately 95 km north north-west of Slave Lake.

The precise origin of the name of this lake is unknown; the name is likely descriptive of the local fauna.

Mink Lake (lake)
84 A/14 - Mink Lake
22-91-21-W4
56°54′N 113°17′W
Approximately 115 km west north-west of Fort McMurray.

The precise origin of the name of this lake is unknown; the name is likely descriptive of the local fauna.

Mink Lake (lake)
84 I/5 - Ruis Lake
NE-19-108-22-W4
58°24′N 113°39′W
Approximately 198 km east of High Level.

Officially approved in 1963, the name had been in local use for many years, and is descriptive of the animal found in the area.

Mink River (river)
83 O/13 - Atikameg
11-9-80-11-W5
55°55′N 115°40′W
Flows south into Utikumasis Lake approximately 87 km north-west of Slave Lake.

Recorded in 1910 by A.H. Hawkins as Mink Creek, it is likely descriptive of the fur-bearing animal prevalent in the area.

*****Mirage Lake** (lake)
83 M/14 - Blueberry Mountain
31-32-79-8-W6
55°53′N 119°13′W

---

*denotes rescinded name or former locality.

Approximately 26 km north-west of Spirit River.

The origin is likely descriptive, and was shown as Mirage Lake on the early maps compiled from the survey in the 1910s. The name was changed in 1983 due to local usage of the name Moonshine. (see Moonshine Lake)

*****Mirror Landing** (former post office)
83 O/1 - Smith
23-71-1-W5
55°10′N 114°02′W
Approximately 70 km north-west of Athabasca.

The post office operated under this name from October 1913 through April 1957. The origin of the name is not known, and the name was later changed. (see Smith)

Misery Mountain (hill)
83 L/9 - Latornell
34,35-64-2-W6
54°35′10″N 118°12′30″W
Approximately 75 km south south-east of Grande Prairie.

Officially approved in 1991 after research conducted in the area found the name well established and in local use. Its elevation is 914 metres. This feature was named Misery Mountain when a road was built on its west side. The road was often impassable during periods of bad weather – the journey was miserable.

Mission Creek (creek)
83 O/5 - Driftpile
13-8-74-13-W5
55°24′N 115°58′W
Flows north into Lesser Slave Lake approximately 75 km west of Slave Lake (town).

This name, adopted in the early 1950s, refers to the Joussard Roman Catholic Mission by which it flows. (see also Joussard)

Holy Angels Residential School picnic at Fort Chipewyan, near Mission Point, n.d.

■ **Mission Point** (point)
74 L/11 - Fort Chipewyan
3-7-112-7-W4
58°42′N 111°11′W
Approximately 215 km north of Fort McMurray.

It is named for the Fort Chipewyan Roman Catholic Mission founded in 1847. The Holy Angels Residential School operated from the late 19th century until the mid-1970s. This site was originally the location of Colin Fraser's Fort Chipewyan trading post. Because of this, it was at one time known as Colin Fraser's Point.

Mistanusk Creek (creek)
83 L/12 - Lingrell Lake
5-64-13-W6
53°30′15″N 119°55′15″W
Flows north-west into British Columbia approximately 100 km south-west of Grande Prairie.

Recorded in 1918 by the surveyors on the Alberta-British Columbia Boundary Commission, *mistanusk* is a Cree word referring to the badger, which were abundant in the area.

Mistehae Lake (lake)
83 O/16 - Mistehae Lake
18-80-2-W5
55°56′N 114°19′W
Approximately 75 km north north-east of Slave Lake.

It is from the Cree language meaning big.

Mitsue (locality)
83 O/7 - Slave Lake
30-72-4-W5
55°16′N 114°37′W
Approximately 10 km east south-east of Slave Lake.

This Edmonton, Dunvegan, and British Columbia Railway station was established here in 1914, taking its name from the nearby lake and creek. The post office was established in June 1931. The postmaster was E. Kirkpatrick. (see also Mitsue Creek)

Mitsue Creek (creek)
83 O/7 - Slave Lake
5-34-72-5-W5
55°17′N 114°42′W
Flows north-west into Lesser Slave River approximately 5 km east of Slave River.

It is a form of the Cree word meaning "eating." It was named before 1900, and along with nearby Eating Creek attests to the abundance of game in the area.

Mitsue Lake (lake)
83 O/7 - Slave Lake
12-19-72-4-W5
55°15′N 114°37′W
Approximately 10 km south-east of Slave Lake.
(see Mitsue Creek)

Moberly Rapids (rapids)
74 D/11 - Fort McMurray
17-89-9-W4
56°43′N 111°24′W
Approximately 2.5 km west of Fort McMurray on the Athabasca River.

These rapids are named for Henry John Moberly (1835-1931), the founder of Fort McMurray. Henry Moberly, born in Penetanguishene, Upper Canada, entered the service of the Hudson's Bay Company in 1854 as a clerk. He served at the once-abandoned Jasper House post, 1855-1861. Moberly similarly re-established a post at Fort McMurray in 1870. He served the HBC until 1894 when he retired and settled in Saskatchewan. During his career as fur trader his service with the company had been intermittent, as he also worked as a free trader. Moberly Lake and Moberly River in the Peace Country in British Columbia, as well as Moberly Creek, Moberly Flats and Moberly Hill in Alberta, are also named after him and members of his family. An elder brother, Walter Moberly (1832-1915), was one of the major explorers in British Columbia, and discovered Eagle Pass between the present Revelstoke and Shuswap Lake. Other brothers, Frank and Clarence W. Moberly, were railway location and construction engineers across North America. The name Moberly Rapids appears as early as 1892 on federal government maps. (see also Fort McMurray)

Modere Creek (creek)
84 I/8 - Pointe de Roche
14-2-109-15-W4
58°27′N 112°23′W
Flows north into Birch River approximately 190 km north north-west of Fort McMurray.

The origin of this name is not known, but it does show on maps as early as the 1940s.

Mons Lake (lake)
83 J/12 - Swartz Lake
5-65-12-W5
54°36′N 115°47′W
Approximately 30 km west south-west of Swan Hills.

It likely commemorates the capture of the Belgian city by Canadian troops shortly before the Armistice in 1918.

Montagneuse Lake (lake)
84 D/9 - Sulphur Lake
31-86-3-W6
56°30′N 118°28′W
Approximately 48 km north of Fairview.

It is the source of the Montagneuse River. (see Montagneuse River)

Montagneuse River (river)
84 D/7 - Eureka River
6-84-6-W6
56°15′N 118°57′W
Flows south-west into Peace River approximately 105 km west of Peace River.

Although the precise origin is not known, it may refer to the nearby Clear Hills, or the more distant Rocky Mountains. The name appears on federal government maps as early as 1914. The word *montagneuse* means "mountainous" in French.

Moody Creek (creek)
84 L/15 - Big Mountain Creek
1-114-5-W6
58°52′N 118°41′W
Flows south south-west into Hay Lake approximately 54 km north-east of Rainbow Lake.

Named in honour of Private William D. Moody, killed in action in 1945. The lower portion of the water body where it enters Hay Lake is known locally as *Wozaa Zahéh* or Muskeg Creek.

Mooney Creek (creek)
83 O/7 - Slave Lake
14-2-73-6-W5
55°18′N 114°48′W
Flows north into Lesser Slave Lake just west of Slave Lake.

The origin of the name is not precisely known; however, it is likely named for John Mooney who worked at the Sawridge (now Slave Lake) Hudson's Bay post in the early 1920s, or it may have been named after E. Mooney who served as rear chainman with W.G. McFarlane in his surveys along the 19th and 20th Baselines.

Moonshine Lake (lake)
83 M/14 - Blueberry Mountain
31,32-79-8-W6
55°53'N 119°13'W
Approximately 30 km north-west of Spirit River.

This small lake was on what was known during the 1910s and 1920s as the Moonshine Trail. During the 1920s two local residents were transporting moonshine along the trail when some of the brew spilled from the wagon and ran into the lake. The name of the lake was changed to the current one in 1983. Before it had been officially called Mirage Lake.

Moonshine Lake Provincial Park (provincial park)
83 M/14 - Blueberry Mountain
29-32-79-8-W6
55°53'N 119°13'W
Approximately 26 km north west of Spirit River.

The 847-hectare park was established in 1979 and was named for its proximity to the lake. (see Moonshine Lake)

Moose Bay (bay)
74 D/8 - Gipsy Lake
1-86-2-W4
56°26'N 110°11'W
Approximately 87 km east south-east of Fort McMurray.

The precise origin of the name of this bay is unknown; it is likely descriptive of the animal in the area. The word moose comes from the Algonkian language meaning browser or stripper, referring to its method of eating. Found in the northern forests across most of Canada, this ruminant, *Alces alces*, is the largest member of the deer family. The moose and the loon are two enduring symbols of the Northern wilderness. The moose has the distinct honour of having more features named after it in Canada than anything else.

Moose Creek (creek)
74 E/11 - Firebag River
30-99-7-W4
57°37'10"N 111°08'58"W
Flows north into the Firebag River 100 km north north-east of Fort McMurray.

One of several creeks in Alberta with this name, the creek has been known by this name for a long time. It is apparently called Moose Creek because many moose have been lost in the quicksand on the bed of the creek while trying to cross it.

Moose Creek (creek)
83 K/14 - Asplund Creek
6-11-68-22-W5
54°52'20"N 117°15'00"W
Flows east into Asplund Creek approximately 107 km south-east of Grande Prairie.

Officially approved in 1991, the name is descriptive of the large moose population around it. The name was found to be well established and in local use when field research was conducted in the area.

Moose Creek (creek)
83 J/11 - Swan Hills
19-65-7-W5
54°38'N 115°03'W
Flows south-east into Timeu Creek approximately 24 km east south-east of Swan Hills.

Officially named in the late 1950s the name is descriptive of the animal found in the area.

***Moose Creek** (creek)
83 K/14 - Asplund Creek
3-25-68-22-W5
54°55'N 117°13'W
Flows north-east into Little Smoky River approximately 18 km south south-east of Valleyview.

Officially renamed Asplund Creek in 1960; this former name was applied to Moose Creek at 6-11-68-22-W5 above. (see Asplund Creek)

Moose Island (island)
84 K/2 - Moose Island
31-104-16-W5
58°05'N 116°37'W
Approximately 56 km south-east of High Level in Peace River.

The name likely refers to the animal, which may live on the island.

Moose Island (island)
74 L/13 - Baril River
26-114-11-W4
58°56'N 111°45'W
Approximately 236 km north of Fort McMurray in Peace River.

Officially named in 1971 the name is descriptive of the animal found in the area.

Moose Lake (lake)
84 J/1 - Harper Creek
26-106-3-W5
58°14'N 114°22'W
Approximately 163 km east south-east of High Level.

This name of this lake is the English translation of the early French name Lac d'Orignal, where Angus Shaw built a trading post for the North West Company

---

*denotes rescinded name or former locality.

in 1789. The post was called Fort Lac d'Orignal or Shaw's House. The lake was reached from the Beaver River up Moose Lake River; although the river was only 15 miles long it took nine days to transport goods as there were 36 rapids with swamps on either side. The lake was named for the abundance of moose in the area.

Moose Lake (lake)
83 K/14 - Asplund Creek
2-14-67-23-W5
54°47'40"N 117°23'20"W
Approximately 98 km south-east of Grande Prairie.

Officially approved in 1991, the name was found to be well established and in local use when field research was conducted. The name has been in use since at least the early 1920s and likely refers to the large moose population which used to feed from the lake.

*****Moose Lake** (lake)
83 P/5 - Fawcett Lake
73-25,26-W4
55°18'N 113°53'W
Approximately 55 km east of Slave Lake.

It was recorded as early as 1892 on a map of the Geological Survey of Canada and is likely descriptive of the animal in the area. The name was changed in 1912. (see Fawcett Lake)

Moose Point (point)
74 L/9 - Old Fort Bay
NW-21-111-3-W4
58°39'N 110°27'W
Approximately 210 km north north-east of Fort McMurray.

The name was well known and in use by the early part of the 20th century, and is likely descriptive of the number of the animals found in the area. It lies on the north shore of the narrows separating Lake Athabasca from Old Fort Bay.

Moose Portage (locality)
83 P/4 - Pelican
SW-14-72-26-W4
55°13'N 113°52'W
Approximately 55 km east of Slave Lake.

Originally this was a post office established in 1928, the first postmaster being J. V. Logan. The "moose portage" was mentioned by the Dominion Land Surveyors in 1913 close to where the post office was established. A 1918 map does show a trail running from near the Athabasca River

Moose Portage, Peace River Country, June-July 1913

north to Paul Lake and Fawcett Lake. The surveyor's field notes mention the plenitude of moose, so the post office likely took the older name.

*****Moose Portage** (former post office)
83 N/4 - Sturgeon Heights
12-72-26-W5
55°14N 117°52'W
Approximately 60 km east of Grande Prairie.

Likely established in the 1920s or 1930s, the name was rescinded in 1964. The name was descriptive of the animal population in the area.

Moose River (river)
83 L/9 - Latornell River
1-64-1-W6
54°35'N 118°08'W
Flows north-west into Latornell River approximately 70 km south south-east of Grande Prairie.

Officially named in 1957 and is descriptive of the animal found in the area.

*****Moose River** (river)
83 O/8 - Driftwood River
6-27-72-2-W5
55°15'N 114°14'W
Flows south-west into Driftwood River approximately 33 km east of Slave Lake.

Originally referred to as Moose River when the Geological Survey of Canada was first in the area in 1892, the name had changed by 1912. (see Fawcett Lake and Fawcett River)

*****Moose River** (river)
83 K/13 - Long Lake
14-69-27-W5
54°58'N 118°00'W
Flows east into Simonette River approximately 55 km east south-east of Grande Prairie.

This descriptive name was recorded by the Dominion Land Surveyors and appears on a federal government map of 1917. It was changed around 1920 to honour a war casualty. (see Latornell River)

Moosehorn River (river)
83 J/14 - Deer Mountain
21-68-9-W5
54°54'N 115°19'W
Flows east into Swan River approximately 50 km south-west of Slave Lake.

---
*denotes rescinded name or former locality.

Named in the 1930s or 1940s the origin is likely descriptive.

Morrison Island (island)
74 E/5 - Bitumount
31-97-10-W4
57°27′30″N 111°36′30″W
In Athabasca River approximately 84 km north north-west of Fort McMurray.

Named for G.A. Morrison, early resident of Fort McMurray, who was at one time the district Crown Land Agent.

Morse Lake (lake)
83 J/11 - Swan Hills
9-66-10-W5
54°43′N 115°27′W
Approximately 4km west of Swan Hills.

This was named before 1928 after C.H. Morse, former Inspector of Forest Reserves.

Morse River (river)
83 J/6 - Christmas Creek
36-63-8-W5
54°30′N 115°04′W
Flows north north-east into Freeman River approximately 24 km south south-east of Swan Hills.
(see Morse Lake)

Morton Island (island)
74 E/4 - Fort MacKay
21-93-10-W4
57°05′N 111°33′W
In Athabasca River approximately 40 km north north-west of Fort McMurray.

This island is named for Lou Morton, longtime captain on the northern rivers, by S.C. Ells. Morton was an engineer for McInnes Fisheries, who ran small fishing craft from Lake Athabasca to their icehouse at Waterways. In 1924 the company introduced freezer barges so that the freezing and packing operation could be carried out at the lake itself. Morton was a well-known character, and when he retired to Vancouver during the 1960s, the call of the sea beckoned. He signed on as a crew member on a ship even though he was in his eighties. (see also Tokyo Snye Channel)

Mount Valley (locality)
83 M/4 - Rio Grande
24-70-13-W6
55°05′N 119°50′W
Approximately 54 km west of Grande Prairie.

Originally a post office, established in January 1938, the name is descriptive, it being in a valley near the mountains. The first postmaster was Mrs. E. Lengrell.

Mountain Lake (lake)
83 N/5 - Puskwaskau River
SW-36-74-25-W5
55°27′N 117°43′W
Approximately 70 km north-east of Grande Prairie.

It is named for its location on a high spot of land. The name was made official in 1953 after a field survey was conducted.

Mountain Rapids (rapids)
74 M/13 - Fitzgerald
35-126-11-W4
59°59′N 111°45′W
Approximately 354 km north of Fort McMurray in Slave River.

The name shows on federal government maps as early as 1930, but the name likely predates that time. After which mountain it is named is not known.

Mountain Rapids (rapids)
74 D/12 - Cascade Rapids
33-88-10-W4
56°40′N 111°31′W

On the Athabasca River, 6 km south-west of Fort McMurray.

These rapids take their name from proximity to a bluff or "mountain" that rises from a bank of the river. Charles Mair in *Through the Mackenzie Basin* (1908) relates how on his way up the river they "came to the first rapid 'the Mountain' – *watchikwe powistic* – so called from a peak at its head which towered to great height above the neighbouring bank." The name was recorded by the Geological Survey of Canada in 1892, and appears on Father Petitot's map of 1883.

Mouse Island (island)
74 L/11 - Fort Chipewyan
1-5-112-7-W4
58°41′N 111°08′W
Approximately 212 km north of Fort McMurray in Lake Athabasca.

It shows on maps as early as 1923, and is likely descriptive.

Mud Creek (creek)
83 J/9 - Flatbush
32-65-3-W5
54°40′N 114°26′W
Flows north-east into Akuinu River approximately 60 km north of Barrhead.

Officially named in 1958; it is descriptive of the water in the creek.

Mud Creek (creek)
83 N/9 - Grouard
8-24-75-15-W5
55°31′N 116°10′W
Flows north into Lesser Slave Lake approximately 20 km east north-east of High Prairie

Named around 1916-1918; the name is descriptive.

Mud Lake (lake)
74 L/14 - Rivière des Rochers
8-113-8-W4
58°47'N 111°20'W
Approximately 222 km north of Fort McMurray.

The name derives from treacherous mud formation along the shore, and the water in the lake is full of greyish, muddy sediment.

Muddy River (river)
84 G/11 - Senex Creek
24-98-10-W5
57°32'N 115°29'W
Flows south-east into Wabasca River approximately 145 km north-east of Manning.

The name of this river is likely descriptive of the sediment found in the river.

Muddyshore Lake (lake)
83 N/5 - Puskwaskau River
19-74-25-W5
55°25'N 117°50'W
Approximately 60 km northeast of Grande Prairie.

Muddyshore Lake is so named because the muskeg surrounding the lake has made the shore of the lake very muddy. The name has been in use since at least 1930, although at one time it was called simply Mud Lake.

Muir Lake (lake)
83 O/12 - Salt Creek
8-77-13-W5
55°40'N 116°00'W
Approximately 85 km west north-west of Slave Lake.

Although the person after whom this lake is named is not known, it may have been for W. Muir, a picketman for W.G. McFarlane, DLS.

Mulligan Creek (creek)
84 D/2 - Hines Creek
12-81-7-W6
56°00'N 118°57'W
Flows south-east into Hamelin Creek approximately 36 km east of Fairview.

J.D. Mulligan served as a cook for J.B. St. Cyr, DLS, who was surveying the area in 1907-1910.

Mulligan Creek (creek)
83 M/6 - La Glace
34-73-8-W6
55°22'N 119°09'W
Flows south into Bear River approximately 29 km north-west of Grande Prairie.

Mulligan Creek was named before 1914 after the first owner of the land adjoining the lake. Although there is no record to substantiate this, since the two are in relative proximity, there may be some connection with the Mulligan Creek above.

Mulligan Lake (lake)
83 M/6 - La Glace
NW-35-73-8-W6
55°22'N 119°07'W
Approximately 30 km north-west of Grande Prairie.

This lake, which is a source of Mulligan Creek, was called at one time by Dave Atkinson, the landowner, "Atkinson Lake." Mr. Atkinson was a veteran of the Boer War. (see Mulligan Creek)

Murchison Lake (lake)
74 M/16 - Andrew Lake
NE-3-126-2-W4
59°55'N 110°15'W
Approximately 353 km north of Fort McMurray.

The name was submitted in 1958 by the Research Council of Alberta, and is one of a series of features in the area named after prominent geologists. This lake was "named after Sir Roderick Impey Murchison (1792-1871), director-general of the Geological Survey of Great Britain, who recommended James Hector to the Palliser Expedition." Holmgren, 1976.

Murdock Creek (creek)
74 M/6 - Bocquene Lake
2-9-120-9-W4
59°24'N 111°28'W
Flows north-east into Slave River approximately 287 km north of Fort McMurray.

The name appears on federal government maps as early as the 1920s, but after whom the creek is named is not known.

Murray Creek (creek)
83 J/13 - Wallace Mountain
1-69-11-W5
54°56'N 115°32'W
Flows north-east into Sutherland Creek approximately 60 km south-west of Slave Lake.

It is named in 1906 after David Murray, a chainman on a survey party who worked in the area.

Mushikitee Island (island)
84 C/4 - Grimshaw
22-81-24-W5
56°02'N 117°40'W
In Peace River approximately 17 km south of Grimshaw.

This name is likely Cree in origin and may be a variation of the Cree word *muskitiw*. The feature is known locally as Big Island. However, *mushikitee* does not closely enough sound like *mistehae*, the Cree word for big, or large, as it was translated in one source.

Muskeg Creek (creek)
74 E/6 - Kearl Lake
4-96-9-W4
57°18'15"N 111°23'25"W
Flows north-west into Muskeg River approximately 62 km north north-east of Fort McMurray.

This creek is named descriptively for the extensive amount of muskeg in the area. Muskeg, an Algonkian term meaning "grassy bog", is commonly used to describe the large, poorly drained areas that cover much of northern Alberta. In these areas black spruce and sphagnum moss grow on the surface of peat deposits, which are of variable thicknesses and types because of incomplete decomposition of plant material in a wet acid environment. The rate of peat accumulation and the distribution of muskeg are dependent on climatic conditions. Most muskeg in Canada is found in areas covered during the last glaciation and is less than 10,000 years old. Muskeg provides important habitat for many of the bird and animal species found in northern Alberta. Reclamation of muskeg is possible, and proper management of organic soils on peat allows for agricultural and forestry operations. *Muskego sipisis* is the well-established Cree name for this creek.

Muskeg Creek (creek)
83 O/7 - Slave Lake
4-7-73-4-W5
55°18'N 114°37'W
Flows south-east into Lesser Slave River approximately 10 km east of Slave Lake.

The name was recorded as early as 1892 by the Geological Survey of Canada as the Muskeg River; the name is descriptive of the area through which the stream flows.

---

*denotes rescinded name or former locality.

*****Muskeg Creek** (creek)
84 L/15 - Big Mountain Creek
1-114-5-W6
58°52'N 118°41'W
Flows south south-west into Hay Lake approximately 54 km north-east of Rainbow Lake.

(see Moody Creek)

Muskeg Lake (lake)
83 O/7 - Slave Lake
15-73-5-W5
55°19'N 114°42'W
Approximately 5 km north-east of Slave Lake.

A tributary of Muskeg Creek, the name is descriptive of the area and is recorded as early as 1892 on a Geological Survey of Canada map.

Muskeg Lake (lake)
73 M/5 - Behan Lake
33-74-11-W4
55°28'N 111°38'W
Approximately 80 km north of Lac La Biche.

The locally well-established name for this lake is descriptive.

Muskeg Lake (lake)
84 H/4 - Osi Lake
28-93-23-W4
57°06'N 113°38'W
Approximately 143 km west north-west of Fort McMurray.

This remote lake has been known by this descriptive name for a long time.

Muskeg Lake (lake)
74 D/7 - Cheecham
31-84-5-W4
56°19'26"N 110°46'15"W

Approximately 58 km south-east of Fort McMurray.

Muskeg Lake is takes its name from the swamp area in which it lies. The name is descriptive.

Muskeg Lake (lake)
84 H/4 - Osi Lake
28-93-23-W4
57°06'N 113°38'W
Approximately 143 km west north-west of Fort McMurray.

The descriptive name for this lake well established by local use, was officially adopted September 23, 1991.

Muskeg Lake (lake)
74 E/15 - I.D. 18
5-104-6-W4
57°59'57"N 110°57'50"W
Approximately 140 km north north-east of Fort McMurray.

This lake, descriptively named for the muskeg around, it was named by Edward Cyprien, who first trapped the line here. (see also Muskeg Creek)

Muskeg Lake (lake)
74 E/15 - I.D. 18
32-104-6-W4
57°59'57"N 110°57'50"W
Approximately 140 km north of Fort McMurray.

The precise origin of the long established name of this lake is unknown; the name is probably descriptive. (see also Muskeg Creek)

*****Muskeg Lake** (lake)
74 E/6 - Kearl Lake
33-95-8-W4
57°17'N 111°14'W

Approximately 62 km north north-east of Fort McMurray.

(see Kearl Lake)

Muskeg Lakes (lakes)
83 N/7 - Triangle
74-19-W5
55°24′N 116°49′W
Approximately 18 km west of High Prairie.

Officially adopted in 1954 after field research, the name is, of course, descriptive.

Muskeg River (river)
83 P/14 - Muskeg River
14-32-78-20-W4
55°48′N 113°04′W
Flows south into Pelican River approximately 120 km north-east of Slave Lake.

This is a descriptive name for the river, which was shown named on a map from 1897.

Muskeg River (river)
74 E/4 - Bitumount
6-94-10-W4
57°08′N 111°36′W
Flows south-west into Athabasca River approximately 47 km north north-west of Fort McMurray.

The name is likely descriptive as it flows from a lake that was called Muskeg Lake, but is now known as Kearl Lake.

Muskrat Lake (lake)
84 H/6 - Alberta
1-98-22-W4
57°29′05″N 113°25′19″W
Approximately 147 km north-west of Fort McMurray.

The name of this lake, which has always been known locally as Muskrat Lake, is likely to be descriptive of the ubiquitous muskrat. The word muskrat comes from the Ojibwa, referring to the aquatic rodent, *Ondatra zibethica*, which has been trapped for its fur. (see also entries under "Rat" for more references to features named after this animal)

Muskwa Lake (lake)
84 B/2 - Muskwa Lake
36-82-5-W5
56°09′N 114°38′W
Approximately 93 km north of Slave Lake.

The name is probably descriptive of the fauna in the area. *Muskwa* is Cree for bear.

Muskwa Lake (lake)
74 D/8 - Gipsy Lake
5-84-2-W4
56°15′N 110°16′W
Approximately 85 km south-east of Fort McMurray.

Muskwa is the Cree word meaning bear. The lake is named for a local trapper with the nickname Muskwa.

Muskwa River (river)
84 A/4 - North Wabasca Lake
1-84-25-W4
56°15′N 113°48′W
Flows north-east into Wabasca River approximately 156 km west south-west of Fort McMurray.

The name is likely descriptive of the prevalence of bear in the area.

Musreau Lake (lake)
83 L/10 - Cutbank River
13-64-5-W6
54°33′N 118°37′W
Approximately 65 km south of Grande Prairie.

There are two differing meanings for this name. Both are aboriginal in origin. The first states the word means something noisy or devil-like. This is in reference to the pockets of gas that form at the bottom of this lake and rise to the surface. During the winter months, this pressure cracks the ice, making a loud noise. The other meaning may be that it is a variation of the Cree word for a young moose. Moose River is nearby. The name was recorded by the Dominion Lands Survey, and appears on a federal government map of 1915.

Mustus Lake (lake)
84 K/1 - Mustus Lake
27-105-15-W5
58°08′N 116°23′W
Approximately 58 km south-east of High Level.

Mustus is derived from the Cree name *puskwaw mostos* meaning buffalo. Mustus Lake is annotated on a 1875 Geological Survey of Canada Map of the Peace and Athabasca Rivers to illustrate the report of James Macoun.

Mustus Lake (locality)
84 K/1 - Mustus Lake
35-105-15-W4
58°09′N 116°22′W
Approximately 60 km south-east of High Level.

(see Mustus Lake)

Myers Lake (lake)
74 M/11 - Hay Camp
14-123-8-W4
59°41′N 111°15′W
Approximately 321 km north of Fort McMurray.

It was named in 1929 after Captain Myers of the steamer *Athabasca River*.

Mylonite Lake (lake)
74 M/16 - Andrew Lake
31-124-2-W4
59°49'N 110°20'W
Approximately 340 km north of Fort McMurray.

The name was submitted in 1965 by the Research Council of Alberta, and is descriptive of the lake where the location and outline is controlled by a major mylonite band. Mylonite is rock that has formed along a fault zone. It is composed of ground rock that has been reconstituted into rock.

Mystery Lake (lake)
74 D/6 - Gregoire Lake
33-85-7-W4
56°24'45"N 111°02'00"W
Approximately 32 km south south-east of Fort McMurray.

This lake appears to be hidden among a variety of different kinds of trees, making it very difficult to locate when on the ground. Local lore has it that the lake is a mystery to locate hence the name.

Nampa (village)
84 C/3 - Peace River
19-81-20-W5
56°02'N 117°08'W
Approximately 24 km south south-east of Peace River.

Nampa was named by Robert Perry "Pa" Christian (1869-1951), through whose homestead the Central Canada Railway extended its line in 1916, building a water tank and pump house. Christian, who originated in Missouri, opened a store and operated the pump house and the area became known as Tank. In July 1924, he opened a post office for the district, and it was decided that Tank needed a new name. According to one source, Christian in consultation with an aboriginal leader Johnny Gladue chose Nampa, an aboriginal word meaning "the place." According to another source, it was named after the community in Idaho. There are at least two other places in the world named Nampa, one in Finland, and one in Peru.

Namur Lake (lake)
84 H/7 - Legend Lake
15-97-17-W4
57°25'N 112°40'W
Approximately 108 km north-west of Fort McMurray.

The precise origin of the name Namur for this trophy fishing lake is unknown. There may be some connection to the Allies' offensive of Artois in 1915, in which the Belgian city of Namur was the target. It is known locally as Buffalo Lake. According to an aboriginal story, long ago the people were tracking eight buffalo that went out onto the lake. The hunters walked all around the lake looking for the spot where the buffalo came out but never found it.

Namur Lake Indian Reserve No. 174B
(Indian reserve)
84 H/7 - Legend Lake
24-97-17-W4
57°26'N 112°37'W
Approximately 98 km north-west of Fort McMurray.

Named for its proximity to Namur Lake. (see Namur Lake)

Namur River (river)
84 H/10 - Legend Lake
18-98-16-W4
57°30'N 112°34'W
Flows north-east into Gardiner Lakes approximately 111 km north-west of Fort McMurray.

Its source is Namur Lake. (see Namur Lake)

Namur River Indian Reserve 174 A
(Indian reserve)
84 H/8 - Chelsea Creek
11-98-16-W4
57°29'N 112°29'W
Approximately 104 km north-west of Fort McMurray.

Named for its proximity to Namur River. (see also Namur Lake)

Nanuche Creek (creek)
84 J/8 - Fox Lake
11-107-1-W5
58°16'N 114°02'W
Flows south into Harper Creek approximately 182 km east south-east of High Level.

This creek takes its name from the lake. Local residents call this stream *Sekwes Sepesis* which is Cree for Mink Creek. Only the lake is known as "Nanooch." (see Nanuche Lake)

Nanuche Lake (lake)
84 J/8 - Fox Lake
23-107-1-W5
58°17'N 114°10'W
Approximately 182 km east south-east High Level.

Named for Peter Nanuche, a member of the Fox Lake Indian Band Council who died in 1929. He was an outstanding leader of his people and a skilled trapper. Nanuche Lake, which was reported in 1908 by Dominion Land Surveyor A. W. Ponton to be a meadow, marsh and hay area with a channel, is almost in the centre of the Nanuche family's traditional trapping grounds.

Narrows Creek (creek)
83 O/6 - Kinuso
10-75-10-W5
55°29'N 115°28'W

Flows south-east into Lesser Slave Lake approximately 50 km north-west of Slave Lake.

The creek flows into The Narrows of Lesser Slave Lake. It appears on a Geological Survey of Canada map in 1892.

Narrows Creek (creek)
84 H/7 - Legend Lake
27-95-16-W4
57°16′N 112°32′W
Flows south-west into Ells River approximately 91 km north-west of Fort McMurray.

(see Chelsea Creek)

Narrows, The (narrows)
83 O/6 - Kinuso
36-74-10-W5
55°27′N 115°23′W
Approximately 45 km west north-west of Slave Lake, found in Lesser Slave Lake.

The name is descriptive of the middle area of Lesser Slave Lake and was well established when the Geological Survey of Canada was in the area in 1892.

Narrows, The (narrows)
84 H/10 - Alberta
14-98-16-W4
57°30′30″N 112°30′50″W
Approximately 65 km north-west of Fort McMurray.

These narrows are descriptively named; they form a neck of water located between Upper and Lower Gardiner Lakes.

Nash Lake (lake)
84 P/6 - Merryweather Lake
24-118-21-W4
59°16′N 113°26′W
Approximately 225 km east north-east of High Level.

It was named in 1948 after Sub-Lieutenant Robert Arthur Nash, born in Killam, Alberta, in 1922. He joined the Royal Canadian Navy in 1941, and was killed in April 1944, in the torpedoing of the destroyer *Athabaskan*, off Brittany. He was mentioned in despatches.

Nash Lake (lake)
74 L/2 - Larocque Lake
NE-2-105-5-W4
58°05′N 110°42′W
Approximately 148 km north of Fort McMurray.

The name shows on maps as early as 1919, it was likely named after J. Nash, and axeman on F.V. Seibert's surveying crew. Seibert and G.H. Blanchet, DLS, and their crews worked on the 27th Baseline during the seasons from 1915 to 1918.

Naylor Hills (hills)
84 F/12 - Kemp River
27-99-24-W5
57°37′N 117°50′W
Approximately 78 km north north-west of Manning.

These hills were named for an Anglican missionary, Canon R. K. Naylor of Montreal. He came to the Notikewin area and set up camp with a student. His work was sponsored by the Fellowship of the West, a group of Montreal businessmen who financed missionary endeavours. Naylor presided at the first service held in the St. John's Church in 1929. He returned to Montreal some time later, and the hills were named as testimony to his work.

Neath Creek (creek)
73 M/8 - Grist Lake
15-13-73-1-W4
55°19′N 110°01′W
Flows south-west into Calder River approximately 100 km north of Cold Lake.

This name appears on a federal government map as early as 1913. J. N. Wallace, DLS, stated in 1916 that it was named after a place in Wales.

Negus Creek (creek)
84 L/16 - Alberta
28-113-2-W6
58°51′N 118°17′W
Flows north north-west into Hay River approximately 76 km north-west of High Level.

The precise origin of the name of this creek is unknown. According to the *Concise Oxford Dictionary*, Negus is the historical title of a ruler of Ethiopia, or a drink of hot sweetened wine and water. The creek may have been named after a person.

New Fish Creek (locality)
83 N/6 - Whitemud Creek
12-73-22-W5
55°18′N 117°15′W
Approximately 100 km east north-east of Grande Prairie.

The name of the locality of New Fish Creek came about when the area was then known as Fish Creek. The local citizenry applied for a post office; there was already a Fish Creek post office in Alberta, so the residents decided on the name New Fish Creek for the post office here, to avoid complication. The name Fish Creek which had been originally applied to a nearby creek, later became known as Clouston Creek. Local stories state the name Fish Creek came from a man who settled (South-west quarter of Section 26, Township 72, Range 22, West of the 5th Meridian) on the bank of the creek now known as Clouston Creek. The man could not write, so he made a sign of a fish. Any time he went away, he would point the fish in the direction he was headed. If he was in the area, he'd take the sign down. The aboriginal people started calling the creek Artificial Fish Creek because there were no fish in it.

Newby River (river)
74 D/2 - Quigley
22-81-4-W4
56°01'53"N 110°31'43"W
Flows south-west into Winefred River via Hook Lake approximately 93 km south south-east of Fort McMurray.

This river is named after W. Newby, a member of a survey party. Earlier names for the river were recorded by the surveyor Philip Turnor. In his journal on June 10, 1791, he noted, "...another small river or creek falls into this on the left hand side which comes from Grizzle Bear Hill mentioned in the 1st inst. and is called by the Southern Indians Mis-ta-hay Mus-qua-a seepe [large bear river] and by the Chipewyan Hot-hale-zag-za Sheth Dez-za or the Grizzle Bear Hill River...."

Newcomen Point (point)
74 D/8 - Gipsy Lake
30-86-3-W4
56°29'N 110°28'W
On the west shore of Gordon Lake approximately 62 km east south-east of Fort McMurray.

The precise origin of the name of this point is unknown.

Ney Lake (lake)
74 M/16 - Andrew Lake
NW-12-124-1-W4
59°46'N 110°01'W
Approximately 339 km north north-east of Fort McMurray on Alberta-Saskatchewan boundary.

The name has appeared on federal government maps since at least 1946, and is named after Cecil Herman Ney, DLS, from Ontario.

Nice Creek (creek)
84 H/3 - Alberta
2-94-22-W4
57°08'00"N 113°25'30"W
Flows from Sick Hill Lake into an unnamed lake, 130 km west north-west of Fort McMurray.

The name is likely descriptive.

Nicholls Creek (creek)
83 N/7 - Triangle
11-12-74-20-W5
55°24'N 116°56'W
Flows south-west into Little Smoky River approximately 30 km west of High Prairie.

Officially adopted in January 1954 after field research. Nicholls Creek is named for two bachelor brothers who lived on the creek for a short period beginning in 1930 or 1931. Alfred Nicholl tried homesteading for awhile. During the war he worked on the construction of the Alaska Highway near Whitehorse in the Yukon.

Niggli Lake (lake)
74 M/16 - Andrew Lake
NW-25-125-1-W4
59°54'N 110°02'W
Approximately 351 km north of Fort McMurray.

The name was submitted in 1958 by the Research Council of Alberta, and is one of a series of features in the area named after deceased prominent geologists. Niggli was a German petrologist, famous for his work on igneous rocks and ore deposits.

Nikik Lake (lake)
84 H/4 - Osi Lake
2-94-23-W4
57°07'N 113°35'W
Approximately 140 km west north-west of Fort McMurray.

The name of this lake translates from Cree as Otter.

Nina Lake (lake)
84 F/6 - Nina Lake
14-97-21-W5
57°25'N 117°17'W
Approximately 58 km north north-east of Manning.

The precise origin of the name of this lake is unknown, although the name does appear on provincial government maps as early as 1930.

Ninemile Point (point)
83 O/7 - Slave Lake
26-73-7-W5
55°21'N 114°58'W
Approximately 12 km west north-west of Slave Lake.

On the shore of Lesser Slave Lake, Ninemile Point was a well-established stopping place for freighters when the Dominion Land Surveyors were working in the area in 1913. It was named for its distance from Sawridge (later the community of Slave Lake).

Ninishith Hills (hills)
84 P/14 - Preble Lake
124-20-W4
59°50'N 113°25'W
Approximately 256 km north-east of High Level.

The name was officially approved in 1949, and is likely Chipewyan in origin.

Niobe (locality)
83 M/6 - La Glace
13-73-8-W6
55°20'N 119°05'W
Approximately 21 km north-west of Grande Prairie.

The post office was established here in January 1915 and was named in commemoration of one of two cruisers bought by Canada from the British government in 1910. The first postmaster was R. E. Bezanson. The name Niobe comes from Greek mythology. She was the daughter of Tantalus, who turned to stone while weeping for her slain children. (see also Buffalo Lake and Spitfire)

Niobe Creek (creek)
83 M/6 - La Glace
10-7-73-7-W6
55°18′N 119°04′W
Flows south into Bear Creek approximately 17 km north-west of Grande Prairie.

Originally known as Buffalo Creek, the name was officially changed to Niobe Creek in the early 1950s to coincide with the name of the nearby community. (see also *Buffalo Creek)

Nipisi Lake (lake)
83 O/15 - Brintnell Lake
23-78-6,7-W5
55°47′N 114°57′W
Approximately 55 km north north-west of Slave Lake.

This may be an abbreviation of the Cree word *nipisikopau*, "the place of many willows," which is descriptive of the area. It is the source of Nipisi River.

Nipisi River (river)
84 B/2 - Muskwa Lake
36-82-5-W5
56°08′N 114°38′W
Flows north-east into Muskwa Lake approximately 98 km north of Slave Lake.

(see Nipisi Lake)

Nisbet Lake (lake)
73 M/8 - Winefred Lake
34-73-2-W4
55°22′N 110°13′W
Approximately 95 km north or Cold Lake.

The origin of the name of this lake is unknown; the name appears on the Baseline surveys of 1912. It may have been named for a survey crew member.

Nixon Lake (lake)
83 P/1 - Wandering River
11-72-16-W4
55°13′N 112°22′W
Approximately 55 km north-west of Lac la Biche.

After whom it is named is not known, but it has been in use since at least the 1940s.

No Name Ridge (ridge)
83 L/11 - Alberta
11-29-65-9-W6
54°39′27″N 119°18′54″W
Approximately 67 km south south-west of Grande Prairie.

This ridge was named locally in 1984-85 to fulfil the need for a landmark in the area. The name was officially approved in 1991.

Noel Lake (lake)
83 J/6 - Christmas Creek
7-62-7-W5
54°21′N 115°03′W
Approximately 50 km north-west of Barrhead.

It shows on federal government maps as early as 1917; its origin is not precisely known. It may have been named after a person, or the feast, for *Noël* is the French word for Christmas. The name of the lake may also have something to do with the nearby Christmas Creek.

Noon Creek (creek)
83 N/7 - Triangle
5-32-74-18-W5
55°27′N 116°44′W
Flows north-east into Maurice Lake approximately 15 km west of High Prairie.

There are two variations about the origin of this name. According to one, Noon Creek was named by Mrs. R. Smyth, her husband, mother, father, sister and brother-in-law who were the first people to cut a road north of the present highway. They always stopped at the creek for their mid-day meal, hence the name Noon Creek. The other story is that the creek is roughly halfway between High Prairie and Little Smoky Settlement on the old settlement road. Being a convenient place to water horses, the noon stop was usually made at this creek.

Nora Lake (lake)
74 D/7 - Cheecham
28-86-4-W4
56°29′N 110°34′W
Approximately 57 east south-east km of Fort McMurray.

After whom this is named is not known.

Normandville (locality)
83 N/14 - Lac Magloire
NE-27-79-22-W5
55°52′N 117°22′W
Approximately 18 km north north-west of Falher.

This was possibly named after the Maurice Normand family who farmed nearby. A post office was established there for less than a year in 1931. The postmaster was A. Parent.

North Heart River (river)
84 C/2 - Harmon Valley
15-82-19-W5
56°07′N 116°52′W
Flows south-west into Heart River approximately 29 km south-east of Peace River.

The name of this river comes from its status as a tributary of the Heart River. (see Heart River)

North Muskeg Creek (creek)
74 E/6 - Kearl Lake
30-95-8-W4
57°16'25"N 111°18'20"W
Flows west into Muskeg Creek approximately 68 km north north-east of Fort McMurray.

It is so named because it is a tributary of Muskeg Creek. (see also Muskeg Creek)

North Star (hamlet)
84 C/13 - Manning
32-90-23-W5
56°51'N 117°38'W
Approximately 7 km south of Manning.

In 1929 the settlement of Little Prairie needed a new name for the post office that was to be opened. Several people apparently discussed possibilities, and the suggestion of Nord for Oscar Nord Sr. who lived in the area was put forward. The name was rejected by those present on the basis that the post office should not be called after someone living in the district. The name North Star was then brought forward and met with approval. It became the official name for the post office and subsequent hamlet. The North Star is the bright star at the tip of the tail of Ursa Minor, variously referred to as Polaris, the polestar. The first postmaster was O. Monrad.

North Steepbank River (river)
74 D/14 - Wood Creek
32-90-7-W4
56°51'N 111°05'W
Flows south into Steepbank River approximately 29 km north-east of Fort McMurray.

This river is so named because it is a tributary of Steepbank River. It was formerly known as Dugout Creek, but this name is no longer used.

North Vermilion Settlement (settlement)
84 K/8 - Fort Vermilion
25-108-13-W5
58°24'N 116°02'W
Approximately 65 km east south-east of High Level.

It was originally surveyed in river lots in 1906 by J.B. St. Cyr, DLS. Locally the settlement has the nickname of "Buttertown" after an incident during the late 19th century or early 1900s when some rancid butter was sold. (see Fort Vermilion Settlement)

North Wabasca Lake (lake)
83 P/13 - South Wabasca Lake
1-80-25-W4
55°59'N 113°55'W
Approximately 95 km north-east of Slave Lake.

The name was recorded by the Dominion Lands Survey in 1913; it is from the nearby river. (see Wabasca River)

North Watchusk Lake (lake)
74 D/1 - Watchusk Lake
23-83-3-W4
56°13'N 110°21'W
Approximately 82 km south-east of Fort McMurray.

This lake is named because of its location to the north of Watchusk Lake. Watchusk is the Cree word for muskrat, literally translating as "little devil creature." (see also South Watchusk Lake)

Northmark (locality)
83 M/10 - Woking
20-76-6-W6
55°36'N 118°54'W
Approximately 46 km north of Grande Prairie.

Northmark post office was opened in 1931 and its first postmaster was E. C. Baker. The Saddle River School District, later Northmark School District, was established in 1930. Although information on its origin is not known, it may have something in common with the establishment of the Westmark School District, nine kilometres to the west, in 1937.

Notikewin (hamlet)
84 C/13 - Manning
16-92-23-W5
56°59'N 117°38'W
Approximately 6 km north of Manning.

The name Notikewin was given in 1925 to this hamlet, formerly known as Battle River Prairie, on the request of the postal authorities who wished to avoid confusion with Battle River farther south in Alberta. The hamlet was named for its proximity to the Notikewin River to the south. The first postmaster was J. Rousseau. (see Notikewin River)

Notikewin Provincial Park (provincial park)
83 F/3 - Cadomin
33-94-20-W5
57°14'N 117°08'W
Approximately 40 km north-east of Manning.

Created in 1979, this 9700-hectare park was named for the nearby town and river. (see Notikewin River)

Notikewin River (river)
84 F/6 - Nina Lake
35-95-20-W5
57°17'N 117°08'W
Flows north-east into Peace River approximately 49 km north-west of Manning.

Notikewin is an anglicised derivative of *Notenaygewn*, meaning Battle River, named after an early battle in the area between the

Beaver and Cree. Surveyor J.A. Buchanan annotated the river as Battle River, the name was then changed in 1915 to Notikewin to avoid duplication with the Battle River to the south. This river was known locally as the First Battle River. The Second and Third Battle rivers in this area were named Hotchkiss and Meikle, respectively, during the 1915 survey. (see also Second Battle River, Third Battle River, Hotchkiss River and Meikle River)

■ **O'Brien Provincial Park** (provincial park)
83 M/2 - Grande Prairie
15-70-6-W6
55°03′N 118°50′W
Approximately 8 km south of Grande Prairie.

This 65-hectare park established in 1954, south of Grande Prairie on the Wapiti River, was named in honour of Dr. Louis J. O'Brien (1868-1958), long-time medical practitioner in the area. He was born in Ontario and taught school for some time in order to earn money to study medicine. He went to Germany for this and graduated from Wurzburg in 1902. Following practice at Nanaimo, B.C., he pursued further studies in London, England. At the beginning of World War I he joined the army, and in 1915 went overseas and served at Salonika. In 1918 that he moved to the Peace River Country where he remained until his death. His first hospital was a log building. Dr. O'Brien soon became both a respected and familiar figure and the subject of many tales. He had boundless interest in nature and was never tired of pointing out the beauty and potential of the country to newcomers. In 1939 he was president of the Canadian Medical Association (Alberta Division) and was awarded an honorary fellowship of the Royal College of Surgeons of Canada as well as an honorary doctorate by the University of Alberta. He served as Independent MLA for Grande Prairie from 1940-1944. He could have built up a successful practice in any large city but preferred to remain in the Peace River Country as he felt that there was a need for him there. Holmgren. 1976.

***O'Donnell Lake** (lake)
84 P/6 - Merryweather Lake
35-120-18-W4
59°28′N 113°00′W
Approximately 260 km north-east of High Level.

This name was originally applied to the lake known now as Robertson Lake. (see Robertson Lake)

Oakley Lake (lake)
74 E/12 - Asphalt Creek
7-100-10-W4
57°39′30″N 111°37′00″W
Approximately 104 km north north-west of Fort McMurray.

Oakley Lake takes its name from the Oakley family who lived in the area. Mr. Oakley died in his trapper's cabin on Crooked Lake in 1969.

Ochre Creek (creek)
84 C/9 - Golden Lake
29-87-15-W5
56°33′N 116°22′W
Flows south-west into Golden Lake approximately 67 km north-east of Peace River.

The name likely indicates either the presence of ochre on the creek's banks or possibly ochre-coloured water. Ochre is a product of the weathering of a mineral resulting in a powder that is used as a pigment. Red ochre is the result of the weathering of hematite. The name was recorded as early as 1912 by A.H. Hawkins, DLS.

Odisque Lake (lake)
84 H/4 - Osi Lake
14-94-23-W4
57°09′N 113°34′W
Approximately 142 km west north-west of Fort McMurray.

This remote lake has always been known by the local people by this name and was officially named September 23, 1991. According to one source the name apparently translates as "where the wolverine tore up the beaver house."

***Old Fort** (former locality)
74 L/5 - Welstead Lake
16-13-108-10-W4
58°23′N 111°31′W
Approximately 173 km north of Fort McMurray.

This may be the site of the North West Company's Fort Athabaska River, built by Peter Pond in 1778 on the west bank of the Athabasca River about 50 kilometres upstream from Lake Athabasca. It was known as the Old Pond Fort, or the Old Establishment for many years. It was the only fort in the area until 1788 when the first Fort Chipewyan was built.

Old Fort Bay (bay)
74 L/9 - Old Fort Bay
22-111-3-W4
58°38′N 110°25′W
Approximately 214 km north north-east of Fort McMurray on Lake Athabasca.

(see Old Fort Point and Fort Chipewyan)

Old Fort Point (point)
74 L/10 - Big Point
SE-21-111-4-W4
58°39′N 110°36′W
Approximately 211 km north north-east of Fort McMurray on Lake Athabasca.

This was the first site of Fort Chipewyan as chosen by Roderick Mackenzie in 1788. In

---
*denotes rescinded name or former locality.

Emporium of the North, Jim Parker wrote: "The site was surrounded by water on three sides; the only approach by land was from the south. The fort was built on the west side of the point, where it was sheltered from the east winds blowing off the lake. The route of the canoes to the main channel was protected by islands and bays along the south shore. ...The fisheries around Old Fort Point provided an abundance of [fish] for the fort's residents. ...Although the south shore site had many advantages, the expansion of the trade made relocation of the fort necessary." The fur traders had to move north. (see also Fort Chipewyan)

Old Fort River (river)
74 L/9 - Old Fort Bay
14-4-111-3-W4
58°37'N 110°27'W
Flows north-west into Old Fort Bay approximately 209 km north north-east of Fort McMurray.

(see Old Fort Point)

Old Man Lake (lake)
84 A/14 - Mink Lake
22-90-21-W4
56°49'25"N 113°15'45"W
Approximately 113 km west of Fort McMurray.

The well-established name for this lake comes from a story that is told by old-timers in the area of two old men who had a race by this lake. The lake was then named Old Man for this reason.

*Old Wives Lake (lake)
84 H/16 - Bayard Lake
13-101-14-W4
57°47'N 112°08'W
Approximately 123 km north north-west of Fort McMurray.

*denotes rescinded name or former locality.

There are two different stories as to the origin of this local name, recorded as early as 1892 by the Geological Survey of Canada. One holds that a long time ago five women went out on the lake in a birchbark canoe and never came back. The canoe was found but the women were lost. The other story tells how these women found a large quantity of fish at the mouth of Moose River where it enters Old Wives Lake.

Ole Lake (lake)
84 D/5 - Boundary Lake
30-84-12-W6
56°19'N 119°53'W
Approximately 87 km north-west of Spirit River.

Named for a trapper Ole Klundby, who had a cabin here. The Ole Lake Recreation Association has built a campground on the shores of this lake.

Omega River (river)
84 L/15 - Habay
16-113-5-W6
58°49'N 118°46'W
Flows south south-east into Hay River approximately 50 km north-east of Rainbow Lake.

The precise origin of the name of this river is unknown. It may refer to this being the farthest point of someone's ventures, since omega is the last letter of the Greek alphabet 'Ω.' It may also relate to a time when surveyors would, for purposes of temporarily differentiating one unnamed body from another, assign numbers or Greek letters to features.

One Week Lake (lake)
74 M/16 - Andrew Lake
29-125-2-W4
59°53'N 110°20'W
Approximately 348 km north of Fort McMurray.

The name was submitted in 1965 by the Research Council of Alberta, and is suggestive of the time involved in geological survey work at this lake.

Ooho Lake (lake)
74 D/3 - Alberta I.D. #18
2-83-10-W4
56°10'02"N 111°28'28"W
Approximately 63 km south of Fort McMurray.

Ooho is the Cree word for owl, and is likely descriptive of the bird in the area.

Orloff Lake (lake)
83 P/5 - Fawcett Lake
32-73-23-W4
55°22'N 113°30'W
Approximately 83 km east north-east of Slave Lake.

Reportedly this was named after a Russian nobleman who first came to the area to fish but liked it so much that he decided to live in the district. The name was first considered for the lake in 1927.

Osborn River (river)
84 D/13 - Betts Creek
16-90-13-W6
56°48'N 112°00'W
Flows west into British Columbia approximately 130 km north-west of Peace River.

It was named after G. Osborn, a chainman on the 1911 survey party of James R. Akins, DLS.

Osi Creek (creek)
84 A/14 - Mink Lake
18-92-21-W4
56°59'N 113°22'W
Flows south into Chipewyan Lake approximately 125 km west north-west of Fort McMurray.

The precise origin of the name of this creek, which flows out of Osi Lake, is unknown.

Osi Lake (lake)
84 H/4 - Osi Lake
25-94-23-W4
57°11′N 113°34′W
Approximately 142 km north north-west of Fort McMurray.

The precise origin of the name of this lake is unknown. Local people refer to the lake as Big Lake.

Osland Lakes (lakes)
84 E/6 - Osland Lakes
25-95-10-W6
57°16′N 119°28′W
Approximately 118 km north-west of Manning.

This is a war memorial name for Private John E. Osland, killed in action on May 23, 1944.

Otasan Lake (lake)
84 H/9 - Alberta
27-100-15-W5
57°42′N 112°23′W
Approximately 123 km north north-west of Fort McMurray.

This lake received its name as the winning entry in the geographical naming contest held to commemorate the International Year of the Child in 1979. The name Otasan was submitted by Smoky Lake Elementary School. Otasan is a compound name using the first letter of **O**il, the first two letters of **ta**r and the first three letters of **san**d.

Otauwau Lake (lake)
83 O/3 - Adams Creek
5-70-7-W5
55°02′N 115°01′W
Approximately 30 km south-west of Slave Lake (town).

(see Otauwau River)

Otauwau River (river)
83 O/8 - Driftwood River
3-33-72-3-W5
55°16′N 114°25′W
Flows north into Lesser Slave River approximately 23 km east of Slave Lake.

This name is likely Cree in origin, although what it means is not known. It was recorded by George Dawson in 1879 as *Pow-wow*, and in 1880 as *Tow-i-now*. By 1897, it appeared on a Geological Survey of Canada map as *O-Tow-Wow*. The name was officially approved in 1904 in its current form. At one time the name was also listed as Corteri (variant spelling of Courte-oreille?) River. The 1897 map also placed the *Tow-i-now-si-pi* farther to the south, what is now called the Saulteaux River.

Otter Lake (lake)
84 A/11 - Blanchet Lake
33-86-22-W4
56°30′30″N 113°25′20″W
Located approximately 125 km west south-west of Fort McMurray.

The name for this lake is derived from the large population of otters found at one time on the lake. The river otter, *Lutra canadensis*, is a playful fur-bearing, aquatic mammal of the weasel family. Prized by the fur trade for its pelt, it can reach a length of 1.3 metres, and a weight of eight kilograms.

Otter Lake (lake)
74 L/12 - Hilda Lake
110-10-W4
58°33′N 111°34′W
Approximately 195 km north of Fort McMurray.

Approved in 1971, the name likely refers to the prevalence of the animal in the area.

Otter Lake (lake)
83 P/5 - Fawcett Lake
26-73-24-W4
55°21′N 113°35′W
Approximately 80 km east of Slave Lake.

The name is descriptive of the animal found in the area.

Otter Lakes (lakes)
74 E/8 - Trout Creek
33-95-2-W4
57°17′30″N 110°15′05″W
Approximately 93 km north north-east of Fort McMurray.

The name Otter Lakes is used to identify this group of lakes of varying sizes, which lie in an area 9 kilometres by 4 kilometres, by local residents, trappers, pilots and forestry personnel. They are also known by the name Otter Lake Area or Otter Area.

Otter Lakes (lakes)
84 C/9 - Golden Lake
18-89-13-W5
56°43′N 116°03′W
Approximately 94 km north-east of Peace River.

The name indicates that the otter is abundant in the area. The name was noted on a federal government map as early as 1905.

Otter River (river)
84 C/8 - Cadotte Lake
33-86-16-W5
56°30′N 116°26′W
Flows south into Cadotte River 59 km north-east of Peace River.

The name is an indication that the otter frequents its banks.

Outlet Creek (creek)
83 K/10 - Atikkamek Creek
15-64-19-W5
54°33′N 116°47′W

Flows north-east into Iosegun River approximately 17 km north of Fox Creek.

Officially named in 1958, it is descriptive of the fact it is the outlet draining Iosegun Lake into Iosegun River.

Owl Creek (creek)

84 G/14 - Alberta
33-101-8-W5
57°48′N 115°14′W
Flows north-west into Mikkwa River approximately 135 km south-east of High Level.

The precise origin of the name of this creek is unknown; it suggests that owls are common in the area. The name was recorded in 1890 by the Geological Survey of Canada as Owl River.

Owl Lake (lake)

84 E/4 - Mearon Creek
23-94-12-W6
57°10′40″N 119°48′50″W
Approximately 135 km west north-west of Manning.

This lake became known as Owl Lake because of the large number of owls that congregate there to roost.

P~Q~R

Paddle Prairie (hamlet)
84 F/14 - Carcajou
18-103-21-W5
57°57'N 117°29'W
Approximately 76 km south south-west of High Level.

This hamlet takes its name from the days when the Beaver and Slavey people used to live here. The land was swampy and they used canoes to get about. Later the swamp dried up and the people moved north, leaving their canoes and paddles behind. When white settlers found the canoes and paddles hanging in the trees they named the place Paddle Prairie. A post office was established here in 1945, and the first postmaster was Mme A. Martineau.

Paddle Prairie Metis Settlement
(Metis settlement)
84 F/12 - Kemp River
18-103-21-W5
57°57'N 117°29'W
Approximately 75 km south of High Level.

The Metis Settlement was established in 1990, and was named for its proximity to the hamlet. From 1939 to 1990, the administrative area was known as the Keg River Metis Colony.

Pair Lakes (lakes)
74 L/11 - Fort Chipewyan
4-110-9-W4
58°31'N 111°26'W
Approximately 192 km north of Fort McMurray.

It is descriptive of the lakes.

Pakashan Indian Reserve No.150 D
(Indian reserve)
83 N/9 - Grouard
28-76-15-W5
55°37'N 116°16'W
Approximately 23 km north-east of High Prairie.

This was named for John "Pakashan" Chalifoux and his family, who attended the signing of Treaty No. 8 in 1899 at Grouard. The name Pakashan was the nickname of John Chalifoux and means "gambler." It is derived from "pakishe" a game played by the Indians, the idea being to guess the number of beads or small bones held by one's opponent hands so to amass more bones or points. The Pakashan Reserve, which remained in the Chalifoux family since its formation, is probably the smallest reserve in Canada and has been operated by the family as a successful farming operation. Holmgren, 1976. It forms part of the Kapawe'no (Grouard) First Nation.

Pakawtew Ministik (island)
84 J/9 - Fifth Meridian
17-110-3-W5
58°32'51"N 114°27'25"W
Mid-channel in Peace River approximately 152 km east of High Level.

A Cree Indian name meaning Ground-Fire Island or Burnt-Under-Island. This island received its name as the result of a fire that destroyed its vegetation in the early 1950s. The fire is said to have continued to burn under the ground throughout the winter, which would indicate that the island has a peat soil.

Pakwanutik River (river)
84 I/12 - Buchanan Lake
10-1-112-24-W4
58°42'N 113°54'W
Flows east into Peace River approximately 184 km east of High Level.

The Cree name for *Heracleum lanatum* or Cow Parsnip. This plant is very common in the rich, damp soil along the river and was used as a vegetable by the Cree living in the vicinity. (see also *Garden River)

Panny River (river)
84 G/2 - Bad Rapids
2-94-6-W5
57°08'N 114°51'W
Flows south-west into Wabasca River approximately 158 km south-east of Manning.

The precise origin of the name of this river is unknown; the name appears as early as 1905 on a federal government map.

Pans Lake (lake)
74 M/16 - Andrew Lake
18-124-2-W4
59°46'N 110°20'W
Approximately 335 km north of Fort McMurray.

The name was submitted in 1965 by the Research Council of Alberta. In a humorous way, it was named for its proximity to Potts Lake.

Parallel Creek (creek)
83 P/15 - Pelican Portage
19-78-17-W4
55°47'N 112°37'W
Flows east into Athabasca River approximately 125 km north north-east of Lac La Biche.

This name is found as early as 1918 on a federal government map. It is likely descriptive. However, depending on the portion of the creek, it may be paralleling the Pelican or Athabasca rivers.

Parker Creek (creek)
83 J/16 - Chisholm
26-69-3-W5
55°00′N 114°21′W
Flows east into Saulteaux River approximately 42 km south-east of Slave Lake.

It appears on a provincial government map as early as 1930, but after whom it is named is not known.

Parker Lake (lake)
83 O/2 - Florida Lake
5-25-70-5-W5
55°05′N 114°37′W
Approximately 25 km south south-east of Slave Lake (town).

After whom this was named is not known; it was named some time between 1914 and 1922, so this might mean it was named after a survey crew member.

Parma Creek (creek)
84 K/6 - Parma Creek
2-108-20-W5
58°21′N 117°13′W
Flows south-east into Bede Creek approximately 18 km south south-east of High Level.

The precise origin of the name of this creek is unknown, although it might have some reference to the city in Italy.

Parsons Creek (creek)
74 D/14 - Wood Creek
7-90-9-W4
56°47′N 111°25′W
Flows east into Athabasca River approximately 4 km north of Fort McMurray.

This creek is named after E.G. Parsons, manager of the Union Bank Branch in Fort McMurray. The Union Bank of Canada, founded in 1865, was absorbed by the Royal Bank of Canada in 1925. The name was on a list of names submitted by geologist S.C. Ells in 1924.

Pass Creek (creek)
83 K/1 - Windfall Creek
1-61-16-W5
54°15′N 116°16′W
Flows south-east into Athabasca River approximately 36 km east south-east of Fox Creek.

It shows as early as 1916 on federal government maps; the origin of the name likely refers to the area through which the creek flows.

Pass Creek (railway point)
83 K/2 - Marsh Head Creek
35-60-20-W5
54°13′N 116°53′W
Approximately 75 km west north-west of Edson.

Officially established in 1973, this Alberta Resources Railway point was named for its proximity to nearby Pass Creek.

Passed Away Creek (creek)
74 D/8 - Gipsy Lake
26-85-4-W4
56°23′20″N 110°30′01″W
Flows west into Gordon River approximately 65 km south-east of Fort McMurray.

According to local legend, an old trapper died on this creek around 1850. Since that time it has been referred to as Passed Away Creek or Dead Man's Creek. When the name was submitted for approval Passed Away Creek was chosen.

Pastecho Lake (lake)
83 O/16 - Mistehae Lake
16-80-3-W5
55°56′N 114°24′W
Approximately 75 km north north-east of Slave Lake.
(see Pastecho River)

Pastecho River (river)
84 B/1 - Godin Lake
21-82-2-W5
56°07′N 114°15′W
Flows north-east into Muskwa River, 99 km north north-east of Slave Lake.

Although likely aboriginal in origin, the meaning is unknown; both the river and the lake appear on federal government maps as early as 1914.

Patenaude Lake (lake)
84 P/3 - Patenaude Lake
23-117-20-W4
59°11′N 113°17′W
Approximately 230 km east north-east of High Level.

Named in 1949 after Private George Patenaude, MM, of Ponoka, who was killed in World War II.

Pats Creek (creek)
84 C/3 - Peace River
31-83-21-W5
56°14′00″N 117°17′40″W
Flows west through the town of Peace River into Peace River.

Named after Patrick Wesley, a Métis whose scrip land covered the present grounds of the Anglican Church, built in 1911. Wesley made a grant of his land to the Anglican Church, asking that his body be laid to rest in the shadow of the church to be built on the land he had given. A.H. Hawkins, DLS, in 1911 noted the name for this as Wesley Creek.

Patterson Lake (lake)
74 L/1 - Archer Lake
SW-28-106-1-W4
58°13′N 110°07′W
Approximately 177 km north north-east of Fort McMurray.

The origin of the name is not known; the name appears on maps as early as 1916.

Paul Lake (lake)
83 P/5 - Fawcett Lake
28-72-26-W4
55°16′N 113°57′W
Approximately 50 km east of Slave Lake.

Officially adopted in 1945, the name was known as Lake Paul as early as the mid 1910s. The origin is unknown, but it may relate to the nearby Peter Lake.

Paxton Lake (lake)
74 L/7 - Keane Creek
2-107-5-W4
58°16′N 110°42′W
Approximately 169 km north north-east of Fort McMurray.

The lake was named in 1917 after F.R. Paxton who likely worked on a survey crew.

Peace-Athabasca Delta (delta)
74 L/11 - Fort Chipewyan
112-9-W4
58°45′N 111°25′W
Approximately 211 km north of Fort McMurray.

This is a large freshwater delta composed of three smaller ones: the Athabasca (2000 square kilometres); the Peace (1700 square kilometres); and the Birch (170 square kilometres). Since the composition of the delta is overwhelmingly comprised of the Peace and Athabasca, the name is descriptive. The first recorded reference to the delta comes from Philip Turnor's Lake Athabasca post journal, 1790-1792, in which he stated: "....low swampy ground on the south side with a few willow growing upon it, from which the Lake in general takes its name. Athapaskan in the southern tongue signifies open country such as lakes with willows and grass growing about them or swampy land without woods."

Peace Grove (locality)
84 D/7 - Eureka River
28-84-5-W6
56°18′N 118°43′W
Approximately 33 km north north-west of Fairview.

Established as a post office in 1931 it was named for its location near the Peace River in a grove of trees. The first postmaster was J.W. Bayliff.

Peace, Municipal District of, No. 135 (municipal district)
84 C/3 - Peace River
82-23-W4
56°10′N 117°40′W
Centred around the town of Peace River.

Established in 1945, it was named after the area in which it is situated.

Near Peace Point - Gypsum series cliffs on Peace River, late 1920s

Peace Point (locality)
84 P/1 - Square Lake
35-116-15-W4
59°08′N 112°27′W
Approximately 263 km north north-west of Fort McMurray.

(see Peace River)

■ Peace River (river)
74 L/14 - Rivière des Rochers
2-23-115-9-W4
59°00′N 111°25′W
Flows north-east into Slave River approximately 45 km north of Fort Chipewyan.

D.A. Thomas on the Peace River, ca. 1923-1930

The Peace River is 1923 kilometres long, and traverses the Province of Alberta, from Williston Lake in British Columbia to its mouth at the junction of the Slave River. It takes its name from Peace Point near Lake Athabasca which was where the Knisteneaux (Cree) and Beaver settled a dispute. Alexander Mackenzie noted in 1792-1793 that "On the 13th at noon we came to the Peace Point from which, according to the report of my interpreter, the river derives its name. It was the spot where the Knisteneaux and Beaver Indians settled their dispute. The real name of the river and point being that of the land which was the object of contention. When this country was formerly invaded by the Knisteneaux, they found the Beaver Indians inhabiting the land about Portage la Loche; and the adjoining tribe were those they called Slavey. They drove both tribes before them; when the latter proceeded down the river from Lake of the Hills [Lake Athabasca] in consequence of which that part of it obtained the name of the Slave River. The former proceeded up the river and then the

Knisteneaux made peace with them, this place was settled to be the boundary."

Peter Pond's maps of 1785 and 1787 refer to it as the "River of Peace", while Philip Turnor recorded the name a few years before as "Beaver Indian River." Other names have included *Un-ja-ga/Unjigah*, as recorded on a map to accompany Alexander Mackenzie's *Voyage to the Pacific,...1793*. It apparently means Large River in the Beaver language. In 1927, Father Morrice, OMI, corroborates this translation by saying the Peace River was known to the Sekani Indians as *Thû-tcî-Kah*, or Water Great (or Important) River. Another source stated it was a translation of the Slavey word *Chin-ch-ago*, meaning Beautiful River. The Fort Chipewyan Hudson's Bay Company post journal of 1822 also refers to it as Rivière de Brochet. *Brochet* in French refers to the northern pike, which were likely found in the river.

■ **Peace River** (town)
84 C/3 - Peace River
31-83-21-W5
56°14′N 117°17′W
Approximately 152 km north-east of Grande Prairie.

The town of Peace River is at the junction of the Peace and Little Smoky rivers. St. Mary's House, the first Hudson's Bay Company trading post to be built in the Peace River Country in 1818, was located near here. Before 1919 the community was called Peace River Crossing. The settlement on the east bank of the Peace River was known as Peace River Landing Settlement. On December 1, 1919, part of this settlement was incorporated as the town of Peace River. An area north of the town was still referred to as Peace River Landing Settlement. The town later expanded to include all of the original settlement, and the name

---
*denotes rescinded name or former locality.

was rescinded. A post office was established in 1916, and the first postmaster was C. Fredrich. (see also Peace Point and Peace River)

*Peace River Crossing Indian Reserve No. 151A (Indian Reserve)
84 C/4 - Grimshaw
16-82-23-W5
56°06′N 117°51W
Approximately 15 km south-west of Grimshaw.

Established in 1907, this reserve was at one time known as Peace River Crossing Indian Reserve, due to its proximity to the crossing. Its official name is Duncan's Indian Reserve No. 151A. (see under the official name)

*Peace River Landing Settlement
(settlement)
83 C/3 - Peace River
32-83-21-W5
56°14′N 117°17′W
Approximately 152 km north-east of Grande Prairie.

Before 1919 the settlement was on the east side of Peace River at the point of the river crossing. On a map from 1915, it is noted as Peace River Crossing Settlement. In 1919 part of the settlement became the Town of Peace River, however, the area north of town was still referred to as Peace River Landing Settlement. The name was rescinded in 1978 since the entire area fell within the town boundaries.

Pearson Lake (lake)
74 E/14 - Pearson Lake
22-103-8-W4
57°57′N 111°14′W
Approximately 137 km north of Fort McMurray.

Named in 1914 after H.E. Pearson, DLS, it is also known locally as Sandy Lake.

Peavine Creek (creek)
83 N/11 - Donnelly
14-16-76-22-W5
55°36′N 117°21′W
Flows south-west into Little Smoky River approximately 60 km west of High Prairie.

The name was recorded by the Dominion Land Surveyors in 1905, and is descriptive of the prevalence of the plant in the area. Found in scrubby wooded areas in Alberta, the pea vine is excellent wild fodder.

Peavine Metis Settlement
(Metis settlement)
83 N/16 - Pentland Lake
79-15-W5
55°50′N 116°10′W
Approximately 30 km north or High Prairie.

This Metis Settlement, established by provincial statute in 1990 is the east portion of what was once called Utikuma Lake Metis Colony, and Utikuma Lake Metis Settlement Area 3. Utikuma Lake Metis Colony was created by order-in-council in 1938.

Peden's Point (point)
74 D/11 - Fort McMurray
28-89-9-W4
56°44′55″N 111°22′55″W
Approximately 1 km east of Fort McMurray.

Peden's Point is a point on Rocke Island at the confluence of the Athabasca and Clearwater rivers and is used as a navigational point for the Fort McMurray area. The name is for Claire Peden, the person upon whose land the point is situated. The point was known earlier as Ben Screen's Point after the man who owned the land at the time. Over the course of years; the point became known as Peden's. In keeping with the principle of official naming that required names to be in current local use, the name Peden was applied to the feature when it was officially named in 1992.

Peel Creek (creek)
84 I/6 - Lake Dene
NW-8-107-20-W4
58°17′N 113°19′W
Flows north into Birch River approximately 197 km north north-west of Fort McMurray.

The name appears on federal government maps as early as 1916; its origin is unknown.

Peerless Lake (hamlet)
84 B/10 - Peerless Lake
33-88-4-W5
56°40′N 114°35′W
Approximately 156 km north of Slave Lake.

This hamlet was named for its proximity to the lake. (see Peerless Lake)

Peerless Lake (lake)
84 B/10 - Peerless Lake
13-88-5-W5
56°37′N 114°40′W
Approximately 142 km north north-east of Slave Lake.

This lake was apparently named in 1912 for the "peerless" beauty of the blue water. The surveyor who was working in the area that year recorded the name as Trout Lake, and it is under that name it appeared on a map in 1905.

***Pegasus Lake** (lake)
83 J/5 - Carson Lake
31-61-11-W5
54°19′N 115°38′W
Approximately 20 km north of Whitecourt.

The name was originally applied in 1961 to this lake which lies to the north-east of

---

*denotes rescinded name or former locality.

Carson Lake. It was named at the request of Mobil Oil of Canada, which was drilling for oil in the area. In Greek mythology, Pegasus is the winged horse whose hoof struck Mount Helicon, and caused the fountain Hippocrene to flow. The Pegasus is the symbol of the company. The historical and locally accepted name for the lake was Little McLeod Lake, and the name was officially changed back in 1986. (see also Little McLeod Lake)

Pelican Island (island)
84 H/7 - Alberta
36-97-17-W4
57°27′19″N 112°37′54″W
Located in Namur Lake approximately 111 km north-west of Fort McMurray.

This island is a bird sanctuary whose name is descriptive of the many pelicans in the area. The white pelican is a magnificent bird with a breeding range over much of eastern Alberta. It can grow to between 140 and 180 centimetres in length with a wingspan of 250-300 centimetres. W. Earl Godfrey, in *Birds of Canada*, writes "Canadian bird life offers few more spectacular sights than a long line or V of precisely spaced White Pelicans flying majestically across the prairie sky."

Pelican Lake (island)
84 H/10 - Alberta
28-99-16-W4
57°37′22″N 112°46′03″W
Located in Big Island Lake approximately 122 km north-west of Fort McMurray.

This name of this small island describes the presence of the bird in the area.

Pelican Lake (lake)
83 N/4 - Sturgeon Heights
SW-1-70-25-W5
55°02′N 117°40′W
Approximately 25 km west of Valleyview.

Named officially in 1952 after field research conducted; the name is descriptive of the bird found there.

Pelican Lake (lake)
83 P/14 - Muskeg River
30-78-21-W4
55°48′N 113°15′W
Approximately 110 km north-east of Slave Lake.

The name is descriptive of the bird in the area.

***Pelican Mountain** (hamlet)
83 P/14 - Muskeg River
5-79-22-W4
55°49′N 113°25′W
Approximately 110 km north-east of Slave Lake.

(see Sandy Lake)

Pelican Mountain (mountain)
83 P/12 - Pelican Mountain
76-24-W4
55°35′N 113°40′W
Approximately 85 km north-east of Slave Lake.

The name also applies to the surrounding area, it refers to the 945-metre-high feature which rises 355 metres from the valley below. The name Pelican Mountain was recorded by the Geological Survey of Canada in 1892, but it was likely in use by the aboriginal people long before. (see also Pelican Lake)

Pelican Portage (locality)
83 P/15 - Pelican Portage
31-78-17-W4
55°48′N 112°37′W
Approximately 120 km north-west of Lac La Biche.

The post office was opened here in August 1934. Mrs. R. Gamber was the first post

Pelican Rapids settlement and trading post near Athabasca River, 1912

master. It was named after the nearby portage to get around the Pelican Rapids. The portage is shown on the 1892 Geological Survey of Canada map compiled by R.G. McConnell. (see also Pelican Rapids)

Pelican Rapids (rapids)

74 M/13 - Fitzgerald
16-126-10-W4
59°57′N 111°41′W
Approximately 350 km north of Fort McMurray in Slave River.

The name appears on federal government maps as early as 1930, it is likely descriptive of the bird found there at certain times of the year.

Pelican Rapids (rapids)

83 P/15 - Pelican Portage
79-17-W4
55°52′N 112°38′W
Approximately 120 km south-west of Fort McMurray on the Athabasca River.

The rapids are found just north of the mouth of the Pelican River and are noted on R. G. McConnell's map of 1892.

Pelican River (river)

83 P/15 - Pelican Portage
16-7-79-17-W4
55°50′N 112°39′W

Flows east into Athabasca River approximately 125 km north north-west of Lac La Biche.

The name shows on Petitot's map of 1883. (see Pelican Lake)

Pelican Settlement (settlement)

83 P/15 - Pelican Portage
36-78-17-W4
55°48′N 112°39′W
Approximately 140 km north north-east of Slave Lake.

The settlement was first surveyed in 1911, and is named after the nearby features. (see Pelican Lake)

Peltier Creek (creek)

74 M/4 - Peltier Creek
6-25-116-10-W4
59°06′N 111°33′W
Flows south-east into Murdock Creek approximately 247 km north of Fort McMurray.

This is a World War II casualty name officially adopted in 1963, commemorating Sgt. Joseph M. E. Peltier of Lac La Biche.

Pemmican Creek (creek)

74 E/3 - Hartley Creek
6-95-8-W4
57°12′45″N 111°18′15″W
Flows north into Shelley Creek approximately 48 km north of Fort McMurray.

Named for pemmican the food indigenous to North America as a staple for trappers and traders. *Pemmican* or *pimikan* literally means "manufactured grease" in the Cree language. It is made by mixing equal amounts of powdered dried meat, traditionally bison, and melted fat. Saskatoon berries or other edibles may be added. The mixture is cooled and traditionally stored in large hide bags, which are easy to transport. It provided a very nutritious and energy-rich food source.

Pentland Lake (lake)

83 N/16 - Pentland Lake
1-79-14-W5
55°49′N 116°03′W
Approximately 92 km south-east of Peace River.

This lake was named in 1947 after Squadron Leader W.H. Pentland, DFC. He was born in Lake Saskatoon, Alberta, in 1917. He enlisted in Calgary in 1940 and received his commission after completing a pilot training course. He received the Distinguished Flying Cross in September 1944, and was reported missing in action a month later, and was presumed dead.

Peoria (hamlet)

83 M/9 - Peoria
36-73-3-W6
55°37′N 118°17′W
Approximately 35 km north-east of Grande Prairie.

It was originally a post office established in October 1928. The origin of the name has at least two possible explanations. It is likely taken after Peoria, Illinois, either because some of the early settlers had lived there or worked there, or because some were admirers of machinery manufactured there. The name Toftner was first suggested for this post office, since Mr. Toftner was one of the area's earliest settlers, but he suggested Peoria instead. The city in Illinois takes its name from the group of aboriginal peoples in the area, the Peoria, who called that area Iliniwek.

Perfume Lake (lake)
84 H/4 - Osi Lake
5-93-22-W4
57°01′55″N 113°31′00″W
Approximately 135 km west of Fort McMurray.

The well-established local name for this lake was officially adopted September 1991, and is likely descriptive of the area. Whether it is a positive or negative appellation is not known.

Perry Creek (creek)
84 N/10 - Perry Creek
16-123-16-W5
59°41′N 116°43′W
Flows north into James Creek approximately 132 km north of High Level.

This name was taken after Pilot Officer Woodrow J. Perry, of Grimshaw, Alberta, who was killed during World War II.

Pert Creek (creek)
84 M/16 - Thurston Lake
2-125-1-W6
59°50′N 118°02′W
Flows north into Beatty Lake approximately 158 km north north-west of High Level.

The origin of this name is not known.

Pert Lake (lake)
84 M/9 - Pert Lake
14-123-1-W6
59°40′N 118°02′W
Approximately 137 km north north-west of High Level.

The lake is the source of Pert Creek; the origin of the name is not known.

Pete Lake (lake)
83 N/5 - Puskwaskau River
34-73-25-W5
55°22′N 117°46′W
Approximately 80 km east of Grande Prairie.

Pete Lake may be named for someone who trapped near or on the lake. A story states that at one time he was sure he heard someone calling him and he spent days trying to find the person. The person was never found.

Peter Lake (lake)
83 P/5 - Fawcett Lake
NW-31-72-26-W4
55°17′N 114°00′W
Approximately 50 km east Slave Lake.

The name was recorded as early as 1914; after whom it is named is not known. (see also Paul Lake)

Peters Lake (lake)
74 M/8 - Wylie Lake
1-121-1-W4
59°29′N 110°02′W
Approximately 310 km north north-east of Fort McMurray on the Alberta-Saskatchewan boundary.

Two explanations have been given for the origin of the name. The first states it is named after World War II casualty Major Francis L. Peters, Canadian Army, who came from North Battleford, Saskatchewan. Since it was named in 1939 and since it lies just to the west of the Alberta-Saskatchewan border, the more likely explanation is that it was named after F.H. Peters, the chairman of the Saskatchewan-Alberta Boundary Commission.

Peterson's Place (point)
74 E/12 - Asphalt Creek
24-99-10-W4
57°36′20″N 111°30′15″W
Approximately 104 km north of Fort McMurray.

This point on the river is locally well known as Peterson's Place. It is likely named for the people who originally settled in the area.

Petitot River (river)
84 M/11 - Dickins River
9-122-12-W6
59°35′N 120°00′W
Flows west into British Columbia approximately 160 km north north-west of High Level.

This tributary of the Liard River was named after Father Émile Petitot, OMI (1838-1917). Born near Dijon, France, Petitot came to the Northwest in 1862 as an Oblate missionary in the Mackenzie district serving at several missions including Fort Good Hope, Fort Rae, Fort McPherson and Fort Norman. Petitot was a talented artist and during the 1870s he designed the lavish decoration of the Church of Our Lady of Good Hope at Providence. His painting of Fort Edmonton (ca. 1867) hangs in the Alberta Legislature Library. Between 1862 and 1873 Petitot undertook several missionary expeditions and explorations, which took him as far as the Yukon. His diaries, geographical, anthropological and linguistic publications, which included his exploration of the Great Slave Lake area and a monograph on the theory of the origin of the Dene, received international attention when they were published in France between 1876 and 1893. Petitot in fact travelled to Paris in 1874 where he worked for two years to arrange publication of some of his important works in native languages to bring back to the Canadian Northwest. Exhausted from the rigours of northern life by the mid-1880s, Petitot returned to France in 1886, where he served as a parish priest until his death in 1917.

Philomena (hamlet)
73 M/4 - Philomena
27-71-11-W4
55°10′N 111°38′W
Approximately 40 km north-east of Lac La Biche.

According to the records of the Alberta and Great Waterways Railway, the station established here in 1916 was named after a nearby lake; however, no reference to that lake has ever been found. Who Philomena was, is not recorded.

Piché Lake (lake)
73 M/4 - Philomena
14-3-70-11-W4
55°02′09″N 111°35′57″W
Located approximately 38 km north north-east of Lac La Biche.

(see Piché River)

Piché River (river)
73 M/4 - Philomena
15-36-69-13-W4
55°02′N 111°51′W
Flows west into Owl River approximately 30 km north of Lac La Biche.

This river was named after a Chipewyan person or family who lived on the nearby Heart Lake Indian Reserve.

*****Pierre au Calumet** (former fur trade post)
74 E/5 - Bitumount
13-97-11-W4
57°25′N 111°39′W
Approximately 78 km north north-west of Fort McMurray.

The old North West Company post of Pierre au Calumet was founded before 1819 below the mouth of the MacKay River on the banks of the Athabasca. John Franklin travelled the river in 1820 and met John Stuart who was in charge of the post.

---

*denotes rescinded name or former locality.

Franklin recorded that the post received its name "from the place where the stone is procured of which many of the pipes used by the Canadians and Indians are made...." There were apparently pipestone cliffs lower down the Athabasca. The calumet or pipe of peace is an ornamented ceremonial pipe traditionally used as a symbol of peace. The Hudson's Bay Company post at the site was Berens House, which George Simpson referred to as being deserted in 1820. *Pierre au calumet* literally translates to pipestone.

Pierre Lake (lake)
84 P/8 - Pierre Lake
30-119-12-W4
59°22′N 112°04′W
Approximately 286 km north of Fort McMurray.

Officially named in 1949; its origin is not known. It may have been named after a person, or it may refer to the French word for stone or rock.

Pierre River (river)
74 E/5 - Bitumount
30-97-10-W4
57°27′N 111°38′W
Flows west into Athabasca River approximately 83 km north north-west of Fort McMurray.

The name Pierre River refers to the abundance of pipestone along its banks. (see Calumet River and Pierre au Calumet)

*****Pine Creek** (creek)
83 M/7 - Sexsmith
10-19-72-6-W6
55°15′N 118°54′W
Flows south into Bear River approximately 8 km north-west of Grande Prairie.

When the Dominion Lands Survey went through the area in 1909, the name was recorded as Pine Creek. This was corroborated by Provincial Archivist Katherine Hughes when she went on a trip to the north country the same year. When the first detailed federal map of the area was produced in 1912, the name was shown as Spruce Creek. In the 1950s it was not the policy to have the same name on more than one feature. Since there was another Spruce Creek nearby, it was decided to change the name. In 1952 the name Grande Prairie Creek was adopted because it flows through the area known as the Grande Prairie. (see Grande Prairie and Grande Prairie Creek)

Pine Island (island)
74 L/11 - Fort Chipewyan
4-15-112-7-W4
58°43′N 111°06′W
Approximately 213 km north of Fort McMurray in Lake Athabasca.

The name for this island was recorded in 1884 by Dr. Robert Bell of the Geological and Natural History Survey of Canada. It is descriptive of this feature which is adjacent to the Chipewyan Settlement.

Pine Lake (lake)
84 P/9 - Peace Point
30-121-13-W4
59°33′N 112°15′W
Approximately 300 km east north-east of High Level.

Officially adopted in 1949, the name is likely descriptive of the trees found in the area.

Pingle (locality)
73 M/15 - Bohn Lake
8-80-6-W4
55°55′N 110°55′W
Approximately 90 km south south-east of Fort McMurray.

This Alberta and Great Waterways Railway station was established here in 1925, and was named after Charles Stewart Pingle, a Medicine Hat druggist and Liberal Member of the Legislative Assembly. He was elected in 1913, re-elected in 1917, and became Speaker in 1920, but was defeated in the United Farmers of Alberta victory in 1921. He was re-elected in a bye-election in 1925, and again in the 1926 general election. He stayed in the Legislature until his death at age 48 in 1928.

Pinto Creek (creek)
83 L/14 - Wapiti
8-16-69-10-W6
54°58′00″N 119°28′00″W
Flows north into Wapiti River approximately 45 km west south-west of Grande Prairie.

When Arthur St. Cyr, DLS, was surveying the 6th Meridian he worked south from Grande Prairie and arrived in this area in the fall. Supplies were becoming low so he sent two men ahead with horses to pick up supplies at a cache on Prairie Creek. The men became lost and matters grew desperate. St. Cyr kept on and where the meridian crossed what is now Pinto Creek he shot a horse for food. Holmgren, 1976. *Pinto* is the Spanish word for painted, referring to the colouration on the horses.

Pinto Mountain (mountain)
83 L/14 - Wapiti
SE-11-67-10-W6
54°46′52″N 119°23′45″W
Approximately 57 km south south-west of Grande Prairie.

Officially adopted in 1991 after field research was conducted in the area, at an elevation of just over 1000 m; it is named after the nearby creek. (see Pinto Creek)

Pipe Creek (creek)
83 N/1 - East Prairie
SW-14-70-16-W5
55°03′N 116°20′W
Flows north into West Prairie River approximately 60 km east of Valleyview.

---

*denotes rescinded name or former locality.

The origin of the name is not known; it is likely aboriginal in origin. It was officially adopted in 1952 after field research was conducted.

Pipestone Creek (creek)
83 M/3 - Wembley
10-11-70-8-W6
55°06′N 119°03′W
Flows south-east into Wapiti River approximately 22 km south-west of Grande Prairie.

The aboriginal people of the area used to use the soft, fine-grained, grey-blue argillite from the shores of this stream to make pipes.

Pipestone Creek (locality)
83 M/3 - Wembley
NW-14-70-8-W6
55°04′N 119°04′W
Flows south-east into Wapiti River approximately 20 km south-west of Grande Prairie.

The post office opened in 1933, and took its name from the nearby creek. The first postmaster was A.K. Watts. (see Pipestone Creek)

Pitchimi Lake (lake)
84 O/2 - Alberta
28-115-5-W5
59°01′N 114°47′W
Approximately 144 km east north-east of High Level.

Likely aboriginal, the precise origin of the name of this lake is unknown. The name was suggested in 1946 by local game wardens who said the name was in local use.

Pitlochrie (locality)
73 M/4 - Philomena
2-70-12-W4
55°02′N 111°43′W
Approximately 30 km north north-east of Lac La Biche.

An Alberta Great Waterways Railway station, Pitlochrie was established in 1916 and likely named after Pitlochry in Perthshire (now Tayside), Scotland. The name means "stony place."

Pleasant View (locality)
83 I/14 - Sawdy
31-68-20-W4
54°56′N 113°03′W
Approximately 30 km north-east of Athabasca.

Established as a post office in 1951, the name is descriptive. The first postmaster was J.A. Irla.

Pluvius Lake (lake)
84 C/12 - Dixonville
28-87-23-W5
56°34′N 117°35′W
Approximately 41 km north north-west of Peace River.

The precise origin of the name of this lake is unknown. It was first recorded in 1913 as Plevius, by G.A. Tipper, DLS. By 1915, the spelling had changed to its current form. Pluvius is an ancient Roman epithet for Jupiter the rainmaker, so perhaps the survey crew encountered rainy weather when working in the area.

Poacher's Creek (creek)
74 D/9 - Bunting Bay
34-88-3-W4
56°40′40″N 110°22′40″W
Flow east into Edwin Creek approximately 64 km east south-east of Fort McMurray.

The name was given to this creek because it runs through two adjacent traplines and the trappers sometimes extend their trapping privileges.

*Point aux Trembles (point)
74 E/14 - Pearson Lake
33-102-9-W4
57°54′10″N 111°25′05″W

Approximately 130 km north of Fort McMurray.

Now known by its English translation, Poplar Point, it is descriptive of a point on the Athabasca River in the Chipewyan Indian Reserve. The Geological Survey of Canada recorded the name in 1890. (see Poplar Point)

Point Brule (locality)
74 L/3 - Embarras
1-13-104-9-W4
58°01′N 111°20′W
Approximately 137 km north of Fort McMurray.

Point Brule is a location on the Athabasca River a short distance south of the 27th Baseline, just across the Athabasca River from Berdinskies, which was the original site of the community called Point Brule. It was at one time a noted overnight stopping place for river travellers. The name was officially approved in 1954. *Brûlé* usually refers to an area that has been burnt out by forest fires.

***Point Brule** (locality)
74 L/3 - Embarras
16-23-104-9-W4
58°03′N 111°22′W
Approximately 139 km north of Fort McMurray.

(see Berdenskies and Point Brule above)

Police Point (point)
83 N/9 - Grouard
6-76-14-W5
55°33′N 116°10′W
Approximately 25 km north-east of High Prairie, on Buffalo Bay of Lesser Slave Lake.

Mounted Police barracks were constructed on the shore of Buffalo Bay at this point before 1901.

---

*denotes rescinded name or former locality.

***Ponder Creek** (creek)
74 L/14 - Rivière des Rochers
7-26-114-8-W4
58°56′N 111°13′W
Flows north into Rivière des Rochers approximately 236 km north of Fort McMurray.

This local name was changed in 1971 at the suggestion of the Fort Chipewyan chief. There was some confusion with Powder Lake some miles to the north-east. (see Sanderson Creek)

Ponita Lake (lake)
83 M/12 - Boone Lake
SE-19-75-12-W6
55°31′N 119°50′W
Approximately 72 km west north-west of Grande Prairie.

It is apparently a Cree word, the root of which means terminate or end. In 1916, J.N. Wallace, DLS, said the lake represented the finish of the survey season when the Dominion Lands Surveys first came through the area in 1909.

Ponton River (river)
84 K/8 - Fort Vermilion
12-109-14-W5
58°27′N 116°11′W
Flows south-east into Boyer River approximately 56 km east south-east of High Level.

This river was named after Dominion Land Surveyor A.W. Ponton. The Beaver name for this stream is *Kaska Sake* or *Kaska Woti Sake*. The name dates to the 1800s. A number of possible meanings have been suggested. It may refer to the aboriginal group known as the Kaska, who formed part of the Nahanni. They dwelt to the north and west in the vicinity of the Liard River in the Yukon. Diamond Jenness translated *kaska* as "rags wrapped around the feet in lieu of stockings" or possibly "long moss hanging from a tree." It is likely the Beaver Indians encountered the Kaska people at this river. According to a Beaver elder, the word translates to "water flowing through many hills." In northern British Columbia, the Carrier people refer to steep cutbanks on a river as *kaska*. Another suggestion came from a priest who was in the north for many years, Father Mariman. He stated the name may be a derivative of the French word *cascade* meaning waterfall.

Pony Creek (creek)
73 M/15 - Bohn Lake
14-15-79-6-W4
55°51′N 110°51′W
Flows east into Christina River approximately 90 km south south-east of Fort McMurray.

The name was recorded on a map as early as 1917; the name likely refers to an incident involving a member of the equine family.

Poplar Creek (creek)
74 D/14 - Wood Creek
30-91-9-W4
56°55′N 111°27′W
Flows north-east into Athabasca River approximately 22 km north of Fort McMurray.

The precise origin of the name of this creek is unknown; it is probably descriptive. It was noted as early as 1914 in the field notes of A.D. Griffin, DLS. The poplar is a genus of the willow family (*Salicaceae*) of which there are at least six species in Alberta. The trees are known for the sound their leaves make in even the slightest breeze, and for their brilliant yellow autumn foliage. Species of poplar are found all over most of Canada. So wide-spread is the tree, it has been suggested that the aspen or poplar leaf would be a more fitting national symbol that the maple leaf.

Poplar Hill (locality)
83 M/6 - La Glace
SW-27-73-9-W6
55°21'N 119°18'W
Approximately 34 km north-west of Grande Prairie.1966, population nil.

Originally a post office opened in December 1930, the name is descriptive. The first postmaster was A.J. Axleson.

Poplar Island (island)
74 D/14 - Wood Creek
20-90-9-W4
56°49'N 111°24'W
On the Athabasca River approximately 10 km north of Fort McMurray.

The name is descriptive of the trees found on the island and was recorded by the Geological Survey of Canada in 1892.

Poplar Lake (lake)
74 E/15 - I.D. 18
4-104-4-W4
57°59'30"N 110°36'30"W
Approximately 148 km north north-east of Fort McMurray.

The precise origin of the name of this lake is unknown; it is probably descriptive.

Poplar Point (point)
74 E/14 - Pearson Lake
33-102-9-W4
57°54'10"N 111°25'05"W
Approximately 130 km north of Fort McMurray.

This descriptive name for a point on the Athabasca River in the Chipewyan Indian Reserve. It is well established in local usage. The Geological Survey of Canada recorded the name in 1890 by the French translation, *Point* (sic) *aux Trembles*.

---

*denotes rescinded name or former locality.

Poplar Ridge (locality)
83 M/15 - Rycroft
11-80-7-W6
55°56'N 118°59'W
Approximately 18 km north north-west of Spirit River.

A post office was established here in June 1951; the name is descriptive of the area. The first postmaster was Mrs. M. L. Jardine.

Popular Point Lake (lake)
74 L/11 - Fort Chipewyan
31-110-8-W4
58°36'N 111°21'W
Approximately 198 km north of Fort McMurray.

No, this is not a misspelling; it may be a variation on the name for the poplar tree found in great abundance in all forested regions in Alberta. It was officially named some time in the late 1960s, and may also refer to the fact the lake was a popular place for people to go.

Portage Lake (lake)
84 I/14 - Big Slough
NW-33-114-19-W4
58°57'N 113°09'W
Approximately 231 east north-east of High Level.

It was named this because it is the source of the river of the same name. (see Portage River)

Portage River (river)
84 I/14 - Big Slough
NE-15-114-19-W4
58°55'N 113°06'W
Flows south-east into Peace River approximately 238 km east north-east of High Level.

The name is likely descriptive, and was recorded as early as 1890 by the Geological Survey of Canada, but probably comes from an earlier time.

Potato Island (island)
74 L/11 - Fort Chipewyan
SE-6-112-7-W4
58°42'N 111°09'W
Approximately 211 km north of Fort McMurray in Lake Athabasca.

In Lake Athabasca near Fort Chipewyan; so named as potatoes were grown there in fur trade days to supply the post. Holmgren, 1976.

***Potts Creek** (creek)
74 D/11 - Fort McMurray
18-89-9-W4
56°43'N 111°26'W
Flows east south-east into Athabasca River, at Fort McMurray.

(see Little Fishery River)

Potts Lake (lake)
74 M/16 - Andrew Lake
NE-3-124-3-W4
59°45'N 110°25'W
Approximately 332 km north of Fort McMurray.

It was named in 1925 by S.C. Ells after Cyril Potts, one of the early homesteaders in the Fort McMurray district and police magistrate. He became president of the Fort McMurray Board of Trade in 1922. Potts lived on the west side of the Athabasca River near Moberly Falls. Here he kept the meteorological records for the Dominion Government and cultivated a beautiful garden. His garden was famous throughout the Northwest and featured sweetpeas, honeysuckle, hops, pansies, roses, poppies and herbs. (see also Pans Lake)

Gorge on the Pouce Coupé River near Imperial Oil Company well location, ca. 1920s

Pouce Coupé River (river)

84 D/4 - Cherry Point
26-82-13-W6
56°08′N 119°54′W
Flows north from British Columbia into Peace River approximately 77 km north-west of Spirit River.

This river is named for a Sikani trapper. He was given the nickname of *Pouce Coupé* (Cut Thumb) by French-Canadian voyageurs as he had lost a thumb as a result of an accident with his gun. Pouce Coupé is mentioned by Simon Fraser in his journal for 1806. George M. Dawson recorded an alternate name for it, Eschafaud River.

Powder Creek (creek)

74 M/3 - Ryan Lake
12-35-116-9-W4
59°07′N 111°25′W

---

*denotes rescinded name or former locality.

Flows north-west into Slave River approximately 257 km north of Fort McMurray.

The name was noted in 1916 by J.A. Fletcher; its origin is not known. It may refer to actual powder, or it may refer to the Powder family.

Powell Lake (lake)

83 M/5 - Hythe
5-74-12-W6
55°23′N 119°49′W
Approximately 65 km west north-west of Grande Prairie.

Named in 1947 after Flying Officer L.W. Powell, DFC, of Edmonton, killed in World War II. He was born in Pickardville, Alberta, on November 15, 1918, the son of Mr. and Mrs T.A. Powell. He joined the RCAF on March 6, 1940, and proceeded overseas a year later as a pilot. He married Christiana Mary Ashton on April 22, 1942. FO Powell was reported missing after air operations on June 17, 1943.

Prairie Creek (creek)

74 D/11 - Fort McMurray
27-88-9-W4
56°39′N 111°21′W
Flows north north-west into Hangingstone River approximately 8 km south of Fort McMurray.

This creek was probably named at a time when it ran through a prairie area, an uncommon topographical feature in the vicinity of Fort McMurray. The name was recorded in 1912 by A.J. Tremblay, DLS.

Prairie Echo (locality)

83 N/9 - Grouard
SE-22-76-16-W5
55°36′N 116°23′W
Approximately 20 km north north-east of High Prairie.

Originally a post office that opened in January 1928. The name of the locality is poetically descriptive. The first postmaster was J.F. Low.

Prairie Lake (lake)

84 H/6 - Alberta
11-96-22-W4
57°18′45″N 113°27′47″W
Approximately 142 km north-west of Fort McMurray.

This name is well established locally and is descriptive. The Liége River, also known as Prairie River, flows out of this lake.

Prairie Point (point)

84 K/8 - Fort Vermilion
5-107-15-W5
58°16′N 116°28′W
Approximately 46 km south-east of High Level.

This is a descriptive name, probably given by the Sheridan Lawrence family who farmed on the point during the late 19th century.

Prairie River (river)

74 L/12 - Hilda Lake
6-14-111-10-W4
58°38′N 111°34′W
Flows east into Mamawi Lake approximately 204 km north of Fort McMurray.

Officially named some time in the 1950s, the name is descriptive of the land through which it flows. Some earlier sources listed it as Hay River.

*__Prairie River__ (river)

84 A/13 - Liége River
30-90-24-W4
56°50′N 113°49′W

Flows south into Wabasca River, 148 km west of Fort McMurray.

(see Liége River)

Preble Creek (creek)
84 P/14 - Preble Lake
32-126-19-W4
60°00′N 113°17′W
Flows north-east into NWT approximately 269 km north-east of High Level.

The name was officially approved in 1965; its origin is unknown.

Preble Lake (lake)
84 P/14 - Preble Lake
NW-29-126-20-W4
59°59′N 113°27′W
Approximately 265 km north-east of High Level.

The name was officially approved in 1965, and the lake was named because it is the source of the creek of the same name.

Preston Lake (lake)
83 M/5 - Hythe
NW-34-73-13-W6
55°22′N 119°55′W
Approximately 70 km west north-west of Grande Prairie.

Preston Lake is named after Elsworth Preston, who homesteaded land bordering on the lake. Messrs Preston and Twombly had cattle that ranged between Ray Lake and Preston Lake. Before 1920 the lake was known locally as Wolf Lake.

Prestville (locality)
83 M/10 - Woking
7-78-4-W6
55°44′N 118°37′W
Approximately 15 km west south-west of Spirit River.

---
*denotes rescinded name or former locality.

Originally a station established in 1916 on the Edmonton, Dunvegan and British Columbia Railway line, it was named after, and likely by, J. B. Prest, a civil engineer for the company. He was born in England in 1884 and received his training there. After working on railway construction in Alberta, he worked for the Alberta government for a number of years until his retirement in 1950. He died in 1967. Mr. Prest was also responsible for naming other stations in the area including Esher, Surbiton, Woking and Wanham. These all were place names from his area of birth in Surrey, England. The post office was established here in 1917, and the first postmaster was J. Johnston.

Prichuk Hill (hill)
83 O/6 - Kinuso
24-73-9-W5
55°20′N 115°15′W
Approximately 30 km west of Slave Lake.

The following is the information supplied by a long-time resident of the area. "In 1925 Mr. and Mrs. Fred Prichuk moved into the Kinuso (Swan River) area and settled on the west side of a large hill to the east of Kinuso. The trail from Slave Lake to Kinuso crossed over this hill and on the Kinuso side of the hill it was very steep and often caused problems for people travelling between Slave Lake, Kinuso and the Peace River Area. People at that time began to refer to the hill as 'that hill near Prichuks' and this was eventually shortened to Prichuk's Hill which it has been called every since." This is a relatively high hill on the south shore of Lesser Slave Lake approximately 12 kilometres east of the Village of Kinuso. The top of the hill is approximately 700 metres above sea level, and 140 metres above the level of Lesser Slave Lake.

Providence, Point (mountain)
84 I/16 - Point Providence
12-115-13-W4
58°58′N 112°03′W
Approximately 243 km north of Fort McMurray.

The name was recorded by the Geological Survey of Canada in 1890; why it was named this is not known. "Providence" has a number of related meanings. It may refer to the act of providing, or provision. If so, it may have been a point where food was found. It also means foresight, so it might have been a landmark to travellers. It also is a synonym for God, therefore there may be some religious significance to the feature.

***Pruden's Crossing** (former post office)
83 N/12 - Watino
35-77-24-W5
55°43′N 117°37′W
Approximately 98 km north-east of Grande Prairie.

The post office opened here in August 1917, the first postmaster being C. Donis. In November 1925, the name was changed to Watino. Pruden's Crossing takes its name from a local farmer and the fact it was situated at a crossing point on the Smoky River. (see Watino)

Purdy Lake (lake)
74 L/8 - Brander Lake
4-109-3-W4
58°26′N 110°26′W
Approximately 191 km north of Fort McMurray.

It was named after E.B. Purdy, a leveller on D.F. McEwen's survey crew working in the area in 1916.

Pushup Lake (lake)
74 D/3 - I.D. #18
12-83-9-W4
56°11′07″N 111°17′35″W

Approximately 63 km south of Fort McMurray.

This is a descriptive name. The term "pushup" is used to describe the dome-like minihouses of vegetation over plunge holes in the ice, which are built by muskrats in which to eat in winter. In these pushups the muskrat can be trapped for its durable pelt.

Pushup Lake (lake)
74 L/14 - Rivière des Rochers
15-113-9-W4
58°49′N 111°26′W
Approximately 224 km north of Fort McMurray.

(see Pushup Lake above)

Pushup Lake (lake)
74 D/7 - Cheecham
19-85-6-W4
56°23′05″N 110°57′05″W
Approximately 47 km south-east of Fort McMurray.

(see Pushup Lake above)

Puskwaskau Lake (lake)
83 N/5 - Sturgeon Heights
20-72-24-W5
55°15′N 117°39′W
Approximately 30 km north-west of Valleyview.

Puskwaskau is a Cree word roughly translated as "short grass." This describes some of the land surrounding the lake and how the lake and river were named. Documentation shows the name has been in use since at least 1914 when it is referred to in the field notebooks of the Dominion Land Surveyor who went through the area during that season.

Puskwaskau River (river)
83 M/8 - Smoky Heights
12-12-75-2-W6
55°29′N 118°10′W

Flows north into Smoky River approximately 50 km north-east of Grande Prairie.

(see Puskwaskau Lake)

Pythagoras Lake (lake)
74 M/16 - Andrew Lake
SE-35-126-2-W4
59°59′N 110°13′W
Approximately 359 km north of Fort McMurray.

The name was submitted in 1958 by the Research Council of Alberta. Pythagoras was a Greek philosopher and mathematician who lived in the 6th century B.C. It was he who developed the theorem regarding right angled triangles (the square of the hypotenuse is equal to the sum of the squares of the other two sides). The lake named after the philosopher, when viewed with imagination, is in the shape of a right-angled triangle.

Quatre Fourches (locality)
74 L/11 - Fort Chipewyan
7-20-111-8-W4
58°39′N 111°18′W
Approximately 205 km north of Fort McMurray.

(see Quatre Fourches, Chenal des)

Quatre Fourches, Chenal des (channel)
74 L/13 - Baril River
14-16-114-10-W4
58°54′N 111°37′W
Flows north into Peace River approximately 232 km north of Fort McMurray.

It is an old name, dating back to the time of the French fur traders. It is referred to in the 1822 Hudson's Bay Company post journal from Fort Chipewyan. The "channel of the four forks" links the Peace River, Mamawi Lake and Lake Athabasca. The four forks are at the southern end of the channel in the narrow strip of land separating these two lakes.

Queen Elizabeth Provincial Park, Lac Cardinal (provincial park)
84 C/4 - Grimshaw
22-83-24-W5
56°13′N 117°41′W
Approximately 6 km north north-west of Grimshaw.

This park was formerly Lac Cardinal Provincial Park when it was established in 1977. When it became known that Queen Elizabeth would visit the area in 1978 it was decided that a park would make an ideal gathering place for the people of the area. It was decided to change the name of the park to honour the Queen as well, so the name was changed to Queen Elizabeth Park, Lac Cardinal. (see also Cardinal Lake)

Quigley (locality)
74 D/2 - Quigley
27-82-6-W4
56°08′N 110°52′W
Approximately 75 km south south-east of Fort McMurray.

The locality of Quigley was originally established as an Alberta and Great Waterways Railway station in 1917. It was named for James N. Quigley, one of the railway contractors for the company.

Quitting Lake (lake)
84 B/9 - Quitting Lake
35-88-3-W5
56°40′N 114°20′W
Approximately 155 km north north-east of Slave Lake.

The precise origin of the name of this lake is unknown; the name of the lake was noted as early as 1912 in the survey notes of A.H. Hawkins. It may refer to the point at which a survey season ended, or the point where someone gave up on whatever project they were working at the time.

Rabbit Lake (lake)
84 H/3 - Alberta
2-93-20-W4
57°02′45″N 113°05′40″W
Approximately 104 km north-west of Fort McMurray.

The name is likely descriptive of the animal found in the area, and was noted as early as 1915 on a federal government map. An earlier map identifies it as Gull Lake.

*****Racing Creek** (creek)
83 N/13 - Tangent
8-4-79-23-W5
55°49′N 117°32′W
Flows north-west into Smoky River approximately 40 km west north-west of McLennan.

(see Hunting Creek)

Raft Lake (lake)
74 D/8 - Gipsy Lake
36-85-1-W4
56°25′N 110°01′W
On Alberta-Saskatchewan border approximately 93 km east south-east of Fort McMurray.

This lake apparently takes its name from the time when surveyors used a raft to cross it. There were survey crews working in the area between 1910 and 1915.

*****Rahab** (former station and post office)
83 M/16 - Codesa
22-78-1-W6
55°46′N 118°05′W
Approximately 49 km east of Spirit River.

This was an Edmonton, Dunvegan and British Columbia Railway station established in 1916, and is Biblical in origin. In the Old Testament, Rahab was a prostitute in the city of Jericho. It was she who helped the escape of two Israelite spies who had

---

*denotes rescinded name or former locality.

been sent in by Joshua on a reconnaissance mission. Because of her efforts, the spies were able to provide enough information for Joshua to defeat the defenders of the walled city. In the New Testament, Rahab is revered as one of the early people of great faith. A post office was established here in 1931, and the name was changed to Codesa in 1938. (see Codesa)

Rainbow Creek (creek)
83 J/11 - Swan Hills
1-65-9-W5
54°36′N 115°13′W
Flows south into Morse River approximately 17 km south-east of Swan Hills.

Officially named in the 1950s; the origin of the name is unknown. It may refer to there being fish in the stream, or the rainbow made by droplets of spray in rough water along the creek, or it may have something to do with fossil fuel seepage into the water causing a rainbow effect on the surface of the water.

Rainbow Creek (creek)
74 D/11 - Fort McMurray
31-88-7-W4
56°40′N 111°06′W
Flows south into Clearwater River approximately 19 km east south-east of Fort McMurray.

The precise origin of the name of this creek is unknown.

Rainbow Lake (lake)
84 L/6 - Rainbow Lake
16-107-8-W6
58°17′N 119°16′W
Approximately 21 km south of the town of Rainbow Lake.

The Slavey, Beaver and Cree have traditionally known this lake as Long Lake in their respective languages, and is still called Long Lake today. According to the files of the Geographic Board of Canada, the name for the lake was supplied by C.B.C. Donnelly, DLS. According to his notes, this lake was called Rainbow by local Cree and Slavey because of its shape. Another source states the name Rainbow lake was apparently borrowed from a lake 24 kilometres to the east (Basset Lake), which was originally named after Rainbow Fournier, who trapped around this lake during the late 19th century. In Cree it is known as *Kinokamak Sakahikun* and in Slavey as *Mieh Dedhe*.

Rainbow Lake (town)
84 L/11 - Zama Lake
34-109-9-W6
58°30′N 119°23′W
Approximately 132 km west of High Level.

The post office was established here in 1967 and was named for its proximity to Rainbow Lake. The first postmaster was A.G. Hislop. (see also Rainbow Lake)

Rambling Creek (creek)
84 D/16 - Cub Lakes
31-91-3-W6
56°57′N 118°27′W
Flows north-east into Notikewin River approximately 97 km north of Fairview.

The precise origin of the name of this creek is unknown; it may be descriptive of the nature of most creeks.

Randall Lake (lake)
83 O/14 - Utikuma Lake
4-81-7-W5
55°59′N 115°02′W
Approximately 77km west north-west of Slave Lake.

Robert Cheetham Randall was born in Saskatoon and started his commercial flying career with the Saskatoon Flying Club. After working for a number of companies he eventually became a pilot for Canadian Pacific Airlines Limited. In 1942, he was on loan to the Canol Project where he was manager of flight operations. After the war, he returned to Canadian Pacific Airlines and he flew trans-oceanic runs. This lake is one of a number named after bush pilots. (see also Berry Lake, Brintnell Lake, Calder Lake, Dickins Lake, Farrell Lake, Lake May, McConachie Lake, McMillan Lake, McMullen Lake and Sawle Lake)

Raspberry Lake (lake)
83 K/7 - Iosegun Creek
13-63-19-W5
54°27′N 116°44′W
Approximately 155 km south-east of Grande Prairie.

It first appears in the records as Raspberry Lake in 1942. It shows as Bear Lake as early as 1916 on federal government maps, and some sources referred to the lake by that name into the 1950s. However the name Raspberry may have been chosen because the name Bear Lake is duplicated 125 kilometres to the east south-east. The current name is likely descriptive for there are a number of species of wild raspberry that grow in Alberta. (see also Bear Lake)

Rat Creek (creek)
84 G/14 - Alberta
16-102-9-W5
57°51′N 115°25′W
Flows east north-east into Wabasca River approximately 124 km south-east of High Level.

The precise origin of the name of this creek is unknown; it is likely named for the prevalence of the muskrat. The name was noted as early as 1908 by J.B. St. Cyr, DLS. (see also Muskrat Lake)

Rat Creek (creek)
83 L/10 - Cutbank River
5-21-64-6-W6
54°26′35″N 118°47′00″W

---

*denotes rescinded name or former locality.

Flows north into Cutbank River, 80 km south of Grande Prairie.

This creek is named for its proximity to Rat Lake. (see Rat Lake and Muskrat Lake)

*****Rat Creek** (creek)
83 M/15 - Rycroft
11-19-79-5-W6
55°51′N 118°46′W
Flows north into Ksituan River approximately 10 km north north-east of Spirit River.

Because of the numbers of muskrats in the creek, it is known locally as Rat Creek. a 1917 federal map of the area shows it as Rat Creek. By the late 1920s, the map shows the name as Howard Creek. (see also Howard Creek and Muskrat Lake)

Rat Lake (lake)
83 L/7 - Prairie Creek
16-11-63-6-W6
54°26′28″N 118°46′50″W
Approximately 82 km south of Grande Prairie.

The locally well-established name for this creek is derived from the large muskrat population that used to inhabit the area surrounding the lake. The name was officially adopted in 1991 after field research was conducted. (see also Muskrat Lake)

Rat Lake (lake)
84 N/15 - Lessard Creek
23-125-18-W5
59°52′N 117°00′W
Approximately 149 km north of High Level.

The precise origin of the name of this lake is unknown; it may well indicate, as do other lakes of the same name, that it has a large muskrat population. (see also Muskrat Lake)

Rat Lake (lake)
73 M/6 - Wiau Lake
30-74-9-W4
55°26′N 111°23′W
Approximately 84 km north north-east of Lac La Biche.

The name for this lake is used by the local residents and refers to the abundance of muskrat. It is also known by some as Island Lake. (see also Muskrat Lake)

*****Rat Lake** (lake)
83 M/5 - Hythe
29-74-12-W6
55°26′N 119°48′W
Approximately 69 km west north-west of Grande Prairie.

Originally known as this for the abundance of muskrats in the area. The name was changed before 1930. (see Updike Lake)

*****Rat Lake** (lake)
83 M/6 - La Glace
1-74-9-W6
55°23′N 119°14′W
Approximately 33 km north-west of Grande Prairie.

(see La Glace Lake)

Rattail Lake (lake)
83 P/1 - Wandering River
15-9-71-14-W4
55°08′N 112°04′W
Approximately 41 km north north-west of Lac La Biche.

The well-established, recently adopted name for this lake is likely descriptive of its shape.

Rattlepan Creek (creek)
74 D/9 - Bunting Bay
12-89-2-W4
56°42′N 110°11′W

Flows north-west into Clearwater River approximately 74 km east of Fort McMurray.

The precise origin of the name of this creek is unknown; it was noted as early as 1910 in the field notes of J.N. Wallace, DLS.

Raup Lake (lake)
74 M/12 - Caribou Islands
NE-22-123-12-W4
59°43′N 111°59′W
Approximately 324 km north of Fort McMurray.

It was named in 1929 after "the well known botanist, Hugh Miller Raup (1901-?), field botanist for the National Museum of Canada during the summers of 1928-30. He later undertook botanical expeditions in the Mackenzie Basin and ultimately became professor at forestry at Harvard University. He published a number of books in his field." Holmgren, 1976.

Ray Lake (lake)
83 M/5 - Hythe
26-74-13-W6
55°26′N 119°53′W
Approximately 71 km west north-west of Grande Prairie.

Ray Lake is named after Tom Ray, one of four early settlers in the area. He and his wife built a cabin on the lake. Mr. Ray was a fur trader. He had left the area by 1919. The lake appears on a 1917 federal government map as Rays Lake.

Ray Lake (lake)
84 D/11 - Worsley
25-88-8-W6
56°39′N 119°07′W
Approximately 79 km north-west of Fairview.

After whom this lake is named is not known.

---

*denotes rescinded name or former locality.

Raymond Creek (creek)
84 H/13 - Raymond Creek
3-103-24-W4
57°55′N 113°52′W
Flows west into Birch River approximately 199 km north-west of Fort McMurray.

The precise origin of the name of this creek is unknown.

Red Clay Creek (creek)
74 E/11 - Firebag River
21-100-9-W4
57°42′N 111°24′W
Flows east south-east into Athabasca River 108 km north of Fort McMurray.

This name, recorded as early as 1890 by the Geological Survey of Canada, is descriptive of exposed red shale along the bank rather than of a red clay.

Red Earth Creek (hamlet)
84 B/11 - Loon Lake
18-87-8-W5
56°33′N 115°15′W
Approximately 143 km north north-east of Slave Lake.

It is named for its proximity to Redearth Creek. A post office was established here in 1970, the first postmaster being A.R. Moore. (see also Redearth Creek)

***Red River** (river)
74 E/4 - Fort MacKay
24-94-11-W4
57°10′N 111°38′W
Flows north-east into Athabasca River approximately 53 km north north-west of Fort McMurray.

Now known as MacKay River, the name Red River was recorded as early as 1890 by the Geological Survey of Canada. Although the origin of this name is not known, it may refer to red soil caused by oxidized iron in the rocks. (see MacKay River)

Red Star (locality)
84 D/1 - Fairview.
8-81-2-W6
56°01′N 118°16′W
Approximately 12 km south-east of Fairview.

This locality takes its name from a former post office near Fairview. The post office, which opened in 1927, took its name from the School District. The postmaster was W.A. Henstock. The red star was a generic symbol of Communists, and was used by some factions in Alberta. Whether there is any connection between the name of the locality and the political persuasion of the early area residents is not known.

***Red Water Lake** (lake)
84 H/7 - Legend Lake
7-97-18-W4
57°24′N 112°55′W
Approximately 118 km north-west of Fort McMurray.

(see Legend Lake)

Redbeaver Creek (creek)
83 O/3 - Adams Creek
16-32-70-9-W5
55°07′N 115°19′W
Flows north into Swan River approximately 43 km west south-west of Slave Lake (town).

Named before 1922; the name is likely descriptive of the animal found in the area.

Redearth Creek (creek)
84 B/11 - Loon Lake
13-88-9-W5
56°37′N 115°18′W
Flows west into Loon River, 129 km east north-east of Peace River.

The name Redearth Creek is descriptive of the red ochre found in places on its banks. It formerly had the descriptive name of Vermilion, but the name was changed at the suggestion of G.M. Dawson to avoid duplication. Holmgren 1976.

Redwillow River (river)
83 M/3 - Wembley
7-4-70-9-W6
55°02′N 119°18′W
Flows south-east into Wapiti River approximately 30 km west of Grande Prairie.

Named for the abundance of red willow along the feature. The name has been in use since at least 1909 when a Dominion Land Surveyor went through the area. Some sources record the spelling of the name as Red Willow.

Reid Creek (creek)
74 E/10 - Audet
18-100-5-W4
57°41′N 110°50′W
Flows south-west into Marguerite River approximately 110 km north north-east of Fort McMurray.

After whom it is named is not known. It has been in use since at least 1916 when it was marked on a federal government map, and likely has some connection with survey work.

*Reid Lake (lake)
74 E/9 - Johnson Lake
34-100-3-W4
57°44′N 110°24′W
Approximately 128 km north-east from Fort McMurray.

(see Line Lake)

*Reid Lake (lake)
74 L/7 - Keane Creek
25-107-5-W4
58°19′N 110°41′W
Approximately 168 km north north-east of Fort McMurray.

---
*denotes rescinded name or former locality.

The name was officially changed in 1953 from Reid Lake to Scot Lake, but after whom it was named is not known.

Rene Creek (creek)
84 F/4 - Hotchkiss
26-92-23-W5
57°01′N 117°35′W
Flows east into Soldar Creek approximately 11 km north of Manning.

The precise origin of the name of this creek is unknown; the name is recorded on a township plan as early as 1919.

René Lake (lake)
74 L/1 - Archer Lake
13-104-1-W4
58°02′N 110°01′W
Approximately 160 km north north-east of Fort McMurray.

It shows on a 1919 federal government map as Réné Lake. After whom it is named is not known.

Rennie Creek (creek)
84 J/9 - Alberta
1-111-3-W5
58°36′N 114°22′W
Flows south-east into Waldo Creek approximately 161 km east north-east of High Level.

Named after J. Rennie by J.R. Akins, DLS, during his 1914 survey of the 29th Baseline. Rennie was a packer on Akins' crew.

Reno (hamlet)
83 N/15 - Springburn
1-81-20-W5
56°00′N 117°00′W
Approximately 32 km south-east of Peace River.

This Central Canada Railway station was established in 1915. The post office opened in 1925 with J. Schneider as the first postmaster. The records of the railway do not give any explanation of the name origin, but it has been speculated it was named after Reno, Nevada which in turn was named after Maj.-Gen. Jesse Lee Reno, a Union commander killed in 1862 at the battle of South Mountain in Maryland. Although Union casualties were nearly twice those of the Confederates, it was viewed as a victory for the North.

Revillon Coupé (channel)
74 L/13 - Baril River
16-22-114-10-W4
58°55′N 111°35′W
Flows north-west into Peace River approximately 235 km north of Fort McMurray.

It was named after the Revillon Frères Trading Company originally founded in 1723 in France. The firm's name dates from 1806 when Louis Victor Revillon assumed control; he was the son of Count Louis Victor d'Apreval who at the time of the French Revolution changed his name to Louis Victor Revillon and bought a farm, which he worked himself. It is said that when on a visit to Paris he witnessed the sale of his former estates. The company grew and ultimately became one of the world's leading fur trade companies. It commenced operations in Edmonton in 1899 and with the city as a base established fur trading posts throughout northern Alberta and the Northwest Territories and conducted trading there for a number of years. In 1936 the Hudson's Bay Company bought its Canadian operation. Holmgren, 1976.

Richardson Lake (lake)
74 L/6 - Richardson Lake
22-108-7-W4
58°24′N 111°04′W
Approximately 177 km north of Fort McMurray.

Named after a member of a survey party, it appears on a federal government map as early as 1919. It was first noted as Jackfish Lake by J.R. Akins, DLS, in 1917.

Richardson River (river)
74 L/6 - Richardson Lake
15-34-108-8-W4
58°25'N 111°14'W
Flows north into Athabasca River approximately 180 km north of Fort McMurray.

Named after a member of J.B. McFarlane's 1911 survey crew, it appears on a federal government map of 1919. It has been identified by a Chipewyan as Whitefish River, and was noted by J.R. Akins, DLS, in 1917 as Silva Creek.

Richmond Park (locality)
83 I/14 - Sawdy
20-68-21-W4
54°53'N 113°11'W
Approximately 25 km north-east of Athabasca.

Originally established as a post office in 1935, it likely took its name from the nearby school district that had been established eight years earlier in 1927. The first post master was C. Gora.

Ridgevalley (hamlet)
83 N/4 - Sturgeon Heights
22,23-71-26-W5
55°10'N 117°54'W
Approximately 60 km east of Grande Prairie.

The likely descriptive name was first used for the Ridge Valley School District established by the Mennonite community in 1931. The community grew around the school and was declared a hamlet in 1992.

Rings Creek (creek)
84 D/2 - Hines Creek
8-81-4-W6
56°00'N 118°35'W

---

*denotes rescinded name or former locality.

Flows south-west into Hines Creek approximately 14 km south-west of Fairview.

The precise origin of the name of this creek is unknown; the name shows as Ring Creek on a 1914 federal government map.

Rio Grande (locality)
83 M/4 - Rio Grande
36-70-12-W6
55°06'N 119°42'W
Approximately 55 km west of Grande Prairie.

The name is a compound one. Rio, the Spanish word for river, forms the first part and may allude to the locality's proximity to the Wapiti River. Grande refers to the fact it is in the Grande Prairie Country. The post office was established in 1919, and the first postmaster was B. Scully.

Ritson Island (island)
74 D/11 - Fort McMurray
33-88-7-W4
56°40'N 111°04'W
At the mouth of Christina River, where it joins the Clearwater approximately 22 km east south-east of Fort McMurray.

Although likely named after an individual, who is not known.

*Riverview (locality)
74 L/13 - Baril River
13-9-115-11-W4
58°59'N 111°49'W
Approximately 240 km north of Fort McMurray.

This was one of the names proposed for the "scaler's establishment" in Wood Buffalo National Park but was rejected because this name did "not at all sound 'northernly,'" according to one government official. (see Carlson Landing)

Robert Creek (creek)
74 E/16 - Robert Creek
4-104-2-W4
57°59'N 110°16'W
Flows north-west into Maybelle River approximately 151 km north north-east of Fort McMurray.

The precise origin of the name of this creek is unknown.

Robertson Lake (lake)
84 P/6 - Merryweather Lake
35-120-18-W4
59°28'N 112°58'W
Approximately 257 km east north-east of High Level.

This lake was named in 1949 after Private James Peter Robertson, VC, born in Pictou County, Nova Scotia, in 1883. He enlisted at Fort Macleod, Alberta, in June 1915 and served with the 27th Battalion of the Canadian Expeditionary Force. He was killed in action at Passchendaele on November 6, 1917, and was awarded the Victoria Cross posthumously in 1918. The medal was presented to his mother in April 1918 by the Lieutenant-Governor, Dr. R.G. Brett.

Roche Lake (lake)
83 J/15 - Upper Saulteaux
66,67-6,7-W5
54°56'N 114°54'W
Approximately 55 km south of Slave Lake.

The name was not recorded until the 1940s, and whether it refers to a geological formation or a person is not known. *Roche* is the French word for rock.

Roche, Pointe de (point)
84 I/8 - Pointe de Roche
12-16-108-13-W4
58°23'N 112°07'W
Approximately 180 km north north-west of Fort McMurray.

Located on Lake Claire, and likely dating from the time of the fur trade, the name is descriptive of the point.

Rochers, Rivière des (river)
74 L/14 - Rivière des Rochers
1-23-115-9-W4
59°00′N 111°25′W
Flows north-west into Slave River approximately 244 km north of Fort McMurray.

This name, which has been in use since the time of the fur trade, is descriptive of the many rocks and rapids found along its course.

Rock Island Lake (lake)
83 P/6 - Alberta
75-22,23-W4
55°30′N 113°23′W
Approximately 92 km east north-east of Slave Lake.

The name is likely descriptive.

Rock Rapids (rapids)
74 D/12 - Cascade rapids
27-87-12-W4
56°35′N 111°50′W
On Athabasca River, 31 km south-west of Fort McMurray.

The name is likely descriptive, and was recorded by the Geological Survey of Canada in 1892, and was identified by Father Petitot in 1883 as Stony Rapids.

Rocke Island (island)
74 D/11 - Fort McMurray
28-89-9-W4
56°45′N 111°22′W
North of McDonald Island, at the confluence of the Athabasca and Clearwater rivers, at Fort McMurray.

This island was named for G.V.R. Rocke, postmaster and notary public at Fort McMurray, by S.C. Ells. Rocke was listed as postmaster 1924-1934.

Rocky Island Lake (lake)
84 O/3 - Adams Creek
4-117-7-W5
59°08′N 115°07′W
Approximately 132 km north-east of High level.

The precise origin of the name of this lake is unknown, although it is likely descriptive.

Rocky Lane (locality)
84 K/8 - Fort Vermilion
16-109-14-W5
58°27′N 116°17′W
Approximately 52 km east of High Level.

It was named for the narrow strip of rock formation that runs through the district. A post office was established here in 1955, and the first postmaster was Mrs. A. Sarapuk.

Rocky Point (point)
74 L/13 - Baril River
16-15-114-10-W4
58°54′N 111°35′W
Approximately 234 km north of Fort McMurray.

Officially named in 1971, it is descriptive of the point in the Peace River. The 1822 Hudson's Bay Company post journal refers to it as Pointe des Roches.

Rod Creek (creek)
84 A/14 - Mink Lake
26-91-21-W4
56°55′N 113°16′W
Flows south into Mink Lake approximately 117 km west of Fort McMurray.

(see Rod Lake)

Rod Lake (lake)
84 A/14 - Mink Lake
35-91-21-W4
56°56′N 113°15′W
Approximately 118 km west north-west of Fort McMurray.

The origin of this name is not known. It may refer to a unit of measurement used in surveying equalling 16 feet. Local residents have indicated they are certain the feature was not named for a person.

Roderick Lake (lake)
74 M/8 - Wylie Lake
7-121-1-W4
59°29′N 110°10′W
Approximately 306 km north north-east of Fort McMurray.

It was named in 1929 after Roderick Fraser of Fort Chipewyan, son of Colin Fraser.

Roe River (river)
84 N/3 - Roe River
36-117-21-W5
59°13′N 117°26′W
Flows north-west into Hay River approximately 79 km north north-west of High Level.

The precise origin of the name of this river is unknown but was likely named by J.R. Akins during the 1914 survey of the area. The name is referred to in his field correspondence. Roe may refer to a person, or it may refer to fish eggs, which, under the name of caviar, is considered a delicacy by some. The local name for the stream is *Tl'odek'alli Zah*, which in Slavey means Whitehay Creek. This name apparently originates in the early 19th century when buffalo were present in the area. According to local Slavey hunters they would check the grassy edge of this creek to see if any bison had churned up the mud, which was very white. If the grassy part of the creek was white this would indicate that bison had been feeding here recently. The Beaver Indians call this stream Whitemud Creek.

Roma (locality)
84 C/3 - Peace River
21-83-22-W5
56°13′N 117°25′W

Approximately 9 km west south-west of Peace River.

Named in 1922 after Stanley Roma Lamb, a former resident railway engineer of the Central Canada Railway. A post office was established here in November 1928 and the first postmaster was W. H. Cameron.

Roma Junction (locality)
84 C/3 - Peace River
24-83-23-W5
56°14′N 117°29′W
Approximately 14 km west of Peace River.

(see Roma)

Romeo's Creek (creek)
74 D/7 - Bunting Bay
19-89-3-W4
56°44′00″N 110°27′40″W
Flows north north-west into Clearwater River approximately 57 km east of Fort McMurray.

This creek was named after Romeo Eymundson who trapped this area. The Eymundsons were homesteaders who ran the telephone system as a private operation 1924 to 1956. Romeo owned and operated his own company to provide the only electricity available in the area.

Ronald Lake (lake)
74 E/13 - Ronald Lake
25-103-11-W4
57°58′N 111°40′W
Approximately 138 km north north-west of Fort McMurray.

After whom it is named is not known; it appears on federal government maps as early as 1916.

Rosebush Creek (creek)
74 L/12 - Hilda Lake
1-29-112-10-W4
58°45′N 111°38′W

---
*denotes rescinded name or former locality.

Flows west into Baril Lake approximately 214 km north of Fort McMurray.

This area in summer is literally overgrown with rose bushes. This is a significant landmark and area and so named by the aboriginal peoples.

Rossbear Creek (creek)
84 F/8 - Rossbear Creek
30-97-13-W5
57°27′N 116°05′W
Flows north-west into Buffalo River approximately 109 km north-east of Manning.

The precise origin of the name of this creek is unknown; both it and the lake appear on a federal government map as early as 1916.

Rossbear Lake (lake)
84 G/5 - Rossbear Lake
19-96-11-W5
57°21′N 115°45′W
Approximately 152 km north-east of Peace River.

It is the source of the creek. (see Rossbear Creek)

Round Lake (lake)
74 D/13 - Ruth Lake
2-89-13-W4
56°46′20″N 111°56′00″W
Approximately 34 km west of Fort McMurray.

The name for this very shallow lake is descriptive of its round shape.

Round Lake (lake)
84 B/15 - Kidney Lake
34-89-4-W5
56°45′N 114°34′W
Approximately 161 km north north-east of Slave Lake.

The name is descriptive of its shape, and appears as early as 1905 on a federal government map.

*****Round Lake** (lake)
83 N/15 - Springburn
14-8-78-19-W5
55°45′N 116°55′W
Immediately to the north of McLennan.

This was the original, descriptive name for the lake, but in 1914 the name was recorded as Kimiwan Lake. (see Kimiwan Lake)

Rousseau Creek (creek)
84 C/14 - Fairacres
13-91-22-W5
56°54′N 117°24′W
Flows north into Buchanan Creek approximately 14 km east of Manning.

The precise origin of the name of this creek is unknown.

Roxana (locality)
83 N/15 - Springburn
14-23-78-20-W5
55°47′N 116°58′W
Approximately 13 km north-west of McLennan.

Originally an Edmonton, Dunvegan and British Columbia Railway station, which was established here in 1915; after whom it is named is not known.

Royce (locality)
84 D/2 - Hines Creek
26-83-6-W6
56°13′N 118°50′W
Approximately 31 km north-west of Fairview.

Established as a post office in 1930, it was named after the nephew of F.L. Smith, the first postmaster.

Royemma Lake (lake)
73 M/8 - Grist Lake
8-75-1-W4
55°28′50″N 110°07′30″W
Approximately 150 km south south-east of Fort McMurray.

The lake is named in honour of a well known area pioneer, Royemma (Mitchell) Yanczura. Miss Mitchell was born in May 1906 at Humboldt, Saskatchewan. In 1925, she moved to Lac La Biche with her father, William Mitchell, where she worked as a labourer repairing and hanging fish nets. She moved to Winefred Lake in the fall of the same year and helped in the construction of fish camps and headquarters to fish the lake.

Ruis Creek (creek)

84 I/5 - Ruis Lake
NE-21-107-22-W4
58°18′N 113°36′W
Flows south into Birch Creek approximately 203 km east of High Level.

It was named after J. Ruis, a packer on the J.R. Akins survey team, which worked in this area in the summer of 1918 along the 28th Baseline.

Ruis Lake (lake)

84 I/5 - Ruis Lake
32-108-23-W4
58°25′N 113°48′W
Approximately 190 km east of High Level.

It is the source of the creek. (see Ruis Creek)

*Running Beaver Lake (lake)

84 M/7 - Elsa Lake
33-120-4-W6
59°28′N 118°37′W
Approximately 115 km north-east of Rainbow Lake.

(see Elsa Lake)

Running Lake (lake)

84 D/11 - Worsley
34-88-7-W6
56°40′N 119°02′W

---

*denotes rescinded name or former locality.

Approximately 77 km north north-west of Fairview.

The precise origin of the name of this lake is unknown.

Russell Creek (creek)

84 F/8 - Rossbear Creek
19-96-13-W5
57°20′N 116°06′W
Flows north-west into Wolverine River approximately 103 km east north-east of Manning.

Named in 1915 after John Russell, DLS.

Russell Lake (lake)

84 G/4 - Russell Lake
10-93-12-W5
57°03′N 115°51′W
Approximately 125 km north-east of Peace River.

(see Russell Creek)

Russenholt Bay (bay)

74 D/10 - Hollies Creek
10-87-4-W4
56°32′N 110°33′W
North-west bay on Gordon Lake approximately 55 km east south-east of Fort McMurray.

The precise origin is unknown, although it is likely named after an individual.

Russet Creek (creek)

84 N/5 - Russet Creek
26-119-23-W5
59°22′N 117°50′W
Flows south-east into Steen River approximately 101 km north north-west of High Level.

The precise origin of the name of this creek is unknown, although it may be descriptive of the reddish-brown or yellowish-brown colour of the water. The name appears in the 1915 field notes of J.R. Akins, DLS.

Ruth Lake (lake)

74 D/13 - Ruth Lake
16-92-10-W4
56°58′N 111°33′W
Approximately 29 km north north-west of Fort McMurray.

After whom it is named is not known; it appears in the 1914 field notes of A.D. Griffin, DLS.

Rutledge Lake (lake)

74 M/16 - Andrew Lake
SE-11-125-2-W4
59°50′N 110°13′W
Approximately 343 km north of Fort McMurray.

The name was submitted in 1958 by the Research Council of Alberta, and is one of a series of features in the area named after deceased prominent geologists, in this case after a distinguished English geologist, Harold Rutledge, who was killed in the early stages of a promising career in igneous-metamorphic geology.

Ryan Creek (creek)

74 M/6 - Bocquene Lake
5-36-118-9-W4
59°17′N 111°24′W
Flows north-east into Slave River approximately 276 km north of Fort McMurray.

The creek, island and lake were named after the brothers, Pat and Mickey Ryan, who were pioneer freighters on the Slave and Athabasca rivers. They came to Edmonton in 1910 from Muncie, Indiana. In 1916, the brothers ventured north and started a mail route from Athabasca to Fort McMurray, and over the years it became a flourishing transportation enterprise. They did much to further the economic development of the north country. In 1937, they staked a gold claim at what eventually became the Con Mine in Yellowknife.

Ryan Island (island)
74 M/13 - Fitzgerald
31-124-9-W4
59°49'N 111°33'W
Approximately 339 km north of Fort McMurray in Slave River.

The Ryan brothers cut hay for their horses on this island. (see Ryan Creek)

Ryan Lake (lake)
74 M/3 - Ryan Lake
23-117-7-W4
59°10'N 111°05'W
Approximately 265 km north of Fort McMurray.

(see Ryan Creek)

Rycroft (village)
83 M/15 - Rycroft
16-78-5-W6
55°45'N 118°43'W
Approximately 8 km south south-east of Spirit River.

According to the records of Canada Post, the post office was originally called Spirit River and opened September 15, 1905. The name changed to Roycroft January 1, 1920 and finally to Rycroft on August 1, 1931. A local history of the area recounts the following story. When the time had come to have a name, four residents placed their names in a hat. These were W.S.O. English, "Doc" Calkin, George Garnett and Robert Henry Rycroft. It is obvious who was the winner.

S Bend (bend)
74 D/15 - Alberta I.D. 18
33-89-4-W4
56°45'58"N 110°34'30"W
In Clearwater River approximately 51 km east of Fort McMurray.

This is a descriptive name for a spot in the river where it winds in the shape of an S.

Saddle (Burnt) River (river)
83 M/16 - Codesa
15-6-80-1-W6
55°55'N 118°08'W
Flows north into Peace River approximately 45 km north north-east of Spirit River.

The name Burnt River was well established when the Dominion Lands Survey came through the area in the early 1910s. George Dawson referred to it a generation before by its French name Rivière Brûlé. In 1925 the Geographic Board of Canada adopted the name Saddle River for the feature. Although extant records do not record the reason, it was probably changed due to the existence of another Burnt River to the north and the name chosen reflected the fact that the source of the river was in the Saddle Hills. By 1948, the river was still being called locally as Burnt River, so the decision was made to recognise both names, and thus it became the Saddle (Burnt) River.

Saddle Hills (hills)
83 M/11 - Saddle Hills
76-6-8-W6
55°31'N 119°05'W
Approximately 40 km north north-west of Grande Prairie.

The name for the Saddle Hills was well known and in use when the Dominion Land Surveyors came through the area in 1912. Although the origin information of the name is not precisely known, it may be descriptive, because the long set of hills look like a saddle from a distance.

Saddle Hills, Municipal District of, No. 20
(municipal district)
83 M/14 - Blueberry Mountain
75-84-5-13-W6
55°50'N 119°00'W
North of Grande Prairie.

It includes the hamlet of Woking, and the settlements of Gundy, Bonanza, East Doe River, Cotillion, Silver Valley, Fourth Creek, Blueberry Mountain, Ksituan, Whitburn, Happy Valley, Northmark, Westmark and Savanna, and was created in 1994. The name is descriptive of the prominent landmark within its boundaries.

St. Agnes Lake (lake)
74 M/9 - Colin Lake
11-123-2-W4
59°41'N 110°14'W
Approximately 326 km north north-east of Fort McMurray.

It was named in 1929 after the St. Agnes Roman Catholic Mission at Chipewyan. St. Agnes who was a Christian Roman noble who, at the age of 13, was martyred in 304 A.D.

St. Germain, Lake (lake)
84 C/6 - Weberville
24-85-23-W5
56°23'N 117°29'W
Approximately 19 km north north-west Peace River.

St. Germain Lake takes its name from the St. Germain family who settled at Shaftesbury in 1893. Charles St. Germain (1850-1911), his wife Angelique, née Lefournaise (1854-1942), and their eight children operated a farm, ranch and stopping place from river lot II 39 on the Peace River. Their twin sons Charles Jr. (1874-1958) and Joseph (1874-1959)

Charles St. Germain and Alex McKenzie, n.d.

remained in the district throughout their lives. In addition to working as freighters on the Grouard-Peace River route, they maintained livestock and hay camps in the vicinity of the lake that bears the family name. During the time of the survey of 1914, this was one of a pair of lakes named Germain Lakes. (see also Leddy Lake)

St. Isidore (locality)
84 C/3 - Peace River
21-83-20-W5
56°12'N 117°06'W
Approximately 11 km east south-east of Peace River.

The name St. Isidore was adopted for this locality by French-Canadian settlers from Lac St. Jean, Quebec, in honour of the name saint of Msgr. Isidore Clut, an Oblate of Mary Immaculate missionary. A post office opened here in 1965, with its first postmaster being Léon Lavoie. St. Isidore (1090-1130) spent all his life working on a farm at Torrelaguna just north of Madrid. Known variously as Isidore the Farm Servant, Isidore the Labourer, Isidore the Husbandman and Isidore the Farmer, he was canonized in 1622. St. Isidore is venerated as the patron saint of Madrid and of farmers everywhere.

Sakwatamau River (river)
83 J/4 - Whitecourt
3-60-12-W5
54°10′N 115°43′W
Flows south-east into Athabasca River approximately 2 km north of Whitecourt.

One source has stated this is an aboriginal word meaning hawk, and may be descriptive of the bird found in the area. It has shown on federal government maps as early as 1917, but likely was recorded by the Geological Survey of Canada whose crews were in the area in the 1870s and 1880s.

Saline Creek (creek)
74 D/11 - Fort McMurray
10-89-9-W4
56°42′N 111°20′W
Flows north-west into Hangingstone River, at Fort McMurray.

This creek takes its name from the salt in the water.

Saline Lake (lake)
74 E/4 - Fort MacKay
22-93-10-W4
57°05′N 111°32′W
Approximately 39 km north of Fort McMurray.

Saline Lake was named for the salt in its waters. The French La Saline, rather than Saline Pond, was originally approved for this feature December 2, 1924. The Geographic Board of Canada noted that La Saline or the salt place was noted on old maps. The change to Saline Lake was approved June 2, 1950.

Sall River (river)
74 L/12 - Hilda Lake
13-5-111-10-W4
58°37′N 111°40′W
Flows east into Prairie River approximately 200 km north of Fort McMurray.

Officially named in the 1960s; the origin of the name has not been recorded.

Salmond's Flat (flat)
83 L/15 - Big Mountain Creek
SE-25-68-5-W6
54°54′40″N 118°36′50″W
Approximately 30 km south south-east of Grande Prairie.

This flat was officially named in 1991 after field research was conducted. It was named after Billy Salmond who had a grazing lease along the Smoky River where he kept cattle.

Salt Creek (creek)
83 N/9 - Grouard
16-12-76-14-W5
55°35′N 116°10′W
Flows south-west into South Heart River approximately 25 km north-east of High Prairie

Descriptive of the mineral content in the water, the name was recorded as early as 1892 when the Geological Survey of Canada was in the area.

Salt Creek (creek)
74 D/11 - Fort McMurray
2-35-87-9-W4
56°34′53″N 111°19′00″W
Flows north-west into Hangingstone River approximately 15 km south of Fort McMurray.

The name was officially approved in 1992 after field research concluded the name was well established and in local use. It likely refers to the mineral found in the creek. On the map of the 1819-1820 Franklin, Ross and Perry expedition, there is reference to Salt Spring quite close to this creek.

Salt Prairie (locality)
83 N/9 - Grouard
2-77-14-W5
55°38′N 116°04′W
Approximately 35 km north-east of High Prairie.

The post office was established here in 1938 with J.A. Moore as first postmaster. (see Salt Prairie Settlement)

Salt Prairie Settlement (settlement)
83 N/9 - Grouard
28-76-14-W5
55°37′N 116°07′W
Approximately 33 km north-east of High Prairie.

It is named for its location on a Salt Prairie, created by large springs that leave alkali and salt.

Salt River (river)
84 P/16 - Brine Creek
NW-33-126-14-W4
60°00′N 112°22′W
Flows north-west into NWT approximately 312 km east north-east of High Level.

Officially named in 1949, it is descriptive of the saline nature of the water. One of its tributaries is Brine Creek.

Sand Hill Lake (lake)
84 D/2 - Hines Creek
9-32-82-4-W6
56°10′N 118°35′W
Approximately 15 km north-west of Fairview.

The precise origin of the name of this lake is unknown, although it is likely descriptive. It was noted as early as 1914 on a federal government map.

Sand Lake (lake)
84 H/9 - Sand Lake
3-100-15-W4
57°38′N 112°21′W
Approximately 117 km north-west of Fort McMurray.

This lake is named because of the numerous sandy beaches along its perimeter.

Sand Point (point)
74 L/15 - Burntwood Island
36-114-5-W4
58°56′N 110°42′W
Approximately 241 km north of Fort McMurray.

The name is descriptive of the feature and shows on federal government maps as early as 1884.

Sand River (river)
84 H/9 - Alberta
7-99-15-W4
57°34′N 112°27′W
Flows south-west into Gardiner Lakes approximately 129 km north north-west of Fort McMurray.

The precise origin of the name of this river is unknown; it is probably descriptive. William Christie, DLS, during his survey of the area referred to it as Punk River. The Surveyor General found the term objectionable, therefore Sand River remained its official name. "Punk" has a number of definitions, according to *Webster's New 20th Century Dictionary*. These include: "decayed wood or dried fungus used for tinder" and "any substance that smolders when ignited, usually in the form of a stick used to light fireworks, etc." These are obviously not objectionable, and is likely the reason Christie used the name. An obsolete definition refers to punk as meaning prostitute. Also it had been used as a term for a male prostitute. Considering these definitions, the Surveyor General may have had a case.

Sander Lake (lake)
83 O/16 - Mistehae Lake
13-80-2-W5
55°56′N 114°10′W
Approximately 80 km north north-east of Slave Lake.

The name appears on a 1918 federal government map; the origin is not known.

Sanderson Creek (creek)
74 L/14 - Rivière des Rochers
7-26-114-8-W4
58°56′N 111°13′W
Flows north into Rivière des Rochers approximately 236 km north of Fort McMurray.

It was suggested in 1967 by the chief of the Fort Chipewyan Indian Band that it be called Sanderson Creek, after an old, highly respected trapper who had this as his trapping ground and was dead by that time. It was at one time known as Ponder Creek.

Sandy Lake (hamlet)
83 P/14 - Muskeg River
5-79-22-W4
55°49′N 113°25′W
Approximately 110 km north-east of Slave Lake.

It takes its name from the nearby lake. At one time there was a petition to change the name of the hamlet to Pelican Mountain. Because there was equal use of both names, the petition was not accepted. (see Sandy Lake)

Sandy Lake (lake)
83 P/14 - Muskeg River
9-79-22-W4
55°50′N 113°25′W

---

*denotes rescinded name or former locality.

Approximately 105 km north-east of Slave Lake.

This descriptive name was recorded as early as 1892 by the Geological Survey of Canada.

*****Sandy Lake** (lake)
74 E/14 - Pearson Lake
22-103-8-W4
57°57′N 111°14′W
Approximately 137 km north of Fort McMurray.
(see Pearson Lake)

Saprae Creek (creek)
74 D/11 - Fort McMurray
32-88-8-W4
56°40′N 111°14′W
Flows north-west into Clearwater River approximately 5 km east of Fort McMurray.

Although the precise origin of the name is not known, it may derive from the Latin word for "rotting" or "putrefaction." It travels through a marshy area characterised by rotting vegetation. It appears on a federal government map as early as 1917. Correspondence of the Geographic Board of Canada from 1924 mentions the name was known locally as Deep Creek, a name still used by local residents.

Sara, Lake (lake)
83 J/9 - Flatbush
15-65-2-W5
54°38′N 114°13′W
Approximately 60 km west of Athabasca.

The name for this lake was originally proposed in 1933 to commemorate Sara Hughes of Flatbush.

Sarah Creek (creek)
83 J/11 - Swan Hills
22-64-9-W5
54°33′N 115°17′W

Flows south-east into Freeman River approximately 55 km north-west of Barrhead.

(see Sarah Lake)

Sarah Lake (lake)
83 J/11 - Swan Hills
25-65-10-W5
54°39′N 115°23′W
Approximately 70 km north-west of Barrhead.

The name for this lake appeared on a federal government map of 1946, but after whom it is named is not known. It is the source of Sarah Creek. (see also Agnes Lake)

Saskatoon Hill (hill)
83 M/3 - Wembley
9-10-72-9-W6
55°13′N 119°17′W
Approximately 40 km west of Grande Prairie.

The name for this hill, 912 metres in altitude, is descriptive of the abundance of saskatoon bushes in the area. The name was recorded by the Dominion Lands Survey when its crews were in the area in the early 1910s. (see also Saskatoon Lake)

Saskatoon Island Provincial Park (provincial park)
83 M/3 - Wembley
7-1-72-8-W6
55°13′N 119°05′W
Approximately 15 km west north-west of Grande Prairie.

Established in 1973, this 101-hectare park is sandwiched between Saskatoon Lake and Little Lake. (see also Saskatoon Lake)

---

*denotes rescinded name or former locality.

Saskatoon Lake (lake)
83 M/3 - Wembley
24-72-8-W6
55°13′N 119°05′W
Approximately 15 km west north-west of Grande Prairie.

The word *saskatoon* is a variation of the Cree word *misaskatomina* meaning "fruit of the tree of many branches." It is well known in most parts of Alberta, and was used by the aboriginal peoples to add flavour and nutrients to pemmican, which was pounded buffalo meat mixed with melted animal fat – a highly nutritious dish easily transported and long lasting. It is a species of serviceberry, *Amelanchier canadensis*. Other serviceberries include juneberry and shadbush. The area is referred to by George Dawson as Service Berry Lakes, or *Gets-i-mi-ne* Lake in Beaver, and *Mus-sa-kwat-sa-ka-gun* in Cree.

Sass Lake (lake)
84 P/13 - Sass Lake
16-126-21-W4
59°57′N 113°35′W
Approximately 254 km north-east of High Level.

Officially named in 1949 it is a source of Sass River. In 1801 Alexander Mackenzie recorded the name as Zass River. It is an aboriginal word, likely Chipewyan, meaning bear.

Saulteaux (locality)
83 O/1 - Smith
13-72-3-W5
55°14′N 114°19′W
Approximately 30 km east south-east of Slave Lake (town).

The Edmonton, Dunvegan and British Columbia Railway station, established here in 1926, may have been built on an earlier site known as Saulteaux Landing or Norris' Landing. (see also Saulteaux River)

Saulteaux River (river)
83 O/8 - Driftwood River
12-25-72-3-W5
55°16′N 114°20′W
Flows north-west in Lesser Slave River approximately 28 km east of Slave Lake.

The Saulteaux are of the Ojibwa group, and their language forms part of the Algonkian family. Although the group originated near Lake Huron and Lake Superior, they may have travelled west in search of better hunting, or with the fur trade. Some sources state the Cree referred to the Saulteaux as *Nak-aw-ew-iy-i-new*, which was a generic term for the tribal groups south of the Chipewyan. This is reflected some kilometres south of the river in the Akuinu River. The river appears on the 1892 map of R.G. McConnell of the Geological Survey of Canada as *Tow-i-now-si-pi* or Saulteaux River. The name was officially approved in 1906.

*Sausage Lake (lake)
74 M/13 - Fitzgerald
13-125-1-W4
59°52′N 110°00′W
Approximately 350 km north north-east of Fort McMurray.

This name was suggested in 1958 and was descriptive of its shape. After research was done, it was determined that the lake had already been given a name 20 years earlier. (see Doze Lake)

Sawdy (locality)
83 I/14 - Sawdy
2-68-23-W4
54°51′N 113°24′W
Approximately 15 km north north-west of Athabasca.

Originally established as a post office in 1913, it was named after the first postmaster, W.E. Sawdy.

Sawdy Creek (creek)
83 I/14 - Sawdy
35-67-22-W4
54°51′N 113°15′N
Flows east into Athabasca River approximately 15 km north of Athabasca.

Officially named in the 1950s, it takes its name from the nearby locality. (see Sawdy)

Sawle Lake (lake)
83 O/15 - Brintnell
29-80-6-W5
55°58′N 114°55′W
Approximately 75 km north of Slave Lake.

North Sawle was born in Athabasca Landing and educated in Edmonton. He had received his commercial pilot's licence in 1931. In 1934 he joined United Air Transport Service (which later became part of Canadian Pacific Airlines Limited) as a mechanic. In 1946 he was named superintendent of pilot training for Canadian Pacific Airlines and in 1949 became chief of Pacific services for the airline. He was killed in March 1953, at Karachi, Pakistan, while testing a Comet IA jetliner for CPA. This is one of the lakes named after bush pilots. (see also Berry Lake, Brintnell Lake, Calder Lake, Dickins Lake, Farrell Lake, Lake May, McConachie Lake, McMillan Lake, McMullen Lake and Randall Lake)

Sawmill Island (island)
74 L/13 - Baril River
NW-21-114-10-W4
58°55′N 111°38′W
Approximately 235 km north of Fort McMurray in Peace River.

It was officially named in 1971 for a nearby sawmill.

---

*denotes rescinded name or former locality.

Sawn Lake (lake)
84 B/13 - Peerless Lake
17-92-12-W5
56°58′N 115°54′W
Approximately 115 km north-east of Peace River.

Officially approved in 1944, the precise origin of the name of this lake is unknown.

***Sawridge** (former post office)
83 O/7 - Slave Lake
35-72-6-W5
55°02N 115°32′W
Approximately 187 km south-east of Peace River.

This was the earliest name for the town of Slave Lake. Some have said the name of Sawridge was given to the community by old-timer Walter Thompson, who settled there at the time of the 1898 gold rush. The name was taken from the nearby hill. The post office opened in May 1909 with Mr. Thompson as the first postmaster. (see also Sawridge Hill and Slave Lake)

Sawridge Creek (creek)
83 O/7 - Slave Lake
11-5-73-5-W5
55°18′N 114°44′W
Flows north-east into Lesser Slave River approximately 10 km east of Slave Lake.

Shown in a 1914 map as Little Prairie Creek, by 1922 it had changed to Sawridge Creek. It is likely named because its source is in Sawridge Hill. (see also Sawridge Hill and Little Prairie Creek)

Sawridge Hill (hill)
83 O/3 - Adams Creek
4-72-7-W5
55°13′N 115°02′W
Approximately 20 km south-west of Slave Lake (town).

Known by this name since at least the turn of the century, and likely descriptive of its sawtoothed appearance.

Sawridge Indian Reserve No. 150G (Indian reserve)
83 O/7 - Slave Lake
2-73-5-W5
55°17′N 114°40′W
Approximately 10 km east of Slave Lake.

Located north of Mitsue, this reserve is the smaller of the two reserves where the Sawridge Band lives. Members of the Sawridge Band are descendants of the Woodland Cree. The signing of Treaty No. 8 in 1899 allocated the land near Lesser Slave Lake in 1912. The name is taken from the nearby hill and creek. (see also Sawridge Hill)

Sawridge Indian Reserve No. 150H (Indian reserve)
83 O/7 - Slave Lake
8-73-6-W5
55°19′N 114°52′W
Approximately 7 km west of Slave Lake.

The name is taken from the nearby hill and creek. (see Sawridge Hill and Sawridge Indian Reserve No. 150G)

Saxon Creek (creek)
83 L/5 - Calahoo Creek
61-14-W6
54°16′N 120°00′W
Flows west into British Columbia approximately 70 km north-west of Grande Cache.

Although it is likely named after a person, the origin of the name is not precisely known. The Saxons were Germanic people who conquered parts of England in the 5th and 6th centuries.

Scheltens Lake (lake)
73 M/1 - Scheltens Lake
1-27-70-1-W4
55°05′N 110°04′W
Approximately 75 km north of Cold Lake.

Officially adopted in 1963, it is named after Pilot Officer Gordon J. Scheltens of Lac La Biche, Alberta, killed in World War II.

Schmidt Creek (creek)

74 D/14 - Wood Creek
8-90-9-W4
56°47'20"N 111°24'10"W
Flows west into Athabasca River approximately 4 km north of Fort McMurray.

Schmidt was a familiar figure in oil sands development, who arrived in Fort McMurray circa 1911 from Athabasca. He was elected Mayor of Fort McMurray in 1951 and served until 1953 when he became the first person to be elected mayor for a second term (1953-55). He died in Fort McMurray in June 1957.

Schuman Lake (lake)

83 J/6 - Christmas Creek
36-61-8-W5
54°19'N 115°05'W
Approximately 47 km north-east of Whitecourt.

The name was officially approved in 1976, and although the origin of the name is not known, it was given by local sources as early as 1963. It was at one time known as Long Lake.

Scooter Lake (lake)

84 A/14 - Mink Lake
8-90-21-W4
56°47'04"N 113°19'30"W
Approximately 118 km west of Fort McMurray.

The origin of the name of this lake is unknown; the lake is, however, popularly used to hunt black ducks. Scoters are sometimes called Black Ducks because they are largely black, unlike the Black Duck,

---

*denotes rescinded name or former locality.

which is in fact brown. The Black Scoter has been reported in Alberta, but is among those species for which material evidence of their occurrence is limited.

Scot Lake (lake)

74 L/7 - Keane Creek
25-107-5-W4
58°19'N 110°41'W
Approximately 168 km north north-east of Fort McMurray.

The name was officially changed in 1953 from Reid Lake to Scot Lake, but after whom it was named is not known.

Scotswood (locality)

84 D/2 - Hines Creek
13-82-5-W6
56°07'N 118°39'W
Approximately 17 km west north-west of Fairview.

The precise origin of the name of this locality is unknown; it might refer to people of Scottish descent in the area. A post office was established here in 1935, and the first postmaster was J.S. Keddie.

Scow Channel (channel)

74 M/3 - Ryan Lake
2-10-116-9-W4
59°03'N 111°26'W
Flows north into Slave River approximately 250 km north of Fort McMurray.

It has shown on federal government maps since at least the 1920s. The name may refer to the channel being passable only by these flat-bottomed boats used for transportation of goods.

Scully Creek (creek)

84 F/11 - Scully Creek
25-100-20-W5
57°43'N 117°08'W
Flows east north-east into Peace River, 89 km south of High Level.

After Pilot Officer John J. Scully, of Grande Prairie, killed in World War II.

Seaforth Creek (creek)

84 A/13 - Liége River
2-91-24-W4
56°52'N 113°45'W
Flows south into Wabasca River approximately 149 km west of Fort McMurray.

The precise origin of the name of this creek is unknown although it may refer to the Seaforth Highlanders of Canada, a regiment based in Vancouver. The name appears as early as 1930 on a provincial government map. Aboriginal people have always called this creek Tawatchaw Creek because it flows out of the Tawatchaw Valley.

Seal Lake (lake)

84 C/1 - Seal Lake
30-82-14-W5
56°08'N 116°10'W
Approximately 68 km east of Peace River.

The precise origin of the name of this lake is unknown.

*Second Battle River (river)

84 F/3 - Crummy Lake
5-93-22-W5
57°02'N 117°28'W
Flows south-east into Notikewin River approximately 16 km north north-east of Manning.

(see Hotchkiss River, Meikle River and Notikewin River)

Sederholm Lake (lake)

74 M/16 - Andrew Lake
3-125-1-W4
59°50'N 110°05'W
Approximately 345 km north north-east of Fort McMurray.

The name was submitted in 1958 by the Research Council of Alberta, and is one of a series of features in the area named after deceased prominent geologists. It was named "after Jacob Johannes Sederholm (1863-1934), Finnish geologist, famous for his petrologic studies of precambrian rocks in Finland." Holmgren, 1976.

Selwyn Lake (lake)
74 M/16 - Andrew Lake
20-126-3-W4
59°58′N 110°29′W
Approximately 356 km north of Fort McMurray.

The name was submitted in 1965 by the Research Council of Alberta, and is one of a series of features in the area named after deceased prominent geologists. It was suggested in recognition of the contributions made to the knowledge and development of Canada by Richard Cecil Selwyn (1824-1902), director of the Geological Survey of Canada from 1869 to 1895. The Selwyn Mountains along the Yukon-Northwest Territories border also bear his name.

Semo Lake (lake)
84 J/14 - Margaret Lake
30-113-6-W5
58°51′N 115°00′W
Approximately 126 km east north-east of High Level.

This lake is named after a man named Semo. There is some confusion as to whether this is Semo Utinowatum or Semo Peechweemow, both of whom apparently trapped in the area in the early 1900s.

Senex Creek (creek)
84 G/11 - Senex Creek
22-99-9-W5
57°36′N 115°23′W
Flows north-west into Wabasca river

---

*denotes rescinded name or former locality.

approximately 144 km south-east of High Level.

The precise origin of the name of this creek is unknown, although it appears on federal government maps as early as 1916. It may refer to John Senex (d. 1740) an English geographer, surveyor, engraver and publisher. If this is the origin, it was therefore likely given by a surveyor in honour of an early practitioner of his craft. *Senex* is also the Latin word for old man.

Sergeant Creek (creek)
83 M/13 - Bonanza
3-17-79-13-W6
55°50′N 119°59′W
Flows north into Henderson Creek approximately 70 km west of Spirit River.

It was named after Mr. Sergeant, a picketman on the 1919 Alberta-British Columbia Boundary Survey crew of R.W. Cautley.

Sexsmith (town)
83 M/7 - Sexsmith
25-73-6-W6
55°21′N 118°47′W
Approximately 15 km north of Grande Prairie.

The original Sexsmith post office was located six kilometres south of the present town. The surrounding area had been surveyed for homesteads in 1909 and the townsite was surveyed by the Edmonton, Dunvegan and British Columbia Railway in 1915. When the railway arrived in 1916 the community was originally called Benville, but the name that finally prevailed was that of David Sexsmith, who arrived in the district in June, 1911. A native of Lennox County, Ontario, he came west to Manitoba in 1890. In 1898 he travelled west as far as Spirit River with a group of men heading for the Klondike, and he was the first to drive a wagon from Spirit River to the site of

Grande Prairie, which he did in 1898. In 1914-1915 the Sexsmiths operated a stopping house, and in 1916, they moved into the village of what became Sexsmith, where they stayed until 1920, operating the first general store. (see also Benville)

Shadow Creek (creek)
83 N/7 - Triangle
11-13-74-18-W5
55°25′N 116°38′W
Flows north-east into Iroquois Creek approximately 10 km west of High Prairie.

This creek showed on maps from the 1940s as Harvey Creek; however, field research showed it was known as Shadow Creek. The change was made in 1954.

***Shaftesbury** (former post office)
84 C/4 - Grimshaw
13-82-24-W5
56°06′45″N 117°36′27″W
Approximately 25 km south-west of Peace River.

It takes its name from the nearby settlement. The post office was established in September 1911; the first postmaster was L. Lynn. (see Shaftesbury Settlement)

■ **Shaftesbury Settlement** (settlement)
84 C/3 - Peace River
83-22-W5
56°10′N 117°24′W
At Peace River (town).

Established in 1905, the settlement takes the name first used by the Reverend J.G. Brick, an Anglican missionary who began the Shaftesbury Farm in 1889. This farming operation, complete with grist mill, was early evidence of the agricultural potential of the region. Although the origin is not precisely known, he may have named it after a town in Dorset, England.

Shallow Lake (lake)
83 J/9 - Flatbush
3-64-3-W5
54°31′N 114°21′W
Approximately 68 km east south-east of Swan Hills.

This is a descriptive name.

Shannon Creek (creek)
83 O/3 - Adams Creek
13-17-71-9-W5
55°09′N 115°21′W
Flows north-east into Swan River approximately 40 km south-west of Slave Lake (town).

No origin information is known for this name which was recorded some time between 1914 and 1922. It may have taken its name from the River Shannon in Ireland.

Shaver (railway point)
83 M/2 - Grande Prairie
6-23-70-5-W6
55°05′N 118°39′W
Approximately 11 km south-east of Grande Prairie.

This Northern Alberta Railways point name was approved in 1971, and was named for a Canadian soldier from the Grande Prairie area, Private Donald F. Shaver, who died on October 25, 1944. The spur line was constructed to the Procter & Gamble pulp mill.

Shaw Creek (creek)
83 O/8 - Salt Creek
16-75-11-W5
55°29′N 115°38′W
Flows south into Lesser Slave Lake approximately 60 km west north-west of Slave Lake.

It shows on federal government maps as early as 1892; possibly named after a Hudson's Bay Company employee. (see also Shaw Point)

Shaw Point (point)
83 N/8 - High Prairie
4-12-75-14-W5
55°29′N 116°03′W
Approximately 30 km east of High Prairie.

This feature, on the north shore of Lesser Slave Lake, was named for a Hudson's Bay factor who at one time was in charge of the district. According to Charles Mair he appeared "to be a man of many eccentricities, one of which was the cultivation *à la Chinois* of a very long fingernail, which he used as a spoon to eat his egg." Holmgren, 1976. It shows on a Geological Survey map from 1892.

Shekilie River (river)
84 M/5 - Bootis Hill
16-119-12-W6
59°21′N 120°00′W
Flows west into British Columbia approximately 100 km north north-west of Rainbow Lake.

It was labelled Shikile River on a Peace River sketch map of 1913, and is an aboriginal word meaning "between two hills" and is descriptive. It was noted by a surveyor on the Alberta-British Columbia Boundary Commission 1950-1953 as being locally known as Rabbitt Creek.

Shelley Creek (creek)
74 E/6 - Kearl Lake
33-95-9-W4
57°17′10″N 111°24′45″W
Flows north-west into Muskeg River approximately 63 km north of Fort McMurray.

The precise origin of this name, given to the creek by surveyors, is unknown. The creek is also called Cheeka Pidica at the mouth. Further downstream it is known as Opiahtan, for the Cree who apparently spent his life attempting to build a canoe for travelling on this creek. He is said to have disappeared but the creek is still associated with his endeavour.

Shelter Point (point)
74 L/15 - Burntwood Island
19-113-5-W4
58°49′N 110°50′W
Approximately 229 km north of Fort McMurray.

This descriptive name has been in use since the 1880s, and possibly long before that.

Shetler Creek (creek)
83 L/5 - Two Lakes
2-63-11-W6
54°25′N 119°33′W
Flows north-west into Nose Creek approximately 95 km south-west of Grande Prairie.

Officially named in 1947; its origin is unknown.

***Shiningbank Lake** (lake)
73 M/5 - Behan Lake
12-75-11-W4
55°29′N 111°35′W
Approximately 81 km north of Lac La Biche.

(see Steepbank Lake)

Shipyard Lake (lake)
74 D/14 - Wood Creek
7-92-9-W4
56°57′55″N 111°26′10″W
Approximately 25 km north of Fort McMurray.

At one time the Hudson's Bay Company and Mackenzie River Transport had a shipyard on the Athabasca River where this lake is situated. The lake became known by this name.

---
*denotes rescinded name or former locality.

Shoal Lake (lake)
84 B/2 - Muskwa Lake
19-83-6-W5
56°13′N 114°56′W
Approximately 102 km north of Slave Lake.

It is the source of Shoal River. (see Shoal River)

Shoal River (river)
84 B/2 - Muskwa Lake
16-83-6-W5
56°12′N 114°53′W
Flows south into Muskwa River approximately 103 km north of Slave Lake.

The name is likely descriptive of the submerged sandbanks in the river. Both the lake and the river appear on a federal government map as early as 1905.

Shortt Lake (lake)
74 D/8 - Gipsy Lake
27-86-2-W4
56°29′00″N 110°13′30″W
Approximately 75 km east south-east Fort McMurray.

The precise origin of the name of this lake is unknown.

Shott Island (island)
74 E/11 - Firebag River
34-100-9-W4
57°42′30″N 111°23′30″W
In Athabasca River approximately 111 km north of Fort McMurray.

This island is named after the celebrated Captain Shott, a colourful figure on the Athabasca River. Captain Shott was in fact a nickname, said to have been bestowed as a result of his "shooting" the Grand Rapids on the Athabasca River in 1867 with a fully loaded scow without loss of life, scow, or cargo – a feat never before accomplished. Another version as to why he was named Shott was that he was "a crack shot" in his youth. Captain Shott was said to be Louis Foursseneuve or Villeneuve. It has been suggested that these were only two of his aliases. He was apparently born in 1841 in the Red Deer area, grew to a height of six feet three inches and, as a Hudson's Bay Company voyageur, saw service on most rivers in the Saskatchewan and Athabasca drainage basins. He piloted scows, canoes and steamboats. It is said he had the swashbuckling manner of a pirate, but in spite of this he was warm and friendly. When Captain Shott died in 1914 at Athabasca Landing, the entire populace turned out for his funeral.

Shuttler Flats (flats)
83 L/13 - Calahoo Creek
8-2-67-11-W6
54°46′04″N 119°33′10″W
Approximately 66 km south south-west of Grande Prairie.

These flats are named after Peter Chatelaine, or Shuttler, who lived along Pinto Creek.

Sick Hill Lake (lake)
84 H/3 - Alberta
23-94-22-W4
57°10′35″N 113°24′40″W
Approximately 132 km north-west of Fort McMurray.

This lake has been locally known by this name for many years. The story goes that someone became ill by the high hill beside the lake.

Side Lake (lake)
83 K/13 - Long Lake
16-5-68-26-W5
54°51′40″N 117°55′00″W
Approximately 65 km south-east of Grande Prairie.

The name was officially approved in 1991 and is descriptive of its position located on the side of a hill. The feature has been known locally by this since at least 1912. According to one old-time trapper in the area, the Cree name for the lake translates to "sitting crossway with the world."

Sides Lake (lake)
83 K/3 - Berland River 12-60-21-W5
54°10′N 117°01′W
Approximately 29 km south south-west of Fox Creek.

The lake was named after the foreman of a road gang. The name was officially approved February 28, 1980.

Sidney Creek (creek)
83 K/16 - Wallace River
2-69-14-W5
54°57′N 116°02′W
Flows north-west into East Prairie approximately 60 km south south-east of High Prairie.

It appears on a federal government map of 1917, and the creek crosses the 18th Baseline. It is named after Sidney Parnall, of Edmonton, a member of a survey party.

Silver Creek (creek)
84 D/9 - Sulphur Lake
33-87-2-W6
56°35′N 118°15′W
Flows south into Whitemud River approximately 59 km north of Fairview.

The precise origin of the name of this creek is unknown.

Silver Creek (railway point)
83 K/1 - Windfall Creek
29-60-16-W5
54°13′N 116°21′W
Approximately 52 km north-west of Whitecourt.

Officially adopted in 1973 for a Canadian National Railways spur line point, it was possibly named after the appearance of the water on a nearby creek.

Silver Valley (locality)
84 D/4 - Cherry Point
28-81-11-W6
56°02′N 119°34′W
Approximately 54 km north-west of Spirit River.

The precise origin of the name of this locality is unknown.

Silverleaf Creek (creek)
83 N/2 - Snipe Lake
13-14-71-17-W5
55°09′N 116°31′W
Flows north into Golden Creek approximately 45 km east of Valleyview.

According to the Geographic Board of Canada in 1953, the name was an old one and well known to the trappers, rangers and lumbermen. It is possibly descriptive.

Silverwood (locality)
83 M/10 - Woking
20-77-5-W6
55°41′N 118°43′W
Approximately 10 km south east of Spirit River.

The locality took its name from the nearby post office, opened in November 1926. It in turn took its name from the school district established in 1916 near there, that was named for the local abundance of silver birch. It is approximately one kilometre south of an old Edmonton, Dunvegan and British Columbia Railway station, Esher. The first postmaster was Mrs. M. Cashback.

*****Silvestre** (former locality)
83 L/13 - Calahoo Creek
19-69-11-W6
55°00′N 119°41′W

___
*denotes rescinded name or former locality.

Approximately 60 km west south-west of Grande Prairie.

(see Sylvester)

*****Silvestre Creek** (creek)
83 L/13 - Calahoo Creek
27-68-12-W6
54°55′N 119°44′W
Flows north-east into Red Willow Creek approximately 63 km west south-west of Grande Prairie.

(see Sylvester Creek)

Simon Lakes (lakes)
84 C/7 - Simon Lakes
20-86-17-W5
56°29′N 116°38′W
Approximately 42 km north-east of Peace River.

After whom these lakes are named is not known.

Simon Lakes (locality)
84 C/7 - Simon Lakes
29-86-17-W5
56°29′N 116°38′W
Approximately 44 km north-east of Peace River.
The locality takes its name from the nearby lakes.

Simonette River (river)
83 M/1 - DeBolt
SW-21-71-2-W6
55°09′N 118°15′W
Flows north west into Smoky River approximately 35 km east of Grande Prairie.

Some sources state the Simonette River may have been named by the pioneers in the area who found a man named Simon Walker living on the river, as a result it was called the Simonette River in 1936. According to the notebooks of George Dawson, of the Geological Survey of Canada, this river was called Simonette or Moose River. He also writes the name as *Si-mon-et-si-pi*. Dawson was surveying in the area in 1879.

Sinclair Creek (creek)
83 M/5 - Hythe
19-20-73-12-W6
55°20′N 119°49′W
Flows south into Beaverlodge River approximately 65 km west north-west of Grande Prairie.

In 1916, J. N. Wallace, DLS, stated it was named after Tom Sinclair or Grande Prairie, a member of a survey party.

*****Sinclair Lake** (lake)
83 M/5 - Hythe
10-74-12-W6
55°24′N 119°45′W
Approximately 65 km west north-west of Grande Prairie.
(see Sinclair Creek and Brainard Lake)

Skunk Lake (lake)
84 B/16 - Goosegrass Lake
35-90-3-W5
56°51′N 114°21′W
Approximately 175 km north of Slave Lake.

The precise origin of the name is unknown; it probably indicates the presence of skunks in the area. The striped skunk (*Mephitis mephitis*) is a member of the weasel family, black with conspicuous white stripes. Skunks are nocturnal creatures and spend most of the day in burrows, hibernating in winter. The skunk is best known for its foul-smelling liquid which in self-defence, can be projected three or four metres.

Slave Lake (town)
83 O/7 - Slave Lake
31-72-5-W5
55°02′N 115°27′W
Approximately 190 km south-east of Peace River.

It was originally known as Sawridge before the Edmonton, Dunvegan and British Columbia Railway station was established here in 1921. The name was changed to that of the nearby lake. The Slave Lake post office opened in 1922, the first postmaster being A. L'Hirondelle. (see also Sawridge and Lesser Slave Lake)

Slave River (river)
74 M/13 - Fitzgerald
NW-35-126-11-W4
60°00′N 111°48′W
Flows north-west into the NWT approximately 355 km north of Fort McMurray.

The name is applied to the river on the Peter Pond map of 1790. (see Lesser Slave Lake)

Slavey Creek (creek)
84 N/3 - Roe River
27-117-21-W5
59°12′N 117°29′W
Flows north-west into Hay River approximately 79 km north of High Level.

Slavey Creek is locally known as *Gotloh Chateh Zahéh* which is translated as Second Slavey Creek. The Melvin River, which flows parallel to Slavey Creek, is known locally as *Hahteh Chateh Zahéh*, or First Slavey Creek. Chatéh was the Slavey Chief who signed Treaty No. 8 on behalf of his people in the area. These local names have been in use since the late 19th century.

Slavey Creek (station)
84 N/4 - Meander River
33-117-21-W5
59°13′N 117°30′W
Approximately 80 km north north-west of High Level.

Established in 1962 as a Great Slave Lake Railway station; it was named for the nearby creek. (see Slavey Creek)

Sled Island (island)
84 J/5 - Sled Island
13-108-11-W5
58°23′N 115°42′W
In Peace River approximately 82 km east south-east of High Level.

Sled Island is a translation of the Cree name *Otapanask ministik*. In the late 19th century the Cree used to make their toboggans here due to the excellent birch trees that grew on the island. This island was recorded as Sledge Island in 1883 by W.T. Thompson, DLS, during a survey of the Peace River. It was annotated as Sled Island on the 1915 Township map, following the surveys of A.W. Ponton (1910) and J.S. Galletly (1913).

Sled Island (island)
74 E/12 - Asphalt Creek
2-98-10-W4
57°33′30″N 111°30′50″W
In Athabasca River approximately 92 km north of Fort McMurray.

Sled Island takes its name from the practice of acquiring birch there to make sleds. The name was recorded by the Geological Survey of Canada in 1890, but the name likely dates from an earlier part of the 19th century, during the heyday of the fur trade.

Slim's Lake (lake)
84 D/11 - Worsley
4-87-9-W6
56°31′N 119°21′W
Approximately 75 km north-west of Fairview.

Named some time before 1956, after whom is not known.

Slims Creek (creek)
84 F/3 - Crummy Lake
13-94-22-W5
57°09′N 117°24′W
Flows south-east into Meikle River approximately 33 km north north-east of Manning.

Officially named in 1953, after whom is not known.

Sloan Creek (creek)
83 O/3 - Adams Creek
33-69-10-W5
55°02′N 115°27′W
Flows north into Inverness River approximately 55 km south-west of Slave Lake (town).

It has shown on maps since 1942, but no origin information is known.

Sloat Creek (creek)
84 E/10 - Vader Creek
25-98-7-W6
57°32′N 118°59′W
Flows north-west into Chinchaga River approximately 117 km north-west of Manning.

A war memorial name, to commemorate Private James C. Sloat killed in action on December 27, 1944.

Slough Lake (lake)
84 A/14 - Mink Lake
36-89-22-W4
56°45′N 113°21′W
Approximately 130 km west of Fort McMurray.

The well-established local name for this lake is descriptive of the marshy slough that surrounds it.

Slug Lake (lake)
84 H/12 - Alberta
34-99-23-W4
57°37′48″N 113°40′40″W
Approximately 171 km north-west of Fort McMurray.

The local people in this remote area have always known this lake by this name, and it was apparently named for the bullets from a gun found there, or perhaps for the occurrence of the snail-like creature around the lake.

Small Creek (creek)
84 K/6 - Parma Creek
16-108-10-W5
58°23′N 117°15′W
Flows south south-east into Parma Creek approximately 17 km south south-west of High Level.

The name is descriptive of the feature.

Small Sandy Lake (lake)
74 E/12 - Asphalt Creek
5-100-10-W4
57°39′30″N 111°35′30″W
Approximately 104 km north north-west of Fort McMurray.

The name is descriptive of the feature.

Smeaton Creek (creek)
84 F/12 - Kemp River
12-101-23-W5
57°45′N 117°38′W
Flows north-east into Keg River 90 km south south-west of High Level.

Although it is found under this name on federal government maps as early as 1922, after whom it is named is not known.

Smith Creek (creek)
83 L/13 - Calahoo Creek
9-69-11-W6
54°57′N 119°36′W
Flows east into Wapiti River approximately 50 km west south-west of Grande Prairie.

---
*denotes rescinded name or former locality.

It is likely named after an early homesteader in the area, Frank Smith. One longtime resident of the area stated the creek may be named after a bootlegger who lived on the creek. The name has been in use since the 1920s.

***Smith Landing Settlement** (settlement)
74 M/13 - Fitzgerald
13-125-10-W4
59°52′N 111°36′W
Approximately 340 km north of Fort McMurray.

Likely named for its proximity to Fort Smith, a short distance away just north of

Smith Landing on Slave River, 1901

the 60th Parallel, which forms the boundary between the Northwest Territories and Alberta. Fort Smith was established in 1874 as a Hudson's Bay Company post. The name of the settlement was changed in 1915. (see Fitzgerald Settlement)

Smithmill (locality)
84 C/5 - Chinook Valley
19-86-24-W5
56°28′N 117°47′W
Approximately 39 km north north-west of Grimshaw.

This locality is reputed to be named after Harry Smith who ran a sawmill in the area.

Smoke Lake (lake)
83 K/7 - Iosegun Lake
19-62-20-W5
54°22′N 116°56′W
Approximately 150 km south-east of Grande Prairie.

The name was officially adopted in 1960, and was taken from local sources. Its origin is not precisely known, but it is speculated the name was chosen for its proximity to the Little Smoky River. The name might also refer to mist rising from the lake at certain times of the year. At one time it was also known as Buck Lake, but the name was changed to avoid duplication. (see also Buck Lake)

Smoky Heights (locality)
83 M/8 - Smoky Heights
13-74-3-W6
55°24′N 118°18′W
Approximately 30 km north-east of Grande Prairie.

The post office was established here in August 1932 and closed in August 1958. It was situated at the top of the bank above the Smoky River. (see Smoky River)

■ **Smoky River** (river)
84 C/3 - Peace River
12-83-22-W5
56°11′N 117°19′W
Flows north-east into Peace River approximately 7 km south of Peace River.

The descriptive name for this river refers to the smouldering beds of coal in the river banks, in Cree *kas-ka-pi-te si-pi*. This river is referred to in Alexander Mackenzie's 1793 *Voyage to the Pacific Ocean* as *Quiscatina-Sepy*.

Smoky River and Peace River Junction, 1961

Smoky River, Municipal District of, No.
130 (municipal district)
83 N/11 - Donnelly
78-21-W5
55°40'N 117°10'W
Approximately 55 km south of Peace River.

The municipal district was established in 1952, and took its name from the predominant feature within its boundaries.

Smuland Creek (creek)
83 L/9 - Latornell River
22-65-2-W6
54°38'43"N 118°13'34"W
Flows north-east into Latornell River approximately 65 km south-east of Grande Prairie.

Named in 1950 by a road gang working in the area, after their supervisor Reinhard Smuland.

Snake Lake (lake)
84 O/9 - Alberta
7-123-1-W5
59°40'N 114°10'W
Approximately 210 km north-east of High Level.

This name was officially approved in 1964 due to an abundance of snakes in the area.

Sneddon Creek (creek)
84 D/4 - Cherry Point
5-83-11-W6
56°10'N 119°41'W
Flows north into Peace River approximately 68 km north-west of Spirit River.

This is a war memorial name in honour of Flying Officer J.A. Sneddon, born in Edmonton on June 11, 1923. He enlisted in the RCAF in 1941 and was posted overseas in 1942. He completed 115 operational sorties with 115 Squadron. On July 1, 1943, he received the DFM and was cited as a rear gunner of the highest order. He was later raised to a commissioned rank. He was reported missing after air operations on January 14, 1944.

Snipe Creek (creek)
84 H/2 - Snipe Creek
13-93-19-W4
57°04'N 112°55'W
Flows south-west into Dunkirk River approximately 101 km north-west of Fort McMurray.

It likely refers to the presence of the common snipe, a shorebird of the sandpiper family characterised by a long straight bill. Marshes, muskegs and the grassy margins of creeks are the favourite habitat of the snipe in all seasons. Snipe take off in erratic flight when disturbed. They remain until well after the first frosts have killed the marsh grasses, but when their bills can no longer probe the mud they take off southward for warmer climes.

Snipe Creek (creek)
84 H/2 - Snipe Lake
2-73-20-W5
55°18'N 116°57'W
Flows north-west into Little Smoky River approximately 60 km north of Athabasca.

This is descriptive of the bird found on the shores of the lake. (see also Snipe Creek)

Snipe Lake (lake)
83 N/2 - Snipe Lake
12-71-19-W5
55°08'N 116°47'W
Approximately 30 km west of Valleyview.

The lake is named after the birds that live on the lake. The name is likely a translation from an aboriginal word. The name appears on federal government maps as early as 1915. (see also Snipe Creek)

Snowfall Creek (creek)
84 L/4 - Chasm Creek
13-104-13-W6
58°02'N 120°00'W
Flows north north-west into British Columbia approximately 64 km south south-west of Rainbow Lake.

This name was given by surveyors because of a snowfall occurring in August while they were camped at this creek during the Alberta-British Columbia Boundary Survey, 1950-51.

Snowshoe Lake (lake)
84 E/4 - Mearon Creek
14-94-13-W6
57°10'35"N 119°58'00"W
Approximately 143 km west north-west of Manning.

As the area surrounding this lake is very wet and is only accessible in winter by snowshoe, it has been known locally as Snowshoe Lake since the 1920s when the area was trapped extensively.

Snuff Mountain (hill)
83 K/12 - Ante Creek
3-66-24-W5
54°40'40"N 117°32'00"W

Approximately 101 km south-east of Grande Prairie.

The name, originally in Cree, was probably translated into English in the 1950s when a Forestry tower was built on the top of the hill. Snuff refers to a type of root that, when dried and ground into a powder, was used by the aboriginal people to induce sneezing. This was done to cure respiratory ailments. The name was officially approved in 1991 after field research was conducted.

Snye, The (channel)
74 D/11 - Fort McMurray
21-89-9-W4
56°44′N 111°22′W
Between the mainland and McDonald Island, at Fort McMurray.

The Snye is the descriptive name used to describe this channel of water. A snye is a subsidiary channel to the main channel of a watercourse. (see also Tokyo Snye)

Sock Lake (lake)
84 E/12 - Sock Lake
13-99-13-W6
57°36′N 119°59′W
Approximately 118 km south south-west of Rainbow Lake.

This name was applied during the Alberta-British Columbia Boundary Commission survey as descriptive of its shape.

Soda Creek (creek)
74 D/9 - Bunting Bay
20-89-3-W4
56°44′05″N 110°27′00″W
Flows south-west into Clearwater River approximately 58 km east of Fort McMurray.

This name is descriptive of the effect created by the mixture of sulphur in the lake water that causes it to appear to be bubbling and white like soda water.

Soldar Creek (creek)
84 F/4 - Hotchkiss
20-92-22-W5
57°00′N 117°30′W
Flows east south-east into Notikewin River approximately 15 km north-east of Manning.

Its origin is unknown; it appears on a federal government map as early as 1919.

Sousa Creek (creek)
84 L/15 - Habay
15-113-5-W6
58°58′N 118°45′W
Flows north into Hay River approximately 51 km north-east of Rainbow Lake.

The precise origin of the name of this creek is unknown; the name was first applied to it in 1921 by a surveyor in the area and may be an incorrect spelling of a local Slavey family called Southa. Another possible explanation is it was named after John De Sousa an accountant for the Hudson's Bay Company. He left the company in April 1899. The Slavey name for this stream is *Tééht'o Zahé* and means Gun Creek. Cree speaking Métis from Paddle Prairie know the east branch of the river as *Paskisikan Sepe* which means Gun River. The creek and prairie through which it flows were so named after a rifle was either found on the prairie or one that was lost in the stream.

South Heart River (river)
83 N/9 - Grouard
12-76-15-W5
55°34′N 116°11′W
Flows south into Buffalo Bay approximately 25 km north-east of High Prairie.

Surveyors' field notes from 1911 show this as Heart River; however, some time before 1950 that name was changed to Harmon River. This may have been named at the same time the Harmon Valley Post Office was established in 1931. In 1950, the name was changed to South Heart River, which referred to its position relative to the Heart River and better reflected local usage.

South Shekilie River (river)
84 M/4 - South Shekilie River
29-116-12-W6
59°06′N 120°00′W
Flows west into British Columbia approximately 75 km north north-west of Rainbow Lake.

Likely named for its proximity to Shekilie River, the precise origin of the name of this river is unknown.

South Wabasca Lake (lake)
83 P/13 - Pelican
6-80-24-W4
55°55′N 113°45′W
Approximately 95 km north-east of Slave Lake.

This is named for its relation to North Wabasca Lake and Wabasca River. The name was well established and in local use when the Dominion Land Surveyors were in the area in 1913. (see also Wabasca River)

South Watchusk Lake (lake)
74 D/1 - Watchusk Lake
6-83-2-W4
56°10′N 110°18′W
Approximately 90 km south-east of Fort McMurray.

Previously known as Watchusk Lake; the name was officially changed to reflect current local usage and to distinguish it from North Watchusk Lake. Watchusk Lake is mentioned by surveyor Philip Turnor in his journal, 1790-1792. Watchusk is the Cree word for "little devil creature" or "muskrat." (see also North Watchusk Lake)

South Whitemud Lake (lake)
84 D/10 - South Whitemud Lake
27-88-6-W6
56°39′N 118°51′W
Approximately 70 km north north-west of Fairview.

The precise origin of the name of this lake is unknown; it is probably descriptive of the silt in the lake.

South Whitemud River (river)
84 D/9 - Sulphur Lake
2-89-3-W6
56°41′N 118°22′W
Flows east into Whitemud River approximately 69 km north of Fairview.

The precise origin of the name of this river is unknown; it is probably descriptive of the silt carried in the river.

Spark Plug Creek (creek)
74 D/15 - Alberta I D # 18
31-89-4-W4
56°45′30″N 110°37′00″W
Flows north into Clearwater River approximately 48 km east of Fort McMurray.

This creek was named Spark Plug Creek in 1979 when a spark plug blew in a local resident's snowmobile. The vehicle was abandoned and when the owner went to retrieve it at a later date, an overflow from the Clearwater River had covered it. The snowmobile was frozen in the creek. This event is commemorated in the now official name for the creek.

Spawn Lake (lake)
84 M/16 - Thurston Lake
32-126-3-W6
59°59′N 118°29′W
Approximately 172 km north north-west of Rainbow Lake.

Officially named in 1956, the precise origin is unknown, although the name may refer to the spawning ground of local fish species.

Spider Lake (lake)
74 M/16 - Andrew Lake
NE-14-124-2-W4
59°47′N 110°13′W
Approximately 337 km north of Fort McMurray.

The name was submitted in 1958 by the Research Council of Alberta, and is derived from the shape of the lake.

Spirit Creek (creek)
83 N/6 - Whitemud Creek
13-24-73-22-W5
55°20′N 117°15′W
Flows north-east into Clouston Creek approximately 30 km north of Valleyview.

The name was officially approved in 1960, although the name was known locally for many years before by trappers in the area. It is likely aboriginal in origin.

Spirit Ridge (ridge)
83 M/11 - Woking
17-77-7-W6
55°40′N 119°02′W
Approximately 16 km south-west of Spirit River.

Officially named in 1958 at the request of Alberta Surveys and Mapping, this 914 metre hill was probably named for its proximity to Spirit River. J.B. St. Cyr recorded the name for this feature in 1904 as Old Ranch Mountains. (see Spirit River)

Spirit River (river)
83 M/16 - Codesa
7-3-79-3-W6
55°48′N 118°22′W
Flows east into Saddle (Burnt) River approximately 30 km east of Spirit River.

The name is a translation of a Cree phrase *chepi-sipi* or *chepi-sepe* meaning ghost, or spirit river. It evokes powerful images from aboriginal legends. In one of the more eerie, it was believed that a body of a woman was buried in a hill close to the river. It is said it is the voice of her spirit in the wind that blew through the trees on the nearby hill. Another story tells of a man who, while washing his face at the river, noticed spots of light flashing around him. Not realizing that what he saw was sunlight sparkling off the "fool's gold" on the banks, he thought the lights to be from the spirits. The third legend tells of a camp of aboriginal people situated on the hills near the river. They were there to hunt game to feed their people. Three of the men had gone hunting while the others set up camp. Each of the three set off in a different direction following a different animal trail. As night approached one man who had killed a deer, called to his comrades for assistance in carrying the deer back to camp. As he shouted, he heard many voices. In fact, it was only the sound of his own voice echoing and re-echoing. Because of the confusion in the darkness he thought the voices were those of the spirits chasing after him. He ran back to his people, they broke camp and quietly slipped away. Although the river was likely known by the aboriginal name many years before, the name was recorded in the Hudson's Bay Company Fort Dunvegan post journal as early as 1854.

Spirit River (town)
83 M/15 - Rycroft
22-78-6-W6
55°47′N 118°50′W
Approximately 65 km north of Grande Prairie.

The Edmonton, Dunvegan and British Columbia Railway station was established there in 1916. Before the railway reached this point, the Village of Spirit River was located on the bank of the river about two miles south and two miles east, but after the steel was laid and the townsite laid out, the residents and storekeepers of the village moved to the present site and also moved the name "Spirit River" along with them. The post office was established in 1920. J. M. Fildes was the first postmaster. It was incorporated as a town in 1951. (see also Spirit River and Rycroft)

Spirit River, Municipal District of, No. 133 (municipal district)
83 M/10 - Woking
22-78-6-W6
55°45′N 118°40W
Centred on the town of Peace River.

Established in 1945, the municipal district took its name from the town and the river, both predominant features within its boundaries.

Spirit River Settlement (settlement)
83 M/10 - Woking
12-78-5,6-W6
55°45′N 118°47′W
Approximately 62 km north of Grande Prairie.

First surveyed in 1907, the settlement takes its name from the river. (see also Spirit River)

***Spitfire Lake** (former post office)
83 M/6 - La Glace
4-74-7-W6
55°23N 119°01W
Approximately 23 km north-west of Grande Prairie.

The post office opened here in January 1915, and was named for a locally known lake, which in turn was named after a British destroyer. The name of the post office was changed in 1917. (see Buffalo Lake and Niobe Creek)

---

*denotes rescinded name or former locality.

Split Lakes (lakes)
74 M/16 - Andrew Lake
SW-25-125-2-W4
59°53′N 110°13′W
Approximately 345 km north of Fort McMurray.

The name was submitted in 1958 by the Research Council of Alberta and is descriptive of the lakes.

Spoon Lake (lake)
84 H/3 - Alberta
7-93-19-W4
57°03′10″N 113°03′25″W
Approximately 107 km west north-west of Fort McMurray.

This lake has been known as Spoon Lake because long ago people gathered the shells from this lake to use for spoons.

Spring Creek (creek)
83 K/13 - Long Lake
8-27-68-26-W5
54°54′45″N 117°52′01″W
Flows west into the Simonette River approximately 68 km south-east of Grande Prairie.

Officially approved in 1991 after field research was conducted; this creek was named because it originates in a muskeg fed by a natural spring. The name is locally well established and has been in use since at least the early 1930s.

Spring Creek (creek)
83 M/2 - Grande Prairie
24-70-7-W6
55°05′N 118°57′W
Flows south-east into Wapiti River approximately 10 km south-west of Grande Prairie.

The name was first recorded in 1951; it is descriptive of the source of the creek.

***Spring Lake** (lake)
83 M/3 - Wembley
NE-16-71-7-W6
55°09′N 119°00′W
Approximately 10 km west of Grande Prairie.

This lake was renamed Dimsdale Lake to coincide with the local railway station. (see Dimsdale Lake)

Springburn (locality)
83 N/15 - Springburn
16-80-19-W5
55°56′N 116°55′W
Approximately 25 km north of McLennan.

Originally it was a Central Canada Railway station established in 1915. A post office opened here in 1935, and the first postmaster was A. Lytle. The origin of the name is not known; however, a burn in Scots Gaelic is a brook, so perhaps the name was inspired by a nearby creek which was fed by a spring.

Spruce Creek (creek)
83 M/3 - Wembley
NW-8-71-9-W6
55°08′N 119°21′W
Flows south-west into Beaverlodge River approximately 35 km west of Grande Prairie.

It has been known by that name since at least the 1940s and is likely descriptive of the vegetation in the area.

***Spruce Creek** (creek)
83 M/7 - Sexsmith
10-19-72-6-W6
55°15′N 118°54′W
Flows south into Bear River approximately 8 km north-west of Grande Prairie.

(see Grande Prairie Creek)

Spruce Island (island)
73 L/12 - Beaver Lake
66-13-W4
54°44′N 111°53′W
In Beaver Lake approximately 5 km south-east of Lac La Biche.

The name is descriptive of the predominant vegetation on the island.

Spruce Lake (lake)
74 D/13 - Ruth Lake
18-90-12-W4
56°47′57″N 111°55′00″W
Approximately 33 km west north-west of Fort McMurray.

This lake in the Thickwood Hills is surrounded by spruce trees.

Spruce Point (point)
84 I/9 - Spruce Point
9-14-110-15-W4
58°33′N 112°22′W
Approximately 202 km north north-west of Fort McMurray.

Descriptive of the flora found there, the name appeared on maps as early as the 1940s.

Spur Lake (lake)
74 M/16 - Andrew Lake
12-126-2-W4
59°56′N 110°12′W
Approximately 353 km north of Fort McMurray.

The name was submitted in 1958 by the Research Council of Alberta and is descriptive of its shape.

Spurfield (hamlet)
83 O/1 - Smith
8-72-2-W5
55°13′N 114°16′W

Approximately 33 km east south-east of Slave Lake.

Originally established as a Central Canada Railway siding in 1926; the name is a combination of spur, describing the railway line to serve the Canyon Creek Lumber Company, and field, after Mr. Field, the manager of the company. The post office opened here in 1926, and Mr. Field was the first postmaster.

Sputina River (river)
84 G/9 - Alberta
33-99-2-W5
57°37′N 114°16′W
Flows north-west into Wabasca River approximately 195 km south east of High Level.

The precise origin of the name of this river is unknown; however, it may be a variation of the Cree word for high hill. The name appears on a federal government map as early as 1915.

Square Creek (creek)
84 E/3 - Halverson Ridge
8-93-8-W6
57°03′N 119°14′W
Flows north-east into the Notikewin River approximately 20 km west of Manning.

Officially named in the 1960s; it is descriptive. Several of its tributaries meet it a right angles.

Square Lake (lake)
84 P/1 - Square Lake
SW-10-116-15-W4
59°04′N 112°28′W
Approximately 257 km north north-west of Fort McMurray.

Officially named in the 1950s; the name is descriptive of its shape.

Squirrel Mountain (mountain)
84 D/8 - Deer Hill
11-86-2-W6
56°27′N 118°12′W
Approximately 46 km north north-east of Fairview.

The precise origin of the name of this mountain is unknown; it may refer to the abundance of the mischievous rodents on the feature.

Stanley Creek (creek)
74 E/6 - Kearl Lake
23-96-9-W4
57°21′N 111°21′W
Flows west into Muskeg River approximately 67 km north north-east of Fort McMurray.

Named in 1925 after Stanley Wood, son of Thomas Wood, of Fort McMurray.

Stebbing Creek (creek)
83 K/16 - Wallace River
36-69-14-W5
54°56′N 116°01′W
Flows west into Sidney Creek approximately 57 km south-east of High Prairie.

It appears on a federal government map of 1917, and since the creek follows the 18th Baseline, it is likely the name of a survey crew member.

Steen River (hamlet)
84 N/11 - Steen River
27-122-19-W5
59°38′N 117°10′W
Approximately 120 km north of High Level.

Named after the Steen River which joins the Hay River near the settlement. A post office operated here between 1957 and 1963. The first postmaster was D.B. McDonald. (see Steen River)

Steen River (river)
84 N/11 - Steen River
3-122-19-W5
59°35′N 117°10′W
Flows north-east into Hay River approximately 117 km north of High level.

It was named by J.R. Akins, DLS, in his 1915 survey of the 6th Meridian. A.S. Steen was the cook on Akins' survey. The local name for this stream is *Tza Zahéh*, which in Slavey means Beaver River.

Steen River (station)
84 N/11 - Steen River
22-122-19-W5
59°36′N 117°10′W
Approximately 125 km north of High Level.
(see Steen River)

Steep Creek (creek)
83 N/7 - Triangle
20-72-19-W5
55°15′N 116°53′W
Flows north into Snipe Creek approximately 32 km north-east of Valleyview.

Officially adopted in the early 1950s after field research, the name is likely descriptive.

Steep Creek (creek)
83 L/10 - Cutbank River
21-66-6-W6
54°44′N 118°50′W
Flows north-east into Big Mountain Creek approximately 45 km south of Grande Prairie.

Officially named in 1957, it is descriptive of the creek.

Steepbank Lake (lake)
73 M/5 - Behan Lake
12-75-11-W4
55°29′N 111°35′W

Approximately 81 km north of Lac La Biche.

The appropriately descriptive name for this lake has been associated with the feature since 1932. It is sometimes referred to as Shiningbank Lake. The Cree refer to the feature as *Wayenenau Sagahegan*, which may be translated as Deep Hole Lake.

Steepbank River (river)
84 I/8 - Pointe de Roche
9-22-107-13-W4
58°18′N 112°04′W
Flows north-east into Lake Claire approximately 171 km north north-west of Fort McMurray.

The name for this river is descriptive and was recorded by the Geological Survey of Canada as early as 1890.

Steepbank River (river)
74 E/3 - Hartley Creek
36-92-10-W4
57°01′N 111°28′W
Flows north-west into Athabasca River approximately 33 km north of Fort McMurray.

This is a descriptive name for this river, which flows through a narrow gorge before entering the Athabasca River. The name was recorded as early as 1890 by the Geological Survey of Canada.

Steephill Creek (creek)
84 K/2 - Moose Island
10-105-16-W5
58°06′N 116°33′W
Flows north into the Peace River approximately 57 km south south-east of High Level.

The name of this creek is descriptive of the steep-banked valley it flows through on its way into the Peace River.

Steeprock Creek (creek)
83 M/5 - Hythe
5-3-73-12-W6
55°17′N 119°44′W
Flows east into Beavertail Creek approximately 56 km west of Grande Prairie.

This likely descriptive name was well established and in local use in 1909 when the Dominion Lands Survey went through.

*****Sterner Lake** (lake)
73 M/7 - Kirby Lake
6-75-5-W4
55°28′N 110°46′W
Approximately 110 km north-east of Lac La Biche.

According to local stories, Sterner was a fisherman, one of the first involved in commercial fishing in the area. The name was changed in the late 1940s or early in the 1950s to commemorate a casualty from World War II. (see Kirby Lake)

Stomach Lake (lake)
84 A/14 - Mink Lake
13-91-22-W4
56°53′N 113°24′W
Approximately 123 km west north-west of Fort McMurray.

This lake apparently became known as Stomach Lake because of confusion between the Cree word for the perch fish and the English word stomach, which sound very much alike. The story goes that a little girl who lived near the lake with her parents was alone when visitors arrived at the door. When they asked her where her parents were, she said they had gone to the lake for some stomach. This story came to be associated with the lake, and the name Stomach Lake received widespread local usage.

---

*denotes rescinded name or former locality.

Stone Lake (lake)
84 H/3 - Alberta
5-95-19-W4
57°13′20″N 113°02′30″W
Approximately 113 km north-west of Fort McMurray.

The precise origin of the name of this lake, always known as Stone Lake to local people, is unknown. It may be descriptive.

Stone Point (point)
74 L/16 - Stone Point
SW-32-113-2-W4
58°51′N 110°19′W
Approximately 236 km north north-east of Fort McMurray.

The name is descriptive or the feature and shows on Dr. Robert Bell's map of 1884 as Rolling Stone Point. It is referred to as Stony Point in the 1822 Hudson's Bay post journal from Fort Chipewyan.

Stoney Creek (creek)
83 O/3 - Adams Creek
14-21-70-9-W5
55°05′N 115°18′W
Flows north-west into Swan River approximately 40 km south-west of Slave Lake (town).

The name is likely descriptive and was adopted some time between 1922 and 1954. There is another stream flowing into the Swan River approximately 6 kilometres to the south called Boulder Creek. Both these names give evidence of rocky watercourses in the area.

Stoney Island (island)
74 D/14 - Wood Creek
8-91-9-W4
56°52′N 111°26′W
On Athabasca River approximately 18 km north of Fort McMurray.

*denotes rescinded name or former locality.

The name was recorded in 1914 as Stony Island by A.D. Griffin, DLS, and is likely descriptive.

Stoney Lake (lake)
74 D/6 - Gregoire Lake
14-12-84-8-W4
56°16′25″N 111°08′00″W
Approximately 79 km south-east of Fort McMurray.

The name for this lake comes from an extremely large boulder found on the banks of the lake.

Stoney Lake (lake)
84 H/11 - Bergeron Creek
13-99-21-W4
57°35′15″N 113°19′00″W
Approximately 150 km north-west Fort McMurray.

This lake is so named because of the large number of stones in it, unusual for most lakes in this area.

***Stoney Lake** (lake)
84 H/9 - Alberta
6-101-13-W4
57°44′N 112°07′W
Approximately 119 km north north-west of Fort McMurray.

(see Clear Lake)

***Stoney Point** (former locality)
83 N/9 - Grouard
19-75-14-W5
55°31′N 116°09′W
Approximately 24 km north-east of High Prairie.

In 1903, when the post office was established, the name for this locality, based on an earlier Cree name, was changed to Lesser Slave Lake, and again in 1909 to its current name, Grouard. (see Lesser Slave Lake and Grouard)

Stony Creek (creek)
83 L/14 - Wapiti Creek
11-28-67-9-W6
54°50′20″N 119°18′25″W
Flows north-west into Pinto Creek approximately 45 km south south-west of Grande Prairie.

The origin of the name of Stony Creek is not clear. Some people claim that it is named after an aboriginal family named Stony who lived near the creek. Others claim the creek is named after Stoney people in the area. A 1951 map documents the name of Stony Creek, so another explanation for the name might be descriptive.

Stony Creek (creek)
83 N/7 - Triangle
9-36-73-20-W5
55°17′N 116°56′W
Flows north into Little Smoky River approximately 30 km west of High Prairie.

The origin of the name is unknown; it may be descriptive. It was officially adopted in the early 1950s after field research conducted in the area found it was an old name, well known by the local residents.

Stony Islands (islands)
74 M/11 - Hay Camp
SW-13-122-9-W4
59°35′N 111°25′W
Approximately 311 km north of Fort McMurray in Slave River.

The name appears on federal government maps as early as 1917, but the name was likely in use much earlier. It is descriptive.

Stony Rapids (rapids)
83 P/15 - Pelican Portage
SE-31-79-17-W4
55°54′N 112°39′W
Approximately 120 km south-west of Fort McMurray on the Athabasca.

The name for these small rapids North of Pelican Rapids is descriptive, and was well known to travellers along the Athabasca in the 19th century. It was recorded on a Geological Survey of Canada map of 1892.

Stony Woman Creek (creek)
83 K/13 - Long Lake
7-23-68-26-W5
54°53′55″N 117°51′00″W
Flows west into Simonette River approximately 70 km south-east of Grande Prairie.

The creek and lake were officially named in 1991 after field research determined the name to be well established and in local usage. At that time two stories concerning the origin of the name arose. One states that early aboriginal people in the area found a woman made of stone near the lake. The other story refers to a Stoney woman who married into a Cree family in the area. She may have camped by the river, and because she was always seen as an outsider, the lake and creek became known as Stony Woman.

Stony Woman Lake (lake)
83 K/13 - Long Lake
12-20-68-25-W5
54°54′08″N 117°47′04″W
Approximately 73 km south-east of Grande Prairie.

The lake takes its name from the creek that drains it. (see Stony Woman Creek)

Stovel Lake (lake)
84 I/11 - Stovel Lake
18-111-19-W4
58°39′N 113°12′W
Approximately 225 km east of High Level.

Officially named in 1949, it commemorates Flight Lieutenant C. C. Stovel, DFC, born in Craigmyle, Alberta in 1917. He enlisted in the RCAF in Calgary, Alberta, trained as a pilot, and went overseas where he received his commission. He was reported missing and subsequently presumed dead after air operations on July 28, 1943, just three weeks after having received the Distinguished Flying Cross.

Stowe Creek (creek)
84 C/13 - Manning
7-92-22-W5
56°58′N 117°32′W
Flows south-east into Notikewin River approximately 8 km north-east of Manning.

The precise origin of the name of this creek is unknown, it likely was named after a survey crew member. The name appears on a federal government map as early as 1919.

Strawberry Creek (creek)
83 O/5 - Driftpile
17-73-10-W5
55°20′N 115°34′W
Flows north-east into Swan River approximately 40 km west of Slave Lake.

The name was mentioned in the Dominion Land Surveys report of 1908, and is likely descriptive of the wild strawberries found along its banks.

Strong Creek (creek)
84 C/3 - Peace River
4-83-22-W5
56°10′N 117°25′W
Flows south into Peace River approximately 11 km south-east of Grimshaw.

The name appears on a federal government map as early as 1915, and is descriptive of the salty, strong taste of the water.

*Strong Creek (former post office)
84 C/3 - Peace River
36-83-23-W5
56°15′N 117°26′W
Approximately 6 km south of Grimshaw.

The post office took its name from the nearby creek, and was in operation here for 21 months in 1923 and 1924. The postmaster was Clara Taylor.

Stump Lake (lake)
83 N/3 - Valleyview
18-71-21-W5
55°09′N 117°13′W
Approximately 10 km north north-east of Valleyview.

The name was officially approved in May 1953 after field research was conducted. Perhaps it describes the remains of a felled tree in the lake.

Sturgeon Creek (creek)
83 N/3 - Valleyview
6-2-71-21-W5
55°06′N 117°07′W
Flows east into Little Smoky River approximately 11 km north-east of Valleyview.

(see Sturgeon Lake)

Sturgeon Heights (hamlet)
83 N/4 - Sturgeon Heights
25-70-25-W5
55°05′N 117°40′W
Approximately 25 km west of Valleyview.

Originally a post office which was named because of its location on high ground overlooking Sturgeon Lake. It opened in October 1931, its first postmaster being N. Stepanick.

Sturgeon Lake (lake)
83 N/4 - Sturgeon Heights
70-71-23-23-W5
55°06′N 117°32′W
Approximately 15 km west of Valleyview.

---

*denotes rescinded name or former locality.

The name was well established and in local use long before George Dawson of the Geological Survey of Canada was in the area in 1879. It is likely named for the abundance of fish in the lake.

Sturgeon Lake Indian Reserve No. 154

(Indian reserve)
83 N/3 - Valleyview
17-70-23-W5
55°04'N 117°28'W
Approximately 80 km south south-east of Grande Prairie.

This reserve takes its name from the nearby lake. The people who live on the reserve are of Woodland Cree descent. (see Sturgeon Lake)

Sturgeon Lake Indian Reserve No. 154A

(Indian reserve)
83 N/3 - Valleyview
9-71-23-W5
55°07'N 117°28'W
Approximately 90 km east of Grande Prairie.

This reserve takes its name from the nearby lake. The people who live on the reserve are of Woodland Cree descent. (see Sturgeon Lake)

Sturgeon Lake Indian Reserve No. 154B

(Indian Reserve)
83 K/13 - Long Lake
22-69-24-W5
54°59'N 117°59'W
Approximately 80 km east south-east of Grande Prairie.

This reserve takes its name from the nearby lake. The people who live on the reserve are of Woodland Cree descent. (see Sturgeon Lake)

Sucker Creek (creek)

83 N/8 - High Prairie
5-18-74-14-W5
55°24'N 116°08'W

Flows east into Arcadia Creek approximately 23 km east south-east of High Prairie.

Sucker Creek was mentioned in the field notebook of the Dominion Land Surveyor who went through the area in 1907. Old-timers in the area feel that the creek may have been named because in the spring it used to be full of suckers, a type of bottom-feeding fish.

Sucker Creek (creek)

84 P/10 - Upland Lake
SW-2-124-17-W4
59°45'N 112°50'W
Flows north-west into Little Buffalo River approximately 277 km east north-east of High Level.

Likely descriptive of the fish found there, this name appears on federal government maps as early as 1917.

Sucker Creek Indian Reserve No. 150A

(Indian reserve)
83 N/8 - High Prairie
30-74-14-W5
55°28'N 116°10'W
Along the shore of Lesser Slave Lake approximately 20 km east of High Prairie.

The Cree reserve takes its name from the nearby creek. It is one of the Cree bands living on the Lesser Slave Lake shore who were under the leadership of Chief Kinosayo. The reserve was resurveyed in 1912, when more lands were allocated to it. (see Sucker Creek)

Sucker Lake (lake)

73 M/4 - Philomena
7-25-71-13-W4
55°10'N 111°51'W
Approximately 45 km north of Lac La Biche.

The locally well-established name for this lake is descriptive of the many sucker fish contained within it. The Cree equivalent is *Namepi Sagahegan*.

Sucker Lake (lake)

74 D/7 - Cheecham
34-85-6-W4
56°25'10"N 110°51'40"W
Approximately 47 km south-east of Fort McMurray.

This name comes from the many fish, locally called sucker fish, to be found in the lake.

Sulphur Lake (lake)

84 D/9 - Sulphur Lake
12-89-3-W6
56°42'N 118°19'W
Approximately 71 km north of Fairview.

The name may refer to the existence of the mineral in the lake.

Sunday Creek (creek)

73 M/10 - Christina Lake
3-76-7-W4
55°37'N 110°52'W
Flows north into Christina Lake approximately 120 km north-east of Lac La Biche.

This name was officially adopted for the creek in 1955. Apparently the survey party that came through the area in the 1910s camped on the creek's banks on a Sunday.

Sunset House (locality)

83 N/2 - Snipe Lake
SW-5-71-19-W5
55°07'N 116°54'W
Approximately 25 km east of Valleyview.

It was the name chosen for the post office established here in 1929. The origin is unknown. Sam Pasicka was the first postmaster.

Supertest Hill (hill)
74 D/14 - Wood Creek
25-91-10-W4
56°55'30"N 111°27'55"W
Approximately 22 km north of Fort McMurray.

This is descriptive name for the man-made hill on the highway, now Highway 63, from Fort McMurray to the Syncrude and Suncor site. The grade was so steep that the road kept subsiding, and was completed with great difficulty. It was hard to manage, especially driving in winter, and so it became known locally as "Supertest Hill."

*****Surbiton** (former railway point)
83 M/10 - Woking
29-75-5-W6
55°32'N 118°44'W
Approximately 39 km north of Grande Prairie.

This Edmonton, Dunvegan and British Columbia Railway station was established around 1916. The name was later changed to Braeburn. It is named after a town near Wimbledon, south of London, in Surrey, England. The name means "southern grange, or outlying farm." It was most likely named by J.B. Prest, an engineer for the railway, who was responsible for naming other stations in the area after his home area. These include Esher, Prestville, Wanham and Woking. (see also Braeburn)

Surette Lake (lake)
84 K/7 - Child Lake
1-108-17-W5
58°20'45"N 116°41'00"W
Approximately 32 km south-east of High Level.

Named in 1914 by P.M.H. Le Blanc, DLS, after his field assistant, Germain Augustin Surette, during a township survey. Surette, a native of Ottawa, received his commission from the Dominion Lands Survey in March 1927.

Surmont Creek (creek)
74 D/6 - Gregoire Lake
11-86-8-W4
56°26'N 111°09'W
Flows north into Gregoire Lake approximately 33 km south south-east of Fort McMurray.

The precise origin of the name of this lake is unknown; the name appears on federal government maps as early as 1919.

Surmont Lake (lake)
74 D/6 - Gregoire Lake
27-84-8-W4
56°19'N 111°10'W
Approximately 47 km south south-east of Fort McMurray.

The precise origin of the name of this lake is unknown; the name appears on federal government maps as early as 1913.

Susan Lake (lake)
74 E/5 - Bitumount
19-97-10-W4
57°26'N 111°38'W
Approximately 80 km north north-east of Fort McMurray.

Named by A.W. Wheeler after Susan Berryman, a resident of Fort McMurray. (see also Bitumount)

Sutherland Creek (creek)
83 O/4 - House Mountain
35-69-10-W5
55°01'N 115°31'W
Flows north into Inverness River approximately 55 km south-west of Slave Lake.

Officially named in 1906 after Robert Sutherland, a member of a survey party.

Sutherland Island (island)
74 E/5 - Bitumount
14-96-11-W4
57°19'30"N 111°40'10"W
In Athabasca River, 70 km north north-west of Fort McMurray.

Named after John Sutherland, chief engineer of the Hudson's Bay Company steamer *Athabasca River*, who was a resident of Fort McMurray.

Sutton Creek (creek)
74 D/16 - High Hill River
30-90-3-W4
56°50'N 110°27'W
Flows west into High Hill River approximately 59 km east north-east of Fort McMurray.

This creek is named for Gordon Sutton, a member of a survey party in the area. It shows on a federal government map as early as 1914.

Sutton Lake (lake)
83 N/16 - Pentland Lake
27-78-14-W5
55°47'N 116°05'W
Approximately 50 km east of McLennan.

This lake was named in 1947 after Flight Lieutenant H.R. Sutton, DFC, who was born in Winnipeg in 1916 and received his early education in Edmonton. He enlisted in Edmonton in 1940 and received his commission after completing a pilot's training course. In 1941 he was awarded the Distinguished Flying Cross. He was reported missing and presumed dead in May 1943.

*****Swamp Creek** (creek)
83 M/16 - Codesa
15-13-78-4-W6
55°46'N 118°29'W
Flows east into Saddle (Burnt) River approximately 10 km east south-east of Spirit River.

---

*denotes rescinded name or former locality.

Likely descriptive, the name was changed to Bremner Creek in 1912. (see Bremner Creek)

Swan Hills (hills)
83 J/12 - Wallace Mountain
67-12-W5
54°45′N 115°45′W
Approximately 30 km west of the town of Swan Hills.

In aboriginal legends these three hills, known collectively as Swan Hills, and specifically as House Mountain, Deer Mountain and Wallace Mountain, are the home of thunder. In the hills are many huge birds and thunder is the sound of the flapping of their wings. The birds are said never to have harmed man but the aboriginal peoples claim it would be unwise to visit their abode. Since the birds never leave their home, no one has ever seen them. The river and the town take their name from the hills.

Swan Hills (town)
83 J/11 - Swan Hills
14-66-10-W5
54°43′N 115°24′W
Approximately 75 km south-west of Slave Lake.

The New Townsite of Swan Hills was established in 1959 because of the various companies that undertook works in the Swan Hills oilfield. The name for the townsite was officially adopted in 1960. At one point there was consideration being given to name the town Chalmers, after Thomas Chalmers, the Dominion Land Surveyor who came through the area in 1897. (see also Swan Hills and Deer Mountain)

---
*denotes rescinded name or former locality.

Swan Lake (lake)
84 N/15 - Lessard Creek
31-126-16-W5
59°59′N 116°47′W
Approximately 161 km north of High Level.

The name likely refers to the presence of the trumpeter swans in the area. They breed in the Grande Prairie region of Alberta, in and around lakes, large sloughs and rivers.

Swan Lake (lake)
83 N/4 - Sturgeon Heights
19-70-24-W5
55°04′N 117°49′W
Approximately 20 km west of Valleyview.

It was officially named in 1952 after field research was conducted. It is possibly descriptive of the presence of the birds in the area.

Swan Lake (lake)
84 A/11 - Blanchet Lake
15-89-21-W4
56°43′20″N 113°14′45″W
Approximately 113 km west of Fort McMurray.

The precise origin of the name of this lake is unknown; it may refer to the prevalence of the bird in the area.

*****Swan Lake** (lake)
74 D/8 - Gipsy Lake
33-86-3-W4
56°30′N 110°25′W
Approximately 55 km east south-east Fort McMurray.

(see Gordon Lake)

*****Swan Lake River** (river)
74 D/9 - Bunting Bay
15-89-3-W4
56°43′N 110°23′W

Flows north-west into Clearwater River approximately 62 km east of Fort McMurray.

(see Edwin Creek)

Swan Point (point)
83 O/6 - Kinuso
12-22-74-9-W5
55°26′N 115°18′W
Approximately 35 km west north-west of Slave Lake.

Named for the prevalence of swans, which use the area as a resting and nesting place.

*****Swan River** (locality)
83 O/6 - Kinuso
23-73-10-W5
55°55′N 115°35′W
Approximately 40 km west of Slave Lake.

Originally named for the nearby river, the area became known as Kinuso. (see Kinuso)

Swan River (river)
83 O/6 - Kinuso
9-21-74-9-W5
55°26′N 115°19′W
Flows north into Lesser Slave Lake approximately 35 km west north-west of Slave Lake.

The name was recorded by the Geological Survey of Canada in 1892 and is likely named for the abundance of the bird in the area. (see also Swan Hills and Swan Point)

Swan River (river)
84 I/11 - Stovel Lake
SE-10-112-21-W4
58°42′N 113°27′W
Flows south-east into Peace River approximately 211 km east of High Level.

Likely named for the prevalence of the bird in the area. The name was recorded as early as 1890 by the Geological Survey of Canada.

*Swan River (river)
84 I/12 - Buchanan Lake
12-3-112-22-W4
58°42′N 113°38′W
Flows south-east into Peace River approximately 200 km east of High Level.

(see Drolet Creek)

Swan River Indian Reserve No. 150E
(Indian reserve)
83 O/6 - Kinuso
73-10-W5
55°22′N 115°25′W
Approximately 40 km west north-west of Slave Lake.

It is named for its proximity to the river. When Treaty No. 8 was signed in 1899, the five Slave Lake Cree bands shared the lands around Lesser Slave Lake. With the increasing importance of agriculture, people migrated to the more fertile lands around the Driftpile and Swan Rivers. This reserve was surveyed in 1912. (see Swan River)

Swartz Lake (lake)
83 J/12 - Swartz Lake
6-66-11-W5
54°41′N 115°40′W
Approximately 16 km west of Swan Hills.

It appears as early as 1930 on a federal government map; after whom it is named is not known.

Sweathouse Creek (creek)
83 N/3 - Valleyview
3-15-70-21-W5
55°03′N 117°07′W
Flows north into the Little Smoky River approximately 10 km east of Valleyview.

The name comes from the sweat-lodges that the aboriginal people built along the creek. This name has been used since at least 1917.

---

*denotes rescinded name or former locality.

Sweathouse Creek (locality)
83 N/2 - Snipe Lake
69-19-W5
55°01′N 116°53′W
Approximately 70 km east of Valleyview.

The name was adopted in 1954; it takes its name from the nearby creek. (see Sweathouse Creek)

Sweeney Creek (creek)
84 D/5 - Boundary Lake
18-86-11-W6
56°28′N 119°44′W
Flows south into Little Clear River approximately 94 km north-west of Spirit River.

The origin of the name of this creek is unknown.

Sweetgrass Landing (hamlet)
74 L/13 - Baril River
SW-26-114-12-W4
58°56′N 111°55′W
Approximately 237 km north north-west of Fort McMurray.

It was established as a post office in 1961, and took its name for the nearby landing on the Peace River. The origin of the name may refer to the prevalence of the perennial sweet-smelling grass, *Hierchloe odorata* which is used by the aboriginal peoples for ceremonial rites of blessing and purification. Traditionally, it is an area used by the Cree and Chipewyan for hunting, and has been known as a good grazing area for bison, which might also account for the name; good grazing meant sweet grass.

Sweetheart Lake (lake)
74 D/3 - Alberta I D #18
31-83-9-W4
56°14′25″N 111°25′30″W
Approximately 53 km south of Fort McMurray.

The precise origin name of this lake is unknown; nevertheless it conjures up romantic images.

Sweezy Creek (creek)
73 M/16 - Cowper Lake
1-16-79-1-W4
55°50′N 110°05′W
Flows west into Landels River approximately 120 km south-east of Fort McMurray.

The origin of the name is not known; the name appears on a federal map of 1917. The creek may have been named after a survey crew member.

Swift Current Creek (creek)
84 I/7 - Heron Island
7-11-108-17-W4
58°22′N 112°43′W
Flows north-west into Birch River approximately 188 km north north-west of Fort McMurray.

The name shows on federal government maps as early as 1897, and is descriptive.

Swinnerton Lake (lake)
74 M/16 - Andrew Lake
SW-24-126-2-W4
59°57′N 110°13′W
Approximately 355 km north of Fort McMurray.

The name was submitted in 1958 by the Research Council of Alberta, and is named after the British paleontologist, H.H. Swinnerton (1875-1966), researcher and teacher. He was professor of geology, University College, Nottingham (later University of Nottingham), 1912-1946, professor emeritus, 1946-1966.

*Sylvester (former locality)
83 L/13 - Calahoo Creek
19-69-11-W6
55°00′N 119°41′W

Approximately 60 km west south-west of Grande Prairie.

The post office was established here in June 1936, and was named after the nearby feature. The first postmaster was T.R. Elliot. (see Sylvester Creek)

Sylvester Creek (creek)
83 L/13 - Calahoo Creek
27-68-12-W6
54°55'N 119°44'W
Flows north-east into Calahoo Creek approximately 63 km west south-west of Grande Prairie.

The creek is named after one of the early settlers in the area, Sylvester Belcourt. It is likely he was also involved in the fur trade. (see also Iroquois Creek and Calahoo Creek)

***Sylvester Creek** (creek)
83 M/4 - Rio Grande
14-20-70-11-W6
55°05'N 119°39'W
Flows north-east into Redwillow River approximately 51 km west of Grande Prairie.

Originally named after Sylvester Belcourt, an early resident in the area. (see Diamond Dick Creek)

---

*denotes rescinded name or former locality.

Taerum Lake (lake)
84 I/12 - Buchanan Lake
NW-25-110-24-W4
58°35′N 113°52′W
Approximately 186 km east of High Level.

A war casualty name, it was named in 1949 after Flight Lieutenant T.H. Taerum, DFC, born at Milo, Alberta, in 1920. He enlisted in the RCAF in Calgary in 1940, and received his air observer's badge. He proceeded overseas and served until he was reported missing, presumed dead, on September 16, 1943. He was awarded the Distinguished Flying Cross on May 5, 1943.

Talbot Lake (lake)
84 G/5 - Rossbear Lake
33-97-11-W5
57°28′N 115°43′W
Approximately 140 km south-east of High Level.

The name appears as early as 1916 on federal government maps; the lake was likely named after a survey crew member.

Tall Cree Indian Reserve No. 173
(Indian reserve)
84 G/14 - Wadlin Lake
103-9-W5
57°55′N 115°22′W
Approximately 120 km south-east of High Level.

The precise origin of the name of this reserve is unknown.

Tall Cree Indian Reserve No. 173A
(Indian reserve)
84 J/4 - Tall Cree
17-104-10-W5
58°02′N 115°36′W
Approximately 102 km south-east of High Level.

*denotes rescinded name or former locality.

The precise origin of the name of this reserve is unknown.

Tamarack Lake (lake)
73 M/1 - Scheltens Lake
8-72-1-W4
55°13′N 110°07′W
Approximately 90 km north of Cold Lake.

The lake which was referred to as early as 1912; the name is descriptive of the tree in the area. (see also Hackmatack Lake)

Tangent (hamlet)
83 N/13 - Tangent
32-78-24-W5
55°48′N 117°40′W
Approximately 30 km west north-west of Falher.

An Edmonton, Dunvegan and British Columbia Railway station opened here in 1916. It is the start of a 56-kilometre tangent or stretch of straight track.

Tanghe Creek (creek)
84 E/5 - Tanghe Creek
24-96-12-W6
57°21′N 119°48′W
Flows south into Chinchaga River approximately 140 km north-west of Manning.

This creek was named for Private Julius Tanghe killed in action on January 7th, 1944.

*****Tank** (railway point)
84 C/3 - Peace River
19-81-20-W5
56°02′N 117°08′W
Approximately 24 km south south-east of Peace River.
(see Nampa)

Tar Island (island)
74 D/14 - Wood Creek
18-92-9,10-W4
56°59′N 111°27′W

T~U~V

In Athabasca River, 30 km north of Fort McMurray.

The name for the island was recorded as early as 1892 by the Geological Survey of Canada and comes from the presence of the tar sands in the area. The island itself no longer exists since the Suncor plant was built on it.

Tar River (river)
74 E/5 - Bitumount
14-96-11-W4
57°19′N 111°40′W
Flows south-east into Athabasca River approximately 69 km north north-west of Fort McMurray.

This name is probably descriptive of exposed oil sands along the river bank. The name was noted in 1914 by J.B. McFarlane, DLS.

Tate Creek (creek)
84 N/5 - Russet creek
22-119-23-W5
59°21′N 117°52′W
Flows south-east into Steen River approximately 101 km north north-west of High Level.

The precise origin of the name of this creek is unknown. It was noted by J.R. Akins, DLS, during his survey in 1915.

*****Tawatchaw Creek** (creek)
84 A/13 - Liége River
2-91-24-W4
56°52′N 113°45′W
Flows south into Wabasca River approximately 149 km west of Fort McMurray.

(see Seaforth Creek)

Tawatchaw Valley (valley)
84 H/4 - Osi Lake
25-93-23-W4
57°06′N 113°33′W
Approximately 137 km west north-west of Fort McMurray.

The precise origin of the name of this valley is unknown; it may be a variation of a Cree word meaning "valley."

Tea Kettle Creek (creek)
74 E/4 - Fort MacKay
2-93-11-W4
57°02′00″N 111°38′21″W
Flows into Syncrude site, 28 km north north-west of Fort McMurray.

This creek flows west in to the dyke system at Syncrude, which now arrests its natural path to the Beaver River. It apparently received its name because of a tea kettle left hanging in a tree along its bank.

Tea Lakes (lakes)
83 J/14 - Deer Mountain
8-67-7-W5
54°47′N 115°01′W
Approximately 50 km south-east of Slave Lake.

Although the origin of the name is not precisely known, it may refer to the occurrence of the plant commonly known as Labrador Tea, *Ledum groenlandicum*, which can be found in muskegs and moist coniferous woods.

Teepee Creek (locality)
83 M/8 - Smoky Heights
5-74-3-W6
55°22′N 118°24′W
Approximately 30 km north-east of Grande Prairie.

The school district was established in 1920, and the post office was established in 1924. These and the community that grew up around here took their name from a nearby stream. The word tepee is adapted from the Sioux language and refers to the conical tents covered with skins used primarily by aboriginal peoples of the plains. The word came to have a more generic meaning referring to any aboriginal dwelling made from skins.

Telephone Lake (lake)
74 E/1 - Alberta-Saskatchewan
29-94-3-W4
57°10′53″N 110°27′15″W
Approximately 75 km north-east of Fort McMurray.

This lake is shaped like the receiver on a telephone. The lake is locally known as AGT Lake. A similarly shaped lake just across the Saskatchewan border is called Sask Tel Lake. Although the name AGT Lake is well-established through local usage, the Historic Sites Board felt the official name should be descriptive, rather than have the lake take the name of a business.

Tepee Creek (creek)
84 A/5 - Tepee Lake
9-86-24-W4
56°26′N 113°43′W
Flows east into Wabasca River approximately 149 km west south-west of Fort McMurray.

The precise origin of the name of this creek is unknown although it may refer to a time when aboriginal lodgings were found by the creek.

Tepee Creek (creek)
84 N/16 - Alberta-Northwest Territories
18-125-14-W5
59°52′N 116°26′W
Flows north-east into Yates River approximately 154 km north north-east of High Level.

Its source is Tepee Lake. The name was submitted for approval in 1932 by C.B.C. Donnelly, DLS.

Tepee Lake (lake)
84 A/5 - Tepee Lake
36-85-26-W4
56°25′N 113°59′W
Approximately 159 km west south-west of Fort McMurray.

The name for this feature was recorded by A.W. Ponton, DLS, as Woodenhouse Creek in 1908. By 1915 the name is recorded on a map as Tepee Creek; therefore the name is likely descriptive.

Test Lake (lake)
74 E/8 - Trout Creek
15-97-3-W4
57°25′02″N 110°24′10″W
Approximately 97 km north-east of Fort MacKay.

This lake was named by two trappers interested in developing this area and known to have sown cattail seeds in the lake. (see also Cattail Lake and Hopeful Lake)

Tethul River (river)
74 M/14 - Tulip Lake
NE-33-126-9-W4
60°00′N 111°29′W
Flows north into NWT approximately 355 km north of Fort McMurray.

Although it is likely Dene in origin, the meaning is not known. At one time the feature was known locally as Hanging Ice River. The name Tethul River was officially approved in 1926.

Thickwood Hills (hills)
84 A/9 - Boiler Rapids
33-88-15-W4
56°40′N 112°10′W

Approximately 40 km west south-west of Fort McMurray.

The name is likely descriptive.

Thinahtea Creek (creek)
84 M/13 - Lake May
34-125-12-W6
59°54′N 120°00′W
Flows west into British Columbia approximately 159 km north north-west of Rainbow Lake.

The name is aboriginal in origin; its precise meaning is not known. The name appears as early as 1913 on a Peace River sketch map.

*Third Battle River (river)
84 F/3 - Crummy Lake
19-94-21-W5
57°10′N 117°22′W
Flows south-east into Notikewin River approximately 29 km north north-east Manning.

Renamed Meikle River, Third Battle River was its earlier name. Whether it was named because it was the third river called Battle, or whether this was the place where the third battle took place, likely between the Cree and Beaver Indians, is not known. (see also Meikle River and Notikewin River)

Thordarson Creek (creek)
84 E/15 - Waniandy Creek
7-101-5-W6
57°45′N 118°48′W
Flows east into Chinchaga River approximately 89 km south south-east of Rainbow Lake.

Named in commemoration of Sapper Laurence C. Thordarson, killed in action December 12, 1944.

---

*denotes rescinded name or former locality.

Thornbury Lake (lake)
73 M/12 - Thornbury Lake
NW-34-76-11-W4
55°38′N 111°39′W
Approximately 80 km north north-east of Lac La Biche.

William Thornbury was an axeman on the 1912 survey crew working in this area.

Three Creeks (locality)
84 C/6 - Weberville
9-85-20-W5
56°21′N 117°05′W
Approximately 18 km north of Peace River.

This former hamlet took its name from the nearby unofficially named water feature Three Creeks. J.H. Johnston, DLS surveying the township in 1915, described Three Creeks as "a stream averaging ten feet in width and one foot deep runs across the centre of the township, in a valley averaging about eighty feet deep with steep slopes." A post office was established here in 1931, and the first postmaster was T. McCann.

Thultue Lake (lake)
84 P/12 - Thultue Lake
24-122-22-W4
59°37′N 113°39′W
Approximately 230 km east north-east of High Level.

This descriptive name was originally recorded by Alexander Mackenzie in 1801, and is apparently a Chipewyan word meaning bog.

Thurston Lake (lake)
84 M/16 - Thurston Lake
9-126-1-W6
59°56′N 118°07′W
Approximately 163 km north north-west of High Level.

It is not known after whom this lake is named.

Tieland (locality)
83 J/16 - Chisholm
14-67-2-W5
54°48′N 114°11′W
Approximately 58 km west north-west of Athabasca.

The locality was originally established in 1914 as a station on the Edmonton, Dunvegan and British Columbia Railway line. In the area, thousands of ties were cut for railway use during construction.

Timeu (locality)
83 J/10 - Timeu Creek
6-64-4-W5
54°30′N 114°35′W
Approximately 45 km north north-west of Barrhead.

A post office opened here in August 1930 with the spelling Timue. A year later the name was corrected to the spelling of the name of the nearby creek. The first postmaster was A. B. Dieffert. (see also Timeu Creek)

Timeu Creek (creek)
83 J/8 - Shoal Creek
19-63-3-W5
54°28′N 114°27′W
Flows into Athabasca River approximately 44 km north north-west of Barrhead.

This name appears on federal government maps as early as 1917. Its precise origin is not known; it has been speculated that it was named after an early resident of the area. The files of the Geographic Board of Canada state that *timeu* is a Cree word meaning deep. (see also Timeu)

Toad Hill (hill)
83 L/14 - Wapiti
2-14-69-8-W6
54°58′02″N 119°06′05″W
Approximately 30 km south south-west of Grande Prairie.

At one time there was a large toad population on the hill. Although there have been other names for this feature with an elevation of 808 metres, Toad Hill has become the locally established name that is used by all local residents. It was officially approved in 1991 after field research was conducted.

Tokyo Snye Channel (channel)
74 L/10 - Big Point
16-29-110-5-W4
58°35′N 110°47′W
Flows north into Big Point Channel approximately 200 km north north-east of Fort McMurray.

According to one source it was named by the Japanese interned there during World War II; however, there were no internment camps that far north during the war. The more likely explanation dates from around the 1930s. There was a commercial fishing operation there at that time run by Mr. McInnes, who recruited Japanese fisherman to work along with the local aboriginal fishermen. They camped along this channel while working on the freezer barge that was used as a floating fish processing platform. A snye usually refers to a narrow, meandering, sluggish side channel of a river. It may be a corruption of the Canadian French *chenal*, meaning channel. An older spelling of snye makes the connection clearer, i.e., "shnye."

Tolstad (railway point)
83 M/2 - Grande Prairie
6-33-69-4-W6
55°01′N 118°33′W
Approximately 20 km south-east of Grande Prairie.

This was named after John Tolstad, who came to the Grande Prairie district from Norway in 1929. He joined the Signal Corps in 1940, and died in France in September 1944.

Tomato Creek (creek)
83 P/4 - Ranch
3-11-71-24-W4
55°07′N 113°35′W
Flows north-west into Athabasca River approximately 60 km east of Slave Lake.

The origin of the name is not known; the name appears on maps as early as 1918.

Tony Creek (creek)
83 K/6 - Tony Creek
23-62-21-W5
54°22′N 117°03′W
Flows east into Little Smoky River approximately 95 km north-west of Edson.

The name shows on a federal government map as early as 1916; although its origin is not known, it may have been named after a survey crew member.

Topland (locality)
83 J/7 - Fort Assiniboine
23-62-7-W5
54°22′N 114°58′W
Approximately 45 km north-west of Barrhead.

Established as a post office in 1914, it was named because of its situation on a ridge between the Athabasca and Freeman rivers. The first postmaster was E. Couch.

Tourangeau, Lake (lake)
84 K/1 - Mustus Lake
17-106-15-W5
58°12′N 116°26′W
Approximately 2 km north-west of La Crete, 54 km south-east of High Level.

Named for Louis Tourangeau, he was one of the first settlers in the area of La Crête.

Tourangeau Creek (creek)
84 O/14 - Alberta-Northwest Territories
35-126-9-W5
60°00′N 115°27′W
Flows north-west into NWT approximately 187 km north north-east of High Level.

Likely named after a resident in the area, it has been named since at least the 1950s.

Tower Lake (lake)
74 D/13 - Ruth Lake
12-90-12-W4
56°47′00″N 111°47′40″W
Approximately 25 km north-west of Fort McMurray.

The name for this lake comes from its proximity to the local fire tower.

Trading Post Lake (lake)
84 E/4 - Mearon Creek
18-93-11-W6
57°05′N 119°45′W
Approximately 131 km west north-west of Manning.

This lake was named Trading Post Lake by the local trappers and natives for the trading post that operated there during the 1920s and 1930s.

Traverse Creek (creek)
83 N/9 - Grouard
24-75-15-W4
55°31′N 116°12′W
Flows south-east into Lesser Slave Lake approximately 100 km south-east of Peace River.

Common belief states this name is a misspelling of the surname of the homesteaders who lived there, Sidney and Oliver Travers. The Dominion Lands Survey notes do show that Travers̲e Creek bordered the lands cleared by Oliver Travers. A "traverse" was the term used to describe the distance covered on any given day of field work done by a survey crew. Was this a deliberate pun? The Travers brothers moved to the Grouard area in 1899 after having made an unsuccessful attempt at a journey to the Klondike a year before. Oliver fought in the Boer War and upon his return in 1905, he and Sidney started a ranching and freighting business. More Travers brothers followed from their home in Middlesex, England and, through the years, the Travers family became well-known citizens of the High Prairie-Grouard area.

Treasure Loch (lake)
74 M/16 - Andrew Lake
10-126-3-W4
59°56'N 110°25'W
Approximately 352 km north of Fort McMurray.

The name was suggested in the late 1950s by a geological field party due to circumstances encountered. These circumstances were not recorded. *Loch* is the Gaelic word for lake.

Triangle (locality)
83 N/7 - Triangle
NW-21-74-18-W5
55°26'N 116°43'W
Approximately 15 km west of High Prairie.

Highways 2 and 2A form a rough triangle north-west of the locality. These highways would have been built based on existing trails, giving the community a descriptive name. The post office was established here in December 1933, the first postmaster being Mrs. G. E. McIntyre.

Trident Creek (creek)
84 I/14 - Big Slough
SW-1-113-21-W4
58°47'N 113°24'W
Flows south-east into Peace River approximately 219 km east north-east of High Level.

It was officially named in the 1940s. The origin of the name is unknown, but two possible descriptive reasons may be suggested. A trident is a three-tined or three-pronged implement, for example a fish spear, or the sceptre attributed to Poseidon/Neptune, the Greek/Roman god of the sea. Therefore, the name of the creek might come from the fact that three smaller streams, in the shape of a trident, form its headwaters, although this is not obvious when you look at a map. It also may refer to the literal translation of the word, i.e. "three-toothed." When viewed from the air, or on maps, there are three sharp bends in the course of the stream which, with some imagination, resemble canine teeth.

Trout Lake (creek)
74 E/8 - Trout Creek
29-96-1-W4
57°21'N 110°08'W
Flows south-west into Firebag River approximately 104 km north-east of Fort McMurray.

This name is probably descriptive of trout in its waters.

Trout Lake (hamlet)
84 B/7 - Bat Lake
34-86-4-W5
56°30'N 114°32'W
Approximately 157 km north of Slave Lake.

It is likely named for an unofficially named lake nearby. A post office was established here in 1973; the first postmaster was M. Zachary.

Trout Mountain (mountain)
84 B/9 - Quitting Lake
28-89-3-W5
56°45'N 114°25'W
Approximately 160 km north north-east of Slave Lake.

It has been known by this name since at least 1905, and may take its name from the early name of Peerless Lake, Trout Lake. Its elevation is 777 metres above sea level.

Trout River (river)
84 A/5 - Tepee lake
24-84-25-W4
56°18'N 113°49'W
Flows south-east into Wabasca River approximately 120 km south-west of Fort McMurray.

The name appears on federal government maps as early as 1905, and is likely descriptive of the abundance of fish in the river.

Trumpeter (post office)
83 M/3 - Wembley
10-72-9-W6
55°14'N 119°17'W
Approximately 30 km west of Grande Prairie.

This post office was opened on the armed forces base in November 1966. According to one source it is named after the trumpeter swans that nest in this area.

Tulip Lake (lake)
74 M/14 - Tulip Lake
33-125-7-W4
59°54'N 111°08'W
Approximately 345 km north of Fort McMurray.

It was named in 1929; the name is descriptive of the shape.

Turtle Lake (lake)
74 M/7 - Alberta
35-119-4-W4
59°23'N 110°35'W
Approximately 291 km north of Fort McMurray.

It was named in 1929; the name is descriptive of the shape.

Twin Lake (lake)
83 P/10 - Parallel Lake
8-18-76-19-W4
55°35'N 112°58'W

Approximately 90 km north north-west of Lac La Biche.

The origin is not precisely known; however it may date from the time of the survey in 1913 when, owing to water levels, there appeared to be two lakes joined by a narrow strip of water.

Twin Lakes (lakes)
84 F/5 - Gofitt Creek
29-97-22-W5
57°27′N 117°32′W
Approximately 58 km north of Manning.

This name is descriptive.

Twin Lakes (lakes)
74 D/6 - Gregoire Lake
10-84-8-W4
56°16′10″N 110°10′55″W
Approximately 53 km south south-east of Fort McMurray.

This descriptive name for these lakes comes from their proximity, rather than any resemblance to each other in shape or size. A short creek connects the two lakes.

Twin Lakes (lakes)
83 M/4 - Rio Grande
NW-27-69-11-W6
55°00′N 119°35′W
Approximately 60 km west south-west of Grande Prairie.

This name is descriptive and refers to two lakes in close proximity. The name has been official since 1951.

Twin Lakes (lakes)
74 E/14 - Pearson Lake
8-102-7-W4
57°50′30″N 111°06′30″W
Approximately 121 km north north-east of Fort McMurray.

A descriptive name for this lake that is well-known to pilots and all users of the Winter Road that goes from Fort McMurray to Fort Chipewyan.

Twin Lakes Creek (creek)
84 B/15 - Kidney Lake
25-91-4-W5
56°56′N 114°30′W
Flows north into Wabasca River approximately 184 km north of Slave Lake.

The precise origin of the name of this lake is unknown; however, it does flow near a pair of lakes.

Two Creeks (creek)
83 K/8 - Two Creek
12-61-16-W5
54°15′N 116°15′W
Flows south into the Athabasca River approximately 40 km west north-west of Whitecourt.

It appears on a 1916 federal government map, and the name is possibly descriptive of the two tributary streams that join to make Two Creeks.

Two Creeks (locality)
83 K/8 - Two Creek
28-61-16-W5
54°18′N 116°21′W
Approximately 43 km west north-west of Whitecourt.

When established in 1956, it took its name from the nearby creek. It was to become a thriving hamlet along the newly constructed Highway 43.

Two Lakes (lakes)
83 N/5 - Puskwaskau River
12-73-25-W5
55°18′N 117°43′W
Approximately 60 km east north-east of Grande Prairie.

The name was approved in 1952 after field research was conducted. The name is descriptive.

Two Round Lakes (lakes)
74 E/14 - Pearson Lake
21-101-7-W4
57°47′N 111°06′W
Approximately 120 km north north-east of Fort McMurray.

These two descriptively named lakes are used as navigational points for pilots and local trappers.

Tyne Lake (lake)
74 L/8 - Brander Lake
4-109-1-W4
58°26′N 110°07′W
Approximately 196 km north north-east of Fort McMurray.

Likely named after a crew member along a survey of the 28th Baseline that was done in the mid-1910s. The 28th Baseline falls between Townships 108 and 109.

Underwood Lake (lake)
73 M/8 - Grist Lake
5-73-3-W4
55°17′N 110°25′W
Approximately 100 km north of Cold Lake.

The origin of the name is not known; it appears on federal government maps as early as 1917. Perhaps it was named after a member of the survey party.

Updike Creek (creek)
83 M/5 - Hythe
9-75-13-W6
55°29′N 119°56′W
Flows north-west into Albright Creek approximately 76 km west north-west of Grande Prairie.

(see Updike Lake)

Updike Lake (lake)
83 M/5 - Hythe
29-74-12-W6
55°26'N 119°48'W
Approximately 69 km west north-west of Grande Prairie.

Originally known as Rat Lake after the abundance of muskrats in the area. The name Rat Lake was considered "objectionable" for there was a number of other features by the same name in the province, therefore, the name was changed to Updike Lake in the 1920s. Charles Updike Smith was a settler who homesteaded near the lake. It is the source of Updike Creek.

Upland Lake (lake)
84 P/10 - Upland Lake
SE-12-123-17-W4
59°40'N 112°47'W
Approximately 275 km east north-east of High Level.

Officially named in the 1950s, it likely took its name from the fact it is somewhat up slope in the Ninishith Hills.

Upper Hay River Indian Reserve No. 212
(Indian reserve)
84 N/4 - Meander River
6-116-22-W5
59°03'N 117°45'W
Approximately 66 km north north-west of High Level.

Named for its proximity to Hay River, which runs through the reserve.

Uswell Slough (marsh)
83 M/3 - Wembley
S -36-71-8-W6
55°11'N 119°05'W
Approximately 15 km west of Grande Prairie.

This feature was named after the Uswell family, who still live in the area. It was first proposed for naming in 1951, and was made official some time after that.

Utamik Lake (lake)
84 J/5 - Sled Island
7-109-12-W5
58°27'N 115°59'W
Approximately 66 km south south-east of High Level.

This Cree name meaning deep was chosen to replace the name Deep Lake, as there were three other lakes called Deep Lake in Alberta.

Utikoomak Indian Reserve No. 155
(Indian reserve)
83 O/13 - Atikameg
80-11-W5
55°55'N 115°35'W
Approximately 85 km north-west of Slave Lake.

The ancestors of most band members are Woodland Cree who lived in the area in the late 18th century. Later, Métis people followed the fur trade into this area. Under Treaty No. 8 of 1899, the three reserves were surveyed in 1909, and allocated to the band. Utikoomak is a variation of the Cree word for "whitefish" and the reserve takes its name from nearby Utikuma Lake. (see also Utikuma Lake)

Utikoomak Indian Reserve No. 155A
(Indian reserve)
83 O/14 - Utikuma River
17-80-9-W5
55°56'N 115°23'W
Approximately 80 km north north-west of Slave Lake.

(see Utikuma Lake and Utikoomak Indian Reserve 155)

Utikoomak Indian Reserve No. 155B
(Indian reserve)
84 B/4 - Mink River
23-81-11-W4
56°02'N 115°35'W
Approximately 97 km north north-west of Slave Lake.

(see Utikuma Lake and Utikoomak Indian Reserve 155)

Utikuma Lake (lake)
83 O/14 - Utikuma River
79-10-W5
55°50'N 115°25'W
Approximately 73 km north-west of Slave Lake.

The name is a variation of the Cree word for "whitefish" which are plentiful in the lake.

Utikuma River (river)
84 B/2 - Muskwa Lake
2-83-7-W5
56°10'N 114°40'W
Flows north north-east into Muskwa Lake approximately 98 km north of Slave Lake.

This name is a variation of the Cree name for "whitefish," which are likely plentiful in the river. A.H. Hawkins, DLS, records the name Whitefish River for this feature in his notes during the 1910 survey season.

Utikumasis Lake (lake)
83 O/13 - Atikameg
5-80-11-W5
55°5'N 115°41'W
Approximately 89 km north-west of Slave Lake.

The name shows on a 1915 plan as Atikamisis Lake and is a variation of the Cree for "whitefish," of which there are many in the lakes in the area. The "sis" suffix means little or small. P.R.A. Belanger, DLS, records the name as Atikamesis Lake in 1914.

Vader Creek (creek)
84 E/10 - Vader Creek
18-100-5-W6
57°41'N 118°48'W
Flows north-west into Chinchaga River approximately 97 km south-east of Rainbow Lake.

A war memorial name, commemorating Private James D. Vader, killed in action October 10, 1944.

Valhalla (locality)
83 M/6 - La Glace
2-75-10-W6
55°28'N 119°26'W
Approximately 49 km north-west of Grande Prairie.

In Norse mythology, Valhalla is the home of the Viking heroes after death. The name was suggested by Reverend H.N. Ronning (1862-1950), a Lutheran pastor who

Valhalla, n.d.

founded the settlement, where a number of Scandinavians settled. Pastor Ronning was the father of Chester Ronning, the Canadian diplomat who for many years worked in China. The post office was established in 1916; the first postmaster was G.R. Owens.

Valhalla Centre (hamlet)
83 M/6 - La Glace
3-4-18-74-9-W6
55°24'N 119°23'W
Approximately 42 km north-west of Grande Prairie.

The post office was established here in February 1923. The first postmaster was O. Horte. (see Valhalla)

Valhalla Lake (lake)
83 M/6 - La Glace
3-74-10-W6
55°23'N 119°27'W
Approximately 45 km west north-west of Grande Prairie.

Originally known as Glass Lake, due to the way the sunset reflected on its surface. Renamed after the Reverend H.N. Ronning named the district Valhalla. (see Valhalla and Glass Lake)

Valleyview (town)
83 N/3 - Valleyview
70-22-W5
55°04'N 117°17'W
Approximately 100 km east of Grande Prairie.

The area was once known as Red Willow Creek, or *Minghkopower seepesis*, by the Cree. The Valleyview post office was established in February 1929, with D. Williamson as the first postmaster. The name is descriptive, for from the spot could be seen the valleys of the Red Willow and Sturgeon creeks.

Vandersteene Lake (lake)
84 B/9 - Quitting Lake
5-88-3-W5
56°35'30"N 114°25'30"W
Approximately 146 km north north-east of Slave Lake.

Named after Father Rogier Vandersteene (1918-1976), who was known and respected throughout the north-west for his missionary work over 30 years. Vandersteene was born in Belgium and came to Canada in 1946 to Grouard, where he learnt Cree. He served at Atikameg and Wabasca from 1946 to 1949, then at Little Red River and Fort Vermilion from 1949 to 1953. Later he was at Trout Lake and Joussard. He returned to Grouard in 1969 and, five years later, went to Fox Lake, John D'Or Prairie and Garden Creek. Vandersteene was a talented artist. He painted in oils, acrylic and watercolours, as well as working at sculpture, woodcut etchings and glasswork; nearly all his work was related to his missionary activity and reflected a Cree symbolization of Christian beliefs. Vandersteene had eclectic interests, he loved gardening and plants, he published poetry and used Cree melodies for Church hymns. He lectured on aboriginal spirituality and the fundamental conflicts he saw with European values, and was highly critical of both church and government bureaucracy in relation to the Cree.

Vanrena (locality)
84 D/2 - Hines Creek
28-81-4-W6
56°03'N 118°31'W
Approximately 7 km south-west of Fairview.

Originally established as a post office in 1914, the name is a combination of portions of names of early settlers, including Mrs. Van. The first postmaster was H. Propst.

Vardie River (river)
84 L/14 - Vardie River
20-113-7-W6
58°50'N 119°08'W
Flows south south-west into Mega River approximately 39 km north north-east of Rainbow Lake.

The name was recorded by E.W. Hubbell, DLS, during his survey of the Zama-Hay Lakes area. According to the files of the Geographic Board of Canada, when it was to be officially named in 1922, it was then locally known by its Slavey name, which was transliterated into *Vardi*. This means amber, referring to the colour of the water. It "happily coincided" with the maiden name of J.B. O'Sullivan's mother, which was Vardie. The local name for this stream is *Mbehkeetthí Ts'eghee Zahéh* which in Slavey means Shrub, or Bushy Creek.

Vermilion Chutes (chutes)
84 J/7 - Vermilion Chutes
11-108-6-W5
58°22′N 114°53′W
Approximately 134 km east south-east of High Level.

Vermilion Falls, Peace River, ca.1900

The name Vermilion Chutes refers to both the Rapids and Falls, which appear on older maps. The actual name Vermilion is most probably descriptive of the red ochre on the south bank of the Peace River. The name was recorded as early as 1888 by the Geological Survey of Canada.

*Vermilion Chutes (former locality)
84 J/7 - Vermilion Chutes
108-6-W5
58°22′N 114°51′W

---

*denotes rescinded name or former locality.

Approximately 134 km east south-east of High Level.

Because of a small concentration of population at that location, the name was suggested for the community in 1944. It was named for the nearby feature. In 1986 the name was rescinded since there were few people left.

Vermilion Lake (lake)
84 O/15 - Vermilion Lake
SE-4-126-6-W5
59°55′N 114°58′W
Approximately 195 km north-east of High Level.

Officially approved in 1964, it was named after Alexander Vermilion (1895-1962), a trapper in Wood Buffalo National Park.

Vermilion River (river)
84 I/11 - Stovel Lake
SE-2-112-21-W4
58°42′N 113°25′W
Flows north-east into Peace River approximately 213 km east of High Level.

Likely named for iron oxide which would colour the rocks and soil. The name was recorded as early as 1890 by the Geological Survey of Canada.

Verte Island (island)
83 M/16 - Codesa
S -6-80-3-W6
55°54′N 118°27′W
Approximately 27 km north-east of Spirit River in the Peace River.

On a federal government map from 1917, the name is shown as Île Verte, which in French means Green Island. It is likely descriptive of the vegetation.

Vesta Creek (creek)
84 E/9 - Dryden Creek
10-101-1-W6
57°45′N 118°03′W

Flows north-west into Keg River approximately 95 km north north-west of Manning.

When J.R. Akins, DLS, first noted the name in the 1915 survey, it was transcribed as Vista Creek, which may have been in reference to the view from its banks. Somehow, the name changed. There may be another explanation. "Vesta" is defined as a short wooden match, in reference to the Roman household goddess of the hearth. Whether a connection grew between the feature and matches is not known.

Victor Creek (creek)
73 M/1 - Sheltens River
9-36-71-1-W4
55°12′N 110°00′W
Flows into Saskatchewan, approximately 75 km north of Cold Lake.

Possibly named after Victor Gay, of Lloydminster, member of a survey party. The name appears as early as 1914 on a federal government map.

Vixen Creek (creek)
83 M/16 - Codesa
5-20-79-1-W6
55°51′N 118°06′W
Flows north into Fox Creek approximately 45 km east of Spirit River.

The name for this creek was well known and in use by the time the Dominion Land Surveyors were in the area in the early 1910s. Vixen is the word for female fox, and it comes from *fyxen*, the feminine form of the Old English word for fox. It is possible the creek is called this because of the prevalence of the animal in the area. The creek it flows into is called Fox Creek.

Vokes Lake (lake)
84 P/3 - Patenaude Lake
NE-18-117-19-W4
59°10′N 113°13′W

Approximately 233 km east north-east of High Level.

The lake was named in 1950 after Lieutenant-Colonel Frederick Alexander Vokes, who died of wounds sustained in action in Italy in August 1944. Col. Vokes, born in Ceylon in 1906, joined the army in Calgary in September 1939. He commanded the B.C. Dragoons (the 9th Armoured Regiment) in Italy and led a formation known as Vokes Force. His brother, Major-General Christopher Vokes, commanded the 1st Canadian Division.

***Wabasca** (hamlet)
83 P/13 - South Wabasca Lake
32-80-25-W4
56°00′N 113°53′W
Approximately 95 km north-east of Slave Lake.

The post office opened here in August 1908, taking its name from nearby features. The first postmaster was W.T. Livock. In 1982, it amalgamated with the hamlet just south, to form Wabasca-Desmarais. (see also Wabasca River and Wabasca-Desmarais)

Wabasca/Desmarais (hamlet)
83 P/13 - South Wabasca Lake
27-80-25-W4
55°58′N 113°51′W
Approximately 95 km north-east of Slave Lake.

The hamlets of Wabasca and Desmarais combined to make the hamlet of Wabasca-Desmarais in 1982. (see also Wabasca River, Wabasca and Desmarais)

Wabasca Indian Reserve No.166
(Indian reserve)
83 P/13 - South Wabasca Lake
79-23-W4
55°53′N 113°31′W
Approximately 105 km north-east of Slave Lake.

The five Wabasca Reserves are inhabited by the Bigstone Cree Band. In 1899, the Treaty Commission and the Half-Breed Commission established these reserves through Treaty No. 8. In 1901 a mission school was opened by the Oblates of Mary Immaculate and the Sisters of Providence. The reserves take their names from the nearby river. (see Wabasca River)

---

*denotes rescinded name or former locality.

Wabasca Indian Reserve No. 166A
(Indian reserve)
83 P/13 - South Wabasca Lake
19-80-24-W4
55°57′N 113°46′W
Approximately 98 km North-east of Slave Lake.

(see Wabasca Indian Reserve No. 166 and Wabasca River)

Wabasca Indian Reserve No. 166 B
(Indian reserve)
83 P/13 - South Wabasca Lake
26-80-26-W4
55°58′N 113°57′W
Approximately 92 km North-east of Slave Lake.

(see Wabasca Indian Reserve No. 166 and Wabasca River)

Wabasca Indian Reserve No. 166C
(Indian reserve)
84 A/4 - North Wabasca Lake
27-82-25-W4
56°08′N 113°50′W
Approximately 109 km north-east of Slave Lake.

(see Wabasca Indian Reserve No. 166 and Wabasca River)

Wabasca Indian Reserve No.166 D
(Indian reserve)
83 P/13 - South Wabasca Lake
5-80-25-W4
55°55′N 113°53′W
Approximately 92 km north-east of Slave Lake.

(see Wabasca Indian Reserve No. 166 and Wabasca River)

Wabasca River (river)
84 J/6 - Adams Landing
6-108-8-W5
58°22′N 115°20′W

W~X~Y~Z

Flows north into Peace River approximately 107 km south south-east of High Level.

This name is apparently a corruption of an aboriginal word, *wapuskau*, meaning "grassy narrows," however, recently a Cree elder from the Wabasca area said the word referred to a body of water with whitecaps on it. The Wabasca River is called the Loon River or *Makwa Sepe* by residents in the Fort Vermilion area. Alexander Mackenzie (1793) and George Simpson (1828) both record this river as the Loon. R.G. McConnell in his 1893 report, and G. Mair in 1908, both comment on the inaccuracy of this application and point out that it should be named the Wabasca or (Wahpooskow). In 1920, C.P. Hotchkiss, DLS, stated the Wabasca is still locally called the Loon River. In 1892, the Geological Survey of Canada noted that portion of the river between Island Lake and Sandy Lake was called Sandy Lake Creek.

Wabasca Settlement (settlement)
83 P/13 - South Wabasca Lake
5-81-25-W4
55°57′N 113°50′W
Approximately 98 km north-east of Slave Lake.

Named after the features of South and North Wabasca lakes, near the settlement. The settlement was first surveyed in 1913. The name was recorded as Wabiskaw Settlement. (see also Wabasca River and Wabasca/Desmarais)

Wabatanisk Creek (creek)
83 N/11 - Donnelly
24-75-22-W5
55°31′N 117°17′W

Flows north into the Little Smoky River approximately 35 km south-west of McLennan.

Wabatanisk is Cree for "white mud" and was known by that name in 1914 when the Dominion Land Surveyors were working in the area. In the early days the river bottom and bank were a white-muddy clay. Aboriginal people in the area used this mud to chink log buildings.

Waddell Creek (creek)
73 M/15 - Bohn Lake
16-9-79-6-W4
55°50′N 110°52′W
Flows east into Christina River approximately 110 km south of Fort McMurray.

Named after W.H. Waddell, a surveyor who was working in the area in 1915.

Wadlin Lake (lake)
84 G/13 - Alberta
4-101-10-W5
57°44′N 115°35′W
Approximately 124 km south-east of High Level.

Likely named after L.N. Wadlin, DLS, the name appears on a federal government map as early as 1916.

*****Wagner** (hamlet)
83 O/7 - Slave Lake
27-73-7-W5
55°21′N 114°59′W
Approximately 18 km north-west of Slave Lake.

This Edmonton, Dunvegan and British Columbia Railway station was built in 1914 and named after a resident engineer of the company. In 1985 it was formed into the widespread hamlet of Canyon Creek/Widewater/Wagner.

---

*denotes rescinded name or former locality.

Wagon Creek (creek)
84 D/9 - Sulphur Lake
15-87-1-W6
56°32′N 118°05′W
Flows south into Whitemud River approximately 49 km north-west of Grimshaw.

The precise origin of the name of this creek is unknown.

Waldo Creek (creek)
84 J/9 - Fifth Meridian
13-111-2-W5
53°38′N 114°14′W
Flows south-east into Peace River approximately 171 km east north-east of High Level.

The precise origin of the name of this lake is unknown.

Wallace Creek (creek)
74 E/8 - Trout Creek
29-95-1-W4
57°16′N 110°08′W
Flows south-west from Saskatchewan into Firebag River approximately 98 km north-east of Fort McMurray.

This feature was named after J.N. Wallace, DLS, who surveyed the east outline of this township, which is the Alberta-Saskatchewan border, in 1910. By 1914, it appears on a federal government map under this name.

Wallace Island (island)
74 M/16 - Andrew Lake
NE-33-125-1-W4
59°55′N 110°07′W
Approximately 353 km north of Fort McMurray in Andrew Lake.

It was named in the late 1950s after Robert Charles Wallace, an early president of the University of Alberta. Dr. Wallace, a geologist, headed the University of Alberta from 1928 to 1936, when he became principal at Queen's University in Kingston, a post he held until 1951.

Wallace Mountain (mountain)
83 J/13 - Wallace Mountain
69-13-W5
54°58′N 115°48′W
Approximately 60 km south-west of Slave Lake.

Named after James Nevin Wallace, DLS (1870-1941), who had a long experience as a surveyor in the Canadian West. He was a member of the Alberta-British Columbia Boundary Commission from 1913 to 1924. The name was officially approved in 1906. It is one of three features which comprise Swan Hills. (see also Swan Hills)

Wallace River (river)
83 N/1 - Bellrose Lake
15-33-69-14-W5
55°02′N 116°04′W
Flows north-east into East Prairie River approximately 178 km east of Grande Prairie.

Likely named after James Nevin Wallace, DLS (1870-1941), who had a long experience as a surveyor in the Canadian West. He was a member of the Alberta-British Columbia Boundary Commission from 1913 to 1924. The name was officially approved in 1906.

Wally Lake (lake)
84 M/6 - Wally Lake
21-120-8-W6
59°27′N 119°19′W
Approximately 102 km north of Rainbow Lake.

The name Wally Lake was submitted by B. M. Rustad, an Alberta Land Surveyor following his survey in 1964. The lake is probably named after Charles Wilton (Wally) Youngs who was, at the time of naming, Director of Surveys for the Alberta government. The local name for this lake is *Ttetanitthí Mieh*, Slavey for Swanhead Lake. The origin of this name is unknown but has been used by the Slavey since as early as 1900.

Wandering River (hamlet)

83 P/1 - Wandering River
SW-6-72-16-W4
55°12′N 112°28′W
Approximately 58 km north north-west of Lac La Biche.

The name was taken from the nearby river and is descriptive. This locality has a post office, opened in February 1932 and the first postmaster being A.G. Coonan.

Wandering River (river)

83 P/2 - Calling River
NE21-70-17-W4
55°05′N 112°02′W
Flows south-west into La Biche River approximately 55 km north-west of Lac La Biche (town).

Appearing on federal government maps as early as 1917, the name is descriptive of its course.

Wanham (village)

83 M/9 - Peoria
4-78-3-W6
55°44′N 118°24′W
Approximately 69 km north north-east of Grande Prairie.

It was originally established in 1916 as a station on the Edmonton, Dunvegan and British Columbia Railway line. There are at least three explanations of the origin of the name. The first and most well known is that Wanham is an aboriginal peoples' word for "warm winds." However, since this word does not seem to be in the vocabularies of the local language groups of Cree and Beaver, the following may be the more likely origin. The station was named by an engineer who worked for the ED & BCR,

Wanham, 1957 (With nary a ham in sight!)

J.B. Prest. Apparently he named a number of small stations on the line using the names of places he was familiar with in his home region in Surrey, England. One community in Surrey is Wonham, so it is logical to assume that Mr. Prest used this as a name for the station. Other stations named by J.B. Prest include Esher, Prestville, Surbiton and Woking. The post office was established at Wanham in 1918, and Peter Tansem was the first postmaster. When queried in 1929 by the Geographic Board of Canada on the origin of the name, Tansem replied "the head surveyor was trying to figure out a name for this siding while the cook was making supper. Coming to the meat supply he found only one ham, so he called out to the surveyor (wan ham), the cook being a French man."

Waniandy Creek (creek)

84 E/15 - Waniandy Creek
3-103-4-W6
57°54′N 118°35′W
Flows north-east into Chinchaga River approximately 81 km south-east of Rainbow Lake.

Named in commemoration of Trooper George Waniandy, killed in action August 31, 1944.

Wapasu Creek (creek)

74 E/6 - Kearl Lake
14-31-96-8-W4
57°22′40″N 111°17′55″W
Flows north-west into Muskeg River approximately 74 km north of Fort McMurray.

An undocumented source states this is named for the man who, according to the Fort York journal entry of June 12, 1719, was the "Swan." He apparently was the one who introduced the Europeans to the bituminous sands.

Wapiti (locality)

83 L/14 - Wapiti
9-69-8-W6
54°58′N 119°08′W
Approximately 25 km south-west of Grande Prairie.

Established as a post office in November 1931, this locality is named for the Cree word for elk, which can be found in the area. The first postmaster was R.J. Rutledge.

Wapiti River (river)

83 M/1 - DeBolt
NW-7-71-2-W6
55°08′N 118°18′W
Flows east into Smoky River approximately 30 km east of Grande Prairie.

The river is named after the Cree word for elk, which roughly translates to "it is white" referring to the light-coloured rump. This is likely due to the prevalence of the animal in the area. "The Wapiti, Elk, or Lac Biche River, is a large rapid stream with muddy water probably derived from glaciers in the mountains. It pursues a tortuous course in a wide trough-like valley 400 feet deep in its lower part, and is said by Indians to rise near the sources of the Smoky River." From an 1890 map compiled by C.O. Senécal, CE.

Wappau Lake (lake)
73 M/5 - Behan Lake
11-75-11-W4
55°29'N 111°37'W
Approximately 85 km North of Lac La Biche.

The origin is possibly aboriginal, but the meaning is not known. It shows on maps as early as 1917.

Warrensville (locality)
84 C/5 - Chinook Valley
26-84-24-W5
56°18'N 117°40'W
Approximately 13 km north of Grimshaw.

It is named after the first postmaster, E. Warren. The post office was established in February 1921.

Warrensville Centre (locality)
84 C/5 - Chinook Valley
30-84-23-W5
56°18'N 117°37'W
Approximately 13 km north of Grimshaw.

(see Warrensville)

Wash Creek (creek)
83 N/9 - Grouard
21-76-15-W5
55°36'N 116°16'W
Flows south into the South Heart River approximately 25 km north-east of High Prairie.

The creek is mentioned by name in the DLS notes of 1906 in which it was described as having a rapid current. No origin information has been recorded; it may have been a place where washing was done, or it may refer to a geological term meaning soil swept off by water.

Waskahigan River (river)
83 K/14 - Waskahigan River
35-66-22-W5
54°45'N 117°13'W
Flows north-east into Little Smoky River approximately 115 km south-east of Grande Prairie.

The generally accepted story of the origin of the name is that the early settlers who came to the area around 1910 found a dwelling on the side of the river and, as a result, the feature became known as House River. *Waskahigan* is Cree for "house" and it is the Cree form of the word that was recorded by the Dominion Land Surveyors. Because the Cree form has survived, it is likely the name predates settlement. Local residents still refer to it as both House River and Waskahigan River.

*****Watchusk Lake** (lake)
74 D/1 - Watchusk Lake
6-83-2-W4
56°10'N 110°18'W
Approximately 90 km south-east of Fort McMurray.

(see South Watchusk Lake)

Water Hen Lake (lake)
83 N/5 - Puskwaskau River
SW-3-74-25-W5
55°23'N 117°46'W
Approximately 70 km east north-east of Grande Prairie.

Water Hen Lake is named after a type of duck that may have been spotted on the lake; the bird is not common in Canada. This name has been in use since at least 1930.

---

*denotes rescinded name or former locality.

Water-Lily Lake (lake)
84 H/10 - Alberta
4-100-16-W4
57°39'N 112°33'W
Approximately 125 km north north-west of Fort McMurray.

The name is derived from the hundreds of water-lily colonies ranging in size from a few feet to over a hundred feet in diameter. Lily colonies of this size are distinctive. Each would have originated from a single water-lily plant and would thus form a peculiar circular colony that can be identified from aerial photographs.

Waterhole (locality)
84 D/1 - Fairview
9-81-3-W6
56°01'N 118°25'W
Approximately 7 km south of Fairview.

The locality of Waterhole derives its name from a hamlet that once stood on the site of the Waterhole community hall. The hamlet moved to the railroad and was renamed Fairview in 1928. The origin of the name Waterhole lies in a little watering place at the bottom of the creek that flows through the site of the hamlet. One of the few places on the Dunvegan Trail where water was available, it had become known as the waterhole. When a post office near this spot was opened by the Dawson family circa 1911, the postal authorities required a name. D.M. Kennedy, later United Farmers of Alberta, then Co-operative Commonwealth Federation Member of Parliament for Peace River (1921-1935), suggested the name Blair Athol or Athol after his Scottish birthplace. Mrs Sarah French, an American and former Southern belle, on whose land the waterhole was situated, responded: "If we must name it *that*, why not Waterhole!"

Old Waterways Hotel during a flood, 1936

*Waterways (town)
74 D/11 - Fort McMurray
89-9-W4
56°44′N 111°23′W
Approximately 378 km north-east of Edmonton.

(see Fort McMurray)

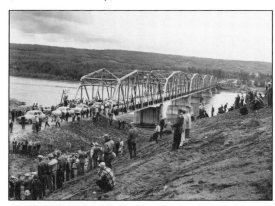

Watino Bridge opening, 1955

Watino (hamlet)
83 N/12 - Watino
35-77-24-W5
55°43′N 117°37′W

---

*denotes rescinded name or former locality.

Approximately 98 km north-east of Grande Prairie.

Originally a post office established in November 1925, it was previously known as Prudens Crossing. One explanation for the name is that Watino is a variation of the Cree word meaning valley.

Watt, Mount (mountain)
84 K/11 - High Level
20-111-21-W5
58°38′N 117°29′W
Approximately 28 km north-west of High Level.

It was likely named by J. R. Akins, DLS, in 1914 after a colleague, G. Watt, DLS. Among local Slavey and Beaver residents this mountain is known as *Deni Ledé Yihé*, which means "partly burnt mountain." In the late 1800s a forest fire destroyed most of the growth on the east side of the slope. The subsequent new growth was distinctly visible throughout the early 1900s, hence the name.

Waugh Lake (lake)
74 M/16 - Andrew Lake
36-124-1-W4
59°48′N 110°01′W
Approximately 343 km north north-east of Fort McMurray.

Officially named in 1939, it takes its name from B.W. Waugh, the surveyor in charge of the portion of the Saskatchewan-Alberta Boundary Commission survey between Lake Athabasca and the 60th Parallel.

Weasone Creek (creek)
83 J/6 - Christmas Creek
10-61-10-W5
54°16′N 115°25′W
Flows south-east into Christmas Creek approximately 155 km north-west of Edmonton.

Named in 1918 after Benjamin Weasone, a trapper in the area at the time.

Weaver Lake (lake)
83 O/16 - Mistehae
27-80-1-W5
55°58′N 114°03′W
Approximately 90 km north north-east of Slave Lake.

The origin of this name is unknown, but the name has appeared on federal government maps as early as 1918.

Webber Creek (creek)
83 M/6 - La Glace
12-7-74-8-W6
55°24′N 119°13′W
Flows south into La Glace Lake approximately 35 km north-west of Grande Prairie.

The creek was named for Fred G. Webber (1866-1943) and family, who arrived in the area in 1914. The Webbers' original homestead was on the same land in which the Beaver Chief La Glace was apparently buried.

Weberville (locality)
84 C/6 - Weberville
24-84-22-W5
56°17′N 117°19′W
Approximately 4 km north of Peace River.

This locality was first established as a post office in 1928 and was named after J.J. Weber, the first postmaster.

Webster (locality)
83 M/7 - Sexsmith
27-74-5-W6
55°26′N 118°41′W
Approximately 32 km north north-east of Grande Prairie.

It was established in 1916 as a station on the Edmonton, Dunvegan and British Columbia Railway and was named for George Webster, who was in 1916 a subcontractor for the railway company. He entered politics eight years later, and served on the

Calgary City Council as an alderman (1920-1922) and Mayor (1923-1926). In 1926 he was elected to the Legislative Assembly, where he stayed until his death in 1933. A post office opened there in October 1929; the first postmaster was A. Hanchery.

Webster Lake (lake)
83 N/16 - Pentland Lake
22-78-14-W5
55°46'N 116°05'W
Approximately 32 km west of McLennan.

The lake was named after Squadron Leader A.E. Webster, DFC, born in Woodville, Ontario in 1910. He and his parents lived in Edmonton for a time. He enlisted in June 1940 in Fort William, Ontario, and in 1943 was awarded the Distinguished Flying Cross. In November 1945 he died in a flying accident.

Weekes Lake (lake)
74 M/9 - Colin Lake
NE-25-123-1-W4
59°43'N 110°01'W
Approximately 334 km north north-east of Fort McMurray.

Named in 1954 in honour of M.B. Weekes, former Director of Surveys in Saskatchewan. In the late 1930s he was the Saskatchewan member of the Saskatchewan-Alberta Boundary Commission.

Wells Lake (lake)
74 M/16 - Andrew Lake
NE-35-126-2-W4
60°00'N 110°13'W
Approximately 361 km north of Fort McMurray on the Alberta-Northwest Territories boundary.

The name was submitted in 1958 by the Research Council of Alberta, and is one of a series of features in the area named after deceased prominent geologists. "A.K. Wells [was a] prominent igneous petrologist." Holmgren, 1976.

Welstead Lake (lake)
74 L/5 - Welstead Lake
32-107-11-W4
58°20'N 111°48'W
Approximately 170 km north of Fort McMurray.

According to the 1928 edition of *Place-Names of Alberta*, in 1914, this lake was named after a reeve of Grantham Township in Ontario. Why this name was chosen is not known. Perhaps Mr. Welstead was a friend or relative of a surveyor working in the area.

Wembley (town)
83 M/3 - Wembley
NW-15-71-8-W6
55°09'N 119°08'W
Approximately 19 km west of Grande Prairie.

The Edmonton, Dunvegan and British Columbia Railway established a station here in 1924. The name was chosen by the Lake Saskatoon Board of Trade at the time of the British Empire Exposition at Wembley in England. The post office opened in November 1924, the first postmaster being R.B. Sinclair.

Wentzel Lake (lake)
84 O/1 - Alberta
32-115-3-W5
59°02'N 114°28'W
Approximately 159 km east north-east of High level.

After Willard Ferdinand Wentzel (d. 1832), fur trader. Wentzel was born in Montreal and in 1799 entered the service of the North West Company. For a number of years he was a clerk in the Athabasca Department. The NWC was taken over by the Hudson's Bay Company in 1821. At the union of the two companies he retired to Canada in 1825. In 1827 he re-entered the service of the HBC and served two years as a clerk in Mingan on the lower St. Lawrence. He retired again in 1829 and died in 1832, victim of a cholera epidemic. Holmgren, 1976. He accompanied Sir John Franklin on his first Arctic expedition in 1821. The lake is locally known as *Mistahe Sakahikun*, which is Cree for Big Lake. It is the largest lake in the immediate area.

Wentzel River (river)
84 J/10 - Wentzel River
13-110-4-W5
58°32'N 114°30'W
Flows south into the Peace River approximately 152 km east of High Level.

Locally this stream is known as *Atikh Sepe*, Cree for Caribou River. Sir George Simpson records the name as Caribou River, and the Caribou River as the Upper Caribou River, in 1828. In 1883, W.T. Thompson, DLS, records the name as Deer River. (see Wentzel Lake)

Werniuk Creek (creek)
84 E/5 - Tanghe Creek
10-96-10-W6
57°18'N 119°32'W
Flows south into the Chinchaga River approximately 114 km west north-west of Manning.

Named in commemoration of Private Stanley Werniuk, killed in action on April 12, 1945.

Wesley Creek (locality)
84 C/3 - Peace River
32-83-20-W5
56°15'N 117°07'W
Approximately 10 km east of Peace River.

Established as a post office in 1939, it was named because of its proximity to the locally known Wesley Creek. Wesley

Creek is named after Pat Wesley. The first postmaster was Mrs. A. Cambridge. (see Pats Creek)

West Creek (creek)
83 N/1 - Bellrose Lake
4-8-71-14-W5
55°08′N 116°08′W
Flows west into East Prairie River approximately 42 km south-east of High Prairie.

Descriptive of direction of flow of water; it was officially named after field research was conducted in the 1950s.

West Golden Creek (creek)
83 N/2 - Snipe Lake
10-70-18-W5
55°03′N 116°40′W
Flows north-east into Golden Creek approximately 43 km south of High Prairie.

Named for its proximity as a tributary to Golden Creek. This name was provided in 1953 by a local trapper and farmer, Gaston Dellazay.

West Iroquois Creek (creek)
83 M/3 - Wembley
5-33-69-9-W6
55°01′N 119°19′W
Flows north-west into Wapiti River 47 km west south-west of Grande Prairie.

Named for its proximity to Iroquois Creek. (see Iroquois Creek)

*****West Peace River** (hamlet)
84 C/3 - Peace River
30-83-22-W5
56°13′35″N 117°27′50″W
Approximately 11 km west of Peace River (town).

Established as a post office in March 1915, its name is descriptive of the area in which it is situated. The first postmaster was G.D. McRae.

*denotes rescinded name or former locality.

West Prairie River Bridge, 1923

West Prairie River (river)
83 N/10 - McLennan
14-75-17-W5
55°30′N 116°31′W
Flows north into South Heart River approximately 10 km north of High Prairie.

The name West Prairie River was known as early as 1911 when the area was surveyed. The name is likely descriptive of the area.

*****Westvale** (former post office)
83 M/9 - Peoria
30-76-3-W6
55°36′50″N 118°26′50″W
Approximately 52 km north-west of Grande Prairie.

The post office opened in December 1946, and took its name from the fact it was located west of Heart Valley. The first postmaster was I.A. Parlee.

Wesukemina Creek (creek)
74 E/6 - Kearl Lake
27-95-8-W4
57°16′20″N 111°13′10″W
Flows north-west into Iyinimin Creek approximately 65 km north north-east of Fort McMurray.

Wesukemina is the Cree word for cranberries. This area is well known for its abundance of highbush cranberries, or *Viburnum opulus* whose bushes yield edible berries.

Whaleback Lake (lake)
74 M/9 - Colin Lake
NE-24-123-3-W4
59°42′N 110°22′W
Approximately 329 km north north-east of Fort McMurray.

The name was suggested in 1965 by the Research Council of Alberta as being descriptive of the outline of the lake.

Wheeler Island (island)
74 E/5 - Bitumount
24-97-11-W4
57°26′N 111°38′W
In Athabasca River approximately 80 km north north-west of Fort McMurray.

This name was originally applied to a post office opened in 1922 by A.W. Wheeler, well known as a trader and trapper. Wheeler lived on the island for many years. (see also Bitumount)

Whiskey Jack Creek (creek)
74 D/13 - Ruth Lake
19-90-12-W4
56°49′10″N 110°54′35″W
Flows north-west into an unnamed creek approximately 33 km west north-west of Fort McMurray.

This creek takes its name from Whiskey Jack Lake from which it flows. (see Whiskey Jack Lake)

Whiskey Jack Lake (lake)
74 D/13 - Ruth Lake
17-90-12-W4
56°48′35″N 111°53′00″W

Lies in Thickwood Hills 34 km west north-west of Fort McMurray.

This lake no doubt took its name from the Whiskey Jack, the grey-and-white bird that inhabits this area year round. Whiskey jacks, alias grey jays, Canada jays or camp robbers, are friendly birds and tend to congregate at campsites. They pilfer food, given a chance, or accept any handout offered. This conspicuous behaviour makes the Whiskey Jack well known to trappers, woodsmen and campers throughout the forested areas of northern Canada. There is a particular variety of pellet-shaped snow described in some areas of northern Canada as being the size of Whiskey Jack brains, possibly alluding to the intelligence of the bird.

Whistwow Lake (lake)
84 A/11 - Blanchet Lake
20-89-22-W4
56°44′N 113°28′W
Approximately 125 km west of Fort McMurray.

It is said *Whistwow* is a Cree word meaning "ducks losing their feathers," and the name was given to this lake because long ago a family went there and found lots of feathers from moulting ducks. The ducks could not fly so the people chased them and killed them.

Whitburn (locality)
83 M/14 - Blueberry Mountain
NW-21-79-8-W6
55°52′N 119°12′W
Approximately 25 km west north-west of Sexsmith.

The name was first given to the post office in February 1929. The first and only postmaster was Mrs. Maplet "Mickey" Scott, and she ran it until it closed in 1967. One source states there is some connection

---

*denotes rescinded name or former locality.

with Whitburn in County Durham, England. Burn is of Scottish origin meaning small stream.

White Cow Lake (lake)
84 A/11 - Blanchet Lake
30-88-21-W4
56°39′56″N 113°26′45″W
Approximately 119 km west of Fort McMurray.

It is said that the name White Cow was given to this lake when a family was travelling through many years ago. A young boy was crying when his mother noticed a tree bent over and covered with snow that looked like a white cow. The boy's mother told him to stop crying or the "white cow" would get him.

***Whitecourt Creek** (creek)
83 J/4 - Whitecourt
35-59-12-W5
54°08′N 115°42′W
Flows north-west into the McLeod River at the town of Whitecourt.

Originally known as Beaver Creek; the name Whitecourt Creek began appearing on federal government maps as early as 1917. It was named for its proximity to the community of the same name, then the name was changed back to Beaver Creek in 1982. (see Beaver Creek, above, and Whitecourt in *Place Names of Alberta, Volume III*)

***Whitefish River** (river)
74 L/6 - Richardson Lake
15-34-108-8-W4
58°25′N 111°14′W
Flows north into Athabasca River approximately 180 km north of Fort McMurray.

(see Richardson River)

***Whitehay River** (river)
84 N/3 - Roe River
36-117-21-W5
59°13′N 117°26′W
Flows north-west into Hay River approximately 79 km north north-west of High Level.

(see Roe River)

Whitelaw (hamlet)
84 D/1 - Fairview
15-82-1-W6
56°07′N 118°04′W
Approximately 20 km east north-east of Fairview.

Originally a station on the Central Canada Railway line, established in 1924, this hamlet was named after a car service accountant of the company. The post office opened here in 1925, with E.L. Davis as first postmaster.

***Whitemud Creek** (former post office)
83 N/6 - Whitemud Creek
SW-1-75-23-W5
55°28′N 117°25′W
Approximately 95 km north-east of Grande Prairie.

The nearby creek contains a white muddy clay on its banks with which the aboriginal people used to chink their cabins. The post office was established here in September 1935, the first postmaster being G.B. Bede. There is a reference in the 1854 Hudson's Bay Company's post journal from Fort Dunvegan referring to Terre Blanche, the French for white earth.

***Whitemud Creek** (creek)
74 E/5 - Asphalt Creek
9-98-10-W4
57°29′30″N 111°34′05″W
Flows south-east into Athabasca River approximately 86 km north of Fort McMurray.

(see Eymundson Creek)

Whitemud Falls (falls)
74 D/9 - Bunting Bay
3-89-1-W4
56°41'30"N 110°03'40"W
On the Clearwater River, 83 km east of Fort McMurray.

The precise origin of the name of these falls is unknown, although it may refer to the silt disturbed at this point in the river.

Whitemud Hills (hills)
84 C/5 - Chinook Valley
17-85-25-W5
56°22'N 117°55'W
Approximately 20 km north-west of Grimshaw.

The precise origin of the name of these hills is unknown; it may refer to the Whitemud River that flows out of the hills.

Whitemud River (river)
84 C/11 - Deadwood
30-88-20-W5
56°40'N 117°10'W
Flows north-east into Peace River approximately 40 km south-east of Manning.

The name is descriptive of the appearance of the river.

*Whitemud River (river)
84 N/3 - Roe River
36-117-21-W5
59°13'N 117°26'W
Flows north-west into Hay River approximately 79 km north north-west of High Level.

(see Roe River)

Whitesand Point (point)
74 M/1 - Winnifred Lake
1-117-3-W4
59°08'N 110°22'W

---
*denotes rescinded name or former locality.

Approximately 266 km north north-east of Fort McMurray.

The name is descriptive of the feature, and appeared on federal government maps as early as 1884.

Whitesand River (river)
84 O/13 - Alberta-Northwest Territories
13-36-126-10-W5
60°00'N 115°36'W
Flows north into NWT approximately 184 km north north-east of High Level.

Likely descriptive, this river was officially named in 1946. The name was suggested by game wardens who said the name was in local use.

Whitham Lake (lake)
83 M/5 - Hythe
13-13-74-12-W6
55°25'N 119°43'W
Approximately 62 km west north-west of Grande Prairie.

The lake was named in 1947 after Flight Lieutenant J. Whitham, DFC, born on May 13, 1919, the son of Mr. and Mrs. C.H. Whitham. After taking a two-year course at the Institute of Art and Technology in Calgary, he enlisted in the RCAF at Edmonton on October 25 1940. He married Margaret Craig of Edmonton in 1941. On August 28, 1942 he was reported missing and subsequently presumed dead. During his tour of duty he was awarded the DFC.

Whyetnow Lake (lake)
84 H/6 - Alberta
11-98-21-W4
57°29'34"N 113°18'20"W
Approximately 143 km north-west of Fort McMurray.

The precise origin of the name of this lake is unknown.

Wiau River (river)
73 M/6 - Wiau Lake
18-73-9-W4
55°19'N 111°23'W
Flows south-west into Clyde Lake approximately 73 km north north-east of Lac La Biche.

The origin is unknown; the name was in use when the area was surveyed in the 1910s.

Widewater (hamlet)
83 O/6 - Kinuso
32-73-7-W5
55°22'N 115°02'W
Approximately 18 km north-west of Slave Lake.

Originally established as an Edmonton, Dunvegan and British Columbia Railway station in 1914; the name is descriptive of its location at the widest portion of Lesser Slave Lake. The post office opened in 1923, and its first postmaster was J.W. Field. In 1985, it was formed into a widespread hamlet. (see Canyon Creek/Widewater/Wagner)

Wildhay River (river)
83 F/14 - Oldman Creek
58-23-W5
53°59'N 117°16'W
Approximately 70 km north north-east of Hinton.

Known to the aboriginal people as *manito-ca-pim-bi-it*, the river Manito (The Great Spirit) straddled as he strode along it. The meadows, lush with wild hay, are said to have been formed where his footsteps flattened the earth; these meadows provided food for the horses. Holmgren, 1976.

*Wilkin Lake (lake)
83 M/6 - La Glace
32-72-9-W6
55°17'N 119°21'W
Approximately 35 km north-west of Grande Prairie.

The long-standing local name for this lake was Bush Lake, but when the Army Survey Establishment was going to produce a detailed map of the area in the early 1950s, it was decided to give the lake the name of a war casualty, which was the policy at that time. The name Wilkin was chosen. Squadron Leader R.P. Wilkin was born in Edmonton, Alberta on September 15, 1919, the son of Mr. and Mrs. W.L. Wilkin. He joined the RCAF at Edmonton on October 15, 1940 for aircrew duties. On completion of the pilot's course he was commissioned and sent overseas. He was reported missing after air operations on September 20, 1943, and was subsequently presumed dead. He was awarded the DFC in 1943. For his outstanding services rendered to the Czech Government he was awarded the Czech Military Cross.

The naming policy since the early 1970s has been to give precedence to local usage. It was determined during a field survey that the local usage was still Bush Lake, so in 1991, the name was officially changed back to its original. (see Bush Lake)

William McKenzie Indian Reserve No. 151K (Indian reserve)

84 C/2 - Harmon Valley
SW-11-81-19-W5
56°00'N 116°52'W
Approximately 37 km south-east of Peace River.

Named after a chief who obtained severalty under Treaty No. 8.

William Smith Lake (lake)

74 M/16 - Andrew Lake
SE-36-125-2-W4
59°54'N 110°11'W
Approximately 351 km north of Fort McMurray.

The name was submitted in 1958 by the Research Council of Alberta, and is one of a series of features in the area named after deceased prominent geologists. "William Smith (1769-1839), [was] an English engineer who became a self-trained geologist. The father of stratigraphy, he made some of the first detailed geological maps." Holmgren, 1976.

Williams Lake (lake)

74 D/14 - Wood Creek
17-90-7-W4
56°48'10"N 110°04'00"W
Approximately 24 km east north-east of Fort McMurray.

This lake was named for William Golosky (1915-1985). The son of George Golosky, one of Fort McMurray's early settlers, he lived with Bill and Christine Gordon (of Gordon and Christina lakes.) William Golosky was well known in the community and the trapline upon which this lake is situated has been owned by the Golosky family for over 65 years.

Williamson Lake Provincial Park (provincial park)

83 N/4 - Sturgeon Heights
23-70-24-W5
55°05'N 117°33'W
Approximately 80 km east of Grande Prairie.

Alexander Williamson, born in Aberdeen in 1882, was an area landowner. He served at sea before coming to Canada in 1910. After working at several jobs, he settled in the Sturgeon Heights area in the early 1910s, bringing his family from Scotland. In honour of his life-long work in the area, the 17-hectare provincial park was named after him when it was established in 1960.

Williscroft Island (island)

74 E/11 - Firebag River
24-99-10-W4
57°36'30"N 111°29'30"W
In Athabasca River approximately 98 km north north-east of Fort McMurray.

Named for Captain C.J. Williscroft.

Willow Island (island)

74 L/9 - Old Fort Bay
8-111-3-W4
58°37'N 110°29'W
Approximately 210 km north north-east of Fort McMurray in Old Fort Bay.

Likely descriptive of flora on the island.

Willow Island (island)

74 D/14 - Wood Creek
6-91-9-W4
56°52'N 111°25'W
On Athabasca River approximately 16 km north of Fort McMurray.

This name is probably descriptive of the willows to be found on the island. There are at least 35 species of willow in Alberta, and in aboriginal medicine, the inside of the bark of some was used as a painkiller. It contains a substance related to modern-day acetasalicylic acid found in a number of over-the-counter pain remedies.

Willow Lake (lake)

74 D/6 - Gregoire Lake
14-86-8-W4
56°27'30"N 111°08'30"W
Approximately 30 km south-east of Fort McMurray.

The origin of the name of this lake is likely descriptive. The name Willow Lake remained in local usage even after the lake was officially named Gregoire Lake in 1927. The name Gregoire was rescinded and the original local name given official status in 1992. It is not clear after whom the lake was named; it is possible that it was named for one of three men: Gregoire Haineault, who lived on the lake, Bill Gregoire or Gregoire Martel who lived near the lake. A federal government map of the McMurray area in 1917 makes a reference to Gregoire Lake, indicating local usage of the name by that date.

Willow Opening (meadow)
83 N/1 - Bellrose Lake
20-71-15-W5
55°10′N 116°15′W
Approximately 161 km east of Grande Prairie.

The well-established name for this opening at the mouth of Willow Opening Creek was in use before 1946. There are large numbers of willow trees in the area.

Willow Opening Creek (creek)
83 N/1 - Bellrose Lake
14-35-71-15-W5
55°10′N 116°16′W
Flows north-east into East Prairie River approximately 164 km east of Grande Prairie.

The name has been established and in local usage since the early 1940s and refers to the large number of willow trees located at the west end of the creek.

Willow Point (point)
74 L/5 - Welstead Lake
16-6-109-12-W4
58°27′N 111°59′W
Approximately 184 km north north-west of Fort McMurray.

The name was officially approved in 1954, the name is descriptive of the flora on this point on Lake Claire.

Willow Point (point)
83 N/9 - Grouard
19-75-14-W5
55°30′N 116°09′W
Approximately 23 km east north-east of High Prairie.

This is a descriptive name for a feature that lies within the Sucker Creek Indian Reserve. It shows as early as 1915 on a federal government map.

Willow River (river)
83 P/13 - South Wabasca Lake
11-31-80-25-W4
55°58′N 113°55′W
Flows north into North Wabasca Lake approximately 95 km north-east of Slave Lake.

Likely descriptive of the flora along its banks, the name for the river was well established and in local use when the surveyors were working in the area in 1913.

Wilson Creek (creek)
83 L/15 - Big Mountain Creek
11-68-7-W6
54°52′N 118°57′W
Flows south-east into Bald Mountain Creek approximately 35 km south south-west of Grande Prairie.

There are two known origins for the name of the feature. The first concerns Harvey Wilson, who attempted to raise cattle in the area but left because of a lack of feed. The other story says that the name was taken after a trapper, Sam Wilson, who lived in the area.

Wilson Lake (lake)
83 L/14 - Wapiti
31-68-7-W6
54°56′N 119°03′W
Approximately 30 km south south-west of Grande Prairie.

It is the source of the nearby feature. (see Wilson Creek)

Wilson Ridge (ridge)
83 L/15 - Big Mountain Creek
26-68-7-W6
54°55′15″N 118°57′58″W
Approximately 40 km south of Grande Prairie.

This 800-metre ridge is named for its proximity to the nearby features. The name was officially adopted in 1991 after field research was conducted in the area. (see Wilson Creek)

Winagami (railway point)
83 N/10 - McLennan
31-77-19-W5
55°43′N 116°57′W
Approximately 42 km north-west of High Prairie just outside McLennan.

An Edmonton, Dunvegan and British Columbia Railway station established in 1915, it was named for its proximity to the lake. (see Winagami Lake)

Winagami Lake (lake)
83 N/10 - McLennan
33-76-18-W5
55°37′N 116°44′W
Approximately 27 km north-west of High Prairie.

It shows in one Dominion Land Surveyor's notebook as *wee-nah-ka-mee*, and was translated as "Stinking Lake." Of it the surveyor Holcroft wrote in 1911, "Winagamei Lake (Stinking Lake) well deserves its cognomen as the water smells strongly of hydrogen sulphide." The name has also been translated to "Dirty-water" Lake.

Winagami Provincial Park (provincial park)
83 N/10 - McLennan
36-76-18-W5
55°37′N 116°40′W
Approximately 25 km north north-west of High Prairie.

This park was established in 1970 and named for its proximity to the lake. (see Winagami Lake)

Windfall Lake (lake)
83 J/10 - Timeu Creek
18-66-5-W5
54°43′N 114°45′W

Approximately 43 km east of Swan Hills.

The name was recorded on a preliminary map from 1944, it likely refers to the trees blown down by the wind in the area.

Windsor Creek (creek)
83 M/4 - Rio Grande
NE-5-72-12-W65
55°12′N 119°48′W
Flows north-east into Beavertail Creek approximately 63 km west of Grande Prairie.

Although the origin of the name is not precisely known, it may have been named after the place in Berkshire, England. The name means "bank or slope with a windlass." A windlass is a horizontal axle wheel used for hauling or hoisting. It shows on a federal government map as early as 1930.

*****Windsor Creek** (former locality)
83 M/4 - Rio Grande
31-70-12-W6
55°06′N 119°49′W
Approximately 72 km west south-west of Grande Prairie.

Named for its proximity to the creek of the same name, the post office opened in October 1929. The first postmaster was G.F. Clarkson. (see Windsor Creek)

Winefred Lake (lake)
73 M/7 - Kirby Lake
75-3,4-W4
55°30′N 110°31′W
Approximately 118 km north north-west of Cold Lake.

It is the source of Winefred River; it was noted in 1910 by William Christie, DLS. (see Winefred River)

---

*denotes rescinded name or former locality.

Winefred River (river)
74 D/2 - Quigley
20-81-4-W4
56°02′N 110°36′W
Flows west into Christina River approximately 90 km south south-east of Fort McMurray.

Named by a Dominion Land Surveyor, R.E. Young, for his wife, Winefred.

Winnifred Lake (lake)
74 M/1 - Winnifred Lake
11-118-3-W4
59°14′N 110°24′W
Approximately 277 km north north-east of Fort McMurray.

It was named in 1929 after one of the daughters of John Wylie of Fort Chipewyan. (see also Florence Lake and Wylie Lake)

Woking (hamlet)
83 M/10 - Woking
19-76-5-W6
55°35′N 118°46′W
Approximately 45 km north of Grande Prairie.

Established in 1916 as a station on the Edmonton, Dunvegan and British Columbia Railway, a post office operated here from June 1932 to 1968. The station was named by J.B. Prest, an engineer for the railway, who came from Woking in Surrey, near London. The name means "area of the family or followers of a man called Wocca." Mr. Prest was responsible for naming a number of stations on the line including Prestville, Surbiton, Wanham and Esher)

*****Wolf Lake** (lake)
74 E/5 - Bitumount
17, 18-97-11-W4
57°25′N 111°46′W
Approximately 75 km north of Fort McMurray

The name which appears on a federal government map as early as 1925, is likely descriptive of the animal found in the area. Because of the number of other features called Wolf Lake in Alberta, the name was changed in 1965. (see Calumet Lake)

Wolfe Lake (lake)
83 M/6 - La Glace
20-74-8-W65
55°26′N 119°11′W
Approximately 39 km north-west of Grande Prairie.

The origin of this name is unknown, although it was in use and well established when it was made official in 1952.

Wolverine Lake (lake)
83 K/13 - Long Lake
9-5-69-25-W5
54°56′55″N 117°45′50″W
Approximately 71 km south-east of Grande Prairie.

It was officially named in 1991. At one time there was a large wolverine population in the area surrounding the lake. By the early 1940s, the wolverine had been trapped out. The wolverine is a large fur-bearing animal of distinctive temperament that inhabits the tundra and northern forests. (see also Carcajou)

Wolverine River (river)
84 F/15 - Steephill Creek
14-101-19-W5
57°45′N 116°59′W
Flows north-west into Peace River approximately 84 km south of High Level.

The precise origin of the name of this river is unknown; it is indicative of the presence of the wolverine. The name was referred to in the 1913 field notes of J.A. Fletcher, DLS.

Wood Buffalo Lake (lake)
84 A/6 - Wood Buffalo Lake
32-84-20-W4
56°19′N 113°07′W
Approximately 115 km south-west of Fort McMurray.

This lake most likely takes its name from its association with the Wood Buffalo River, which has its source in the lake.

Wood Buffalo National Park (national park)
84 P/2 - Boyer Rapids
116-16-W4
59°15′N 113°15′W
Approximately 260 km north north-west of Fort McMurray and east north-east of High Level.

This, the largest national park in Canada, is named for the herds of wood buffalo seen there by surveyors in 1916. They were

Wood Buffalo Park cabin near 27th Baseline at Chenal des Quatre Fourches, n.d.

termed "wood buffalo" because they inhabited the wooded parkland. They have a darker coat than that of the plains buffalo. In 1916 a federal survey party noticed tracks of wood buffalo and as a result of their report the park was established by order-in-council of December 18, 1922. When the herd of 6,000 plains buffalo was moved in from Wainwright between 1925 and 1927, they preferred the open plains near Lake Claire so the park boundaries were extended to include that area. The park has an area of 17,300 square miles (44,804 square kilometres) of which 3,625 (9388) are in the Northwest Territories. Holmgren, 1976.

Wood Buffalo River (river)
84 A/5 - Tepee Lake
23-86-24-W4
56°28′N 113°41′W
Flows north-west into Wabasca River approximately 143 km west south-west of Fort McMurray.

The precise origin of the name of this river is unknown; it is likely due to the prevalence of the animal in the area at one time.

Wood Creek (creek)
74 D/14 - Wood Creek
20-91-9-W4
56°54′N 111°25′W
Flows west into Athabasca River approximately 20 km north of Fort McMurray.

This name was submitted by S.C. Ells after James Wood, a pioneer of Northern Alberta and at one time the mayor of Athabasca.

Wood Lake (lake)
83 M/2 - Grande Prairie
15-17-71-5-W6
55°09′N 118°44′W
Approximately 3 km east of Grande Prairie.

After RSM James Wood, DCM, Calgary, Alberta, the first Calgary fatality of the Korean War where he was killed in a land mine demonstration. He was awarded the Distinguished Conduct Medal for exceptional bravery when he served with Princess Patricia's Canadian Light Infantry in Italy during World War II.

Woodenhouse River (river)
84 A/12 - Woodenhouse River
7-88-23-W4
56°37′N 113°41′W
Flows north-east into Wabasca River approximately 141 km west of Fort McMurray.

The precise origin of the name of this river is unknown although it may refer to a structure on the banks of the river.

Woodman Lake (lake)
74 M/9 - Colin Lake
29-121-3-W4
59°32′N 110°28′W
Approximately 100 km north north-east of Fort Chipewyan.

It was named in 1929 after Thomas Woodman, postmaster and trader of Fort Chipewyan.

Woodpecker Creek (creek)
83 N/3 - Valleyview
31-70-22-W55
55°06′N 117°21′W
Flows north into Sturgeon Creek approximately 5 km north-west of Valleyview.

The name was officially approved in 1953 after field research was conducted. It likely refers to the presence of the bird in the area. A number of species of woodpecker are common in Alberta; and like all of their kin, they perform a valuable service by indulging in their favourite food, wood-boring insects.

Worsley (hamlet)
84 D/11 - Worsley
36-86-8-W6
56°31′N 119°08′W
Approximately 66 km north-west of Fairview.

It was originally established as a post office in 1931, two stories have emerged as to its origins. The first is that it honours Captain

Eric Worsley, a British cavalry officer who at one time trained a private army for an Indian prince. Before World War I, Worsley arrived in the Peace River area, where, with a Mr. Berranger, he was involved in the fur trade. With the outbreak of war, Worsley returned to military life and was killed in action. Another source states the original post office was named after a village in Lancashire, England. The first postmaster was L. O'Neil.

Wylie Lake (lake)
74 M/8 - Wylie Lake
12-119-3-W4
59°20′N 110°22′W
Approximately 287 km north north-east of Fort McMurray.

Officially named in 1929 after John Wylie (1871-1958), at one time a police magistrate at Fort Chipewyan. His father, William Wylie, came from the Orkney Islands in 1863 and was a blacksmith at Fort Chipewyan. Holmgren, 1976. (see also Florence Lake and Winnifred Lake)

"Y", The (river)
84 H/9 - Alberta
18-99-15-W4
57°35′28″N 112°27′05″W
Flows north-west into Big Island Lake approximately 116 km north north-west of Fort McMurray.

The owner of the fishing lodge in this area and the two trappers who operate traplines here call this part of the river by the descriptive name of the "Y." It joins Big Island Lake with the Sand River.

Yates River (river)
84 N/16 - Alberta-Northwest Territories
31-126-12-W5
60°00′N 116°05′W
Flows north-east into the Northwest Territories approximately 175 km north north-east of High Level.

It was officially named in 1946 after it was submitted by M.G. Cameron, DLS, honouring Constable R.N.Yates, of the Royal Canadian Mounted Police who was stationed at Fort Vermilion. His territory included this area. It is known locally as Big River.

Yellowstone Creek (creek)
83 O/4 - Horse Mountain
9-3-71-13-W5
55°07′N 115°54′W
Flows north-west into Little Driftpile River approximately 75 km west of Slave Lake.

The name was adopted some time between 1914 and 1922 and may be descriptive of the rocks found in the creek.

Yoke Lake (lake)
83 M/4 - Rio Grande
7-72-11-W6
55°13′N 119°40′W
Approximately 52 km west of Grande Prairie.

It is named for its shape which resembles the piece of equipment that harnessed oxen to ploughs. The original name suggested in 1951 correspondence was "Horseshoe Lake", but because the name was duplicated in a number of other places, the name Yoke Lake was adopted as an alternative.

Young's Point Provincial Park (provincial park)
83 N/4 - Sturgeon Heights
11-71-24-W5
55°08′N 117°34′W
Approximately 20 km west north-west of Valleyview.

The park is named for Frederick Campbell Young, a local farmer. He served overseas in World War I, attaining the rank of lieutenant and was awarded the Military Cross. Before the war he worked in various areas in Alberta in various jobs. He returned to Alberta in 1919 and took out a homestead/soldier grant. In 1968, the land was sold to the Government of Alberta to make it into park on the shore of Sturgeon Lake. Its area is 1,090 hectares.

Zama City (hamlet)
84 M/2 - Moody Creek
13-117-5-W6
59°09′N 118°41′W
Approximately 115 km north-west of High Level.

(see Zama River)

Zama Lake (lake)
84 L/11 - Alberta
1-113-7-W6
58°46′N 119°01′W
Approximately 27 km north north-east of Rainbow Lake.

Locally the lake is called *Tulonh*, a Slavey word meaning "Where the water ends." The work is descriptive as this lake is the westernmost of the Hay Lakes group. (see Zama River)

Zama Lake Indian Reserve No. 210 (Indian reserve)
84 L/11 - Alberta
22-112-8-W6
58°44′N 119°15′W
Approximately 25 km north north-east of Rainbow Lake.

(see Zama River)

Zama River (river)
84 L/15 - Habay
31-113-5-W6
58°51′N 118°50′W
Flows south into Hay Lake approximately 51 km north north-east of Rainbow Lake.

The Zama River is named for a Slavey chief and was recorded in 1921 during a survey as Zamah River. The local name for the river is *K'olaa Zahéh* which is Slavey for Old

Man River which may refer to the Slavey chief whose name now appears on the river.

Zig Zag Lake (lake)
84 H/4 - Osi Lake
8-95-23-W4
57°13′N 113°42′W
Approximately 151 km west north-west of Fort McMurray.

The name of this lake is descriptive of its shape.

Bibliography

PRIMARY SOURCES:

Alberta. Geographical Names Program correspondence files, 1914-1995. Edmonton: Geographical Names Program.

Alberta. Legislative Counsel. Index to Orders in Council, 1905-1984. Edmonton: Provincial Archives of Alberta.

Alberta. Legislature Library. Records collected by the early archival program as set up by Katherine Hughes, 1822-1950s. (Includes some original and some transcripts of Hudson's Bay Company post journals.) Edmonton: Provincial Archives of Alberta, Ref. No. 74.1.

Alberta. Legislature Library. Records of the first provincial toponymist, librarian and archivist, Katherine Hughes, 1908-1910. Edmonton: Provincial Archives of Alberta Ref. No. 74.350.

Canada. Canadian Permanent Committee on Geographical Names. Correspondence files on microfiche, 1895-1978. Ottawa: National Archives of Canada.

Canada. Department of the Interior. North West Half Breeds and Original White Settlers. Microfilmed files from the National Archives of Canada relating to Métis land scrip issued, 1870-1930. Edmonton: Provincial Archives of Alberta, Ref. No. 90.562.

Canada. Department of the Interior. Microfilmed general indexes to Dominion Land Agencies in Alberta, 1875-1931. Edmonton: Provincial Archives of Alberta, Ref. No. 74.32.

Canada. Department of the Interior. Microfilmed files of Dominion Lands homestead, school lands and settlement records, 1875-1950s. Edmonton: Provincial Archives of Alberta, Ref. No. 70.313.

Canada. Dominion Lands Survey. Township plans, field note books, diaries, correspondence files relating to the Dominion Land Surveyors, 1870s-1920s. Edmonton: Provincial Archives of Alberta, Ref. Nos. 79.27, 83.376, 83.421, 85.34.

Information/clippings files, [1940s-1950s]. Edmonton: Provincial Archives of Alberta.

Northern Alberta Railways. Administrative records of the company and its components, 1922-1981. Edmonton: Provincial Archives of Alberta, Ref. no. 86.587.

Oblates of Mary Immaculate. Administrative, parish, and records relating to individuals in the order, 1840s-1980s. Edmonton: Provincial Archives of Alberta, Ref. Nos. 71.220 and 84.400.

Pereira, Joe. "McLennan, Alberta", interview with Alberta Geographical Names Program staff, 1989.

Polet family. Letter from Robina Polet to Marianne Mack, 1981. Edmonton: Provincial Archives of Alberta, Ref. No. 81.207.

SECONDARY SOURCES:

Across the Smoky, eds. Winnie Moore and Fran Moore. DeBolt, Alberta: DeBolt and District Pioneer Museum Society, 1978.

Alberta. Energy and Natural Resources, Alberta Forest Service. *The Clearwater River. A Map Guide for River Travel*. Edmonton, Alberta: Alberta Energy and Natural Resources, n.d. [1970s].

Alberta. Legislative Assembly. *Alberta Regulations*.

Alberta. Legislative Assembly. *Alberta Gazette*.

Alberta. Legislative Assembly. *Municipal Government Act, 1976*.

Alberta and British Columbia Boundary Commission. *Report of the Commission appointed to delimit the boundary between the provinces of Alberta and British Columbia*. Ottawa, Ontario: Office of the Surveyor General, 1917-1955.

Alberta-Northwest Territories Boundary Commission. *Report of the Commissioners appointed to direct the survey and demarcation of the boundary between the province of Alberta and the Northwest Territories*. Ottawa, Ontario: Queen's Printer and Controller of Stationery, 1956.

Alberta. Travel Alberta. *Canoe Alberta* (map). Edmonton: Alberta Transportation, Surveys and Mapping Branch, 1978.

Along the Wapiti. Wapiti River Historical Society. Grande Prairie, Alberta: The Society, 1981.

Always a River to Cross. Bear Canyon, Alberta: Silver and Gold History Committee, 1981.

Attwater, Donald. *The Penguin Dictionary of Saints.* 2nd edition. Revised and updated by Catherine Rachall John, 1965.

Beaverlodge to the Rockies, E.C. Stacey, et al, eds. Beaverlodge, Alberta: Beaverlodge and District Historical Association, 1974.

Beaverlodge to the Rockies, Supplement, E.C. Stacey, ed. Beaverlodge, Alberta: Beaverlodge and District Historical Association, 1976.

Berwyn Centennial Committee. *Brick's Hill, Berwyn and beyond.* Berwyn, Alberta: Berwyn Centennial Committee, ca. 1968.

Blatherwick, F.J. *Canadian Orders, Decorations and Medals, 3rd ed.,* Toronto: Unitrade Press, 1985.

Bond, Courtney C.J. *Surveyors of Canada, 1867-1967.* Ottawa: Canadian Institute of Surveying, 1966.

Big Bend. Blueberry Mountain, Alberta: Big Bend Historical Committee, 1981.

Brick's Hill, Berwyn and Beyond. Berwyn Centennial Committee, 1968.

Brady, Archange J. *A history of Fort Chipewyan: Alberta's Oldest Continuously Inhabited Settlement,* 2nd ed. Athabasca, Alberta: Chronicle Publishers Athabasca, 1985.

Bryan, Gertrude. *Land of the Spirit.* S.l., s.n. [1970].

Buffalo Trails, Tales of the Pioneers. Buffalo Lake, Alberta: Buffalo Lake Community Society, 1978.

Burnt Embers: A History of Woking and District in the Burnt River Valley. Woking, Alberta: Woking and Area Historical Society, 1985.

by the Peavine...in the Smoky...of the Peace: Local History of Donnelly, Falher and biographies of the pioneers. Marie Cimon Beaupré, ed. *s.l.:* Stuart Brandle Printing Services Limited, 1980.

Canada. Dominion Lands Survey. *Abstracts from Reports on Townships West of the Fourth Meridian.* Ottawa, Ontario: Department of the Interior, 1901-1915.

Canada. Dominion Lands Survey. *Reports – Townships West of the Fifth Meridian, 1909-1914.* Ottawa, Ontario: Department of the Interior, 1909-1914.

Canadian Encyclopedia. Edmonton: Hurtig Publishers Limited, 1988.

Canadian Parliamentary Guide. Ottawa, Ontario: Canada. Parliament, 1905-

Carrière, Gaston. *Dictionnaire Biographique des Oblats de Marie Immaculée au Canada.* 4 Vols. Ottawa: Editions de L'Université d'Ottawa, 1977.

Chalmers, John W. and the Boreal Institute. *The Land of Peter Pond.* Occasional Publication Number 12, Boreal Institute for Northern Studies, University of Alberta, 1974.

Chipeniuk, R.C. *Lakes of the Lac La Biche District.* Calgary, Alberta: D.W. Friesen and Sons Ltd., 1975.

Clark, E. *Fort Vermilion before Alberta: An Early History of the Fort Vermilion District.* Erskine, Alberta: Intercollegiate Press, 1982.

Clear Vision; a history of the Cleardale area, 60 miles west of Fairview. Cleardale, Alberta: Cleardale History Book Committee, 1982.

Comfort, D. J. *Meeting Place of Many Waters. A History of Fort McMurray, Part I, 1835-1931.* Fort McMurray, Alberta: *s.n.,* 1973.

_____. *Ribbons of Water and Steamboats North. A History of Fort McMurray, Part II, 1870-1898.* Fort McMurray, Alberta: S.n., 1974.

_____. *Pass the McMurray Salt Please! The Alberta Salt Company as Remembered by Three Fort McMurray Pioneers.* Fort McMurray, Alberta: *s.n.,* 1975.

Concise Oxford Dictionary of Current English. Oxford, England: Clarendon Press, 1982.

Cormack, R.G.H. *Wild Flowers of Alberta*. Edmonton, Alberta: Hurtig Publishers, 1977.

Crockford's Clerical Directory for 1913. Being a statistical book of reference for facts relating to the clergy and the church. Forty fifth issue. London, England: Horace Cox, 1913.

Crockford's Clerical Directory for 1929 with which is incorporated the clergy list, clerical guide and ecclesiastical directory. London, England: Oxford University Press, 1929.

Davies, Margaret. *Wales in Maps*. Cardiff: University of Wales, 1951.

Dempsey, Hugh. *Indian Names for Alberta Communities*. Occasional Paper No. 4. Calgary, Alberta: Glenbow Alberta Institute, 1969.

Department of the Interior. *Description of Surveyed Townships in the Peace River District in the Provinces of Alberta and British Columbia.* Third Edition. Ottawa, Ontario: Department of the Interior, 1916.

Dickason, Olive Patricia. *Canada's First Nations*. Toronto, Ontario: McClelland and Stewart, 1992.

Dictionary of Canadianisms on Historical Principles. Toronto: W.J. Gage Limited, 1967.

Donahue, Paul F. *Archaeological Research in Northern Alberta*. Occasional Paper No. 32 Edmonton, Alberta: Alberta Culture, 1976.

Dubuc, Denis. *Jean-Côté: histoire et généalogie d'une paroisse canadienne-française du nord Albertain,* 2nd ed. Falher, Alberta: Denis Dubuc, 1982.

Echoes along the Athabasca River: a history of Chisholm, Fawcett Lake, Forest View, Hondo, Lawrence Lake, Moose Portage, Moose River, Otter Creek, Ranch, Smith, Smokey Creek. Smith, Alberta: Smith Half Century Plus Historical Book Committee, 1984.

Ells, S.C. "Wood Smoke," in *Rhymes of the Miner: An Anthology of Canadian Mining Verse*, ed. E.L. Chicanot. Gardenvale, Quebec: Federal Publications Limited, [1930s].

Encyclopedia Britannica. 1929.

Encyclopedia Canadiana. Toronto, Ontario: Grolier, 1958.

Engstrom, E. *Clearwater Winter*. Edmonton: Lone Pine, 1984.

Farm Women's Union of Alberta High Prairie Local 204 Centennial Book Committee. *Pioneers who Blazed the Trail. A History of High Prairie and District*. High Prairie, Alberta: Lithographed by South Peace News, ca. 1968.

Ferguson, Barry Glen. *Athabasca Oil Sands. Northern Resource Exploration, 1875-1951*. Regina, Saskatchewan: Alberta Culture/Canadian Plains Research Centre, 1985.

Fort Vermilion before Alberta: An Early History of the Fort Vermilion District. Erskine, Alberta: Pioneers of Fort Vermilion, 1982.

Fort Vermilion People. In Our Vast Trading North, 1788-1988. Fort Vermilion: Fort Vermilion and District Bicentennial Association, 1992.

Freeman, Randolph. Geographical Naming in Western British North America: 1780-1820. Edmonton, Alberta: Alberta Culture, 1985. (Historic Sites Service occasional paper No. 15).

Friends of Geographical Names of Alberta Society. *Local Histories Mapping Project*. Edmonton, Alberta: The Friends, 1995.

Fryer, Harold. *Ghost Towns of Alberta*. Langley, British Columbia: Stagecoach Publishing Co., 1976.

Gazetteer of Canada, Alberta. Ottawa, Ontario: Canadian Board on Geographical Names, 1958.

Gazetteer of Canada, Alberta. Ottawa, Ontario: Canadian Permanent Committee on Geographical Names, 1974.

Gazetteer of Canada, Alberta. Ottawa, Ontario: Canadian Permanent Committee on Geographical Names, 1988.

Geographic Board of Canada. *Place-Names of Alberta*. Ottawa, Ontario: Department of the Interior, 1928.

Godfrey, W. Earl. *The Birds of Canada*. Ottawa: Supply and Services Canada, 1976.

Golden Years Club of Bezanson. *Smoky River to Grande Prairie*. Grande Prairie, Alberta: Grande Prairie and District Old Timers' Association, 1975.

Grooming the Grizzly: A History of Wanham and Area. Ed. Wallace Tansem. Wanham, Alberta: Birch Hills Historical Society, 1982.

Guy histoire – Guy History: Guy-Ballater-Whitemud Creek. Guy, Alberta: Guy Historical Society, 1987.

Hail, Barbara A. and Kate C. Duncan. *Out of the North*. The Subarctic Collection of the Haffenreffer Museum of Anthropology. Bristol, Rhode Island: Haffenreffer Museum of Anthropology, Brown University, 1989.

Halwreck, F.G. *A Biographical Dictionary of the Saints*. London, St. Louis, Missouri: B. Herder Book Company, 1924.

Hansen, Joe. *The saga of the Battle: the History of the Battle River Country*. s.l.: Four Arrows Ltd., 1983.

Harraps Shorter French and English Dictionary, revised edition. Toronto, Ontario: Clarke, Irwin and Company, 1967.

Histoire de Girouxville/Girouxville History. Lucie St-André and Edith Lorrain, eds. Girouxville, Alberta: Girouxville Historical Society, [1976].

Holmgren, Eric J. and Patricia M. Holmgren. *Over 2000 Place Names of Alberta*. 3rd Edition. Saskatoon, Saskatchewan: Western Producer Prairie Books, 1976.

Holtslander, Dale. *School Districts of Alberta: A Listing of All Protestant Public Schools Organized in the Province of Alberta*. Edmonton, Alberta: D. Holtslander, 1978.

Homesteaders' Heritage, a History of Bay Tree, Bonanza, Gordondale, West Pouce Coupé and East Doe River. Bonanza, Alberta: Fellow Pioneers Historical Society, 1982.

Hopper, A.B. and T. Kearney, comps. *Canadian National Railways, Synoptical History of Organization, Capital Stock, Funded Debt, and other General Information as of Dec. 31, 1960*. Montreal, Quebec: Accounting Department of the CNR, Oct 15, 1962. [unpublished report].

Hosie, R.C. *Native Trees of Canada*. Ottawa, Ontario: Queen's Printer, 1969.

Hughes, Neil. *Post Offices of Alberta, 1876-1986*, unpublished manuscript, 1986.

I remember Peace River, Alberta and adjacent districts, ed. Yvette T. M. Mahé. Peace River, Alberta: Women's Institute of Peace River, Alberta, 1974.

Jenness, Diamond. *Indians of Canada*. Ottawa, National Museum of Canada, 1963.

Johnston, J.B. *Place Names of Scotland,* 2nd ed., Edinburgh, Scotland: David Douglas, 1903.

Kitto, F.H. "The practical management of field Surveys." *Programme of the Association of Dominion Land Surveyors at its Sixth Annual Meeting held at the Carnegie Library, Ottawa.* Ottawa, Ontario: Association of Dominion Land Surveyors, 1911.

Kunitz, Stanley J. and Howard Haycraft. *Twentieth Century Authors*. New York, N.Y.: H.W. Wilson Company, 1942.

La Glace, Yesterday and Today. La Glace, Alberta: The Twilight Club, 1981.

Lacombe, Albert. *Dictionnaire de la langue de Cris*. Montréal, Québec: Beauchemin & Valois, 1874.

_____. *Petit manuel pour apprendre à lire la langue crise*. Montréal, Québec: C.O. Beauchemin, 1886.

Lake Saskatoon Reflections: A History of the Lake Saskatoon District. Sexsmith, Alberta: Lake Saskatoon History Book Committee, 1980.

Land of Hope and Dreams: A History of Grimshaw and Districts. Grimshaw, Alberta: Grimshaw and District Historical Society, 1980.

Lawrence, Sheridan. *Emperor of the Peace, 1870-1952*. Alberta: *s.n.*, 195?.

Leonard, David W. and Victoria L. Lemieux. *A Fostered Dream, the Lure of the Peace River Country, 1872-1914*. Calgary, Alberta: Detselig Enterprises, 1992.

Local History of Donnelly-Falher and Biographies of the Pioneers, ed. Marie Cimon Beaupré. Alberta, *s.n.*: 1980.

Local History of Joussard and biographies of the pioneers. Joussard, Alberta: Joussard Homesteaders, 1986.

MacGregor, J.G. *Paddle Wheels to Bucket Wheels on the Athabasca.* Toronto, Ontario: McClelland and Stewart Ltd., 1974.

_____. *Vision of an Ordered Land. The Story of the Dominion Land Survey.* Saskatoon, Saskatchewan: Western Producer Prairie Books, 1981.

Mackenzie, Alexander (Sir). *Voyage to the Pacific Ocean in 1793.* Chicago: Lakeside Press, R.R. Donnelly and Son, Christmas, 1931.

Macmillan Dictionary of Canadian Biography. Edited by W. Stewart Wallace. 4th edition. Toronto, Ontario: Macmillan, 1978.

Mair, Charles. *Through the MacKenzie Basin. A Narrative of the Athabasca and Peace River Treaty Expedition of 1899.* Toronto, Ontario: William Briggs, 1908.

Mardon, E.G. *Community Names of Alberta.* Lethbridge, Alberta: E.G. Mardon, 1973.

McPherson, Jody. *Tracing Our History through Names.* Fort McMurray, Alberta: Fort McMurray Express, n.d.

Memories and Moments of White Mountain, Willowvale, Bridgeview. Spirit River, Alberta: WWB Historical Society, 1983.

Miles, A.D., *A Dictionary of English Place Names.* Oxford: Oxford University Press, 1991.

Miller, William J. *Report on the Methye Portage and Associated Portages on the Clearwater River,* 1977.

Mosquitoes, Muskegs and Memories: A History of Wesley Creek and Three Creeks. Peace River, Alberta: McKinney Hall History Book Committee, 1985.

Moss, E.H. *Flora of Alberta.* Toronto: University of Toronto Press, 1977.

Moyles, R. G. (ed) *From Duck Lake to Dawson City. The Diary of Eben McAdam's Journey to the Klondike, 1898-1899.* Saskatoon, Saskatchewan: Western Producer Prairie Books, 1977.

Nicholson, Gerald W.L. *The Canadians in Italy, 1943-1945. Official history of the Canadian Army in the Second World War.* Ottawa, Ontario: E. Cloutier, 1950-1960.

Nicholson, Harold. *Heart of Gold: Fairview, 1929-1978.* Edmonton: Bulletin Commercial, 1978.

Ogilvie, William. "Reminiscences of camp life on surveys in the North-West during the last thirty years." *Programme of the Association of Dominion Land Surveyors at its Sixth Annual Meeting held at the Carnegie Library, Ottawa.* Ottawa, Ontario: Association of Dominion Land Surveyors, 1911.

Our bend in the Peace: the Story of Royce and Lubeck. Hines Creek, Alberta: Lubeck Merrymakers Society, 1979.

Owens, Brian M. and Claude M. Roberto. *A Guide to the Archives of the Oblates of Mary Immaculate.* Edmonton: The Missionary Oblates, Grandin Province, 1989.

Paddle Wheels and Moccasins. Sawridge, Alberta: Sawridge Historical Committee, ca. 1980.

Palmer, Howard and Tamara. *Alberta, a New History.* Edmonton, Alberta: Hurtig Publishers, 1990.

Parker, James M. *Emporium of the North: Fort Chipewyan and the Fur Trade to 1835.* Regina, Saskatchewan: Alberta Culture and Multiculturalism/Plains Research Centre, 1987.

Peace River Remembers: Peace River, Alberta, and Adjacent Districts. Peace River, Alberta: Sir Alexander MacKenzie Historical Society, 1984.

Pioneer Round Up. A History of Albright, Demmitt, Goodfare, Hythe, Lymburn, Valhalla. Hythe, Alberta: Pioneer History Society of Hythe and Area, 1972.

Pioneers of the Peace, Isabel M. Campbell, ed. Grande Prairie, Alberta: Grande Prairie and District Old Timers Association, 1975.

Pioneers of the Lakeland. A homespun history of Slave Lake and surrounding communities of Assineau, Canyon Creek, Widewater, Wagner, Mitsue and the North Shore. Slave Lake, Alberta: Slave Lake Pioneers, 1984.

Random House Dictionary of the English Language. New York, New York: Random House, 1966.

Reid, Gordon. *Frontier Notes. s.l., s.n.,* n.d.

Reminisce with Friedenstal. Fairview, Alberta: Friedenstal Historical Society, 1987.

Room, Adrian. Dictionary of Place-names in the British Isles.

Rourke, Louise. *The Land of the Frozen Tide.* London: Hutchinson & Co. Ltd., n.d.

Saga of Battle River – We Came, We Stayed: A History of Deadwood, North Star, Manning, Notikewin, Hotchkiss, and Hawkhills District. Manning, Alberta: Battle River Historical Society, 1986.

Saint Joseph Daily Missal: the Official Prayers of the Catholic Church for the Celebration of Daily Mass. Rev. Hugo H. Hoever, ed. New York, New York: Catholic Book Publishing Co., 1961.

Salt, W. Ray, and Jim R. Salt. *The Birds of Alberta.* Edmonton: Hurtig Publishers, 1976.

Schneider, Ena. *Ribbons of Steel: The Story of the Northern Alberta Railways.* Calgary, Alberta: Detselig Enterprises, 1989.

Shorter Oxford English Dictionary on Historical Principles. Oxford, England: Clarendon Press, 1973.

Smythe, Terry. *Thematic Study of the Fur Trade in the Canadian West, 1670-1870.* Prepared for Historic Sites and Monuments Board of Canada, 1968. [Unpublished manuscript].

Smith, A. *Biological Survey of Lakes in the Caribou Mountains,* Report 11. Edmonton, Alberta: Alberta Lands and Forests, Wildlife Division, 1970.

Sodbusters: a History of Kinuso and Swan River Settlement, Jean Quinn, ed. *S.l.: s.n.,* 1979.

Story, Norah. *The Oxford Companion to Canadian History and Literature.* Toronto, London, New York: Oxford University Press, 1967.

Story of Rural Municipal Government in Alberta, 1909-1969. s.l.: s.n., [ca. 1970].

Switzer, Harvey A. "On the Edson-Grande Prairie Trail," in Hugh Dempsey, ed., *The Best from Alberta History.* Saskatoon, Saskatchewan: Western Producer Books, 1981.

Ten Dollars and a Dream, Mary Almeda Klein, ed. Dixonville, Alberta: L.I.F.E. History Committee, 1977.

Thompson, Don W. *Men and Meridians: The History of Surveying and Mapping in Canada.* Ottawa, Ontario: Queen's Printer, 1967.

Tooley, R.W. *Tooley's Dictionary of Mapmakers.* Tring, Hertfordshire, England: Map Collector Publications Limited, 1979.

Trails and Rails North: History of McLennan and District. McLennan, Alberta: McLennan History Book Committee, 1981.

Turning the Pages of Time. A History of Nampa and Surrounding Districts, 1800-1981. Nampa, Alberta: Nampa and District Historical Society, 1981

Van Kleek, Edith. *Our Trail North, a true story of Pioneering the Peace River Country of Northern Alberta.* Edmonton, Alberta: Co-op Press Limited, 1980.

Voorhis, A. M. *Historic Forts and Trading Posts of the French Regime and of the English Fur Trading Companies.* Ottawa: Department of the Interior, 1930.

Wagon Trails Grown Over: Sexsmith to the Smoky. Jean Fraser Rycroft and Margaret Fraser Thibault, eds. Sexsmith, Alberta: Sexsmith to the Smoky Historical Society, 1980.

Walters, L.M. Lloyd. *My First Trip to the North West Territories. S.l., s.n.,* n.d.

Wandering River History. Wandering River, Alberta: Wandering River Women's Institute, 1983.

Waterhole and the Land North of the Peace. Hec MacLean, ed. Fairview, Alberta: Waterhole Old Timers Association, 1970.

Waugh, Earle. "Vandersteene's Art: Christian Interaction with Cree Culture," in *Proceedings of the Fort Vermilion Bicentennial Conference*, pp.118-127, edited by Patricia A. McCormack and R. Geoffrey Ironside. Edmonton, Alberta: Boreal Institute for Northern Studies, 1990.

Webster's Dictionary. Springfield, Massachusetts: G. & C. Merriam, 1958.

Websters Third New International Dictionary. Springfield, Massachusetts: G. & C. Merriam, 1976.

Wheatfields and Wildflowers: a History of Rycroft and Surrounding School Districts. Rycroft, Alberta: Rycroft History Committee, 1984.

Where the Red Willow Grew: Valleyview and Surrounding Districts. Valleyview, Alberta: Valleyview and District Old Timers Association, 1980.

Appendix

Life on a survey crew

As illustrated in all four volumes of the **Place Names of Alberta** series, surveying was a major factor in the toponymy of Alberta. Much of the early work was accomplished by the Dominion Lands Surveys, which came under the jurisdiction of the Canadian Department of the Interior. The day-to-day life of survey crews epitomises life on the Canadian frontier – a lot of hard work and a bit of fun.

The "ideal" crew consisted of twelve men in all, including the chief, assistant, first and second chainman, picketman, three axemen, two mounders, a cook and a teamster.[1] The head of the survey, a professional engineer, usually was a qualified Dominion Land Surveyor who contracted to be in charge of a crew for the survey season. He was responsible for the hiring and maintenance of the crew, equipment purchase and maintenance, and most important, the recording of all the surveying data. The assistant, or transitman (perhaps also sometimes called instrument man), was often an engineer in training, and was responsible for the use of the transit, which is a surveying instrument for measuring horizontal angles. He also acted as assistant to the chief surveyor. The chainmen were in charge of the chaining: that meant measuring distance with a surveying chain that was 66 feet in length. (There are eighty chains to a mile.) The front chainman kept the pickets, and the picketman gave line for the transitman, as well as establishing a point on the ground for the transitman to put his transit. Mounders would dig pits, build mounds, and place the monuments that marked the boundaries of the units being surveyed. As the name suggests, the axemen were used to cut survey lines through forest and bush. Where there was prairie, there was little need for axemen. The cook, who was considered a very important member of the crew, sometimes had a helper, called the "cookee." Teamsters looked after the horses and wagons. Axemen, mounders, cooks, and teamsters were often hired from localities near the survey sites.

The life of a survey crew member would have been primitive, and it would take a special group of people to work together in harmony for the eight or nine months they would be together in close company. Once on the job, barring serious injury, you were there for the duration of the season. In 1911, F.H. Kitto, DLS, admonished all chiefs of surveys:

How often do we see confusion and discontent abounding in a survey camp, leading at once to loss of time and of interest in the work, and detracting from the good result desired. This should not be so. Something is radically wrong. There is no reason why a party should not spend a season on survey and retain order and good will in its ranks. It is seldom done... Strive to keep the temper of the camp cheerful. Without lessening authority there is much that can be done to keep all hands in good spirits. Let them indulge in a little hunting or fishing. A kodak, (sic) even a football, can be easily carried. Horse shoes can be loaned for pitching. While the chief and assistant have work to do after hours, the men may find the time drag, and without amusement may fall into mischief.[2]

Today, we must be thankful for those men who brought their "kodaks." Without them, we would not have the photographs on the following pages that help to illustrate life on a survey crew. In spite of privation, mosquitoes, muskeg and mud, the men were usually able to manage a smile for the camera.

---

[1] F. H. Kitto, "The practical management of field surveys," *Programme of the Association of Dominion Land Surveyors at its sixth annual meeting held at the Carnegie Library,* Ottawa, 1911, pp. 31-32.
[2] *Ibid.*, pp. 30, 41-42.

Getting there

Scow loaded with horses, supplies, men, ca. 1915

Surveyor with mosquito netting, on canoe, ca. 1915 (Enough said.)

Everyday duties

Humphrey and Tupper survey party cook making dinner on a raft on the Peace River, 1911

Leveller, northern surveying party, 1917

Testing chains, northern surveying party, 1917

Transit and levelling crews, northern surveying party, 1917

The work of the axemen, survey crew in Peace River area, 1912-1916

Dominion Land Survey Party near Peace River, 1915 (Some of the instruments are being shown.)

Camp Life

Communal grooming, survey crew in Peace River area, ca. 1912-1916

Typical camp, survey crew in Peace River area, 1912-1916

Relaxing around the camp fire, survey trip, northern Alberta, ca. 1915

Bath day, survey trip, northern Alberta, ca. 1915

Glossary

These include terms from Volumes I-III.

Basin – Bowl-shaped head of a valley in foothills or mountains.*

Bay – Water area in an indentation of the shoreline of lakes or large rivers.*

Bend – Distinct curve in a water body.*

Bluff – Headland, cliff, or river bank with a steep face.*

Bottom – Level land of a valley floor.*

Buffalo Jump – Vertical side of a coulee, hill, or river bank. Place where Prairie Indians killed herds of bison by driving them over steep cliffs.*

Butte – Conspicuous isolated hill with steep sides and a flat top.*

Canadian Expeditionary Force – Canadian army raised in World War I. It was composed of a number of units, and remained a voluntary force until conscription was enacted in 1917. In all, over 600,000 troops joined the CEF.

Canal – Artificial waterway.*

Canyon – Deep narrow valley with precipitous walls.*

Cape – Prominent elevated projection of land extending into a body of water.*

---

* *Gazetteer of Canada, Alberta,* 3rd ed., Ottawa, Ontario: Energy Mines and Resources Canada, 1988, pp. ix-xi, xv-xviii.

† F.J. Blatherwick, *Canadian orders, decorations and medals,* 3rd ed., Toronto, Ontario: Unitrade Press, 1985, various pages.

Cascade – Series of stepped waterfalls.*

Cave – Natural subterranean chamber open to the surface.*

CEF – See Canadian Expeditionary Force.

Channel – Narrow stretch of water, either an inlet or a connection between two bodies of water.*

Chutes – Narrow and fast flowing descent of a watercourse confined within steep banks.*

City – At the request of the residents, it is an incorporated jurisdiction of more than 10,000 inhabitants.

CMG – Companion, the Most Distinguished Order of St. Michael and St. George. Established in 1818 and awarded to citizens of the Commonwealth who have rendered distinguished services in foreign affairs.†

Coulee – Usually steep-sided valley or ravine.*

County – An incorporated administrative area with legislated boundaries which is operated by an elected council, with jurisdiction over education.

Creek – Watercourse, usually smaller than a river.*

Crossing – A place suitable for traversing a body of water.*

DCM – See Distinguished Conduct Medal.

DFC – See Distinguished Flying Cross.

Distinguished Conduct Medal – Usually awarded when a Victoria Cross has been recommended but not given.

Distinguished Flying Cross – Awarded to Officers and Warrant Officers for and act or acts of valour, courage or devotion to duty performed whilst flying in active operations against the enemy.†

Distinguished Service Order – Established for rewarding individual instances of meritorious or distinguished service in war. This is a purely military order and is only given to officers whose service has been marked by the special mention of his name in despatches for "distinguished services under fire", or under conditions equivalent to service in actual combat with the enemy.†

DLS – Dominion Land Surveyor

Dome – Mass of rock or ice with rounded top, elevated above the surrounding terrain.*

DSO – See Distinguished Service Order.

Elbow – Sharp turn in a watercourse.*

Falls – Perpendicular or steep descent of water.*

Flat – Almost level land, usually found along a valley.*

Foothills – Hilly transition zone between a mountain range and a plain.*

Former locality – A place usually uninhabited or with a very small, scattered population.*

Former post office – Name retained for a post office now closed.*

Former railway point – Name retained for a railway point no longer in use.

Gap – Narrow opening through a ridge or mountain chain.*

Glacier – Mass of permanent snow and ice flowing from an area of snow accumulation on higher ground.*

Hamlet – An unincorporated area of land subdivided into lots and blocks as a townsite, usually containing eight or more occupied dewllings and at least one retail business outlet, the administration of which is handled by the municipality under which it falls – improvement district, municipal district or county.

Hill – Elevation of terrain rising prominently above the surrounding land.*

Hotsprings – Site of a natural flow of hot or warm water issuing from the ground.*

Icefield – Irregularly shaped mass of permanent snow and ice, generally forming the accumulation area of two or more glaciers.*

Improvement District – An administrative area with legislated boundaries, without a large enough taxation base to enable the formation of a Municipal District or County. It is under the jurisdiction of the provincial Department of Municipal Affairs. If a stable population/taxation base becomes available, the ratepayers may petition the government to form a Municipal District or County.

Indian Reserve – Tract of land set apart for the use and benefit of a particular Indian band.*

Island – Land area surrounded by water or marsh.*

Lake, Lac – Inland body of standing water.*

Locality – A place with scattered population or fewer than eight occupied dwellings.*

Marsh – Area of low-lying land, often flooded and usually characterized by growth of grass and reeds.*

MC – See Military Cross.

Meadow – (i) Low-lying flat, seasonally wet grassy area.*
– (ii) Alpine or sub-alpine treeless area characterized by seasonal grasses and wild flowers.*

Member of Parliament – Representative of a constituency elected to the federal House of Commons.

Member of the Legislative Assembly – Representative of a constituency elected to the provincial parliament.

Metis Settlement – An administrative area with legislated boundaries, established under the Metis Settlements Act of 1990.

Military Cross – Awarded to officers of the rank of Captain or lower including Warrant Officers, for gallant and distinguished services in action.†

Military Medal – Awarded to Warrant Officers, NCOs [Non-Commissioned Officers] for individual or asssociated acts of bravery and devotion under fire on the recommendation of a Commander-in-Chief in the Field.†

MLA – See Member of the Legislative Assembly.

MM – See Military Medal.

MP – See Member of Parliament.

Municipal District – An incorporated administrative area with legislated boundaries which is operated by an elected council, but with no jurisdiction over education.

Mount, Mountain – Mass of land prominently elevated above the surrounding terrain, bounded by steep slopes and rising to an summit and/or peaks.*

Muskeg – Waterlogged swamp with deep accumulation of organic material.*

Narrows – Constricted section of a water body.

National Park – Legally defined land area, under federal jurisdiction for camping, outdoor recreation and preservation of wildlife.*

Pass – Low opening in a mountain range or hills, offering a route from one side to the other.*

Peak – Summit of a mountain or hill, or the mountain or hill itself.*

Point, Pointe – Land area jutting into a water feature; also used for a convex change in direction of a shoreline.*

Post office – A Canada Post designation, listed where the post office name differs from the name of the place where it is located.*

Prairie – Area of flat or gently rolling grassland; larger that a meadow and often extensive.*

Provincial Park – Lands designated by Order in Council, for conservation of flora and fauna, or for preservation of areas and objects of geological, cultural, ecological or other specific interest, and to facilitate their use and enjoyment for outdoor recreation.*

Railway point – A named point or intersection of tracks, as designated by a railway company.*

Range – Group or chain of mountains or hills.*

Rapids – Fast-flowing section of a watercourse, usually with turbulent water or exposed rocks.*

Reservoir – Inland body of standing water, often man-made.*

Ridge – Elongated stretch of elevated ground.*

River – Flowing watercourse.*

Rock – Rocky hill, mountain, or cliff; or a large boulder.*

Sapper – A military engineer of the rank of private.

Settlement – A legally designated land subdivision, usually with a scattered population.*

Slide – Scar and/or material from landslide or debris flow.*

Slough – Shallow water-filled or marshy depression with no external drainage.*

Spring – Site of a natural flow of water issuing from the ground.*

Station – An older term referring to a stop on a railway line, usually attended by an agent.

Summer village – At the request of the residents, it is an incorporated jurisdiction of not less than 50 separate dwellings, with seasonal occupancy.

Survey crew – See appendix on Surveying for information on survey crews.

Surveyor – Someone, usually an engineer, hired to oversee the accurate recording of the topography of the land. In the early days of Alberta's history, much of the work was accomplished by the Dominion Land Surveyors. The work is now done by the Alberta Lands Surveyors. See the appendix on Surveying.

Town – At the request of the residents, it is an incorporated jurisdiction of more than 1000 inhabitants.

Valley – Long, relatively narrow depression, commonly containing a river or other water feature.*

VC – See Victoria Cross.

Victoria Cross – Awarded for most conspicuous bravery or some daring or pre-eminent act of valour or self-sacrifice or extreme devotion to duty in the presence of the enemy.†

Village – At the request of the inhabitants, it is an incorporated jurisdiction containing not less than 75 separate buildings with continuous occupation.

Wall – Steep rock face.*

Colour Photographs

Northern Alberta

Athabasca River, 1985

Dog Head, 1985

Athabasca Delta, Athabasca River is in centre, Fletcher Channel to the right, 1985

East Dollar Lake, looking west, 1995

Grand Rapids on Athabasca River, 1985

Dunvegan Bridge over the Peace River from Fort Dunvegan Historic Site, 1995

Northern Alberta

Mission Point, 1985

Guy - Statue of Notre Dame de Fatima, church in background, 1995

The Grande Prairie from atop Richmond Hill, 1992

John D'Or Prairie, 1985

O'Brien Provincial Park and Wapiti River

Peace River and Smoky River Junction, 1992

Peace River looking south-west from Peace River (town), 1995

Toward Shaftesbury Settlement, Peace River Bridge at Peace River (town), 1995

Smoky River 9 km south of Guy, 1995